Multiple Criteria Decision Making in Supply Chain Management

T0384275

The Operations Research Series

Series Editor: A. Ravi Ravindran

Professor, Department of Industrial and Manufacturing Engineering
The Pennsylvania State University – University Park, PA

Published Titles:

Multiple Criteria Decision Making in Supply Chain Management
A. Ravi Ravindran

Operations Planning: Mixed Integer Optimization Models
Joseph Geunes

Introduction to Linear Optimization and Extensions
with MATLAB®
Roy H. Kwon

Supply Chain Engineering: Models and Applications
A. Ravi Ravindran & Donald Paul Warsing

Analysis of Queues: Methods and Applications
Natarajan Gautam

Integer Programming: Theory and Practice
John K. Karlof

Operations Research and Management Science Handbook
A. Ravi Ravindran

Operations Research Applications
A. Ravi Ravindran

Operations Research: A Practical Introduction
Michael W. Carter & Camille C. Price

Operations Research Calculations Handbook, Second Edition
Dennis Blumenfeld

Operations Research Methodologies
A. Ravi Ravindran

Probability Models in Operations Research
C. Richard Cassady & Joel A. Nachlas

Multiple Criteria Decision Making in Supply Chain Management

Edited by A. Ravi Ravindran

CRC Press
Taylor & Francis Group
Boca Raton London New York

CRC Press is an imprint of the
Taylor & Francis Group, an **informa** business

CRC Press
Taylor & Francis Group
6000 Broken Sound Parkway NW, Suite 300
Boca Raton, FL 33487-2742

First issued in paperback 2021

© 2016 by Taylor & Francis Group, LLC
CRC Press is an imprint of Taylor & Francis Group, an Informa business

No claim to original U.S. Government works

ISBN-13: 978-0-367-78294-8 (pbk)
ISBN-13: 978-1-4987-0858-6 (hbk)

Library of Congress Cataloging-in-Publication Data

Names: Ravindran, A. Ravi, editor.
Title: Multiple criteria decision making in supply chain management / A. Ravi Ravindran.
Description: Boca Raton, FL : CRC Press, 2015. | Series: The operations research series ; 12 | Includes bibliographical references and index.
Identifiers: LCCN 2015045362 | ISBN 9781498708586 (alk. paper)
Subjects: LCSH: Business logistics--Decision making | Multiple criteria decision making.
Classification: LCC HD38.5 .M75 2015 | DDC 658.5/036--dc23
LC record available at http://lccn.loc.gov/2015045362

Visit the Taylor & Francis Web site at
http://www.taylorandfrancis.com

and the CRC Press Web site at
http://www.crcpress.com

Contents

Preface

Supply chain management (SCM) decisions are made under the conflicting criteria of maximizing profit, maximizing customer responsiveness, and minimizing supply chain risk. This book provides a comprehensive overview of multiple criteria decision making (MCDM) models and methods that can be used in supply chain decisions. It covers recent developments and applications of MCDM for solving SCM problems. Our focus in this book is on the *design and operation* of the supply chain system, which involves connecting many production and distribution systems, often across wide geographic distances, in such a way that the businesses involved can ultimately satisfy customer demand as effectively as possible, resulting in maximum financial returns to those businesses connected to the supply chain system.

The key features of this book are as follows:

- Single source guide
- Written by leading researchers and practitioners
- Comprehensive resource, but concise
- Covers recent developments and applications
- Quick reference guide for students, researchers, and practitioners
- Bridges theory and practice
- Designed and edited with non-experts in mind
- Unified and up-to-date coverage ideal for ready reference

The supply chain topics that are covered in this volume include

- Supplier selection
- Network design
- Logistics and distribution
- Inventory policies
- Risk management
- Global SCM

Book Overview

The chapters in this book are contributed by internationally known authors, researchers, educators, and practitioners. Chapters 1 and 2 provide an introduction to supply chain management (SCM) and to multiple criteria decision making (MCDM), respectively. These two chapters will standardize the terminology that will be used in this book and set the stage for the various SCM problems that will be covered in the chapters that follow.

Supply chain drivers represent the critical areas of decision making in SCM—those that ultimately generate the outcomes that impact the supply chain performance. The key drivers of supply chain include *inventory, transportation, facilities,* and *suppliers*. Companies maintain inventory to protect against unpredictable demand and unreliable supply. The key decision variables in managing inventory in supply chains are *how much and when to order* (inventory policies) and *where to hold inventory* (locations). Chapters 4, 5, and 12 discuss the supply chain inventory decisions in detail.

Transportation is concerned with the movement of items among the supply chain stages—namely, suppliers, plants, distribution centers (DCs), and retailers. Use of faster transportation modes, such as air and roadways, incurs higher transportation costs, but this reduces delivery times and increases reliability. Chapters 3, 5, 7, and 8 cover the transportation issues in supply chains.

Facilities (plants and DCs) play a key role in managing supply chains. Their numbers and locations are generally considered as strategic decisions and directly affect the supply chain performance. Chapters 3–8 and 11 present multiple criteria integer programming models to make optimal decisions regarding the number and location of supply chain facilities and to determine the optimal distribution strategies.

Selection of suppliers of raw materials and intermediate components is considered a critical area of strategic decision making in SCM. Chapters 3, 4, 7, 9, and 10 discuss the supplier selection models under multiple conflicting criteria.

Managing the *risk in supply chains* has gained a lot of attention in recent years. Man-made events, such as the labor strike in US West Coast ports in 2002, and natural events, such as the Japanese earthquake and tsunami in 2011, have caused companies to realize that a singular emphasis on the cost efficiency of supply chains can actually make the supply chains brittle and much more susceptible to risk from disruptions. Chapters 3, 7, 9, and 10 incorporate supply chain risk as an objective function in multiple criteria optimization models.

Chapter Summaries

Chapter 1 provides an introduction to the meaning of supply chains and to the types of design and operational decisions that are made in SCM.

It introduces a variety of conflicting performance measures that are used in supply chain optimization—namely, supply chain costs, customer responsiveness, and supply chain risk.

Chapter 2 presents an overview of the MCDM models and solution methods. MCDM problems are categorized on the basis of whether (1) the alternatives are *finite and known*, which are called multi-criteria selection problems (MCSP) or (2) the alternatives are *infinite and unknown*, which are called multiple criteria mathematical programming (MCMP) problems. In this chapter, the most common methods that are available for solving both MCSP and MCMP problems are reviewed.

Chapter 3 presents a case study in designing a resilient global supply chain network. With increased globalization, SCM has become strategic for companies striving to maximize the overall value generated by reducing costs, increasing responsiveness to customers, and decreasing risks. The emphasis of this chapter is on developing MCMP models for designing and managing a global supply chain network to support the strategic and tactical decisions within the complex multi-national environment. The models are illustrated by applying them to a global consumer products company listed in the Fortune 500.

Chapter 4 introduces a two-phased approach to multi-objective supply chain design and operation. When designing a production–distribution network, supply chain managers may have only limited knowledge of costs, demand, and other information needed to develop a network's infrastructure and optimize its performance. The model developed and demonstrated in this chapter parallels the supply chain planning process through the formulation of a strategic sub model for infrastructure design and initial operation based on limited inputs followed by a tactical sub model to assist in more refined operational planning once higher resolution information is available. Notably, this model takes into account the decision makers' multiple objectives, allowing them to reprioritize among profit, demand satisfaction, and transit time goals.

Chapter 5 presents a multi-criteria distribution planning model for a consumer products company. Integrating different types of supply chain decisions in optimization models allows the supply chains to operate more efficiently. This chapter presents a multiple criteria mixed-integer linear program to design the best possible supply chain distribution network. The model makes the strategic decisions of determining the optimal configuration of manufacturing plants, distribution centers, distributors, and customers, as well as the tactical decisions of designing the product flows through these distribution stages. The model contains multiple criteria, including customer service objectives, in addition to maximizing profit. Its functionality and applicability are shown by implementation in a real-world case study of a consumer goods company.

Chapter 6 discusses multiple criteria network design in health and humanitarian logistics, where the key challenges include multiple conflicting

objectives and the significant amount of inherent uncertainty. The authors
of this chapter present two detailed applications in this area. The first application optimizes the design of a humanitarian assistance and disaster relief
(HA/DR) supply chain network for military aerial delivery operations under
uncertainty that considers trade-offs between military HA/DR aerial delivery
supply chain efficiency and responsiveness. The second application optimizes
the network for federally qualified community health centers to serve at-risk
populations in Pennsylvania.

Chapter 7 incorporates disruption risk in a supply chain network design
model. Supply chain network design decisions that determine the number
and location of facilities and the selection of transportation modes have a
significant impact on competitive performance. However, facilities and
transportation links are susceptible to disruptions. In addition, they have
different capacities to cope with those disruptions, which contribute to supply chain resilience. This chapter provides a framework to quantify the risk
level of supply chain nodes and links. Then, a multiple objective optimization model is presented for designing a resilient supply chain network, with
an emphasis on balancing the cost, responsiveness, and risk of the supply
chain.

Chapter 8 focuses on the *design of closed loop supply chains*. Integrating forward and reverse supply chains, termed closed loop supply chains (CLSC),
has proven to be a challenging task due to the differences in the nature
of the activities that make up the forward and reverse flows. This chapter
discusses the optimal design of a CLSC with *commercial returns* with the
objectives of maximizing profit and minimizing energy usage. The bi-
criteria network design model considers quality-based classification of the
product returns and also the customer behavior toward buying refurbished
products.

Chapter 9 presents a multiple objective multi-period supplier selection
model with product bundling for low cost/low risk items. The buyer's objective is to decide which products to order from which supplier, in what quantity, and in which period. The multi-objective problem is solved using four
different variants of goal programming, and the results are compared.

Chapter 10 incorporates supply disruptions in a multi-objective supplier
selection model and uses "back-up" suppliers as risk mitigation strategies.
Disruption risks are among the major threats to supply chains. By nature,
disruptive events are either very hard or impossible to prevent, making identification and implementation of mitigation measures much more critical.
This chapter presents a statistical model to quantify the effect of disruption
risks and a multiple objective model to improve supply chain decision making by selecting optimal disruption mitigation strategies.

Chapter 11 discusses the use of MCDM models in planning prevention
services in health care. Prevention services have been widely implemented
in communities to improve mental health care for the youth population,
and to reduce antisocial, criminal, and disruptive behaviors. Under this

circumstance, prioritizing prevention services is crucial for policymakers when allocating a limited budget. In this chapter, a budget allocation problem is solved considering limited budget, preferences of policymakers, and effectiveness of each prevention program.

Chapter 12 investigates optimal inventory policies for *divergent supply chains*, under conflicting criteria. Past research has assumed that orders received by the distributor/manufacturer from its retailers are interchangeable and that replenishment to retailers can happen in any manner, without any consideration to the corresponding orders placed by them. Such an approach, without linking replenishment to order, is not acceptable in many real-life supply chains due to the lack of material traceability. The presentation in this chapter is a significant step toward modeling and solving such real-life supply chain problems with inventory allocation and rationing. It also considers multiple objectives of minimizing the total supply chain cost and maximizing the product fill rate.

Additional material is available from the CRC Press website: http://www.crcpress.com/product/isbn/9781498708586.

Acknowledgments

First and foremost, I thank the authors, who have worked diligently in producing the book chapters that are comprehensive, concise, and easy to read, bridging theory and practice. The development and evolution of this book have also benefited substantially from the advice and counsel of my colleagues and friends in academia and industry, who are too numerous to acknowledge individually. They helped me identify the key topics to be included in this volume, suggested chapter authors, and served as reviewers of the manuscripts.

I would like to express my sincere appreciation to Sharan Srinivas and Suchithra Rajendran, industrial engineering doctoral students at The Pennsylvania State University (Penn State), for serving as my editorial assistants for the book and reviewing all the chapters.

I would also like to thank Cindy Carelli, senior acquisition editor, and Jessica Vakili, project coordinator, at CRC Press for their help from the book's inception until its publication. Finally, I wish to thank my dear wife, Bhuvana, for her patience, understanding, and support when I was focused completely on the book project.

Editor

Dr. A. Ravi Ravindran has been a professor and past department head of the Harold and Inge Marcus Department of Industrial and Manufacturing Engineering at The Pennsylvania State University (Penn State) since 1997. Formerly, he was a faculty member in the School of Industrial Engineering at Purdue University for 13 years and at the University of Oklahoma for 15 years. At Oklahoma, he served as the director of the School of Industrial Engineering for 8 years and as the associate provost of the university for 7 years with responsibility for budget, personnel, and space for the academic area. He earned a bachelor of science degree, with honors, in electrical engineering from the Birla Institute of Technology and Science, Pilani, India. His post-graduate degrees are from the University of California, Berkeley, where he earned a master of science and doctoral degree in industrial engineering and operations research.

Dr. Ravindran's area of specialization is operations research with interests in multiple criteria decision making, financial engineering, healthcare delivery systems, and supply chain optimization. He has published six books: *Operations Research: Principles and Practice* (Wiley, 1987); *Engineering Optimization: Methods and Applications* (Wiley, 2006); *Operations Research and Management Science Handbook* (CRC Press, 2008); *Operations Research Methodologies* (CRC Press, 2009); *Operations Research Applications* (CRC Press, 2009); and *Supply Chain Engineering: Models and Applications* (CRC Press, 2013); and more than 150 journal articles on operations research. His most recent book, *Supply Chain Engineering*, received the Institute of Industrial Engineers (IIE) Book-of-the-Year Award in 2013.

Dr. Ravindran is a Fulbright Fellow and a Fellow of the IIE. In 2001, he was recognized by IIE with the Albert G. Holzman Distinguished Educator Award for significant contributions to the industrial engineering profession by an educator. In 2013, he received the Outstanding Teaching Award in the College of Engineering from the Penn State Engineering Alumni Society. He has been a consultant to AT&T, CNH America, General Motors, IBM, Kimberly Clark, General Electric, the US Department of Transportation, the Cellular Telecommunications Industry Association, and the US Air Force. He currently serves as the series editor for the Operations Research Series for CRC Press.

Contributors

Nathaniel D. Bastian
Harold and Inge Marcus
   Department of Industrial and
   Manufacturing Engineering
The Pennsylvania State University
University Park, Pennsylvania

R. Ufuk Bilsel
The Boston Consulting Group
Istanbul, Turkey

Aixa L. Cintrón
Supply Chain Manager
San Juan, Puerto Rico

Paul M. Griffin
H. Milton Stewart School
   of Industrial & Systems
   Engineering
Georgia Institute of Technology
Atlanta, Georgia

Kurian John
Department of Management
   Studies
Indian Institute of Technology
   Madras
Chennai, India

Yuncheol Kang
Harold and Inge Marcus
   Department of Industrial and
   Manufacturing Engineering
The Pennsylvania State University
University Park, Pennsylvania

Yooneun Lee
Harold and Inge Marcus
   Department of Industrial and
   Manufacturing Engineering
The Pennsylvania State University
University Park, Pennsylvania

Subramanian Pazhani
Senior Engineer – Manufacturing
   Operations
Malta, New York

Rodolfo C. Portillo
Amazon
San Jose, Costa Rica

Vittaldas V. Prabhu
Harold and Inge Marcus
   Department of Industrial and
   Manufacturing Engineering
The Pennsylvania State University
University Park, Pennsylvania

Chandrasekharan Rajendran
Department of Management Studies
Indian Institute of Technology
   Madras
Chennai, India

A. Ravi Ravindran
Harold and Inge Marcus
   Department of Industrial and
   Manufacturing Engineering
The Pennsylvania State University
University Park, Pennsylvania

Kanokporn Rienkhemaniyom
Graduate School of Management
   and Innovation
King Mongkut's University of
   Technology Thonburi
Bangkok, Thailand

Christopher J. Solo
Department of Supply Chain and
   Information Systems
The Pennsylvania State University
University Park, Pennsylvania

Lisa M. Ulan
Harold and Inge Marcus
   Department of Industrial and
   Manufacturing Engineering
The Pennsylvania State University
University Park, Pennsylvania

Vijay Wadhwa
Texas Instruments Inc.
Dallas, Texas

Hans Ziegler
Department of Production,
   Operations and Logistics
   Management
Faculty of Business Administration
   and Economics
University of Passau
Passau, Germany

1

Managing Supply Chains: An Introduction

A. Ravi Ravindran

The Pennsylvania State University, University Park, Pennsylvania

CONTENTS

Our focus in this book is on the *design and operation* of the *supply chain system*, which involves connecting many production and distribution systems, often across wide geographic distances, in such a way that the businesses involved can ultimately satisfy consumer demand as efficiently as possible, resulting in maximum financial returns to those businesses connected to that supply chain system. A good discussion of the supply chain design and operation is given in Warsing (2008, 2009).

Most supply chain design and operational problems are multiple criteria decision making (MCDM) problems. In this chapter, we address the meaning of supply chains and the types of design and operational decisions that are made in supply chain management. We introduce a variety of conflict-ing performance measures that are used in supply chain optimization. In Chapter 2, we provide an overview of MCDM models and methods. These two chapters will standardize the terminology that will be used in the book and will set the stage for the various supply chain management problems that will be covered in the chapters that follow.

1.1 Understanding Supply Chains

Before we formally define *supply chain management*, we begin with the defini-tion of a *supply chain*. A supply chain consists of the following:

1. A series of *stages* (e.g., suppliers, manufacturers, distributors, retail-ers, and customers) that are physically distinct and geographically separated at which inventory is either stored or converted in form and/or in value.

2. A coordinated set of *activities* concerned with the procurement of raw materials, production of intermediate and finished products, and the distribution of these products to customers within and external to the chain.

Thus, a supply chain includes all the partners involved in fulfilling cus-tomer demands and all the activities performed in fulfilling those demands. Figure 1.1 illustrates a typical supply chain.

It is important to recognize that, for a multi-national company with a global supply chain network, the different stages of the supply chain (suppliers, plants, distribution centers [DCs], and retailers) may be located in different countries.

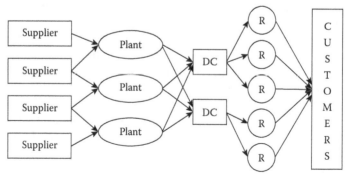

(DC = distribution center, R = retailer)

FIGURE 1.1
Supply chain network.

It is also possible that a firm may employ fewer supply chain stages than those represented in Figure 1.1, or perhaps more. Indeed, some business researchers (e.g., Fine 2000) argue that the supply chains in various industries follow historical cycles that move from periods of significant vertical integration to periods of significantly less integration, where firms in the supply chain rely more on partnerships than on owning substantial portions of the value chain within a single firm. In vertical integration periods, the supply chain may employ only a few stages from raw material extraction to final production, owned primarily or exclusively by a single firm. A good example of this would be the early days of Ford Motor Company in the 1920s. In the less integrated periods, it is the horizontal, across-firm relationships that are prominent. A good example would be in the 1990s and early 2000s, when Dell led the global market for personal computers with a highly decentralized supply chain in which they served only as the final assembler and direct distributor. In this latter case, Dell not only relied heavily on its suppliers to independently manage the production and supply of components but also simply bypassed independent distributors and retailers and dealt with the final consumers directly, without the "middle men." Interestingly, Fine's (2000) hypothesis regarding cycles of change in various industries may be coming to light in the personal computer (PC) industry because Dell has recently added the retail "middle men" back into its supply chain.

1.1.1 Flows in Supply Chains

Following Chopra and Meindl (2001), the key flows in a supply chain are as follows:

- *Products:* Includes raw materials, work-in-progress (WIP), sub-assemblies, and finished goods
- *Funds:* Includes invoices, payments, and credits
- *Information:* Includes orders, deliveries, marketing promotions, plant capacities, inventory, and so on

Thus, the flows in the supply chain are not just "goods." Tracking flows from the suppliers to the customers is called *"moving downstream"* in the supply chain. Tracking flows from the customers to the suppliers is called *"moving upstream"* in the supply chain.

1.2 Managing Supply Chains

Chopra and Meindl (2001, p. 6) define supply chain management (SCM) as "the management of flows between and among supply chain stages to maximize supply chain profitability." A more complete definition of SCM by

Simchi-Levi et al. (2003, p. 1) states, "SCM is a set of approaches utilized to efficiently integrate suppliers, manufacturers, warehouses, and stores, so that merchandise is produced and distributed at the right quantities to the right locations, and at the right time in order to minimize system-wide costs while satisfying service level requirements." Their definition brings out all the key aspects of SCM, including the two conflicting objectives in SCM—minimizing supply chain costs while simultaneously maximizing customer service.

Ravindran and Warsing (2013) define *supply chain engineering*, which encompasses the following key activities for the effective management of a supply chain:

1. Design of the supply chain network, namely the location of plants, DCs, warehouses, and so on
2. Procurement of raw materials and parts from suppliers to the manufacturing plants
3. Management of the production and inventory of finished goods to meet customer demands
4. Management of the transportation and logistics network to deliver the final products to the warehouses and retailers
5. Managing the integrity of the supply chain network by mitigating supply chain disruptions at all levels

Most of the aforementioned activities involved in supply chain engineering (SCE) also come under the rubrics of SCM. An important distinction, however, between SCE and SCM is the emphasis in SCE on the design of the supply chain network and the use of mathematical models and methods to determine the optimal strategies for managing the supply chain.

This emphasis on mathematical models makes sense if one returns to the introductory comments of the chapter, where we point out that our emphasis in this book is really on supply chain design, namely on the design of a relatively complex system of interconnections and flows that move both goods and information around the globe. In order to accomplish that in a systematic way, we must turn to some reasonably precise and verifiable tools of analysis. Hence, our emphasis on design—ultimately, what we hope to characterize as *optimal* design—requires a hand-in-hand emphasis on mathematical models.

Without doubt, commerce has become increasingly global in scope over the past several decades. This trend toward *globalization* has resulted in supply chains whose footprint is often huge, spanning multiple countries and continents. Because products and funds now regularly flow across international boundaries, engineering a global supply chain becomes impractical—or at least ill-advised—without the use of sophisticated mathematical models. The use of MCDM methods for managing the supply chain decisions will be the primary focus of this book.

1.3 Supply Chain Decisions

The various decisions in SCE can be broadly grouped into three types: strategic, tactical, and operational.

1.3.1 Strategic Decisions

Strategic decisions deal primarily with the design of the supply chain network and the selection of partners. These decisions are not only made over a relatively long time period (usually spanning several years) and have greater impact in terms of the company's resources, but they are also subject to significant uncertainty in the operating environment over this lengthy span of time. Examples of strategic decisions include:

- *Network Design:* Where to locate and at what capacity
  - Number and location of plants and warehouses
  - Plant and warehouse capacity levels
- *Production and Sourcing:* To make or to buy
  - Produce internally or outsource
  - Choice of suppliers, subcontractors, and other partners
- *Information Technology:* How to coordinate the chain
  - Develop software internally or purchase commercially available packages, such as SAP, Oracle

1.3.2 Tactical Decisions

Tactical decisions are primarily supply chain planning decisions and are made in a time horizon of moderate length, generally as monthly or quarterly decisions, covering a planning horizon of one or two years. Thus, these decisions are typically made in an environment characterized by less uncertainty relative to strategic decisions, but where the effects of uncertainty still are not inconsequential. Examples of tactical decisions include:

- *Purchasing decisions:* For example, how much to buy and when?
- *Production planning decisions:* For example, how much to produce and when?
- *Inventory management decisions:* For example, how much and when to hold to balance the costs of resupply with the risks of shortages?
- *Transportation decisions:* For example, which modes to choose and how frequently to ship using them?
- *Distribution decisions:* For example, how DC replenishment be coordinated with production schedules?

1.3.3 Operational Decisions

Operational decisions are short-term decisions made on a daily/weekly basis, at which point much of the operational uncertainty that existed when the strategic and tactical decisions were made has been resolved. In addition, because the time scale is so short, most of these decisions involve a significantly lower expenditure of funds. Examples include:

- Setting delivery schedules for shipments from suppliers
- Setting due dates for customer orders
- Generating weekly or daily production schedules
- Allocating limited supply (e.g., between backorders and new customer demand)

It is important to recognize that the three types of supply chain decisions—strategic, tactical, and operational—are interrelated. For example, the number and locations of plants affect the choice of suppliers and the transportation mode for receiving raw materials. Moreover, the number and locations of plants and warehouses also affect the inventory levels required at the warehouses and the delivery times of products to customers. Aggregate production planning decisions affect product availability and customer fulfillment.

1.4 Importance of SCM

SCM can have a significant impact on business performance. Based on a 2003 study conducted by Accenture in conjunction with Stanford University, Mulani (2005) reported the following:

- Nearly 90% of the companies surveyed said that SCM is critical or very important.
- 51% said that the importance of SCM had increased significantly in the five years leading up to the survey.
- SCM accounted for nearly 70% of the companies' operating costs and comprised at least half of all the typical company's assets.

Mulani (2005) also reported that a significant percentage of promised synergies for many company mergers and acquisitions came from SCM. For example, during the HP/Compaq merger, it was estimated that the merger would result in a savings of $2.5 billion, of which $1.8 billion would be due to supply chain efficiency.

Moreover, failure to excel in SCM can negatively affect a company's stock prices. Hendricks and Singhal (2005) found this to be true in a study of 885 supply chain disruptions reported by publicly traded companies from 1989 to 2000. The list included small, medium, and large companies with respect to market capitalization and covered both manufacturing and information technology (IT) industries. A summary of their findings is given here:

- An average loss of over $250 million in shareholder value per disruption
- An average reduction of 10% in stock price
- 92% reduction in return on assets
- 7% lower sales
- 11% increase in cost of doing business
- 14% increase in inventory

SCM has become sufficiently important to business performance to warrant a mantra of sorts, namely that "companies do not compete with each other, but their supply chains do." Although some might debate whether entire supply chains could literally compete with each other, there is no doubt that efficient management of the supply chain has become a competitive differentiator for many companies.

1.5 Enablers and Drivers of Supply Chain Performance

1.5.1 Supply Chain Enablers

Enablers make things happen and, in the case of SCM, are considered essential for a supply chain to perform effectively. Without the necessary enablers, the supply chain will not function smoothly. Simply having the necessary enablers, however, does not guarantee a successful supply chain performance.

Based on a survey of supply chain managers, Marien (2000) describes four enablers of effective management of the supply chain. In order of their ranked importance by the survey respondents, they are organizational infrastructure, information technology, strategic alliances, and human resource management.

- *Organizational infrastructure:* As we mentioned earlier, the essential issue in this case is whether SCM activities internal to the firm, and across firms in the supply chain, are organized in more of a vertical orientation or with greater decentralization. The fact that this enabler ranked first among practicing supply chain managers is clearly consistent with much that has been written in the trade press regarding the fact that intrafirm SCM processes must be in place and operating effectively before there is any hope that interfirm collaboration on supply chain management activities is to be successful.

- *Technology:* Two types of technology are critical to success in designing and managing supply chains effectively—information technology and manufacturing technology. Although the emphasis of many consultants and software providers is on information technology, product design can often have more impact on whether supply chain efficiencies ultimately can be achieved. Prominently, product design should account for manufacturability (e.g., using modular components that utilize common interfaces with multiple final products), and it should allow for efficiencies in managing inventories and distribution processes.

- *Alliances:* The effectiveness of alliances is particularly important in supply chains that are more decentralized, wherein more authority is given to suppliers. In some cases, these suppliers may take on roles that go beyond just supplying components; instead they may become outsourcing partners who assume significant responsibility for product design and manufacturing.

- *Human resources:* Two categories of employees are critical to effective SCM. First, technical employees assume an important role in designing networks that minimize costs while simultaneously achieving high levels of customer service performance. These employees must have a solid understanding of the types of mathematical tools that we discuss in this book. Second, managerial employees must have a solid conceptual grasp on the key issues addressed by the models and tools of the technical staff and must clearly understand how such tools ultimately can be applied to allow the firm to achieve its strategic goals.

1.5.2 Supply Chain Drivers

Supply chain drivers represent the critical areas of decision making in SCM—those that ultimately generate the outcomes that impact supply chain performance. Thus, they appear as the decision/design variables in the optimization models used in SCM decision making. Following Ravindran and Warsing (2013), the key drivers of supply chain performance are described in the following sections.

1.5.2.1 Inventory

Companies maintain inventory of raw materials, WIP, and finished goods to protect against unpredictable demand and unreliable supply. Inventory is considered an *idle asset* of the company and is one of the major portions of supply chain costs. Maintaining large inventories increases supply chain costs but provides a higher level of customer service.

The key decision variables here are what items to hold in inventory (raw materials, WIP, and finished products), how much and when to order (inventory policies), and where to hold inventory (locations). Chapters 4, 5, and 12 discuss the supply chain inventory issues in detail.

1.5.2.2 Transportation

Transportation is concerned with the movement of items among the supply chain stages—suppliers, plants, DCs, retailers. Use of faster transportation modes such as air and roadways incurs higher transportation costs but reduces delivery times and increases reliability. The key decision variables here are:

1. Whether to outsource transportation decision making and execution to a third party logistics (3PL) provider
2. What transportation mode(s) to use (air, sea, road, etc.) for what items (raw materials, WIP, and finished goods)
3. Distribution options for finished goods (either shipped to customers directly or through intermediate distribution centers)

Chapters 3, 5, 7, and 8 discuss the transportation issues in supply chains.

1.5.2.3 Facilities

Facilities (plants and distribution centers) play a key role in managing supply chains. They are generally considered as strategic decisions and directly affect the performance of the supply chain. The key decision variables under facilities are the following:

1. Number of plants and their locations
2. Plant capacities and product mix allocated to plants
3. Number of DCs and their locations
4. Distribution strategies

Chapters 3–8 and 11 discuss the use of multiple criteria integer programming models to make optimal decisions regarding the number and location of supply chain facilities.

1.5.2.4 Suppliers

Raw material cost accounts for 40–60% of the production cost in most manufacturing industries. In fact, for the automotive industry, the cost of components and parts from outside suppliers may exceed 50% of sales (Wadhwa and Ravindran 2007). For technology firms, it could be as high as 80%. Hence, the selection of suppliers for raw materials and intermediate components is considered a critical area of strategic decision making in SCM. Chapters 3, 4, 7, 9, and 10 discuss supplier selection models under multiple conflicting criteria.

1.6 Assessing and Managing Supply Chain Performance

The idea that there are key drivers of supply chain performance is useful in thinking about another theme emphasized by many authors and was first proposed by Fisher (1997) in an important article that advanced the notion that "one size fits all" is not an effective approach to managing supply chains. Fisher (1997) cogently lays out a matrix that matches product characteristics—what he describes as a dichotomy between *innovative* products (such as those that are technology based) and *functional* products (such as toothpaste or other staple goods)—and supply chain characteristics—and another dichotomy between *efficient* (cost-focused) supply chains and *responsive* (customer service-focused) supply chains. Chopra and Meindl (2001) take this conceptual model a step further, first by pointing out that Fisher's product characteristics and supply chain strategies are really continuous spectrums, and then by superimposing the Fisher model, as it were, on a frontier that represents the natural trade-off between responsiveness and efficiency. Clearly, it stands to reason that a firm, or a supply chain, cannot maximize cost efficiency and customer responsiveness simultaneously. Some aspects of each of these objectives necessarily work at cross purposes. A combined version of Chopra and Meindl's frontier and Fisher's product dichotomy is presented in Figure 1.2.

The value of this perspective is that it clearly identifies a market driven basis for strategic choices regarding the supply chain drivers: Should our inventory management decisions be focused more on efficiency (e.g., minimizing inventory levels) or on responsiveness (e.g., maximizing product availability)? Should our transportation choices be focused more on efficiency (e.g., minimizing transportation costs, perhaps through more extensive economies of scale) or on responsiveness (e.g., minimizing delivery lead times and maximizing reliability)? Should our facilities (network design) decisions be focused more on efficiency (e.g., minimizing the number of locations and maximizing their size and scale) or on responsiveness (e.g., seeking high levels of customer service by choosing many focused locations closer to customers)?

In the following, we discuss efficiency and responsiveness in more detail, and we also introduce *supply chain risk* as an additional criterion to consider in designing the supply chain network and its associated operating policies.

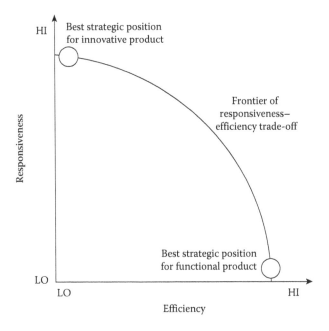

FIGURE 1.2
Responsiveness/efficiency trade-off frontier.

1.6.1 Supply Chain Efficiency

Generally, efficiency is measured by a ratio of the level of output generated to the level of input consumed to generate that output. This concept can be applied to physical systems (e.g., an automobile engine that converts the energy stored in the fuel consumed by the engine into horsepower generated by the engine to drive the wheels of the vehicle) and to businesses (e.g., the conversion of dollar-valued inputs—such as labor, materials, and the costs of owning and/or operating physical assets such as plants and warehouses—into sales revenue). Therefore, the efficiency of a given supply chain focuses on how well resources are utilized across the chain to fulfill customer demand. In Fisher's conceptual framework (1997), discussed earlier, efficient supply chains are focused more on cost minimization—the idea being that a supply chain that requires less cost input to generate the same amount of sales revenue output is more efficient. Therefore, efficiency measures in SCM are often focused on costs, and they include the following:

- Raw material cost
- Manufacturing cost
- Distribution cost

- Inventory holding cost
- Facility operating costs
- Freight transportation costs
- Shortage costs

In addition, other measures that may influence the costs listed here include:

- *Product cycle time:* This is the time that elapses from the start of production of the item up to its conversion into a product that can be shipped to the customer. Clearly, longer cycle times can result in larger costs (e.g., labor costs and/or inventory holding costs).
- *Inventory levels:* Again, higher levels of inventory can result in a number of associated costs, beyond the cost of tying up the firm's cash in currently idle assets. Higher inventory levels generate greater needs for storage space and for labor hours and/or employee levels in order to manage these inventories as they reside in and flow among storage facilities.

Typically, supply chain optimization models focus on minimizing costs because the decisions of supply chain managers often involve choices that directly influence costs, while revenue may often be outside the scope of the supply chain manager's decisions. Some models, however, may appropriately involve maximizing profit—to the extent that it is clear that the decision at hand has both cost and revenue implications.

1.6.2 Supply Chain Responsiveness

Responsiveness refers to the extent to which customer needs and expectations are met and also the extent to which the supply chain can flexibly accommodate changes in these needs and expectations. Thus, in the efficiency–responsiveness trade-off introduced by the Fisher (1997) framework discussed earlier, firms whose supply chains are focused on responsiveness are willing to accept higher levels of cost (i.e., lower cost efficiency) in order to improve their ability to meet and flexibly accommodate customer requirements (i.e., higher responsiveness). Common measures of responsiveness are:

- Reliability and accuracy of fulfilling customer orders
- Delivery time
- Product variety
- Time to process special or unique customer requests (customization)
- Percent of customer demand filled from finished goods inventory versus built to order from raw materials or component inventories

1.6.3 Supply Chain Risk

A third supply chain criterion has gained attention in recent years. The September 11, 2001, terrorist attacks in the United States obviously had broad and lasting impacts on society in general. From the standpoint of managing supply chains, the disruption in material flows over the days and weeks after September 11 caused companies to realize that a singular emphasis on the cost efficiency of the supply chain can actually make the chain brittle and much more susceptible to the risk of disruptions. This includes not only catastrophic disruptions such as large-scale terrorist attacks but even mundane, commonly occurring disruptions such as a labor strike at a supplier. Thus, effective SCM no longer just involves moving products efficiently along the supply chain, but it also includes mitigating risks along the way. Ravindran and Warsing (2013) classify supply chain risks into two types:

1. *Hazard risks:* These are disruptions to the supply chain that arise from large-scale events with broad geographic impacts, such as natural disasters (e.g., hurricanes, floods, blizzards), terrorist attacks, and major political actions such as wars or border closings.
2. *Operational risks:* These are more commonly occurring disruptions whose impacts are localized (e.g., affecting only a single supplier) and are resolved over a relatively short period of time. Examples include information technology disruptions (e.g., a server crash due to a computer virus infection), supplier quality problems, and temporary logistical failures (e.g., temporarily "lost" shipments).

Chapters 3, 7, 9, and 10 incorporate supply chain risk as an objective in multi-criteria optimization models.

1.6.4 Conflicting Criteria in Supply Chain Optimization

It is important to recognize that efficiency and responsiveness are conflicting criteria in managing supply chains. For example, customer responsiveness can be increased by having a larger inventory of several different products, but this increases inventory costs and thereby reduces efficiency. Similarly, using fewer distribution centers reduces facility costs and can also reduce inventory levels across the network through "risk pooling" effects. The downside, however, is that such a network design increases delivery time and thereby reduces responsiveness, and it also increases supply chain risk by concentrating the risk of distribution failure in fewer facilities. Thus, supply chain optimization problems generally are multiple criteria optimization models. In the chapters that follow, we use multiple criteria optimization models to determine the optimal solutions. An overview of MCDM models and methods is given in Chapter 2.

References

Chopra, S. and P. Meindl. 2001. *Supply Chain Management: Strategy, Planning and Operation*. Upper Saddle River, NJ: Pearson Education.

Fine, C. H. 2000. Clock speed based strategies for supply chain design. *Production and Operations Management* 9(3): 213–221.

Fisher, M. 1997. What is the right supply chain for your product? *Harvard Business Review*, March–April, pp. 105–116.

Hendricks, K. B. and V. R. Singhal. 2005. Association between supply chain glitches and operating performance. *Management Science* 51(5): 695–711.

Marien, E. J. 2000. The four supply chain enablers. *Supply Chain Management Review*, March–April, pp. 60–68.

Mulani, N. 2005. High performance supply chains. *Production and Operations Management Society (POMS) Conference*, April 29–May 2, Chicago, IL.

Ravindran, A. R. and D. P. Warsing. 2013. *Supply Chain Engineering: Models and Applications*. Boca Raton, FL: CRC Press.

Simchi-Levi, D., P. Kaminisky, and E. Simchi-Levi. 2003. *Designing and Managing the Supply Chain*. 2nd Edition. New York: McGraw Hill.

Wadhwa, V. and A. Ravindran. 2007. Vendor selection in outsourcing. *Computers and Operations Research* 34: 3725–3737.

Warsing, D. P. 2008. Supply chain management. In *Operations Research and Management Science Handbook*, chapter 22 (pp. 1–63), A. R. Ravindran (Ed.). Boca Raton, FL: CRC Press.

Warsing, D. P. 2009. Supply chain management. In *Operations Research Applications*, chapter 8 (pp. 1–63), A. Ravindran (Ed.). Boca Raton, FL: CRC Press.

2

Multiple Criteria Decision Making: An Overview

A. Ravi Ravindran

The Pennsylvania State University, University Park, Pennsylvania

CONTENTS

Managers are frequently called upon to make decisions under multiple criteria that conflict with one another. For example, supply chain engineers have to consider conflicting criteria—such as supply chain costs, customer responsiveness, and supply chain risk—when making decisions. The general framework of a multiple criteria optimization problem is to simultaneously optimize several criteria that are usually conflicting and subject to a system of constraints that define the feasible alternatives. Multiple criteria decision making (MCDM) problems are categorized on the basis of whether (i) the constraints are implicit (i.e., the feasible alternatives are *finite and known*) or (ii) the constraints are explicit and given by a set of linear and nonlinear inequalities or equations (i.e., the feasible alternatives are *infinite and unknown*). MCDM problems with finite (known) alternatives are called multiple criteria selection problems (MCSPs). MCDM problems with infinite (unknown) alternatives are called multiple criteria mathematical programming (MCMP) problems. In this chapter, we will give an overview of some of the methods that are available for solving both MCSPs and MCMP problems. For a more detailed discussion of multi-criteria optimization methods, the reader is referred to Masud and Ravindran (2008, 2009).

2.1 Multiple Criteria Selection Problems

For MCSP, the alternatives are finite, and their criteria values are known a priori in the form of a *pay-off matrix*. Table 2.1 illustrates the pay-off matrix for an MCSP with n alternatives (1, 2, ..., n) and p criteria ($f_1, f_2, ..., f_p$). The matrix elements, f_{ij}, denote the value of criterion j for alternative i.

TABLE 2.1

Pay-Off Matrix of MCSP

	Criteria/Objectives (Max)				
	f_1	f_2	f_3	$\cdots$	f_p
Alt. 1	f_{11}	f_{12}	f_{13}		f_{1p}
2	f_{21}	f_{22}	f_{23}		f_{2p}
–					
–					
–					
N	f_{n1}	f_{n2}	f_{n3}		f_{np}
Max f_i	f_1^*	f_2^*	f_3^*		f_p^*

2.1.1 Concept of "Best Solution"

In a single objective optimization problem, the "best solution" is defined in terms of an "optimal solution" that maximizes (or minimizes) the objective, compared to all other feasible solutions (alternatives). In MCSP, due to the conflicting nature of the objectives, the optimal values of the various criteria do not usually occur at the same alternative. Hence, the notion of an optimal or best alternative does not exist in MCSP. Instead, decision making in MCSP is equivalent to choosing the "most preferred" alternative or the "best compromise" solution based on the preferences of the decision maker (DM). Thus, the objective of the MCSP method is to rank order the alternatives from the best to the worst, based on the DM's preference structure.

We begin the discussion with some key definitions and concepts in solving MCSP. We will assume that all the criteria in Table 2.1 are to be maximized.

2.1.2 Dominated Alternative

Alternative i is dominated by alternative k if and only if $f_{kj} \geq f_{ij}$, for all $j = 1, 2, \ldots, p$ and for at least one j, $f_{kj} > f_{ij}$. In other words, the criteria values of alternative k are as good as those of alternative i and, for at least one criterion, alternative k is better than i.

2.1.3 Non-Dominated Alternatives

An alternative that is not dominated by any other feasible alternatives is called *non-dominated*, *Pareto optimal*, or an *efficient* alternative. For a non-dominated alternative, an increase in the value of any one criterion is possible only with a decrease in the value of at least one other criterion.

2.1.4 Ideal Solution

The ideal solution is the vector of the best values achievable for each criterion. In other words, if $f_j^* = \max\limits_i f_{ij}$, then the ideal solution $= \left(f_1^*, f_2^*, \ldots, f_p^* \right)$. Because the f_j^* values may correspond to different alternatives, the ideal solution is not achievable for MCSP. However, it provides good target values to compare against for a trade-off analysis.

2.2 Multi-Criteria Ranking Methods

Weighted methods are commonly used to rank the alternatives under conflicting criteria. Based on the DM's preferences, a weight w_j is obtained for criterion j such that

$$w_j \geq 0 \text{ and } \sum_{j=1}^{p} w_j = 1 \tag{2.1}$$

Next, a weighted score of the criteria values is calculated for each alternative as follows:

$$\text{Score}(i) = \sum_{j=1}^{p} w_j f_{ij} \quad \text{for } i = 1, 2, \ldots, n \tag{2.2}$$

The alternatives are then ranked based on their scores. The alternative with the highest score is ranked at the top.

There are two common approaches for determining the criteria weights based on the DM's preferences.

2.2.1 Rating Method

Here the DM is asked to provide a rating for each criterion on a scale of 1–10 (with 10 being the most important and 1 being the least important). The ratings are then normalized to determine the weights as follows:

$$w_j = \frac{r_j}{\sum_{j=1}^{p} r_j} \tag{2.3}$$

where r_j is the rating assigned to criterion j for $j = 1, 2, \ldots, p$.

NOTE: $w_j \geq 0$ and $\sum_{j=1}^{p} w_j = 1$.

2.2.2 Borda Count Method

Under the ranking method devised by Jean Charles de Borda (an eighteenth-century French physicist), the DM is asked to rank the p criteria from the most important (ranked first) to the least important (ranked last). The criterion that is ranked first gets p points, the one that is ranked second gets $(p - 1)$ points, and the last place criterion gets 1 point. The sum of all the points for the p criteria is given by

$$S = \frac{p(p+1)}{2} \tag{2.4}$$

The criteria weights are then calculated by dividing the points assigned to criterion j by the sum S, given by Equation 2.4.

Let us illustrate the basic definitions (dominated, non-dominated, and ideal solutions) and the two weighting methods with a numerical example.

Example 2.1 (Faculty Recruiting)

An industrial engineering (IE) department has interviewed five doctoral candidates for a faculty position and has rated them on a scale of 1–10 (with 10 being the best and 1 being the worst) on three key criteria—research, teaching, and service. The criteria values of the candidates are given in Table 2.2.

1. Determine the ideal solution to this problem. Is the ideal solution achievable?
2. Identify the dominated and non-dominated candidates.
3. Determine the ranking of the candidates using
   a. Rating method
   b. Borda count method

Solution

1. The ideal solution represents the best values achievable for each criterion. Because all the criteria are to maximize, the ideal solution is given by (8, 8, 5). The ideal solution is not achievable because the criteria conflict with one another and no candidate has the ideal values.

TABLE 2.2

Faculty Recruiting for Example 2.1

Candidate	Criteria		
	Research	Teaching	Service
A	8	4	3
B	4	5	3
C	6	6	5
D	2	8	4
E	7	3	2

2. Candidate A dominates E because A has higher values for all three criteria. Similarly, candidate C dominates B. On the other hand, Candidates A, C, and D are non-dominated.
3. Using the two ranking methods, the following are determined.
   a. Rating method: Assume that the ratings for research, teaching, and service are 9, 7, and 4, respectively. Then, the weights for research, teaching, and service are computed using Equation 2.3 as follows:

   $$w_R = 9/(9 + 7 + 4) = 0.45$$

   $$w_T = 7/20 = 0.35$$

   $$w_S = 4/20 = 0.20$$

   Note that the sum of the weights is equal to one. Using the criteria weights, the weighted score for Candidate A is computed using Equation 2.2: Score (A) = (0.45) 8 + (0.35) 4 + (0.2) 3 = 5.6

   Similarly, the scores for the other candidates are computed and are given as follows:

   $$\text{Score (B)} = 4.15$$

   $$\text{Score (C)} = 5.8$$

   $$\text{Score (D)} = 4.5$$

   $$\text{Score (E)} = 4.6$$

   The five candidates are then ranked, using their scores, from the highest to the lowest. Thus, Candidate C is ranked first, followed by candidates A, E, D, and B, respectively.
   b. Borda count method: Assume that the three criteria are ranked as follows:

Rank	Criteria
1	Research
2	Teaching
3	Service

   Thus, research gets 3 points, teaching 2 points, and service 1 point. Their sum (S) is 6, and the weights are

   $$w_R = 3/6 = 0.50$$

   $$w_T = 2/6 = 0.33$$

   $$w_S = 1/6 = 0.17$$

Using the above weights and Equation 2.2, the scores for candidates A, B, C, D, and E are 5.83, 4.17, 5.83, 4.33, and 4.83, respectively. Thus, both candidate A and C are tied for first place, followed by candidates E, D, and B. Note that the rankings are not exactly the same for the two methods. This does happen in practice.

2.2.3 Pairwise Comparison of Criteria

When there are many criteria, it would be difficult for a DM to rank order them precisely. In practice, pairwise comparison of criteria is used to facilitate the criteria ranking required by the Borda count method. Here, the DM is asked to give the relative importance between two criteria C_i and C_j, whether C_i is preferred to C_j, C_j is preferred to C_i or both are equally important. When there are n criteria, the DM has to respond to $\dfrac{n(n-1)}{2}$ pairwise comparisons. Based on the DM's response, the criteria rankings and their weights can be computed, following the steps given here:

Step 1: Based on the DM's response, a pairwise comparison matrix, $P_{(n \times n)}$, is constructed, whose elements p_{ij} are as follows:

$$p_{ii} = 1 \quad \text{for all } i = 1, 2, ..., n$$

$p_{ij} = 1, p_{ji} = 0$, if C_i is preferred to C_j ($C_i > C_j$).
$p_{ij} = 0, p_{ji} = 1$, if C_j is preferred to C_i ($C_i < C_j$).
$p_{ij} = p_{ji} = 1$, if C_i and C_j are equally important.

Step 2: Compute the row sums of the matrix P as

$$t_i = \sum_j p_{ij}, \quad \text{for } i = 1, 2, ..., n$$

Step 3: Rank the criteria based on the t_i values and compute their weights,

$$W_j = \frac{t_j}{\sum_i t_i}, \quad \forall j = 1, 2, ..., n$$

Example 2.2

Five criteria—A, B, C, D, and E—have to be ranked based on 10 pairwise comparisons as follows.

- A > B, A > C, A > D, A > E
- B < C, B > D, B < E
- C > D, C < E
- D < E

Solution

Step 1: Construct the pairwise comparison matrix *P*.

$P_{(5\times5)}$ =	A	B	C	D	E
A	1	1	1	1	1
B	0	1	0	1	0
C	0	1	1	1	0
D	0	0	0	1	0
E	0	1	1	1	1

Step 2: Compute the row sums as $t_A = 5$, $t_B = 2$, $t_C = 3$, $t_D = 1$, and $t_E = 4$.

Step 3: The ranking of the five criteria is A > E > C > B > D and their weights are: $W_A = \dfrac{5}{15}$, $W_B = \dfrac{2}{15}$, $W_C = \dfrac{3}{15}$, $W_D = \dfrac{1}{15}$, and $W_E = \dfrac{4}{15}$.

2.3 Scaling Criteria Values

The major drawback of the ranking methods discussed so far is that they use criteria weights that require the criteria values to be scaled properly. For example, in Table 2.2, all the criteria values ranged between 2 and 8. In other words, they have been already scaled. In practice, the criteria are measured in different units. Some criteria values may be very large (e.g., cost), while others may be very small (e.g., quality, delivery time). If the criteria values are not scaled properly, the criteria with large magnitudes would simply dominate the final rankings, independent of the assigned weights. In this section, we shall discuss some common approaches to scaling the criteria values.

Consider a supplier selection problem with *m* suppliers and *n* criteria, where f_{ij} denotes the value of criterion *j* for supplier *i*. Let *F* denote the supplier criteria matrix:

$$F_{(m \times n)} = [f_{ij}]$$

Determine $H_j = \max_i f_{ij}$
$L_j = \min_i f_{ij}$
H_j will be the ideal value if criterion *j* is maximizing and L_j is its ideal value if it is minimizing.

2.3.1 Simple Scaling

In simple scaling, the criteria values are multiplied by 10^K where "K" is a positive or negative integer, including zero. This is the most common scaling method used in practice. If a criterion is to be minimized, its values should be multiplied by (–1) before computing the weighted score.

2.3.2 Ideal Value Method

In this method, criteria values are scaled using their ideal values as given below:

$$\text{For "max" criterion: } r_{ij} = \frac{f_{ij}}{H_j} \tag{2.5}$$

$$\text{For "min" criterion: } r_{ij} = \frac{L_j}{f_{ij}} \tag{2.6}$$

Note that the scaled criteria values (r_{ij}) will always be ≤ 1, and all the criteria have been changed to maximization. The best value of each criterion is 1, but the worst value need not necessarily be zero. In the next approach, all criteria values will be scaled between 0 and 1, with 1 for the best value and 0 for the worst.

2.3.3 Simple Linearization (Linear Normalization)

Here the criteria values are scaled as follows:

$$\text{For "max" criterion: } r_{ij} = \frac{f_{ij} - L_j}{H_j - L_j} \tag{2.7}$$

$$\text{For "min" criterion: } r_{ij} = \frac{H_j - f_{ij}}{H_j - L_j} \tag{2.8}$$

All the scaled criteria values will be between 0 and 1, and all the criteria are to be maximized after scaling.

2.3.4 Use of L_p Norm (Vector Scaling)

The L_p norm of a vector $X \in R^n$ is given by L_p norm $= \left[\sum_{j=1}^{n} |X_j|^p \right]^{\frac{1}{p}}$, for $p = 1, 2, \ldots, \infty$.

The most common values of p are $p = 1, 2$, and ∞.

$$\text{For } p = 1, L_1 \text{ norm} = \sum_{j=1}^{n} |X_j| \tag{2.9}$$

$$\text{For } p = 2, L_2 \text{ norm} = \left[\sum_{j=1}^{n} |X_j|^2 \right]^{\frac{1}{2}} \text{ (length of vector } X) \tag{2.10}$$

$$\text{For } p = \infty, L_\infty \text{ norm} = \max[|X_j|] \text{ (Tchebycheff's norm)} \tag{2.11}$$

In this method, scaling is done by dividing the criteria values by their respective L_p norms. After scaling, the L_p norm of each criterion will be one. We shall illustrate the different scaling methods with an example.

2.3.5 Illustrative Example of Scaling Criteria Values

Example 2.3 (Scaling Criteria Values)

Consider a supplier selection problem with three suppliers—A, B, and C, and three selection criteria—total cost of ownership (TCO), service, and experience. The criteria values are given in Table 2.3. TCO has to be minimized, while the service and experience criteria have to be maximized.

Solution

Note that the high cost supplier A gives the best service and has the most experience, while supplier C has the lowest cost and experience and gives poor service. The criteria values are not scaled properly, particularly cost measured in dollars. If the values are not scaled, TCO criterion will dominate the selection process irrespective of its assigned weight. If we assume that the criteria weights are equal $\left(\dfrac{1}{3}\right)$, then the weighted score for each supplier would be

$$S_A = \frac{(-125{,}000 + 10 + 9)}{3} = -41{,}660$$

$$S_B = \frac{(-95{,}000 + 5 + 6)}{3} = -31{,}663$$

$$S_C = \frac{(-65{,}000 + 3 + 3)}{3} = -21{,}665$$

Note that the cost criterion (TCO) has been multiplied by (−1) to convert it to a maximization criterion, before computing the weighted score. Supplier C has the maximum weighted score and the rankings will be Supplier C > Supplier B > Supplier A in that order. In fact, even if the weight for TCO is reduced, cost will continue to dominate as long as it is not scaled properly. Let us look at the rankings after scaling the criteria values by the methods given in this section.

2.3.5.1 Simple Scaling Illustration

Dividing TCO values by 10,000, we get the scaled values as 12.5, 9.5, and 6.5, which are comparable in magnitude with the criteria values for service

TABLE 2.3

Supplier Criteria Values for Example 2.3

	TCO (Min)	Service (Max)	Experience (Max)
Supplier A	$125,000	10	9
Supplier B	$95,000	5	6
Supplier C	$65,000	3	3

and experience. Assuming equal weight again for the criteria, the new weighted scores of the suppliers are as follows:

$$S_A = \frac{(-12.5 + 10 + 9)}{3} = 2.17$$

$$S_B = \frac{(-9.5 + 5 + 6)}{3} = 0.5$$

$$S_C = \frac{(-6.5 + 3 + 3)}{3} = -0.17$$

Now, Supplier A is the best, followed by Suppliers B and C.

2.3.5.2 Scaling by Ideal Value Illustration

For Example 2.3 (Table 2.3), the maximum and minimum criteria values are as follows:

$$C_1 - \text{TCO: } H_1 = 125,000, L_1 = 65,000$$

$$C_2 - \text{Service: } H_2 = 10, L_2 = 3$$

$$C_3 - \text{Experience: } H_3 = 9, L_3 = 3$$

The ideal values for the three criteria are 65,000, 10, and 9, respectively. Of course, the ideal solution is not achievable. Using the ideal value method, the scaled criteria values are computed using Equation 2.6 for TCO and Equation 2.5 for service and experience. They are given in Table 2.4.

Note that the scaled values are such that all criteria (including TCO) have to be maximized. Thus, the new weighted scores are

$$S_A = \frac{(0.52 + 1 + 1)}{3} = 0.84$$

$$S_B = \frac{(0.68 + 0.5 + 0.67)}{3} = 0.62$$

$$S_C = \frac{(1 + 0.3 + 0.33)}{3} = 0.54$$

TABLE 2.4

Scaled Criteria Values by the Ideal Value Method (Example 2.3)

	TCO	Service	Experience
Supplier A	0.52	1	1
Supplier B	0.68	0.5	0.67
Supplier C	1	0.3	0.33

The final rankings (in descending order) are Suppliers A, B, and C—the same ranking obtained using the simple scaling.

2.3.5.3 Simple Linearization (Linear Normalization) Illustration

Under this method, the scaled values are computed using Equations 2.7 and 2.8 and are given in Table 2.5.

Note that the best and worst values of each criterion are 1 and 0, respectively, and that all the criteria values are now going to be maximized. The revised weighted sums are

$$S_A = \frac{(0+1+1)}{3} = 0.67$$

$$S_B = \frac{(0.5+0.29+0.5)}{3} = 0.43$$

$$S_C = \frac{(1+0+0)}{3} = 0.33$$

The rankings are unchanged, with Supplier A as the best, followed by B, and C.

2.3.5.4 Scaling by L_p Norm Illustration

We shall illustrate using L_∞ norm for scaling. The L_∞ norms for the three criteria are computed using Equation 2.11:

$$L_\infty \text{ norm for TCO} = \text{Max } (125000, 95000, 65000) = 125{,}000$$

$$L_\infty \text{ norm for service} = \text{Max } (10, 5, 3) = 10$$

$$L_\infty \text{ norm for experience} = \text{Max } (9, 6, 3) = 9$$

The criteria values are then scaled by dividing them by their respective L_∞ norms, and they are given in Table 2.6.

TABLE 2.5

Scaled Criteria Values by Simple
Linearization (Example 2.3)

	TCO	Service	Experience
Supplier A	0	1	1
Supplier B	0.5	0.29	0.5
Supplier C	1	0	0

TABLE 2.6

Scaled Criteria Values Using L_∞ Norm
(Example 2.3)

	TCO	Service	Experience
Supplier A	1	1	1
Supplier B	0.76	0.5	0.67
Supplier C	0.52	0.3	0.33

Note that the scaling by L_p norm did not convert the minimization criterion (TCO) to maximization as the previous two methods (ideal value and simple linearization) did. Hence, the TCO values have to be multiplied by (−1) before computing the weighted score. Note also that the L_∞ norm of each criterion (column) in Table 2.6 is always 1. The new weighted scores are as follows:

$$S_A = \frac{(-1+1+1)}{3} = 0.33$$

$$S_B = \frac{(-0.76+0.5+0.67)}{3} = 0.14$$

$$S_C = \frac{(-0.52+0.3+0.33)}{3} = 0.04$$

Once again, the rankings are the same, namely Supplier A, followed by Suppliers B and C.

It should be noted that even though the scaled values using different scaling methods were different, the final rankings were always the same. Occasionally, it is possible for rank reversals to occur.

2.4 Analytic Hierarchy Process

The analytic hierarchy process (AHP), developed by Saaty (1980), is an MCDM method for ranking alternatives. Using AHP, the DM can assess not only quantitative but also various qualitative factors, such as financial stability, feeling of trust, and so on, in the supplier selection process. The buyer establishes a set of evaluation criteria, and AHP uses these criteria to rank the different suppliers. AHP can enable the DM to represent the interaction of multiple factors in complex and unstructured situations. AHP does not require the scaling of criteria values.

2.4.1 Basic Principles of AHP

- *Design a hierarchy:* Top vertex is the main objective, and bottom vertices are the alternatives. Intermediate vertices are criteria/subcriteria (which are more and more aggregated as you go up in the hierarchy).
- At each level of the hierarchy, a pairwise comparison of the vertices criteria/subcriteria is performed from the point of view of their "contribution (weights)" to each of the higher-level vertices to which they are linked.
- Uses both rating method and pairwise comparison method with a numerical scale of 1 through 9 (1 = equal importance; 9 = most important).
- Uses pairwise comparison of alternatives with respect to each criterion (subcriterion) and gets a numerical score for each alternative on every criterion (subcriterion).
- Computes total weighted score for each alternative and ranks the alternatives accordingly.

We shall illustrate AHP using a case study.

Case Study 1 (Ravindran and Warsing, 2013)
Consider a supplier selection problem involving 20 suppliers and 14 criteria. The supplier criteria have been split into various categories as described here:

- *Organizational criteria:*
  - *Size of company (C1):* Size of the company can be either its number of employees or its market capitalization.
  - *Age of company (C2):* Age of the company is the number of years that the company has been in business.
  - *Research and development (R&D) activities (C3):* This is the company's investment in research and development.
- *Experience criteria:*
  - *Project type (C4):* Specific types of projects completed in the past.
  - *Project size (C5):* Specific sizes of projects completed in the past.
- *Performance criteria:*
  - *Cost overruns (C6):* Cost overruns in the past.
  - *Capacity (C7):* Capacity of the supplier to fulfill orders.
  - *Lead time (C8):* Meeting promised delivery time.
- *Quality criteria:*
  - *Responsiveness (C9):* If there is an issue concerning quality, how fast the supplier reacts to correct the problem.
  - *Acceptance rate (C10):* Perfect orders received within acceptable quality.

- *Cost criteria:*
  - *Order change and cancellation charges (C11):* Fees associated with modifying or changing orders after they have been placed.
  - *Cost savings (C12):* Overall *reduction* in procurement cost.
- *Miscellaneous criteria:*
  - *Labor relations (C13):* Number of strikes or any other labor problems encountered in the past.
  - *Procedural compliances (C14):* Conformance to national/international standards (e.g., ISO 9000).

In this case study, there are 20 suppliers to be ranked. The 14 supplier criteria values for the set of 20 suppliers are given in Table 2.7. Smaller values are preferred for criteria C6, C11, and C13; larger values are preferred for the other criteria. Using this case study, we shall illustrate the key steps of the AHP method.

To design the hierarchy for Case Study 1, the 14 supplier criteria are grouped into six major criteria and several subcriteria as shown in Figure 2.1.

2.4.2 Steps of the AHP Model

Step 1: In the first step, a pairwise comparison of criteria using the 1–9 degree of importance scale shown in Table 2.8 is carried out.

If there are n criteria to evaluate, then the pairwise comparison matrix for the criteria is given by $A_{(n \times n)} = [a_{ij}]$, where a_{ij} represents the relative importance of criterion i with respect to criterion j. Set $a_{ii} = 1$ and $a_{ji} = \dfrac{1}{a_{ij}}$. The pairwise comparisons—with the degree of importance—for the six major criteria in Case Study 1 are shown in Table 2.9.

Step 2: Compute the normalized weights for the main criteria. We obtain the weights using the L_1 norm. The two-step process for calculating the weights is as follows:

1. Normalize each column of A matrix using L_1 norm:

$$r_{ij} = \frac{a_{ij}}{\displaystyle\sum_{i=1}^{n} a_{ij}}$$

2. Average the normalized values across each row to get the criteria weights:

$$w_i = \frac{\displaystyle\sum_{j=1}^{n} r_{ij}}{n}$$

TABLE 2.7

Supplier Criteria Values for Case Study 1

	C1	C2	C3	C4	C5	C6	C7	C8	C9	C10	C11	C12	C13	C14
S1	0.75	1	0.46	1	0.92	0.9	1	0	0.13	0.18	0.18	0.01	0.26	0.79
S2	0.22	0	0.33	1	0.94	0.35	0.9	0.13	0.02	0	0.38	0.95	0.88	0.72
S3	0.53	0	0.74	0	0.03	0.89	0.1	0.12	0	0.3	0.66	0.08	0.86	0.22
S4	0.28	1	0.8	0	0.54	0.75	0.85	1	1	0.87	0.33	0.5	0.78	0.12
S5	0.3	0	0.79	1	0.6	0.49	0.8	0.15	0.97	0.79	0.83	0.13	0.46	0.15
S6	0.5	1	0.27	0	0.43	0.52	0.12	0	0	0.25	0.9	0.07	0.26	0
S7	0.25	1	0.6	1	0.1	0.18	0	0.13	1	0.85	0.51	0.59	0.12	1
S8	0.76	1	0.68	1	0.55	0.87	0	0.14	0	1	0.98	0.19	0.86	0.99
S9	0.25	1	0.5	1	0.26	0.92	0.94	0.03	0.15	1	0.7	0.41	0.95	1
S10	0.16	1	0.7	0	0.46	0.62	0.9	0	0.03	1	0.3	0.68	0.61	1
S11	0.31	0	0.3	0	0.09	0.73	1	1	1	0	0.87	0.3	0.98	0
S12	0.34	1	0.39	1	0.75	0.94	0.78	0.3	0	0.85	0.94	0.61	0.46	0.3
S13	0.08	0	0.27	0	0.14	0.42	1	0.91	0	0.82	0.45	0.42	0.81	1
S14	0.62	1	0.02	1	0.15	0.97	0.15	0.01	0.18	0.92	0.55	0.23	0.12	0.97
S15	0.49	0	0.98	0	0.52	0.68	0	0.24	0.06	0	0.52	0.84	0.05	0.76
S16	0.1	1	0.32	1	0.67	0.21	1	0.85	0.16	0.29	0.49	0.41	0.29	0.27
S17	0.08	0	0.19	1	0.24	0.87	0	0.72	0.26	1	0.84	0.99	0.64	0.04
S18	0.86	0	0.28	1	0.95	0.08	1	0.12	0.2	0	0.4	0.76	0.66	1
S19	0.72	0	0.88	0	0.15	0.93	0.97	1	1	1	0.75	0.64	0.26	1
S20	0.15	1	0.92	1	0.77	0.63	0	0	0.3	0.22	0.22	0.94	0.93	0.26

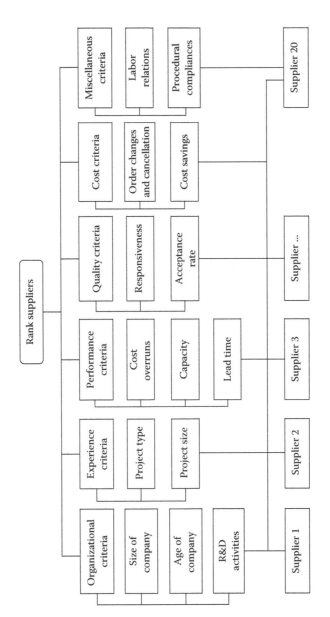

FIGURE 2.1
AHP hierarchy for supplier criteria (Case Study 1).

TABLE 2.8

Degree of Importance Scale in AHP

Degree of Importance	Definition
1	Equal importance
3	Weak importance of one over another
5	Essential or strong importance
7	Demonstrated importance
9	Absolute importance
2,4,6,8	Intermediate values between two adjacent judgments

TABLE 2.9

Pairwise Comparison of Criteria (Case Study 1)

	Organizational	Experience	Performance	Quality	Cost	Miscellaneous
Organizational	1	0.2	0.143	0.33	0.33	1
Experience	5	1	0.5	2	2	5
Performance	7	2	1	5	4	7
Quality	3	0.5	0.2	1	1	3
Cost	3	0.5	0.25	1	1	3
Miscellaneous	1	0.2	0.143	0.33	0.33	1

TABLE 2.10

Final Criteria Weights Using AHP (Case Study 1)

Criteria	Weight
Organizational	0.047
Experience	0.231
Performance	0.430
Quality	0.120
Cost	0.124
Miscellaneous	0.047

Table 2.10 shows the criteria weights for Case Study 1 obtained as a result of Step 2.

Step 3: In this step, we check for consistency of the pairwise comparison matrix using Eigen value theory as follows (Saaty 1980).

1. Using the pairwise comparison matrix A (Table 2.9) and the weights W (Table 2.10), compute the vector AW. Let the vector $X = (X_1, X_2, X_3, ..., X_n)$ denote the values of AW.

2. Compute

$$\lambda_{max} = \text{Average}\left[\frac{X_1}{W_1}, \frac{X_2}{W_2}, \frac{X_3}{W_3}, \cdots, \frac{X_n}{W_n}\right]$$

3. The consistency index (CI) is given by

$$CI = \frac{\lambda_{max} - n}{n - 1}$$

Saaty (1980) generated a number of random positive reciprocal matrices with $a_{ij} \in (1, 9)$ for different sizes and computed their average CI values, denoted by RI, as given here.

N	1	2	3	4	5	6	7	8	9	10
RI	0	0	0.52	0.89	1.11	1.25	1.35	1.4	1.45	1.49

He defines the consistency ratio (CR) as $CR = \frac{CI}{RI}$. If CR < 0.15, then accept the pairwise comparison matrix as consistent. Using these steps, the CR is found to be 0.009 for our sample problem. Because the CR is less than 0.15, the response can be assumed to be consistent.

Step 4: In the next step, we compute the relative importance of the subcriteria in the same way as done for the main criteria. Steps 2 and 3 are carried out for every pair of subcriteria with respect to their main criterion. The final weights of the subcriteria are the product of the weights along the corresponding branch. Table 2.11 illustrates the final weights of the various criteria and subcriteria for Case Study 1.

Step 5: Repeat Steps 1, 2, and 3 and obtain the following:

1. Pairwise comparison of alternatives with respect to each criterion using the ratio scale (1–9).
2. Normalized scores of all alternatives with respect to each criterion. Here, an $(m \times n)$ matrix S is obtained, where S_{ij} = normalized score for alternative i with respect to criterion j, and m is the number of alternatives and n is the number of criteria.

Step 6: Compute the total score (TS) for each alternative as follows: $TS_{(m \times 1)} = S_{(m \times n)} W_{(n \times 1)}$, where W is the weight vector obtained after Steps 3 and 4. Using the total scores, the alternatives are ranked. The total scores and the final rankings of the suppliers obtained by AHP for Case Study 1 are given in Table 2.12.

NOTE: There is commercially available software for AHP called Expert Choice. Interested readers can refer to http://expertchoice.com for additional information.

TABLE 2.11

AHP Subcriteria Weights for Case Study 1

Criteria (Criteria Weight)	Subcriteria	Subcriteria Weight	Global Weight (Criteria Weight × Subcriteria Weight)
Organizational (0.047)	Size of company	0.143	0.006
	Age of company	0.429	0.020
	R&D activities	0.429	0.020
Experience (0.231)	Project type	0.875	0.202
	Project size	0.125	0.028
Performance (0.430)	Cost overruns	0.714	0.307
	Capacity	0.143	0.061
	Lead time	0.143	0.061
Quality (0.120)	Responsiveness	0.833	0.099
	Acceptance rate	0.167	0.020
Cost (0.124)	Order change	0.833	0.103
	Cost savings	0.167	0.020
Miscellaneous (0.047)	Labor relations	0.125	0.005
	Procedural compliances	0.875	0.041

TABLE 2.12

Supplier Ranking Using AHP (Case Study 1)

Supplier	Total Score	Rank
Supplier 1	0.119	20
Supplier 2	0.247	14
Supplier 3	0.325	12
Supplier 4	0.191	18
Supplier 5	0.210	16
Supplier 6	0.120	19
Supplier 7	0.249	13
Supplier 8	0.328	11
Supplier 9	0.192	17
Supplier 10	0.212	15
Supplier 11	0.427	7
Supplier 12	0.661	1
Supplier 13	0.431	6
Supplier 14	0.524	5
Supplier 15	0.422	8
Supplier 16	0.539	4
Supplier 17	0.637	2
Supplier 18	0.421	9
Supplier 19	0.412	10
Supplier 20	0.543	3

2.5 Group Decision Making

Most purchasing decisions, including the ranking and selection of suppliers, involve the participation of multiple DMs, and the ultimate decision is based on the aggregation of DMs' individual judgments to arrive at a group decision. The rating method, Borda count, and AHP discussed in Sections 2.2 and 2.4 can be extended to group decision making as described in the following:

1. *Rating method:* Ratings of each DM for every criterion are averaged. The average ratings are then normalized to obtain the group criteria weights.
2. *Borda count:* Points are assigned based on the number of DMs that assign a particular rank for a criterion. These points are then totaled for each criterion and normalized to get criteria weights. (This is similar to how the college polls are done to get the top 25 football or basketball teams.)
3. *AHP:* There are two methods to get the group rankings using AHP.
   a. *Method 1:* Strength of preference scores assigned by individual DMs are aggregated using geometric means and then used in the AHP calculations.
   b. *Method 2:* First, all the alternatives are ranked by each DM using AHP. The individual rankings are then aggregated to a group ranking using the Borda count method.

2.6 Use of L_p Metric for Ranking Alternatives

Mathematically, the L_p metrics, for $p = 1, 2, ..., \infty$, represent the distance between two vectors **x** and **y**, where $\mathbf{x}, \mathbf{y} \in R^n$, and is given by

$$\|\mathbf{x} - \mathbf{y}\|_p = \left[\sum_{j=1}^{n} | x_j - y_j |^p \right]^{1/p} \qquad (2.12)$$

The ranking of alternatives is done by calculating the L_p metric between the ideal solution (I) and each vector representing an alternative's ratings for the criteria. The ideal solution represents the best values possible for each criterion. Because no alternative will have the best values for all the criteria (e.g., a supplier with minimum cost may have poor quality and delivery time), the ideal solution is an artificial target and cannot be achieved. The L_p metric approach computes the distance of each alternative's attributes from the ideal solution and ranks the alternatives based on that distance (the smaller the better). One of the most commonly used L_p metrics is the L_2 metric ($p = 2$), which measures the Euclidean distance between two vectors. We shall illustrate the steps of the L_2 metric method using the Case Study 1 data in Table 2.7.

2.6.1 Steps of the L_2 Metric Method

Step 1: Determine the ideal solution. The ideal values for the 14 criteria in Table 2.7 are given in Table 2.13.

Step 2: Use the L_2 metric to measure the closeness of each supplier to the ideal values. The L_2 metric for supplier k is given by

$$L_2(k) = \sqrt{\sum_{j=1}^{n}(I_j - Y_{jk})^2} \tag{2.13}$$

where, I_j is the ideal value for criterion j and Y_{jk} is the jth criterion value for supplier k.

Step 3: Rank the suppliers using the L_2 metric. The supplier with the smallest L_2 value is ranked first, followed by the next smallest L_2 value, and so on. Table 2.14 gives the L_2 distance from the ideal for each supplier and the resultant rankings from 1 to 20.

TABLE 2.13

Ideal Values for Case Study 1

Criteria	Ideal Value
C1	0.86
C2	1
C3	0.98
C4	1
C5	0.95
C6	0.08
C7	1
C8	1
C9	1
C10	1
C11	0.18
C12	0.99
C13	0.05
C14	1

TABLE 2.14

Supplier Ranking Using L_2 Metric
(Case Study 1)

Supplier	L_2 Value	Rank
Supplier 1	2.105	7
Supplier 2	2.332	11
Supplier 3	3.011	20
Supplier 4	1.896	3
Supplier 5	2.121	8
Supplier 6	2.800	19
Supplier 7	1.817	1
Supplier 8	2.357	4
Supplier 9	2.206	9
Supplier 10	2.339	12
Supplier 11	2.782	18
Supplier 12	2.083	5
Supplier 13	2.429	15
Supplier 14	2.347	13
Supplier 15	2.517	16
Supplier 16	1.834	2
Supplier 17	2.586	17
Supplier 18	2.092	6
Supplier 19	1.970	4
Supplier 20	2.295	10

2.7 Comparison of Ranking Methods

Different ranking methods can provide different solutions resulting in rank reversals. In extensive empirical studies with human subjects (Powdrell 2003, Ravindran et al. 2010), it has been found that Borda count rankings (with pairwise comparison of criteria) are generally in line with AHP rankings. Given the increased cognitive burden and expensive calculations required for AHP, the Borda count method would be an appropriate procedure for ranking alternatives. Even though rating method is easy to use, it could lead to several ties in the final rankings, thereby making the results less useful.

Velazquez et al. (2010) studied the best combination of weighting and scaling methods for single and multiple DMs. The scaling methods considered were ideal value, linear normalization, and vector normalization using L_p norm for $p = 1, 2, 3$, and ∞. The weighting methods included in the study were rating, ranking (Borda count), and AHP. The L_p metric methods for $p = 1, 2, 3$, and ∞ were also included for ranking. Experiments were done with real DMs. They found that the best scaling method was influenced by the chosen weighting method. The best combination was scaling by L_∞

norm and ranking by Borda count. The worst combination was scaling by L_∞ norm and ranking by L_∞ metric. The conclusions were the same for single and multiple DMs.

___

2.8 MCMP Problems

In the previous sections, our focus was on solving MCDM problems with a *finite* number of alternatives, where each alternative is measured by several conflicting criteria. These MCDM problems were called multiple criteria selection problems. The ranking methods we discussed earlier helped in identifying the best alternative and rank order of all the alternatives from the best to the worst.

In this and subsequent sections, we will focus on MCDM problems with an *infinite* number of alternatives. In other words, the feasible alternatives are not known a priori but are represented by a set of mathematical (linear/nonlinear) constraints. These MCDM problems are called Multi Criteria Mathematical Programming (MCMP) problems.

2.8.1 MCMP Problem

$$\text{Max } F(x) = \{f_1(x), f_2(x), \dots, f_k(x)\}$$

$$\text{Subject to: } g_j(x) \leq 0 \quad \text{for } j = 1, \dots, m$$

(2.14)

where **x** is an *n*-vector of decision variables and $f_i(\mathbf{x})$, $i = 1, \dots, k$ are the k criteria/objective functions. All the objective functions are to maximize.

$$\text{Let } S = \{x/g_j(x) \leq 0, \text{ for all } j\}$$

$$Y = \{\mathbf{y}/F(\mathbf{x}) = \mathbf{y} \text{ for some } x \in S\}$$

S is called the *decision space*, and Y is called the *criteria or objective space* in MCMP.

A solution to MCMP is called a *superior solution* if it is feasible and maximizes all the objectives simultaneously. In most MCMP problems, superior solutions do not exist because the objectives conflict with one another.

2.8.2 Efficient, Non-Dominated, or Pareto Optimal Solution

A solution $\mathbf{x}^o \in S$ to MCMP is said to be *efficient* if $f_k(\mathbf{x}) > f_k(\mathbf{x}^o)$ for some, $x \in S$ implies that $f_j(\mathbf{x}) < f_j(\mathbf{x}^o)$ for at least one other index j. More simply stated, an efficient solution has the property that an improvement in any one objective is possible only at the expense of at least one other objective. A *dominated* solution is a feasible solution that is not efficient. A set of all efficient solutions is called the *efficient set* or *efficient frontier.*

NOTE: Even though the solution of MCMP reduces to finding the efficient set, it is not practical because there could be an infinite number of efficient solutions.

Example 2.4

Consider the following bi-criteria linear program:

$$\text{Max } Z_1 = 5x_1 + x_2$$

$$\text{Max } Z_2 = x_1 + 4x_2$$

$$\text{Subject to: } x_1 \le 5$$

$$x_2 \le 3$$

$$x_1 + x_2 \le 6$$

$$x_1, x_2 \ge 0$$

Solution

The *decision space* and the *objective space* are given in Figures 2.2 and 2.3, respectively. Corner points C and D are efficient solutions, while corner points A, B, and E are dominated. The set of all efficient solutions is given by the line segment CD in both figures.

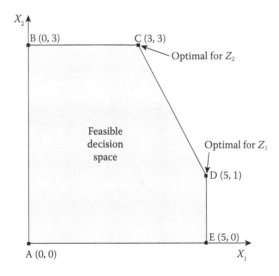

FIGURE 2.2
Decision space (Example 2.4).

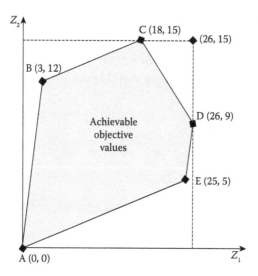

FIGURE 2.3
Objective space (Example 2.4).

An ideal solution is the vector of individual optima obtained by optimizing each objective function separately, ignoring all other objectives. In Example 2.4, the maximum value of Z_1, ignoring Z_2, is 26 and occurs at point D. Similarly, maximum Z_2 of 15 is obtained at point C. Thus the ideal solution is (26, 15), but it is *not* feasible or achievable.

NOTE: One of the popular approaches to solving MCMP problems is to find an efficient solution that comes "as close as possible" to the ideal solution. It is similar to the L_p metric method discussed earlier. We will discuss this approach later in Section 2.12.

2.8.3 Determining an Efficient Solution

For the MCMP problem given by Equation 2.14, consider the following single objective optimization problem, called the P_λ problem. The P_λ problem is also known as the *weighted objective problem*.

$$\text{Max } Z = \sum_{i=1}^{k} \lambda_i f_i(x) \tag{2.15}$$

$$\text{Subject to: } x \in S$$

$$\sum_{i=1}^{k} \lambda_i = 1 \text{ and } \lambda_i \geq 0$$

Theorem 1: Sufficiency

Let $\lambda_i > 0$ for all i be specified. If $\mathbf{x}^o$ is an optimal solution for the P_λ problem (Equation 2.15), then $\mathbf{x}^o$ is an efficient solution to the MCMP problem. In Example 2.4, if we set $\lambda_1 = \lambda_2 = 0.5$ and solve the P_λ problem, the optimal solution will be at D, which is an efficient solution.

Warning: Theorem 1 is only a sufficient condition and is not necessary. For example, there could be efficient solutions to MCMP that could not be obtained as optimal solutions to the P_λ problem. Such situations occur when the objective space is not a convex set. However, for MCMP problems, where the objective functions and constraints are linear, Theorem 1 is both necessary and sufficient.

2.8.4 Test for Efficiency

Given a feasible solution $\bar{x} \in S$ for MCMP, we can test whether or not it is efficient by solving the following single objective problem.

$$\text{Max } W = \sum_{i=1}^{k} d_i$$

$$\text{Subject to: } f_i(x) \geq f_i(\bar{x}) + d_i \quad \text{for } i = 1, 2, ..., k$$
$$x \in S$$
$$d_i \geq 0$$

Theorem 2

1. If Max $W > 0$, then $\bar{x}$ is a dominated solution.
2. If Max $W = 0$, then $\bar{x}$ is an efficient solution (Geoffrion 1968).

NOTE: If Max $W > 0$, then at least one of the d_i's is positive. This implies that at least one objective can be improved without sacrificing on the other objectives.

2.9 Classification of MCMP Methods

In MCMP problems, there are often an infinite number of efficient solutions, and they are not comparable without the input from the DM. Hence, it is generally assumed that the DM has a real-valued preference function defined on the values of the objectives, but it is not known explicitly. With this assumption, the primary objective of the MCMP solution methods is to find the *best compromise solution*, which is an efficient solution that maximizes the DM's preference function.

In the last three decades, most MCDM research have been concerned with developing solution methods based on different assumptions and approaches to measure or derive the DM's preference function. Thus, the MCMP methods can be categorized by the basic assumptions made with respect to the DM's preference function as follows:

1. When *complete* information about the preference function is available from the DM

2. When *no* information is available

3. Where *partial* information is obtainable progressively from the DM

In the following sections, we will discuss the MCMP methods—goal programming, compromise programming, and interactive methods, as examples of Category 1, 2, and 3 type approaches, respectively.

2.10 Goal Programming

One way to treat multiple criteria is to select one criterion as primary and the other criteria as secondary. The primary criterion is then used as the optimization objective function, while the secondary criteria are assigned acceptable minimum and maximum values and are treated as problem constraints. However, if careful considerations were not given while selecting the acceptable levels, a feasible design that satisfies all the constraints may not exist. This problem is overcome by goal programming (Ravindran et al. 2006), which has become a practical method for handling multiple criteria. Goal programming falls under the class of methods that use completely prespecified preferences of the DM in solving the MCMP problem.

In goal programming, all the objectives are assigned target levels for achievement and relative priority on achieving these levels. Goal programming treats these targets as *goals to aspire for* and not as absolute constraints. It then attempts to find an optimal solution that comes as "close as possible" to the targets in the order of specified priorities.

Before we discuss the formulation of goal programming models, we should discuss the difference between the terms *real constraints* and *goal constraints* (or simply *goals*) as used in goal programming models. The real constraints are absolute restrictions on the decision variables, while the goals are conditions one would like to achieve but that are not mandatory. For instance, a real constraint given by

$$x_1 + x_2 = 3$$

requires all possible values of $x_1 + x_2$ to always equal 3. As opposed to this, a goal requiring $x_1 + x_2 = 3$ is not mandatory, and we can choose values of

$x_1 + x_2 \geq 3$ as well as $x_1 + x_2 \leq 3$. In a goal constraint, positive and negative deviational variables are introduced as follows:

$$x_1 + x_2 + d_1^- - d_1^+ = 3 \qquad d_1^+, d_1^- \geq 0$$

Note that, if $d_1^- > 0$, then $x_1 + x_2 < 3$, and if $d_1^+ > 0$, then $x_1 + x_2 > 3$.

By assigning suitable weights w_1^- and w_1^+ on d_1^- and d_1^+ in the objective function, the model will try to achieve the sum $x_1 + x_2$ as close as possible to 3. If the goal were to satisfy $x_1 + x_2 \geq 3$, then only d_1^- is assigned a positive weight in the objective, while the weight on d_1^+ is set to zero.

2.10.1 Goal Programming Formulation

Consider the general MCMP problem given by Equation 2.14. The assumption that there exists an optimal solution to the MCMP problem involving multiple criteria implies the existence of some preference ordering of the criteria by the DM. The goal programming (GP) formulation of the MCMP problem requires the DM to specify an acceptable level of achievement (b_i) for each criterion f_i and specify a weight w_i (ordinal or cardinal) to be associated with the deviation between f_i and b_i. Thus, the GP model of an MCMP problem becomes

$$\text{Minimize } Z = \sum_{i=1}^{k} (w_i^+ d_i^+ + w_i^- d_i^-) \qquad (2.16)$$

$$\text{Subject to: } f_i(x) + d_i^- - d_i^+ = b_i \quad \text{for } i = 1, \ldots, k \qquad (2.17)$$

$$g_j(x) \leq 0 \quad \text{for } j = 1, \ldots, m \qquad (2.18)$$

$$x_j, d_i^-, d_i^+ \geq 0 \quad \text{for all } i \text{ and } j \qquad (2.19)$$

Equation 2.16 represents the objective function of the GP model, which minimizes the weighted sum of the deviational variables. The system of equations (Equation 2.17) represents the *goal constraints* relating the multiple criteria to the goals/targets for those criteria. The variables, d_i^- and d_i^+, in Equation 2.17 are called *deviational variables*, representing *underachievement* and *overachievement* of the ith goal. The set of weights $(w_i^+ \text{ and } w_i^-)$ may take two forms:

1. Prespecified weights (cardinal)
2. Preemptive priorities (ordinal)

Under prespecified (cardinal) weights, specific values in a relative scale are assigned to w_i^+ and w_i^- representing the DM's "trade-off" among the goals. Once w_i^+ and w_i^- are specified, the goal program represented by Equations 2.16

through 2.19 reduces to a single objective optimization problem. The cardinal weights could be obtained from the DM using any of the methods discussed earlier, such as the rating method, Borda count, and AHP. However, in order for this method to work, the criteria values have to be scaled properly.

In reality, goals are usually *incompatible* (i.e., incommensurable), and some goals can be achieved only at the expense of some other goals. Hence, *preemptive goal programming*, which is more common in practice, uses *ordinal ranking* or *preemptive priorities* to the goals by assigning incommensurable goals to different priority levels and weights to goals at the same priority level. In this case, the objective function of the GP model (Equation 2.16) takes the form

$$\text{Minimize } Z = \sum_p P_p \sum_i \left(w_{ip}^+ \, d_i^+ + w_{ip}^- \, d_i^- \right) \tag{2.20}$$

where P_p represents priority p with the assumption that P_p is much larger than P_{p+1} and w_{ip}^+ and w_{ip}^- are the weights assigned to the ith deviational variables at priority p. In this manner, lower priority goals are considered only after attaining the higher priority goals. Thus, *preemptive goal programming* is essentially a sequence of single objective optimization problems in which successive optimizations are carried out on the alternate optimal solutions of the previously optimized goals at higher priority.

In both preemptive and non-preemptive GP models, the DM has to specify the targets or goals for each objective. In addition, in the preemptive GP models, the DM specifies a preemptive priority ranking on the goal achievements. In the non-preemptive case, the DM has to specify relative weights for goal achievements. To illustrate, consider the following bi-criteria linear program (BCLP).

Example 2.5 (BCLP)

$$\text{Max} f_1 = x_1 + x_2$$

$$\text{Max} f_2 = x_1$$

$$\text{Subject to: } 4x_1 + 3x_2 \le 12$$

$$x_1, x_2 \ge 0$$

Maximum f_1 occurs at $\mathbf{x} = (0, 4)$ with $(f_1, f_2) = (4, 0)$. Maximum f_2 occurs at $\mathbf{x} = (3, 0)$ with $(f_1, f_2) = (3, 3)$. Thus the ideal values of f_1 and f_2 are 4 and 3, respectively, and the bounds on (f_1, f_2) on the efficient set will be

$$3 \le f_1 \le 4$$

$$0 \le f_2 \le 3$$

Let the DM set the goals for f_1 and f_2 as 3.5 and 2, respectively. Then the GP model becomes

$$x_1 + x_2 + d_1^- - d_1^+ = 3.5 \tag{2.21}$$

$$x_1 + d_2^- - d_2^+ = 2 \tag{2.22}$$

$$4x_1 + 3x_2 \le 12 \tag{2.23}$$

$$x_1, x_2, d_1^-, d_1^+, d_2^-, d_2^+ \ge 0 \tag{2.24}$$

Under the preemptive GP model, if the DM indicates that f_1 is much more important than f_2, then the objective function will be

$$\text{Min } Z = P_1 d_1^- + P_2 d_2^-$$

subject to the constraints (2.21) to (2.24), where P_1 is assumed to be much larger than P_2.

Under the non-preemptive GP model, the DM specifies relative weights on the goal achievements, say w_1 and w_2. Then the objective function becomes:

$$\text{Min } Z = w_1 d_1^- + w_2 d_2^-$$

subject to the same constraints (2.21) to (2.24).

2.11 Partitioning Algorithm for Preemptive Goal Programs

2.11.1 Linear Goal Programs

Linear GP problems can be solved efficiently by the *partitioning algorithm* developed by Arthur and Ravindran (1978, 1980a). It is based on the fact that the definition of preemptive priorities implies that higher order goals must be optimized before lower order goals are even considered. Their procedure consists of solving a series of linear programming sub problems by using the solution of the higher priority problem as the starting solution for the lower priority problem. Care is taken that higher priority achievements are not destroyed while improving lower priority goals.

2.11.2 Integer Goal Programs

Arthur and Ravindran (1980b) show how the partitioning algorithm for linear GP problems can be extended with a modified branch and bound strategy to solve both pure and mixed integer GP problems. They demonstrate the applicability of the branch and bound algorithm by solving a multiple objective nurse scheduling problem (Arthur and Ravindran 1981).

2.11.3 Nonlinear Goal Programs

Saber and Ravindran (1996) present an efficient and reliable method, called the partitioning gradient based (PGB) algorithm, for solving nonlinear GP problems. The PGB algorithm uses the partitioning technique developed for linear GP problems and the generalized reduced gradient (GRG) method to solve single objective nonlinear programming problems. The authors also present numerical results by comparing the PGB algorithm against a modified pattern search method for solving several nonlinear GP problems. The PGB algorithm found the optimal solution for all test problems—proving its robustness and reliability, while the pattern search method failed in more than half the test problems by converging to a non-optimal point.

Kuriger and Ravindran (2005) have developed three intelligent search methods to solve nonlinear GP problems by adapting and extending the simplex search, complex search, and pattern search methods to account for multiple criteria. These modifications were largely accomplished by using partitioning concepts of GP. The paper also includes computational results with several test problems.

2.12 Method of Global Criterion and Compromise Programming

Method of Global Criterion (Hwang and Masud 1979) and *Compromise Programming* (Zeleny 1982) fall under the class of MCMP methods that do not require any preference information from the DM. Consider the MCMP problem given by Equation 2.14. Let

$$S = \{x/g_j\,(x) \le 0, \text{ for all } j\}$$

Let the ideal values of the objectives $f_1, f_2, ..., f_k$ be $f_1^*, f_2^*, ..., f_k^*$. The global criterion method finds an efficient solution that is "closest" to the idea solution in terms of the L_p distance metric. It also uses the ideal values to normalize the objective functions. Thus, the MCMP reduces to

$$\text{Minimize } Z = \sum_{i=1}^{k} \left(\frac{f_i^* - f_i}{f_i^*} \right)^p$$

Subject to: $x \in S$

The values of f_i^* are obtained by maximizing each objective f_i subject to the constraints $x \in S$ but ignoring the other objectives. The value of p can be 1, 2, 3, ... and so on. Note that $p = 1$ implies equal importance to all deviations from the ideal. As p increases, larger deviations have more weight.

2.12.1 Compromise Programming

Compromise programming is similar in concept to the method of global criterion. It finds an efficient solution by minimizing the weighted L_p distance metric from the ideal point as follows:

$$\text{Min } L_p = \left[\sum_{i=1}^{k} \lambda_i^p \left(f_i^* - f_i \right)^p \right]^{1/p} \tag{2.25}$$

subject to $\mathbf{x} \in S$ and $p = 1, 2, \ldots, \infty,$

where λ_is are weights that have to specified or assessed subjectively. Note that λ_i could be set to $1/(f_i^*)$.

Any point x* that minimizes L_p (Equation 2.25) for $\lambda_i > 0$ for all i, $\sum \lambda_i = 1$, and $1 \le p < \infty$ is called a compromise solution. Zeleny (1982) has proved that these compromise solutions are non-dominated. As $p \to \infty$, Equation 2.25 becomes

$$\text{Min } L_\infty = \text{Min } \underset{i}{\text{Max}} \left[\lambda_i \left(f_i^* - f_i \right) \right]$$

and is known as the Tchebycheff metric.

2.13 Interactive Methods

Interactive methods for MCMP problems rely on the progressive articulation of preferences by the DM. These approaches can be characterized by the following procedure.

- **Step 1:** Find a solution, preferably feasible and efficient.
- **Step 2:** Interact with the DM to obtain his/her reaction or response to the obtained solution.
- **Step 3:** Repeat Steps 1 and 2 until satisfaction is achieved or until some other termination criterion is met.

When interactive algorithms are applied to real world problems, the most critical factors are the functional restrictions placed on the objective functions, constraints, and on the *unknown* preference function. Another important factor is *preference assessment styles* (hereafter, called *interaction styles*). According to Shin and Ravindran (1991), the typical interaction styles are as follows:

1. *Binary pairwise comparison:* The DM must compare a pair of two-dimensional vectors at each interaction.

2. *Pairwise comparison:* The DM must compare a pair of p-dimensional vectors and specify a preference.

3. *Vector comparison:* The DM must compare a set of p-dimensional vectors and specify the best, the worst, or the order of preference. (Note that this can be done by a series of pairwise comparisons.)

4. *Precise local trade-off ratio:* The DM must specify precise values of local trade-off ratios at a given point. It is the *marginal rate of substitution* between objectives f_i and f_j; in other words, trade-off ratio is how much the DM is willing to give up in objective j for a unit increase in objective i at a given efficient solution.

5. *Interval trade-off ratio:* The DM must specify an interval for each local trade-off ratio.

6. *Comparative trade-off ratio:* The DM must specify his preference for a given trade-off ratio.

7. *Index specification and value trade-off:* The DM must list the indices of objectives to be improved or sacrificed, and specify the amount.

8. *Aspiration levels* (or reference point): The DM must specify or adjust the values of the objectives that indicate his/her optimistic wish concerning the outcomes of the objectives.

Shin and Ravindran (1991) also provide a detailed survey of MCMP interactive methods. Their survey includes

- A classification scheme for all interactive methods
- A review of methods in each category based on functional assumptions, interaction style, progression of research papers from the first publication to all its extensions, solution approach, and published applications
- A rating of each category of methods in terms of the DM's cognitive burden, ease of use, effectiveness, and handling inconsistency

2.14 MCDM Software

One of the problems in applying MCDM methods in practice is the lack of commercially available software implementing these methods. There is some research software available. Two good resources for these are:

1. http://www. mcdmsociety.org
2. http://www.sal.hut.fi

The first is the web page of the International Society on Multiple Criteria Decision Making. It has links to MCDM software and a bibliography. Most of the software is available free for research and teaching use. The second link is to the Systems Analysis Laboratory at Aalto University. It also has links to some free software, again for research and instructional use.

References

Arthur, J.L. and A. Ravindran. 1978. An efficient goal programming algorithm using constraint partitioning and variable elimination. *Management Science* 24(8): 867–868.

Arthur, J.L. and A. Ravindran. 1980a. PAGP: An efficient algorithm for linear goal programming problems. *ACM Transactions on Mathematical Software* 6(3): 378–386.

Arthur, J.L. and A. Ravindran. 1980b. A branch and bound algorithm with constraint partitioning for integer goal programs. *European Journal of Operational Research* 4: 421–425.

Arthur, J.L. and A. Ravindran. 1981. A multiple objective nurse scheduling model. *Institute of Industrial Engineers Transactions* 13: 55–60.

Geoffrion, A. 1968. Proper efficiency and theory of vector maximum. *Journal of Mathematical Analysis and Applications* 22: 618–630.

Hwang, C.L. and A. Masud. 1979. *Multiple Objective Decision Making-Methods and Applications*. New York: Springer-Verlag.

Kuriger, G. and A. Ravindran. 2005. Intelligent search methods for nonlinear goal programs. *Information Systems and Operational Research* 43: 79–92.

Masud, A.S.M. and A. Ravindran. 2008. Multiple criteria decision making. In *Operations Research and Management Science Handbook*, chapter 5 (pp. 1–41), ed. A.R. Ravindran. Boca Raton, FL: CRC Press.

Masud, A.S.M. and A. Ravindran. 2009. Multiple criteria decision making. In *Operation Research Methodologies*, chapter 5 (pp. 1–41), ed. A.R. Ravindran. Boca Raton, FL: CRC Press.

Powdrell, B.J. 2003. Comparison of MCDM algorithms for discrete alternatives. M.S. Thesis, Department of Industrial Engineering, The Pennsylvania State University.

Ravindran, A., K.M. Ragsdell, and G.V. Reklaitis. 2006. *Engineering Optimization: Methods and Applications*, 2nd ed. Hoboken, NJ: Wiley.

Ravindran, A.R., U. Bilsel, V. Wadhwa, and T. Yang. 2010. Risk adjusted multicriteria supplier selection models with applications. *International Journal of Production Research* 48(2): 405–424.

Ravindran, A.R. and Warsing, D.P., Jr. 2013. *Supply Chain Engineering: Models and Applications*. Boca Raton, FL: CRC Press.

Saaty, T.L. 1980. *The Analytic Hierarchy Process*. New York: McGraw Hill.

Saber, H.M. and A. Ravindran. 1996. A partitioning gradient based (PGB) algorithm for solving nonlinear goal programming problem. *Computers and Operations Research* 23: 141–152.

Shin, W.S. and A. Ravindran. 1991. Interactive multi-objective optimization: Survey I- continuous case. *Computers and Operations Research* 18: 97–114.

Velazquez, M.A., D. Claudio, and A.R. Ravindran. 2010. Experiments in multiple criteria selection problems with multiple decision makers. *International Journal of Operational Research* 7(4): 413–428.

Zeleny, M. 1982. *Multiple Criteria Decision Making*. New York: McGraw Hill.

3

Designing Resilient Global Supply Chain Networks

Rodolfo C. Portillo

Amazon, San Jose, Costa Rica

CONTENTS

3.1 Introduction

A supply chain consists of (1) a series of physical entities (e.g., suppliers, plants, warehouses, and retailers) and (2) a coordinated set of activities concerned with the procurement of raw material and parts, production of intermediate and final products, and their distribution to the customers (Ravindran and Warsing 2013). The various decisions involved in managing a supply chain can be grouped into three types—*strategic, tactical,* and *operational. Strategic decisions* deal primarily with the design of the supply chain network—namely, the number and location of plants and warehouses and their respective capacities. They are made over a longer time horizon and have a significant impact with respect to the company's assets and resources, such as opening, expanding, closing, and downsizing facilities. *Tactical decisions* are primarily of a planning nature and made over a horizon of one or two years. They involve purchasing, aggregate production planning, inventory management, and distribution decisions. Finally, *operational decisions* are short term and made on a daily or weekly basis, such as setting customer delivery and weekly production schedules as well as inventory replenishment.

Optimal supply chain design needs to balance among multiple conflicting objectives, such as efficiency in terms of costs and profitability as well as speed to source, produce, and distribute products to customers. Resiliency is also an important objective and is measured in terms of the reliability of the supply chain network when there are disruptions to the supply chain. The case study presented in this chapter addresses strategic and tactical decisions in designing and managing an agile global supply chain.

The material in this chapter is based on the doctoral dissertation of the author (Portillo 2009). With increased globalization, global supply chain management has become strategically important for many companies. The objectives of every supply chain continue to be maximizing the overall value generated by reducing the costs of procurement, increasing the responsiveness to customers, and decreasing the risks due to disruptions affecting the supply chain network. The big change now is that global supply chain management involves a company's worldwide interests: manufacturing facilities, distribution centers (DCs), customers, and suppliers located in several countries. Besides the conventional financial aspects, companies are now required to deal with a plethora of other factors for doing business abroad, such as duties, transfer prices, taxes, multiple exchange rates, and disruption risk. Transfer prices are charges among enterprise entities on goods and services. Disruption risk can be due to natural disasters, supplier quality issues, political tensions among countries, civil unrest, economic issues, government controls, and strikes from unions, among others. Within this environment, as part of their global supply chain management strategy, a company must make decisions on its overall outsourcing plan, supplier selection, the number of production plants and DCs that are needed, as well as the locations of those facilities, modes of transportation, and customer allocations to the DCs.

The emphasis of this chapter is on developing mathematical models to determine optimal supply chain design to support specific competitive strategies within the complex multi-national environment. A multi-criteria mixed-integer linear programming model has been developed to aid in a multiple echelon supply chain design, including manufacturing and distribution facilities' location/allocation, capacity and expansion requirements, production and distribution variables, international issues, exchange rates, lead times, and transfer prices. This work also considers a variety of semi-finished goods of a health and hygiene consumer products company (e.g., tissue hard rolls, unpacked diapers, and oily soap solution) and finished products (e.g., facial tissues, toilet paper, toiletries, and gloves). Moreover, it includes the definition of a set of supply chain design criteria that integrates financial aspects, customer service, disruption risk, and strategic factors in the process. Strategic factors may include decisions to open new markets, increase market share, and to strengthen relationships with particular customers.

The methods for designing a resilient and responsive supply chain developed in this chapter have been applied to a leading global health and hygiene company listed in the Fortune 500. The company is a leader in tissue paper manufacturing, baby products (such as diapers), adult personal care, and health care products. More specifically, the case study has focused on developing analysis tools for a market driven supply chain structure so that the global manufacturing and distribution network for the largest international division of the company can be redesigned. This required integrating local structures, as well as distribution and manufacturing networks, into a unique global optimization model with the objective of reducing the supply chain cost and increasing supply chain market responsiveness to customers, thereby enabling a more robust supply chain strategy—including manufacturing, external sourcing, and distribution activities.

3.2 Problem Description

The company employs approximately 55,000 people worldwide, and its sales are close to $20 billion a year. With operations in 37 countries, the company's global brands are sold in more than 150 countries and are used by approximately 1.3 billion people; it holds first or second position in the majority of its markets. This case study focuses on one of the company's international divisions, which sells products across Latin America. The division has several offices, distribution centers, and manufacturing facilities in more than 20 countries. To support its competitive strategy, its supply chain is formed by different types of customers—from multi-national chains and large distributors to thousands of small "mom-and-pop" stores. In the last 15 years, a series of mergers and acquisitions across the continent led to a supply chain with a highly complex internal structure of many production and distribution facilities without standard assets and product technologies, together with redundancy of operational strategies and organizational structures. Currently, the supply chain is comprised of approximately 45 distribution locations spread across the continent and 21 manufacturing facilities located in 10 countries. Most of the products sold in the region are supplied by these 21 manufacturing plants, and the rest are imported from other company facilities located all around the world. In addition, cross-sourcing activity within the continent has increased significantly in the last few years, by blending the advantages of single and multiple sourcing strategies. Today, more than 60% of the production facilities manufacture finished and semi-finished products that are distributed to different countries in addition to the local market. At least three facilities are continent-wide facilities sourcing all markets within the division, and they also export products to other company divisions worldwide. Until now, asset rationalization to improve operational efficiencies and structural reorganization efforts have focused on supply chain distribution designs for specific business units or division-wide designs considering manufacturing facilities for particular products only. In order to better support and enhance the division's competitive strategy, a robust, flexible, and efficient global supply chain design was required to ensure exceptional achievement of customer service levels and financial goals while considering related risk factors.

For a complete strategic and tactical optimization of the manufacturing and distribution network, the model needed to manage more than 100 customer zones or markets, as well as dozens of products manufactured in more than 250 production lines. Because of the diverse international nature of the problem, many global factors needed to be considered, such as domestic and international freights, transfer prices, taxes and duties, among others. Some products have a multi-stage production process and are processed in multiple echelons (Figure 3.1). In other words, the production process involves more than one stage before the final product is

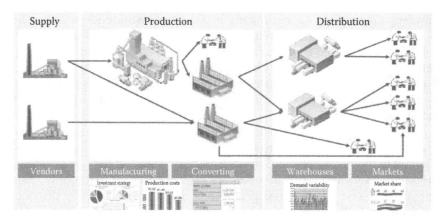

FIGURE 3.1
Supply chain network echelon.

ready, where inventory may need to be managed and production technology and manufacturing lead times may differ. For example, in tissue production, you may have multiple processes to manufacture the paper itself in the form of semi-finished hard rolls that are later converted to finished products such as napkins, facial tissue, toilet paper, and kitchen towels. Multiple production rates are considered for multi-product machines and products. The costs in the optimization process include facility overheads, fixed and variable costs of production lines, and raw materials consumption costs.

3.3 Multi-Criteria Model for Resilient Supply Chain

Decision makers often need to consider multiple criteria in order to determine the best course of action to solve a particular problem. The relationship among these decision criteria can be conflicting, which implies that trade-offs among the conflicting criteria need to be considered and carefully evaluated. As described by Masud and Ravindran (2008), a general multi-criteria decision-making problem can be represented as follows:

$$\text{Maximize } C_1(x), C_2(x), \ldots, C_k(x) \quad x \in X$$

where x is any specific alternative, X is a set representing the feasible region or available alternatives, and C_j is the jth criterion or objective function.

The objective functions (C_j) may conflict with one another, and the difficulty is to maximize all the objectives simultaneously.

According to Masud and Ravindran, multi-criteria decision-making problems can be classified into two types: (1) multi-criteria mathematical programming problems (MCMP) with an infinite number of feasible alternatives determined by a finite number of explicitly stated constraints and (2) multi-criteria selection problems (MCSP) that consist of ranking a finite number of alternatives stated explicitly.

The supply chain network design problem presented in this chapter is a multi-criteria mathematical programming problem. In this case study, goal programming is used as the solution approach for handling multiple criteria. Because there is conflict among the criteria, there is no "optimal solution" to the MCMP problem that will maximize all the criteria simultaneously. This problem is overcome with GP, which finds the "best compromise solution" that is acceptable to the decision maker. In the GP approach, all the criteria are assigned acceptable target levels of achievement and a relative priority on achieving these levels. GP treats these targets as *goals to aspire for* and not as absolute constraints and then attempts to find a solution that comes as "close as possible" to these targets, in the order of importance for the decision maker, by minimizing the weighted deviations from the target values. The criteria relative weights are obtained from the decision makers. For a detailed discussion of GP, the reader is referred to Ravindran et al. (2006) or Chapter 5 of the *Operations Research and Management Science Handbook* (Ravindran 2008). A detailed discussion of the ranking methods for computing criteria weights (Borda count, analytic hierarchy process [AHP], etc.) is available in Chapter 6 of the *Supply Chain Engineering: Models and Applications* by Ravindran and Warsing (2013).

3.3.1 Model Features

The multi-criteria global supply chain network design model integrates customer service levels, strategic factors, and disruption risk criteria along with the financial measure of performance. Customer service level is measured using two factors: (1) *demand fulfillment* and (2) *speed of delivery.* *Demand fulfillment* is defined as the portion of the customer demand that is satisfied—namely, the quantity that is effectively delivered to the customers. The ability to completely fulfill customer demand is modeled as a goal constraint by specifying demand fulfillment targets for all the combinations of products and customer zones. *Speed of delivery* is measured in terms of the *lead time* to deliver the products to the customers. This is also modeled as a goal, by minimizing the quantity weighted lead time, based on volume and the respective delivery lead times.* Weighted lead time targets, for each customer zone, are explicitly considered in the GP model. In addition, the multi-criteria model considers the minimization of *risk associated with supply chain disruptions*. Different measures of risk for domestic and global sourcing are estimated for each manufacturing, converting, and distribution location. These measures incorporate facility and country specific risk factors. Facility specific risk factors are determined based on assessments performed by the decision makers. Country specific risk factors are obtained by considering the weighted average cost of capital rates for each country. A more detailed description of the risk measure estimation is given in Section 3.3.2. The objective of minimizing the risk measure is also modeled as a goal constraint by setting the overall risk target value for the entire supply chain.

Decisions related to supply chain network design may also require the modeler to consider *strategic factors* to open new markets, to increase market share, and to strengthen relationships with customers. This model includes measures for strategic factors for each facility, based on the ratings provided by the decision makers. A goal constraint is set to achieve the maximum possible overall strategic measure for the entire supply chain network.

---

* Corresponding to each arc of the supply chain network that links a facility (plant/DC) to a customer zone.

Among other features, the model allows the evaluation of outsourcing decisions as well as the consideration of different product mix and corresponding productivity rates on different production lines and at different locations. The model supports both strategic and tactical decisions. On the strategic side, the focus is on the design of the supply chain network, in which the optimization model determines the facilities that need to be opened and their locations, as well as the facilities that negatively affect profitability and therefore need to be closed. In the case where current network capacity (measured in product units) is not sufficient to fulfill customer demand, the model provides for manufacturing and distribution decisions, evaluating where and how capacity should be expanded or outsourced. Note that when combining products with significantly different specifications, a common standard unit of measure may be defined within the enterprise, such as weight (i.e., tons) and volume (i.e., cubic meters) for measuring capacity. Also, the ability to perform analysis at the production line level facilitates decisions associated with the transfer of equipment among facilities. Moreover, strategic decisions related to technological changes are supported by the model—such as what technologies are more convenient for the required expansions, or what specific equipment should be considered for write-off and replacement. The model also assists in tactical decisions, such as customer zone assignments to the distribution centers, the development of high level production and distribution plans, product allocation to specific equipment, and cross-sourcing among production facilities. A more detailed description of the model features is presented in the following sections.

The multiple and conflictive decision criteria used in the model will be explained in more detail in Section 3.3.2. The objective then becomes the minimization of the deviations from the specified criteria targets: profit, demand fulfillment, lead time, disruption risk, and strategic factors.

3.3.2 Decision Criteria and Risk Assessment

This section presents a detailed discussion of the supply chain design criteria used in the case study (Figure 3.2) and the methods used to determine the criteria weights and preferences. Assessments of risk and strategic factors are also discussed.

The financial objective of maximizing the gross profit considers revenue from sales less production costs, distribution expenses, and freight expenses. The production costs include facility overhead or fixed costs, fixed and variable machine costs, and raw materials cost. The distribution expenses include all the fixed and variable costs for operating a distribution center (DC). The transportation cost is divided into inbound and outbound freight. Inbound transportation cost is incurred when moving goods among facilities within the firm's supply chain network. Outbound transportation costs are the freight paid for shipping the goods to the end customers.

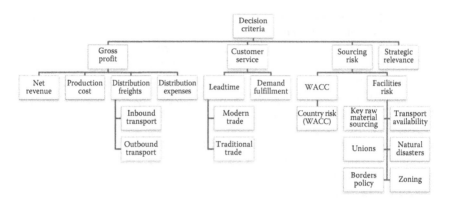

FIGURE 3.2
Decision criteria hierarchy.

The customer service criterion has two sub-criteria: lead time and demand fulfillment. Lead time is defined as the time from when a customer places an order until the moment it is delivered at the customer's facility (used as a proxy for speed of delivery). Demand fulfillment is the proportion of the customer's order that is effectively delivered. Under the lead time criterion, customers are classified as *modern trade* or *traditional trade*. *Modern trade* refers to large customers (e.g., super market chains), while *traditional trade* refers to small customers (e.g., "mom-and-pop" stores).

The supply chain disruption risk criterion includes the facility specific and country specific disruption risk factors. For each facility, the facility specific risk factor is assessed using an expert opinion-based risk rating method. It is a qualitative assessment done by the decision makers considering factors such as key raw material sourcing, transportation availability, existence of labor unions, risk of zoning, and occurrence of natural disasters. The decision makers assign a score for each facility, on a 1–5 scale (see Table 3.1), considering its impact on the domestic and export market. An example of a facility risk rating is given in Table 3.2. The country specific risk factor uses the firm's weighted average cost of capital (WACC) as the risk measure, according to the country in which the facility is located. The WACC is an indicator of risk used primarily for evaluating the exposure of the company's investments. WACC can be used for supply chain design decisions for two reasons: (1) most of the strategic decisions would imply making capital investments to purchase new assets or build new facilities, and (2) WACC is a comprehensive and standard measure of risk when dealing in diverse international environments. WACC is an estimate of the domestic cost of capital, excluding inflation, and is based on US dollar denominated bonds, which are used to determine the spread between the United States and foreign countries. The WACC rates are then adjusted based on political risk (50%), economic risk (25%), and financial risk (25%). The weights associated with the types of risk are defined by

TABLE 3.1

Scale for Facility Risk Rating

Verbal Preference	Score to Assign
No risk	1
Very low risk	2
Medium risk	3
High risk	4
Very high risk	5

TABLE 3.2

Example of Facility Risk Rating

Facilities	Open		Closed	
	Local	Exports	Local	Exports
DC 1	2	2	5	5
Plant 2	2	2	5	5
...	2	2	5	5

the decision makers. *Political risk* considers government stability, corruption, bureaucracy, socioeconomic conditions, involvement of military in politics, investment profile, religious tensions, internal conflicts, law and order, external conflict, ethnic tensions, and democratic accountability. *Economic risk* considers the current account balance and budget balance as a percentage of gross domestic product (GDP), GDP per capita, annual inflation, and real annual GDP growth. *Financial risk* includes the percentage of exports of goods and services (XGS), foreign debt as a percentage of the GDP, net liquidity as months of import cover, foreign debt service as a percentage of XGS, and exchange rate stability. All of these factors are very important for any supply chain strategic decision because—in the long run—they may affect the ability to operate the business from a logistic or financial perspective. For example, imagine a company that needs to pay for imported raw materials in order to produce goods and also needs to repatriate profits from its sales as an expected return on the invested capital. This could be disrupted if the government of the country limits the amount of US dollars the company can convert.

Three methods have been used to obtain criteria weights: simple rating, pairwise comparison using Borda count, and AHP. For a detailed discussion of these methods, the reader is referred to Chapter 6 of *Supply Chain Engineering* by Ravindran and Warsing (2013). In the simple rating method, the experts assign a score from 1 to 10 (the higher the better) for each criterion and for each attribute within a criterion. A sample criteria rating for one decision maker (DM) is given in Table 3.3. Based on this information, a set of criteria weights for a DM is calculated by normalizing the weights, as presented in Table 3.4.

TABLE 3.3

Sample Criteria Ratings for a Decision Maker

	Rating Score (1–10)
Main Criteria	
1 Gross profit	10
2 Lead time	6
3 Demand fulfillment	9
4 Sourcing risk	6
5 Strategic factor	6
Attributes—Lead Time	
1 Modern trade	10
2 Traditional trade	7
Attributes—Risk	
1 WACC	7
2 Facility risk	5

TABLE 3.4

Criteria Weights by Simple Rating Method for a DM

Criteria	Rating	Weight
Gross profit	10	27%
Lead time	6	16%
Demand fulfillment	9	24%
Sourcing risk	6	16%
Strategic factor	6	16%
	37	

In the pairwise comparison method using Borda count, preferences between two criteria and between attribute pairs for each criterion are specified by each DM. For AHP, a pairwise comparison of the criteria, using a strength of preference scale of 1–9 (the higher the better), is done by each DM. Table 3.5 gives the strength of preference scale used for AHP. Based on this, each DM assigns a numerical value representing the importance of one criterion over another, as presented in Table 3.6. Then, two sets of criteria weights are determined: (1) using the ordinal preference by Borda count, based on how the decision makers ranked the criteria, and (2) by AHP, based on the strength of preference between criteria (how much more the DM preferred one criterion over another). Examples of both criteria weights are given in Tables 3.7 and 3.8, respectively. For details on the calculations used to obtain the criteria weights with Borda count and AHP, the reader is referred to Ravindran and Warsing (2013).

A group of 11 DMs were involved in the criteria assessments. For each DM, three sets of criteria weights were computed using the three methods

TABLE 3.5

Strength of Preference Scale Used in AHP

Verbal Preference	Score to Assign
Equally important	1
Slightly more important	3
Strongly more important	5
Very strongly more important	7
Absolutely more important	9

TABLE 3.6

Pairwise Comparison

Criterion Pair	Which is More Important?	How Much More Important (1–9)?
Pairwise Comparison of Criteria and Strength of Preference for a DM		
GP – LT	GP	6
GP – DF	GP	5
GP – RD	GP	3
GP – SF	GP	5
LT – DF	DF	7
LT – RD	LT	7
LT – SF	LT	3
DF – RD	DF	5
DF – SF	DF	5
RD – SF	SF	5
Pairwise Comparison of Response Time (Lead Time)		
Lead time to modern or traditional trade?	MT	7
Pairwise Comparison of Sourcing Risk Attributes		
WACC or facility risk?	WACC	3

Note: GP: gross profit, LT: lead time, DF: demand fulfillment, RD: sourcing risk, SF: strategic factor.

of preference assessment. The DMs were then asked to indicate which of the three methods and their weights best reflected their preferences. In half of the cases, the DMs answered that the simple rating method represented better their preferences, while the pairwise comparison method using Borda count performed better in 30% of the cases, and AHP, with the strength of preference information, did better in 20% of the cases.

The individual set of weights selected by each DM was then combined to obtain the group criteria weights using three different group decision-making

TABLE 3.7

Criteria Weights by Pairwise Preference for
a DM

	GP	LT	DF	RD	SF	Total	%
GP	1	1	1	1	1	5	33
LT	0	1	0	1	1	3	20
DF	0	1	1	1	1	4	27
RD	0	0	0	1	0	1	7
SF	0	0	0	1	1	2	13
						15	

TABLE 3.8

Criteria Weights by Strength of Preference
by AHP for a DM

	GP	LT	DF	RD	SF	%
GP	1	6	5	3	5	
LT	1/6	1	1/7	7	3	
DF	1/5	7	1	5	5	
RD	1/3	1/7	1/5	1	5	
SF	1/5	1/3	1/5	1/5	1	
	1.9	14.5	6.54	16.2	19	
GP	0.53	0.41	0.76	0.19	0.26	43
LT	0.09	0.07	0.02	0.43	0.16	15
DF	0.11	0.48	0.15	0.31	0.26	26
RD	0.18	0.01	0.03	0.06	0.26	11
SF	0.11	0.02	0.03	0.01	0.05	4

approaches: simple averaging, Borda count, and AHP. Group weights with
simple averaging are presented in Table 3.9. In the Borda count approach,
a value from 1 to 5 points (the higher the better) is given to each criterion,
depending on the ranking obtained from the pairwise comparison performed
by each DM, assigning five points to the most important and one to the least
important. The group weights are then calculated based on the total number
of points obtained for each criterion, combining all DMs (see Table 3.10). On
the other hand, the AHP method provided the following results for group
weights: 38% for gross profit, 12% for lead time, 22% for demand fulfillment,
10% for risk, and 18% for strategic factor.

Table 3.11 shows the group weights obtained from the three group decision-
making approaches. In all three approaches, the ranking of the criteria were
the same: gross profit, demand fulfillment, strategic factor, lead time, and risk,
in order from the most important to the least important. The group weights
obtained by each approach were reasonably close. For the case study, the set

TABLE 3.9

Group Weights by Simple Averaging of Each DM's Weights

	DM1	DM2	DM3	DM4	DM5	DM6	DM7	DM8	DM9	DM10	DM11	Overall %
GP	23	36	24	27	40	28	53	33	44	33	33	34
LT	18	18	19	20	4	13	14	12	17	20	13	15
DF	23	27	19	13	9	28	24	14	25	27	27	21
RD	18	9	19	7	14	6	6	10	5	7	13	10
SF	20	9	19	33	32	25	3	31	8	13	13	19

TABLE 3.10

Group Weights by Borda Count

	DM1	DM2	DM3	DM4	DM5	DM6	DM7	DM8	DM9	DM10	DM11	Overall %
GP	1	1	1	2	1	1	1	1	1	1	1	33
LT	4	3	3	3	5	4	3	4	3	4	2	17
DF	2	2	2	4	4	2	2	3	2	2	5	22
RD	5	5	4	5	3	5	4	5	5	5	4	10
SF	3	4	5	1	2	3	5	2	4	3	3	19

TABLE 3.11

Group Weights for the Criteria

Criteria %	Simple Averaging	Borda Count	AHP
Gross profit	34	33	38
Lead time	15	17	12
Demand fulfillment	21	22	22
Sourcing risk	10	10	10
Strategic factor	19	19	18

of weights obtained from the simple averaging method was used in the GP objective function, which minimized the weighted deviations of the criteria from their target levels.

3.3.3 Mathematical Model

3.3.3.1 Notations

A specific index is given to each echelon of the supply chain. For the case study, one or more echelons can be part of the supply chain, depending on the product. The production process is split into two production echelons, manufacturing and converting facilities, and needs one or more distribution centers to reach a market. For example, a manufacturing facility may produce a semi-finished product, such as paper rolls, and a converting facility may convert the paper rolls into finished products, such as facial tissues, napkins, paper towels, and so on. In addition, specific indexes are used to represent different product and production lines.

h	Manufacturing facility index where $h = (1, ..., n_h)$
i	Converting facility index where $i = (1, ..., n_i)$
j	Distribution center (DC) number where $j = (1, ..., n_j)$
l	Receiving DC supplied by a DC where $l = (1, ..., n_j)$
k	Market or customer zone index where $k = (1, ..., n_k)$
p	Product $p = (1, ..., n_p)$
t	Production line $t = (1, ..., n_t)$
g	Goal constraint number $g = (1, ..., 5)$

3.3.3.1.1 Sets

Multiple sets are defined to allow feasible flows among manufacturing, converting, and distribution facilities as well as flows from these facilities at different echelons to different markets. This is based on geographic, infrastructure, or business considerations. In addition, several sets are defined linking products with particular production lines and facilities where they can be produced based on technological constraints. Similarly, sets are created based on marketing strategies to link products with specific markets. The sets definition is particularly valuable for the database build-up process and for computational efficiency because it is not necessary to consider all mathematically possible network combinations as a complete graph.

MFS	Manufacturing facilities, $h = (1, ..., n_h)$
CFS	Converting facilities, $i = (1, ..., n_i)$
DCS	Distribution centers, $j, l = (1, ..., n_j)$
MKS	Markets, $k = (1, ..., n_k)$
PRS	Products, $p = (1, ..., n_p)$
CTS	production lines, $t = (1, ..., n_t)$
PRSS	Semi-finished products
MKSTR	Traditional trade markets (large supermarkets)
MKSMR	Modern trade markets (small retail stores)
$CFSM_h$	Converting facilities supplied by manufacturing facility h
$MKSM_h$	Markets served by manufacturing facility h
$MFSC_i$	Manufacturing facilities supplying converting facility i
$DCSC_i$	Distribution centers supplied by converting facility i
$MKSC_i$	Markets supplied by converting facility i
$CFSD_j$	Converting facilities supplying distribution center j
$MKSD_j$	Markets supplied by distribution center j

$MFSK_k$	Manufacturing facilities supplying market k
$CFSK_k$	Converting facilities supplying market k
$DCSA_j$	Distribution centers supplying distribution center j
$DCSD_j$	Distribution centers supplied by distribution center j
$DCSK_k$	Distribution centers supplying market k
$CTSM_h$	Production lines at manufacturing facility h
$CTSC_i$	Production lines at converting facility i
$CTSP_p$	Production lines that produce product p
$PRSC_i$	Goods produced at conversion facility i
$PRST_t$	Goods produced by production line t
$PRSM_h$	Goods produced at manufacturing facility h
$PRSD_j$	Goods distributed by distribution facility j
$PRSK_k$	Products sold at market k
$MSFP_p$	Manufacturing plants producing product p
$CFSP_p$	Conversion plants producing product p
$DCSP_p$	Distribution centers shipping product p
$MFSTT_{htt'}$	Installed line t at manufacturing facility h and corresponding extension within technology t'
$CFSTT_{itt'}$	Installed line t at converting facility i and corresponding extension within technology t'
$DCSINTERPLANTS$	Distribution centers shipping intercompany
$DCSTOMARKETS$	Distribution centers shipping directly to markets

3.3.3.1.2 Parameters

The following parameters represent the financial and operational data:

D_{kp}	Customer demand in market k for product p, in tons for semi-finished goods and in standard units for finished goods
P_{kp}	Sales price for product p in market k, in \$/standard unit for finished goods and in \$/ton for semi-finished products
FM_h	Facility fixed costs of manufacturing plant h
FMM_{ht}	Fixed costs of production line t at manufacturing plant h
MRC_{hp}	Raw material variable cost per ton for product p in manufacturing site h
MMC_t	Machine cost per hour for manufacturing line t
MPT_{pt}	Production time hours per ton for product p at production line t
MUC_{hp}	Cost, insurance, and freight (CIF) unit cost for product p from manufacturing facility h, includes intercompany markup
$I_{hip}^{(2)}$	Cross-sourcing cost percentage for product p from manufacturing facility h to converting facility i
$T_{hip}^{(2)}$	Freight in \$/ton for product p from manufacturing facility h to converting facility i
$TI_{hip}^{(2)}$	Freight in \$/ton for p from facility h to entry customs when sending goods to facility i

$T_{hkp}^{(3)}$	Freight in \$/ton for product p from manufacturing facility h to market k
MC_{ht}	Manufacturing capacity in hours for production line t at facility h
$DF_{ip}^{(1)}$	Unit of measure conversion factor for product p at conversion facility i (standard units/ton). (Note that different measurement units may be used at different echelons, such as tons or standard units for production, cubic meters for storage and distribution, and standard units or cases for sales.)
$DF_{jkp}^{(2)}$	Conversion factor unit of measure for product p for arc (j, k) (cubic meters/standard units)
$DF_{jlp}^{(3)}$	Conversion factor unit of measure for product p for arc (j, l) (cubic meters/standard units)
FC_i	Facility fixed costs of converting plant i
FCM_{it}	Fixed costs of production line t at converting plant i
CRC_{ip}	Raw material variable cost per ton for product p in converting plant i
CMC_t	Machine cost per hour for production line t
CPT_{pt}	Conversion time hours/ton for product p at production line t
CUC_{ip}	Cost, insurance, and freight (CIF) unit cost for product p in conversion facility i, includes intercompany markup
$I_{ijp}^{(4)}$	Cross-sourcing cost factor for product p from converting facility i to distribution facility j
$T_{ijp}^{(4)}$	Transportation cost for product p from converting facility i to distribution facility j in \$/standard unit
$TI_{ijp}^{(4)}$	Transportation cost for product p from facility i to entry customs when sending to facility j
$T_{ikp}^{(5)}$	Transportation cost for product p from converting facility i to market k in \$/standard unit
CC_{it}	Converting capacity in hours for facility i and production line t
$T_{jkp}^{(7)}$	Transportation cost for product p from DC j to market k in \$ per standard unit
$T_{jlp}^{(6)}$	Transportation cost for product p from DC j to DC l in \$ per standard unit
$TI_{jlp}^{(6)}$	Transportation cost for product p from DC j to entry port or customs when sending goods to DC l in \$ per standard unit
DUC_{jl}	CIF unit cost for product p at DC j, includes intercompany markup
$I_{jlp}^{(6)}$	Cross-sourcing cost percentage for product p from DC j to DC l
FD_j	Fixed operational cost of DC j
VOC_j	Variable operational cost of DC j in \$/cubic meters
SC_j	Shipping capacity of DC j in cubic meters

The following parameters represent the subjective facility risk rating values obtained from the DMs using a numerical scale (1–5), where higher numbers represent higher risk as presented in Table 3.1. The risk values are related to opening or closing a facility and the corresponding impact on fulfilling the demand of local customers and exports. Different parameters are defined for different echelons of the supply chain.

$R\ell_h^{(1)}$	Risk rating for manufacturing facility h if opened to serve local customers
$R\varepsilon_h^{(1)}$	Risk rating for manufacturing facility h if opened to serve exports' demand
$Rc_h^{(1)}$	Risk rating for manufacturing facility h if closed to serve local customers
$R\ell_i^{(2)}$	Risk rating for conversion facility i if opened to serve local customers
$R\varepsilon_i^{(2)}$	Risk rating for conversion facility i if opened to serve exports' demand
$Rc_i^{(2)}$	Risk rating for conversion facility i if closed to serve local customers
$R\ell_j^{(3)}$	Risk rating for distribution facility j if opened to serve local customers
$R\varepsilon_j^{(3)}$	Risk rating for distribution facility j if opened to serve exports' demand
$Rc_j^{(3)}$	Risk rating for distribution facility j if closed to serve local customers

Similar to the facility risk ratings, three rating groups are defined to represent the strategic factor values based on the DMs' assessment for each echelon. The DMs assign a value from 1 to 5 indicating how relevant it is to keep the facility open for strategic purposes (the higher the value the more important it is). For example, consider a facility operating in a country where imports are restricted by the government. Because it is not possible to import cheaper products to this market, it is strategically more important to keep this facility open to serve the local markets.

$St_h^{(1)}$	Strategic rating for manufacturing facility h
$St_i^{(2)}$	Strategic rating for converting facility i
$St_j^{(3)}$	Strategic rating for distribution facility j

Other parameters are defined to incorporate the lead times for shipments between a given facility and a customer zone. These are measured in days and represent the time from when a customer places an order with the sales department until this order is delivered at the customer's facility.

$L_{hk}^{(3)}$	Lead time in days for shipments between manufacturing facility h and market k
$L_{ik}^{(5)}$	Lead time in days for shipments between converting facility i and market k

$L_{jk}^{(7)}$ Lead time in days for shipments between DC j and market k

$L_{jl}^{(6)}$ Lead time in days for shipments between DC j and DC l

Target values for the criteria are determined by identifying the *ideal values* for each criterion. Ideal values represent the best values achievable for each criterion, ignoring the other criteria. For example, the ideal value of the profit criterion is obtained by maximizing the profit function alone and is expressed in dollars. The ideal value of the lead time criterion is obtained by minimizing the lead time objective and is measured in days. Ideal values are then used by the DMs to set the best target values for each criterion. Target values are generally set close to the ideal or at the ideal by the DMs. Because the units of measurement for the criteria are different, it is important to scale the criteria values properly. A common approach to scaling is to divide the criteria by their respective ideal values so that the best values of the criteria are always one. The parameter $T^{(g)}$ is used to denote the target value of the criterion (goal) "g" and its relative weight, assessed by the DMs, is denoted by w_g.

3.3.3.2 Decision Variables

Several continuous variables are defined to represent the flow of goods through the network for both production and distribution volumes, considering different units of measure depending on the echelon where the flows occur. Binary variables are used for opening or closing decisions associated with manufacturing, converting, and distribution facilities, as well as for specific production lines.

Production Stage 1

$x_{hipt}^{(1)}$ Production of product p at production line t at manufacturing facility h sent to converting facility i in tons

$x_{hkpt}^{(2)}$ Production of product p at production line t at manufacturing facility h sent to market k in tons

$\delta_h^{(1)}$ 1 if manufacturing facility h is opened, 0 otherwise

$\gamma_{ht}^{(1)}$ 1 if production line t at manufacturing facility h is opened, 0 otherwise

Production Stage 2

$y_{ijpt}^{(1)}$ Production of product p at converting facility i and line t sent to DC j in standard units

$y_{ikpt}^{(2)}$ Distribution of product p from converting facility i and line t to market k in standard units

$\delta_i^{(2)}$ 1 if converting facility i is opened, 0 otherwise

$\gamma_{it}^{(2)}$ 1 if production line t at converting facility i is opened, 0 otherwise

Distribution Stage

$z_{jlp}^{(1)}$ Distribution of product p from DC j to DC l in standard units

$z_{jkp}^{(2)}$ Distribution of product p from DC j to market k in standard units

$\delta_j^{(3)}$ 1 if distribution facility i is opened, 0 otherwise

3.3.3.3 Decision Criteria

3.3.3.3.1 Gross Profit

The gross profit is given by the total revenue less fixed and variable operating costs, raw material costs, transportation costs, and cross-sourcing costs (Equations 3.1–3.13).

3.3.3.3.2 Total Revenue

The total revenue is given by the demand volume and sales price of a particular product p in a specific customer zone k (Equation 3.1). Shipping a product to a customer zone can be done from three different sources: (1) a distribution center j ships products to customers where the flow is represented by $z_{jkp}^{(2)}$, (2) direct shipments to customers occur from a converting facility i for which the decision variable $y_{ikpt}^{(2)}$ is used, and (3) semi-finished goods are directly shipped to customers from a manufacturing facility h represented by $x_{hkpt}^{(2)}$.

$$\sum_{k\in MKS}\sum_{p\in PRSK_k} P_{kp}\left(\sum_{j\in DCSK_k} z_{jkp}^{(2)} + \sum_{i\in CFSK_k}\sum_{t\in CTSC_i} y_{ikpt}^{(2)} + \sum_{h\in MFSK_k}\sum_{t\in CTSM_h} x_{hkpt}^{(2)}\right) \quad (3.1)$$

3.3.3.3.3 Fixed Operating Costs

The fixed costs associated with the manufacturing and distribution processes are separated into facility overheads (Equation 3.2) and production line fixed costs (Equation 3.3). Facility overheads include all the fixed costs associated with the operation of a manufacturing, converting, or distribution facility—such as plant general management, quality, maintenance, building leasing or depreciation, among others. The product line fixed costs include machine specific fixed costs—such as equipment depreciation, labor required to operate a particular production line, and so on. In the objective function, these fixed cost parameters are multiplied by their corresponding binary variables, which represent the activation status of a facility or a production line.

$$-\left(\sum_{h\in MFS} FM_h\delta_h^{(1)} + \sum_{i\in CFS} FC_i\delta_i^{(2)} + \sum_{j\in DCS} FD_j\delta_j^{(3)}\right) \quad (3.2)$$

$$-\left(\sum_{h\in MFS}\sum_{t\in CTSM_h} FMM_{ht}\gamma_{ht}^{(1)} + \sum_{i\in CFS}\sum_{t\in CTSC_i} FCM_{it}\gamma_{it}^{(2)}\right) \quad (3.3)$$

3.3.3.3.4 Variable Operating Costs

The variable operating costs are given by raw materials consumed; costs incurred for the operation of production lines such as utilities, operating supplies, and spare parts; and some expenses at the distribution centers, such wrapping materials and nonreusable pallets. At a particular production facility h or i, the total raw material costs are determined by the total units produced of each product p and their corresponding unit of raw material costs MRC_{hp} and CRC_{ip}. Then the network total raw material costs are given by Equations 3.4 and 3.5.

$$-\left(\sum_{h\in MFS} \sum_{p\in PRSM_h} MRC_{hp} \left(\sum_{i\in CFSM_h} \sum_{t\in CTSM_h} x_{hipt}^{(1)} + \sum_{k\in MKSM_h} \sum_{t\in CTSM_h} x_{hkpt}^{(2)} \right) \right) \quad (3.4)$$

$$-\left(\sum_{i\in CFS} \sum_{p\in PRSC_i} CRC_{ip} \sum_{t\in CTSC_i} \left(\sum_{j\in DCSC_i} y_{ijpt}^{(1)} + \sum_{k\in MKSC_i} y_{ikpt}^{(2)} \right) \right) \quad (3.5)$$

Total production line operation costs are presented in Equations 3.6 and 3.7. The calculation is based on the total hours of operation required by the volume produced for a particular product p in a production line t and its corresponding productivity rate in hours per unit MPT_{pt} and CPT_{pt}. Then, each production line t has a specific variable operating cost per hour of operation MMC_{pt} and CMC_{pt}. Finally, the total network costs are summarized by facility, based on the production lines operating at each facility.

$$-\left(\sum_{h\in MFS} \sum_{t\in CTSM_h} MMC_t \sum_{p\in PRST_t} MPT_{pt} \left(\sum_{i\in CFSM_h} x_{hipt}^{(1)} + \sum_{k\in MKSM_h} x_{hkpt}^{(2)} \right) \right) \quad (3.6)$$

$$-\left(\sum_{i\in CFS} \sum_{t\in CTSC_i} CMC_t \sum_{p\in PRST_t} CPT_{pt} \left(\sum_{j\in DCSC_i} y_{ijpt}^{(1)} + \sum_{k\in MKSC_i} y_{ikpt}^{(2)} \right) \right) \quad (3.7)$$

Equation 3.8 shows the formula for the distribution variable costs at the warehouse, which converts to cubic meters the volume in standard units shipped from a given distribution center j for a specific product p. The total variable distribution cost is then calculated for all facilities, and the products handled at each DC are multiplied by a unit variable operating cost VOC_j determined for each DC.

$$-\left(\sum_{j\in DCS} VOC_j \left(\sum_{l\in DCSC_j} \sum_{p\in PRSD_l} z_{jlp}^{(1)} DF_{jkp}^{(2)} + \sum_{k\in MKSD_j} \sum_{p\in PRSK_k} z_{jkp}^{(2)} DF_{jkp}^{(2)} \right) \right) \quad (3.8)$$

3.3.3.3.5 Transportation Costs

Equations 3.9 and 3.10 show the inbound and outbound shipment costs, respectively, that are included in the objective function, based on the transportation costs determined for each arc of the network. The outbound shipments are associated with the transportation of semi-finished and finished products directly to customers, regardless of the origin facility type, and the inbound shipments correspond to the inter-plant transactions among production and distribution facilities.

$$
-\left(\sum_{h\in MFS} \sum_{i\in CFSM_h} \sum_{p\in PRSC_i} \sum_{t\in CTSC_h} x_{hipt}^{(1)} T_{hip}^{(2)} + \sum_{i\in CFS} \sum_{j\in DCSC_i} \sum_{p\in PRSD_j} \sum_{t\in CTSC_i} y_{ijpt}^{(1)} T_{ijp}^{(4)} \right.
$$
$$
\left. + \sum_{j\in DCS} \sum_{l\in DCSD_j} \sum_{p\in PRSD_l} T_{jlp}^{(6)} z_{jlp}^{(1)} \right)
\tag{3.9}
$$

$$
-\left(\sum_{h\in MFS} \sum_{k\in MKSM_h} \sum_{p\in PRSK_k} \sum_{t\in CTSC_h} x_{hkpt}^{(2)} T_{hkp}^{(3)} + \sum_{i\in CFS} \sum_{k\in MKSC_i} \sum_{p\in PRSK_k} \sum_{t\in CTSC_i} y_{ikpt}^{(2)} T_{ikp}^{(5)} \right.
$$
$$
\left. + \sum_{j\in DCS} \sum_{k\in MKSD_j} \sum_{p\in PRSK_k} T_{jkp}^{(7)} z_{jkp}^{(2)} \right)
\tag{3.10}
$$

3.3.3.3.6 Cross-Sourcing Costs

Cross-sourcing costs include any amount related to international shipments, with the exception of freight costs that were already considered in Equations 3.9 and 3.10, such as import and export duties, imports agencies' fees, among others. Cross-sourcing costs $I_{hip}^{(2)}$, $I_{ijp}^{(4)}$, and $I_{jlp}^{(6)}$ are expressed as a percentage and are applied to the total unit product cost accumulated at the manufacturing, converting, and distribution echelons represented by the parameters MUC_{kp}, CUC_{ip}, and DUC_{jp}, as shown in Equations 3.11 and 3.12.

$$
-\left(\sum_{j\in DCS} \sum_{p\in PRSD_j} DUC_{jp} \left(\sum_{l\in DCSD_j} I_{jlp}^{(6)} z_{jlp}^{(1)} \right) \right)
$$

$$
-\left(\sum_{h\in MFS} \sum_{p\in PRSM_h} MUC_{hp} \left(\sum_{i\in CFSM_h} I_{hip}^{(2)} \sum_{t\in CTSM_h} x_{hipt}^{(1)} \right) \right)
\tag{3.11}
$$

$$
-\left(\sum_{i\in CFS} \sum_{p\in PRSC_i} CUC_{ip} \left(\sum_{j\in DCSD_i} I_{ijp}^{(4)} \sum_{t\in CTSC_i} y_{ijpt}^{(1)} \right) \right)
\tag{3.12}
$$

In addition, the cross-sourcing rates given by $TI_{hip}^{(2)}$, $TI_{ijp}^{(4)}$, and $TI_{jlp}^{(6)}$ are applied over the transportation costs from a sourcing facility to the customs office at a first entry point to a country (Equation 3.13). Generally, in international trade, the total duties are determined by customs over the total cost of the product at the country's first entry point, considering not only the cost of production of the product but the expenses incurred in its transportation.

$$
-\sum_{i \in CFS} \sum_{j \in DCSC_i} \sum_{p \in PRSD_j} \sum_{t \in CTSC_i} y_{ijpt}^{(1)} TI_{ijp}^{(4)} I_{ijp}^{(4)} - \sum_{j \in DCS} \sum_{l \in DCSD_j} \sum_{p \in PRSD_l} TI_{jlp}^{(6)} I_{jlp}^{(6)} z_{jlp}^{(1)}
$$
$$
-\sum_{h \in MFS} \sum_{i \in CFSM_h} \sum_{p \in PRSC_i} \sum_{t \in CTSM_h} x_{hipt}^{(1)} TI_{hip}^{(2)} I_{hip}^{(2)}
\tag{3.13}
$$

Thus, the gross profit goal constraint is given by Equation 3.14.

3.3.3.3.6.1 Maximize Gross Profit

$$
\left(\text{Gross Profit}\right) + d_1^- - d_1^+ = T^{(1)}
\tag{3.14}
$$

where $T^{(1)}$ is the gross profit target and the objective is to minimize d_1^-, which is the underachievement of the profit target.

3.3.3.3.6.2 Minimize Lead Time to Customers   Equation 3.15 presents a demand-weighted measure of the lead time to ship products to customers, where the lead time parameters for the corresponding facility to customer arcs are weighted by the flow of goods in each arc. Delivery time targets are defined for each customer zone k, and the goal is to not exceed those targets for each customer zone $\left(T_k^{(2)}\right)$. Hence, the deviation variable d_{2k}^+ is minimized, which represents the violation of the lead time goal. All terms in Equation 3.15, except for the deviational variables, are scaled by the total demand at the market to get an approximate value, in days, of the weighted average delivery time.

$$
\frac{\sum_{i \in CFS} L_{ik}^{(5)} \left(\sum_{p \in PRSK_k} \sum_{t \in CTSC_i} y_{ikpt}^{(2)} \right) + \sum_{j \in DCS} L_{jk}^{(7)} \left(\sum_{p \in PRSK_k} z_{jkp}^{(2)} \right)}{\sum_{p \in PRSK_k} D_{kp}} + d_{2k}^- - d_{2k}^+
$$
$$
= \frac{T_k^{(2)} \left(\sum_{p \in PRSK_k} \sum_{t \in CTSC_i} y_{ikpt}^{(2)} + \sum_{p \in PRSK_k} z_{jkp}^{(2)} \right)}{\sum_{p \in PRSK_k} D_{kp}} \quad \text{for all } k \in MKS
\tag{3.15}
$$

3.3.3.3.6.3 Minimize Risk of Supply Chain Disruptions The risk measures, based on the qualitative assessment of the DMs and the quantitative cost of capital measure presented in Section 3.2, are included in Equation 3.16, together with its global goal target and corresponding deviational variables. For this goal, it is required to have the least possible risk level, thereby minimizing the deviation d_3^+ over $T^{(3)}$.

$$\sum_{h \in MFS} R\ell_h^{(1)} \delta_h^{(1)} + \sum_{i \in CFS} R\ell_i^{(2)} \delta_i^{(2)} + \sum_{j \in DCS} R\ell_j^{(3)} \delta_j^{(3)} + \sum_{h \in MFS} Rc_h^{(1)} \left(1 - \delta_h^{(1)}\right)$$

$$+ \sum_{i \in CFS} Rc_i^{(2)} \left(1 - \delta_i^{(2)}\right) + \sum_{j \in DCS} Rc_j^{(3)} \left(1 - \delta_j^{(3)}\right) + d_3^- - d_3^+ = T^{(3)} \tag{3.16}$$

3.3.3.3.6.4 Maximize Strategic Factors Equation 3.17 includes the strategic factor ratings for each manufacturing, converting, and distribution facility, along with a global strategic target and the deviational variables. In this case, the goal is to minimize the underachievement of a predetermined level of the strategic factor measure $T^{(4)}$ for the entire supply chain network.

$$\sum_{h \in MFS} St_h^{(1)} \delta_h^{(1)} + \sum_{i \in CFS} St_i^{(2)} \delta_i^{(2)} + \sum_{j \in DCS} St_j^{(3)} \delta_j^{(3)} + d_4^- - d_4^+ = T^{(4)} \tag{3.17}$$

3.3.3.3.6.5 Maximize Demand Fulfillment at the Markets Equation 3.18 represents the goal constraint for any product and market combination, where the total flow of semi-finished or finished goods shipped to customers from the manufacturing, converting, and distribution facilities should not exceed the predicted customer demand. Hence, the deviational variables d_{5kp}^+ are included in the minimization objective function.

$$\left(\sum_{h \in MKSM_h} \sum_{t \in CTSM_h} x_{hkpt}^{(2)} + \sum_{i \in CFSK_k} y_{ikp}^{(2)} + \sum_{j \in DCSK_k} z_{jkp}^{(2)} \right) + d_{5kp}^- - d_{5kp}^+ = D_{kp} \tag{3.18}$$

for all $k \in MKS, p \in PRSK_k$

In the multi-criteria problem, the objective is to minimize the weighted sum of the deviations from the target values defined for each goal. As presented in Equation 3.19, the objective function considers the minimization of the underachievement of the profit, overall strategic factor value, and demand fulfillment targets, as well as any deviations (overachievements) above the lead time and risk targets. Note that for the demand fulfillment component of the objective function, the sum of all the deviational variables d_{5kp}^-, is arithmetically averaged based on the total number of markets and product combinations with customer demand greater than zero, which is given by the product of the cardinality of the sets *MKS* and *PRS* such that $D_{kp} > 0$ for all k, p. This result is then weighted as a component of the GP objective function. Similarly, the sum of the lead time deviational variables d_{2k}^+ is averaged arithmetically based on the number of markets in the network with customer demand. This is the given by the cardinality of the set MKS such that $D_{kp} > 0$ for all k, p.

3.3.3.3.7 GP Objective Function

$$z = w_1 d_1^- + w_2 \left(\frac{\sum\limits_{k \in MKS} d_{2k}^+}{|MKS|} \right) + w_3 d_3^+ + w_4 d_4^- + w_5 \left(\frac{\sum\limits_{k \in MKS} \sum\limits_{p \in PRS} d_{5kp}^-}{|MKS| * |PRS|} \right) \quad (3.19)$$

$$\sum_{g=1}^{5} w_g = 1 \qquad 0 \le w_g \le 1 \text{ for all } g = 1, \dots, 5. \quad (3.20)$$

$$d_1^-, d_1^+, d_{2k}^-, d_{2k}^+, d_3^-, d_3^+, d_4^-, d_4^+, d_{5kp}^-, d_{5kp}^+ \ge 0 \quad (3.21)$$

For the weighted objective GP formulation, scaling of the goals is necessary for proper optimization. Note that the goal constraints explained here are in different units of measure and can significantly vary in magnitude. For example, gross profit can be in millions of currency units, lead time may be from single to no more than double digits, demand fulfillment is a percentage amount, and risk and strategy are single digit measures. The formulation uses the goals' target values for scaling purposes, assuring that the deviational variables vary between 0 and 1. The group weights obtained in Table 3.9 are used in Equation 3.19. Thus, the objective function minimizes the weighted sum of the scaled deviational variables.

3.3.3.4 Model Constraints

The model constraints represent the distribution and production capacities, mass and flow balance, and binary variables relationships.

3.3.3.4.1 Distribution Capacity Utilization

Equation 3.22 states that the total volume shipped from each distribution center j to other distribution centers l and customer zones k cannot exceed its capacity SC_j, stated in cubic meters. Specific mass factors are considered for each product p and specific arc (j, l) and (j, k).

$$\sum_{l \in DCSD_j} \left(\sum_{p \in PRSD_l} z_{jlp}^{(1)} DF_{jlp}^{(3)} + \sum_{k \in MKSD_j} \sum_{p \in PRSK_k} z_{jkp}^{(2)} DF_{jkp}^{(2)} \right) \le SC_j \quad \text{for all } j \in DCS \quad (3.22)$$

3.3.3.4.2 *Flow Balance at Semi-Finished Manufacturing*

Equation 3.23 represents the balance required between flows, in and out, given the production volumes at a manufacturing facility h, corresponding shipments to converting facilities i, and sales of semi-finished products to customer zones k, considering mass conversion factors. These balance constraints are enforced only for the products p defined as part of the set *PRSS*.

$$\sum_{h \in MFSP_p} \sum_{i \in CFSC_i} \sum_{t \in CTSM_h} DF_{ip}^{(1)} x_{hipt}^{(1)} + \sum_{i \in CFSP_p} \sum_{j \in DCSC_i} \sum_{t \in CTSC_i} y_{ijpt}^{(1)}$$

$$= \sum_{j \in DCSP_p} \sum_{l \in DCSD_j} z_{jlp}^{(2)}, \text{ for all } p \in PRSS \tag{3.23}$$

3.3.3.4.3 *Flow Balance at Conversion Facilities*

Similarly, Equations 3.24 and 3.25 show the balance constraints required between flows, in and out, given the production volumes at a converting facility i, any amount received from a manufacturing facility h, when applicable, corresponding shipments to distribution facilities j, and sales of finished products to customer zones k. Note that Equation 3.24 represents the flow balance for specific products p for which converting facilities receive semi-finished goods from manufacturing facilities. In contrast, Equation 3.25 applies only for products that have a one-stage production process.

$$DF_{ip}^{(1)} \left(\sum_{h \in MFSC_i} \sum_{t \in CTSM_h} x_{hipt}^{(1)} \right) - \sum_{j \in DCSC_i} \sum_{t \in CTSC_i} y_{ijpt}^{(1)} - \sum_{k \in MKSC_i} \sum_{t \in CTSC_i} y_{ikpt}^{(2)} = 0 \tag{3.24}$$

$$\text{for all } i \in CFS, p \in PRSC_i$$

$$\sum_{i \in CFSP_p} \sum_{j \in DCSC_i} \sum_{t \in CTSC_i} y_{ijpt}^{(1)} = \sum_{j \in DCSP_p} \sum_{l \in DCSD_j} z_{jlp}^{(2)}, \quad \text{for all } p \notin PRSS \tag{3.25}$$

3.3.3.4.4 *Flow Balance at Distribution Centers*

At the distribution centers, the flow balance constraints are defined for facilities that receive goods from both production facilities and other distribution centers (Equation 3.26) or only from other distribution centers (Equation 3.27). These flows are balanced with the shipments out to customer zones k or to other distribution facilities. Note that several distribution echelons may be necessary to fulfill demand at some markets.

$$\sum_{i \in CFSD_j} \sum_{t \in CTSC_i} y_{ijpt}^{(1)} + \sum_{l \in DCSA_j} z_{ljp}^{(1)} = \sum_{l \in DCSD_j} z_{jlp}^{(1)} + \sum_{k \in MKSD_j} z_{jkp}^{(2)}, \tag{3.26}$$

$$\text{for all } j \in DCSINTERPLANTS, p \in PRSD_j$$

$$\sum_{l \in DCSA_j} z_{ljp}^{(1)} = \sum_{l \in DCSD_j} z_{jlp}^{(1)} + \sum_{k \in MKSD_j} z_{jkp}^{(2)}, \quad \text{for all } j \in DCSTOMARKETS, p \in PRSD_j$$

(3.27)

3.3.3.4.5 Manufacturing and Conversion Capacity

The production capacity at the manufacturing and converting facilities is given by the total number of hours of operation available for each production line t, represented by MC_{ht} and CC_{it}. The volumes produced for each product p at each production line t, have specific productivity rate MPT_{hpt} and CPT_{ipt}, that give the total required load for the machines. As stated by Equations 3.28 and 3.29, the total required load must be less than or equal to the total number of hours available for a machine t, if the machine is operating, which is determined by the value of the binary variables $\gamma_{ht}^{(1)}$ and $\gamma_{it}^{(2)}$.

$$\sum_{p \in PRST_t} \left(MPT_{hpt} \left(\sum_{i \in CFSM_h} x_{hipt}^{(1)} \right) + \sum_{p \in PRST_t} MPT_{hpt} \left(\sum_{k \in MKSM_h} x_{hkpt}^{(2)} \right) \right) \leq MC_{ht} \gamma_{ht}^{(1)}$$

(3.28)

$$\text{for all } h \in MFS, t \in CTSM_h$$

$$\left(\sum_{p \in PRST_t} CPT_{ipt} \left(\sum_{j \in DCSC_i} y_{ijpt}^{(1)} \right) + \sum_{p \in PRST_t} CPT_{ipt} \left(\sum_{k \in MKSC_i} y_{ikpt}^{(2)} \right) \right) \leq CC_{it} \gamma_{it}^{(2)}$$

(3.29)

$$\text{for all } i \in CFS, t \in CTSC_i$$

3.3.3.4.6 Distribution Capacity

Equation 3.30 represents the shipping capacity constraint, in cubic meters, for the flows out of the distribution facility j, provided it is open.

$$\sum_{l \in DCSD_j} \sum_{p \in PRSD_l} DF_{jlp}^{(3)} z_{jlp}^{(1)} + \sum_{k \in MKSD_j} \sum_{p \in PRSK_k} DF_{jkp}^{(2)} z_{jkp}^{(2)} - SC_j \delta_j^{(3)} \leq 0 \quad \text{for all } j \in DCS$$

(3.30)

3.3.3.4.7 Manufacturing and Conversion Binary Decision Variables

Equations 3.31 and 3.32 ensure that a production line t is not active if the associated manufacturing facility h or converting facility i is not open. However, when a facility is open, the production lines are not necessarily active; they may or may not operate depending on the production needs.

$$\gamma_{ht}^{(1)} \leq \delta_h^{(1)}, \text{ for all } h \in MFS, t \in CTSM_h$$

(3.31)

$$\gamma_{it}^{(2)} \leq \delta_i^{(2)}, \text{ for all } i \in CFS, t \in CTSC_i$$

(3.32)

3.3.3.4.8 Production Expansions Binary Decision Variables

Equations 3.33 and 3.34 ensure that a new production line t, proposed as a capacity expansion, is activated only when all the existing machines of similar technology t are operating. If at least one production line of type t is idle at a given plant, then no capacity expansion can be done. Note that these constraints can be relaxed if the analyst wants to evaluate the replacement of equipment. In such a case, new production lines could be opened even when the existing equipment is idle.

$$\gamma_{ht'}^{(1)} \leq \gamma_{ht}^{(1)}, \text{ for all } (h,t,t') \in MFSTT_{htt'} \tag{3.33}$$

$$\gamma_{it'}^{(1)} \leq \gamma_{it}^{(1)}, \text{ for all } (i,t,t') \in CFSTT_{itt'} \tag{3.34}$$

Finally, Equations 3.35 and 3.36 make sure that at least one production line t is active, in order to open a manufacturing facility h or converting facility i.

$$\sum_t \gamma_{it}^{(2)} \geq \delta_i^{(2)} \text{ for all } i \tag{3.35}$$

$$\sum_t \gamma_{ht}^{(1)} \geq \delta_h^{(1)} \text{ for all } h \tag{3.36}$$

All the decision variables are continuous and nonnegative, except for $\delta_h^{(1)}$, $\delta_i^{(2)}$, and $\delta_j^{(3)}$ that are binary variables, defined as 1 if facility is open and 0 otherwise. Similarly $\gamma_{ht}^{(1)}$ and $\gamma_{it}^{(2)}$ are defined as 1 if production line is operating and 0 otherwise.

3.4 Data Needs, Model Results, and Managerial Insights

3.4.1 Data Collection

Before conducting the analysis, significant effort was required to collect data of both types, historical and planned. Because of the large scale of the analyses, it is important to highlight the effort dedicated to build the databases for the different supply chain network scenarios. Each scenario analysis required extracting thousands of market, finance, and operations related data records from the firm's business systems as well as obtaining information from external sources. At least three employees worked full time directly gathering or requesting information, as well as organizing it appropriately to run the optimization models. In addition, at least a dozen people were contacted to provide information. The historical data was obtained from the company's enterprise resource planning (ERP) system at very low levels of granularity to have the flexibility of aggregating it as required by the optimization model. Sales volume and prices were obtained at stock keeping unit (SKU) and customer levels and then aggregated to the product and customer zone level. Production volume and unit costs were extracted at the SKU and production line levels and then aggregated to a product for each production line. Plant cost information was generated at the financial account level by each cost center associated with each production line and then classified as plant overheads, production line fixed and variable costs, and raw material costs. Transportation and cross-sourcing cost was defined for each arc of the network at the SKU level and then aggregated to products. Also, mass conversion factors were determined to handle different volume units of measure used at the different echelons of the supply chain. Projected information was obtained from the company's most recent business plans, including forecasted demand volume, price, and cost projections. Finally, an aggregated database consisting of approximately 75,000 data records, including marketing, sales, production, distribution, and purchasing information, was built.

The mathematical formulation was coded in ILOG and solved using a CPLEX solver. The optimization model consisted of approximately 7,500 variables, from which 300 were binary and around 7,000 were constraints. Three persons were involved in coding the models in ILOG and then using the CPLEX software to solve the problems. In general, optimal solutions were obtained very efficiently, taking less than three minutes for each scenario analysis to run.

3.4.2 Single Objective (Profit Maximization) Analysis

The model was applied to the manufacturing and distribution network of a leading health care and hygiene company, based on its competitive strategy and corresponding customer demand projections, for a 10-year horizon. Initially, the analysis was executed with the primary objective of maximizing profits, and it consisted of three supply chain scenarios:

- *Scenario 1:* Determine the ability of the company to fulfill current and projected sales levels, based on the current supply chain network.
- *Scenario 2:* Evaluate how the company's ability would be improved by including the potential expansions of plants and DCs already under consideration by the management.
- *Scenario 3:* Optimize the global supply chain network that would deliver the best results for the entire time horizon.

Under the profit maximization assumption, a single objective integer programming problem was solved using the ILOG CPLEX Solver. The optimal solution gave the best values of the decision variables (defined in Section 3.3.2) that would maximize the total profit for the company. The optimal values of the binary variables provided the following information:

- Location of new facilities (manufacturing plants, converting facilities, and DCs) that were to be opened and their capacities
- Status of the existing facilities—whether they have to be expanded, downsized, closed, or operated at the same level

The optimal values of the continuous variables provided the following information:

- Specific products manufactured at the plants and converting facilities
- Products handled by the DCs
- Optimal distribution plans for the products and customers
  - Shipments from a manufacturing plant to a converting facility, to a DC, or directly to the customer
  - Shipments from a converting facility to a DC or directly to customers
  - Shipments from a DC to another DC or directly to customers

Based on these optimal distribution plans, the demand fulfillments for each customer were determined by computing the ratio of the total amount shipped to a customer from all sources to that customer's estimated demand. Besides confirming the supply chain design decisions already made, important outcomes for strategic investment and business tactical plans were obtained regarding the optimal levels of demand fulfillment, location and size of required facility expansions, relocation of production lines, intercompany cross-sourcing, and distribution to strategies. The results of each scenario will be discussed in detail in the next sections.

3.4.2.1 Scenario 1 Analysis

The Scenario 1 analysis, which considered only the existing supply chain network, provided relevant results related to the ability of the current supply chain to support the given competitive strategy of the company. When performing the analysis with current demand levels, the overall results showed a very close to full capacity utilization of the current facilities. Regarding structural changes, as expected from a high utilization of resources, the network design did not have major changes except for the closure of a small facility and a few inter-facility transfer production lines. However, the model suggested modifications to the cross-sourcing strategy. Also, when considering the future demand, the overall results showed that the current supply chain design could fulfill only 70% of the total projected demand, and that it was restricted primarily by the production and distribution capacities. The model used the production and distribution capacities for the most profitable combinations of products and markets, clearly identifying potential shortages in specific products and markets.

3.4.2.2 Scenario 2 Analysis

Analysis of Scenario 2 included capacity expansions in the production and distribution facilities already considered by the management. Close to a dozen new production lines were planned to be installed within a two-year horizon to increase production capacity of different products. Although management had already decided on the location of these machines, multiple options were allowed in the model to confirm their choices. The results showed that the majority of the chosen locations for the production lines were optimal, while others had no significant differences between the chosen location and the optimal location. Although the locations were the best to maximize profit, the supply chain network was capable of meeting only 85% of the projected demand, even after all the approved expansions. Again, the model identified clearly where the demand shortages would occur.

3.4.2.3 Scenario 3 Analysis

For Scenario 3, it was necessary to first perform an assessment of the physical feasibility and strategic convenience of expansions at each of the current facilities. Different levels of expansions were also considered—expanding a facility by incorporating a new machine to the existing infrastructure or acquiring additional support equipment, additional building construction, land, and so on. In addition, locations for potential new facilities were determined based on the opinions of senior management. Similar evaluation was performed for the distribution centers as well. With this information, multiple expansion alternatives were incorporated into the database in the optimization analysis. The results of the Scenario 3 analysis provided optimal levels of production, distribution, and sales, in order to maximize the profits. The optimal demand fulfillment ratio increased from 85% in Scenario 2 to 96% in Scenario 3, again highlighting specific product/market combinations that were not profitable. This opened up opportunities to improve business practices in the company.

3.4.2.4 Other Results

Another outcome very important for investment planning was the determination of the specific location and size of the required expansions or openings of new facilities for different technologies and products. For some products, where economies of scale are more important due to large fixed costs involved in the manufacturing process, the model suggested centralizing the manufacturing at key regional facilities and closing some of the smaller facilities in other countries. For other products, where the operational and technological advances had made the operation of the local plants economically feasible, the model suggested not expanding the regional plants but adopting a local production strategy to save in freight and cross-sourcing costs. The model suggested not only new expansions but also relocation of assets among existing facilities. In addition, the model was useful in determining the need for production lines with new technologies as demand for new technology products increases and that for old technology products decreases.

Based on the optimal supply chain design, optimal distribution strategies, including cross-sourcing and distribution for each product, were obtained. The distribution plans gave the optimal flow of products through the supply chain from the manufacturing facilities to the customers. This analysis involved decisions on the selection of production lines to produce products, sourcing strategy for converting facilities, allocation of distribution centers to production facilities, and on allocation of customer zones to either distribution centers or production facilities. The model suggested a more centralized distribution strategy for customers in two groups of countries, where favorable geographic conditions and trade agreements exist. This implied closing the local warehouses and opening an expanded regional distribution center. The aforementioned results were critical—for determining strategic actions as well as for developing tactical business plans.

3.4.3 Multi-Criteria Analysis

In order to enhance the initial analysis of the profit maximization model, a multi-criteria supply chain optimization model was solved by adding objectives on demand fulfillment, lead time, sourcing risk, and strategic factors (defined in Section 3.3.3). The weights and preferences obtained earlier from the DMs (Table 3.11) were used in solving the GP models. The results obtained in this analysis are similar to the ones generated for the single objective model. However, important differences in the supply chain network design occurred primarily due to the inclusion of the lead time and risk criteria. Also, the size of the facility expansions was affected by the demand fulfillment criterion. In addition, the results led to a trade-off analysis among the conflicting decision criteria. Significant differences in the optimal supply chain network design between the multi-criteria model and the single objective profit maximization model are discussed as follows:

1. The profit maximization model suggested adopting a centralized distribution strategy for some countries. The multi-criteria model suggested a decentralized structure. This change was primarily due to the relative importance given to the lead time criterion. Evidently, a trade-off exists between the profit and lead time criteria. Based on the model results, the marginal benefits in profits may not justify reduction in customer service levels. More specifically, the savings

from efficiencies gained from economies of scale and risk pooling are partially offset by higher transportation costs, making the marginal benefit not large enough to justify a decrease in the responsiveness to customers. The risk of serving local markets increased with the centralized approach because the probability of supply chain disruptions is higher due to increased foreign sourcing, longer intercompany routes, and greater lead times.

2. The multi-criteria model suggested keeping specific facilities open in countries where having local production facilities was crucial for minimizing supply chain disruptions when serving local customer zones. Previously, results from the single criterion optimization (focused on maximizing profit) considered closing facilities in these countries. However, when considering the high values of the WACC of the firm and the risk assessments obtained from the DMs, which were driven primarily by the current political instability in those countries, the optimal solution recommended keeping the facilities open regardless of profit implications.

3. Strategic factors had less impact on the supply chain network design because there were no significant differences in the assessed values among the facilities. However, the results from the multi-criteria models were different in two cases. In one case, the multi-criteria model resulted in opening a production facility with a very high strategic rating. The profit maximization model considered closing that facility due to the cost. In another case, one of the new production facilities opened by the profit maximization model was closed in the multi-criteria model. This was due to the fact that its strategic rating was very low compared to the second sourcing option for that specific country, which had a larger regional plant with a higher strategic rating. The profit maximization model only focused on marginal benefit in profit.

4. In the multi-criteria model, the overall demand fulfillment ratio increased to 99% with some reduction in profits. A valuable outcome of this analysis was the trade-off evaluations for specific product–market combinations where increases in sales reduced profitability. These insights led to valuable managerial implications for the evaluation of the company's competitive strategy.

3.5 Conclusions

This chapter provided relevant insights from modeling to the implementation of designing a resilient global supply chain network. The multi-criteria mixed-integer linear programming model provided robust solutions for supporting strategic decisions related to the design of supply chain networks and tactical plans for manufacturing and distribution within a highly complex global environment. The models focused on optimizing multiple conflicting criteria, such as financial, customer service, risk, and strategic factors. These models were able to handle the complexity of the system (i.e., multiple products sold in several markets in different countries that required dealing with different currencies and commercial practices). Decisions regarding the optimal location, relocation, and allocation of production and distribution facilities as well as specific assets were efficiently addressed.

The case study illustrated several real-world applications. First, the analysis evaluated the current supply chain network and optimized the production and distribution flows within the given network. From the Scenario 1 analysis, it was possible to determine the maximum demand fulfillment potential of the current structure, understand the firm's supply chain design limitations, and to identify opportunities for future business growth. Scenario 2 consisted of running the optimization model with the approved future capacity expansions. This analysis was very valuable to the firm in reviewing the decisions made earlier but not yet implemented. Finally, the Scenario 3 analysis determined several alternative modifications to the current supply chain structure based on the judgments of the senior management and then performed optimization to obtain the best supply chain structure as well as cross-sourcing strategies. Different analyses were performed with different objectives—some focused on profitability, some on supply chain disruption risk, and others on a combination of criteria. The models were capable of delivering optimal solutions for large-scale applications with many products, dozens of facilities, and hundreds of assets and markets.

References

Masud, A. S. M., and A. R. Ravindran. Multiple Criteria Decision Making. In A. R. Ravindran (Ed.), *Operations Research and Management Science Handbook*. CRC Press, Boca Raton, FL, 2008.

Portillo, R. C. Resilient Global Supply Chain Network Design. PhD Dissertation, Pennsylvania State University, University Park, PA, 2009.

Ravindran, A. R. *Operations Research and Management Science Handbook*. CRC Press, Taylor and Francis Group, Boca Raton, FL, 2008.

Ravindran, A. R., K. M. Ragsdell, and G. V. Reklaitis. *Engineering Optimization: Methods and Applications*. Wiley, Hoboken, NJ, 2006.

Ravindran, A. R. and D. P. Warsing, Jr. *Supply Chain Engineering: Models and Applications*. CRC Press, Boca Raton, FL, 2013.

4

A Two-Phased Approach to Multi-Objective Supply Chain Design and Operation

Christopher J. Solo

The Pennsylvania State University, University Park, Pennsylvania

CONTENTS

4.1 Approaches to Multi-Objective Supply Chain Problems

Supply chain designers and managers potentially face a wide array of challenges, such as uncertain costs and unpredictable demand, when developing a supply chain's infrastructure and determining optimal production, shipment, and inventory quantities. To complicate matters, they are also charged with meeting objectives other than maximizing profit, such as minimizing transportation time. Fortunately, given the wide array of available multiple objective optimization techniques—many of which receive additional managerial attention through decision maker participation—supply chain designers and operators have the ability to model and solve supply chain problems in a way that very accurately reflects real-world business goals. Although the literature is ripe with an extensive array of single objective supply chain models and solutions, many authors (e.g., Beamon 1998) have also recognized the advantages of considering multiple objectives when developing solutions to supply chain problems. For instance, Sabri and Beamon (2000) use the ε-constraint method to handle the conflicting objectives of cost, customer service levels (fill rates), and volume/delivery flexibility in a two-stage supply chain problem under production, delivery, and demand uncertainty. Attai (2003) proposes a deterministic multi-criteria supply chain model that seeks to optimize facility locations, production quantities, shipment amounts, shipment routes, and inventory levels. This mixed integer model, solved using both a weighted objective method and compromise programming, considers profits, lead times, and local incentives. Local incentives, in this case, refer to labor quality, tax breaks, loans, and customer buying power (see Melachrinoudis and Min 2000). Min and Zhou (2002) provide a brief overview of several supply chain papers that consider multiple objectives. Ashayeri and Rongen (1997) consider the problem of optimally locating distribution centers and apply the ELECTRE solution method. This effort was extended to the multi-period case by Melachrinoudis and Min (2000). Melachrinoudis et al. (2000) consider a problem similar to the one addressed in Melachrinoudis (1999), this time using physical programming, in which a decision maker expresses criteria preferences in terms of degrees of desirability. In a shift from traditional multi-objective techniques, Altiparmak et al. (2006), Al-Mutawah et al. (2006), and others show how genetic algorithms can be used to provide a set of optimal or near-optimal solutions to a supply chain design problem.

More recently, Cintron et al. (2010) report on an application of a multi-criteria model for designing the distribution network for a major consumer products company. Due to globalization, supply chain networks have expanded beyond national boundaries, with suppliers, distribution centers (DCs), and manufacturing plants located all over the world. This expansion makes the supply chain more vulnerable to disruptions in different countries (Ravindran and Warsing 2013). Indeed, Ravindran et al. (2010) and Bilsel and Ravindran (2011, 2012) have developed multiple objective models for global sourcing considering disruption risk, and Rienkhemaniyom and Ravindran (2014) have formulated goal programming models for designing global supply chain networks incorporating disruptions at facilities (e.g., plants, DCs, and suppliers) and transportation links.

Although the aforementioned multi-criteria optimization techniques can be used to pursue multiple objectives in a supply chain scenario, the method of choice should be one that readily provides optimal solutions while accomplishing the following: (1) placing a minimum amount of input burden on the decision maker and (2) remaining straightforward and easily described to the decision maker, allowing him to gain a sufficient level of confidence in both the technique and accompanying solution. In many scenarios, decision makers require a solution based upon a simple prioritization of goals. A further requirement may include the flexibility to quickly explore alternate solutions based upon a reprioritization of goals. Alternatively, a decision maker may wish to formulate and optimize a supply chain problem in which a particular relative importance has been placed upon the various goals. One method that allows for such solution analysis is goal programming, and this technique will be addressed later in the chapter.

4.2 Two-Phased Mathematical Model for Supply Chain Design and Operation

The remainder of this chapter describes the formulation of a mathematical model developed to aid supply chain managers in the design and operation of a single product, multi-echelon, production–distribution network of suppliers, plants, warehouses, and customer markets. The problem considered here consists of designing the supply chain infrastructure (i.e., selection of suppliers, plants, production capacities, and warehouses) and determining the raw material, production, and inventory quantities needed to optimize profits, supply chain response time, and customer service levels (in terms of demand fulfillment) over a specified planning horizon when all input data is assumed to be known with certainty. In the design phase of the problem, where time periods are assumed to be in the one- to five-year range, managers wish to develop the framework for a production–distribution network that will achieve the maximum possible profit while ensuring market deliveries do not exceed forecasted customer demand. In the operational phase of the supply chain problem, it is assumed that time periods are in the three- to twelve-month range, that raw material and finished product transit times will become available, and that raw material availability, various costs, and customer demand are known with higher resolution (i.e., in terms of shorter time periods). In this phase, managers seek to make additional supplier selections and determine the best compromise raw material, production, inventory, and finished product shipment quantities necessary to achieve or exceed a specified profit level, minimize supply chain response time, and to come as close as possible to exactly meeting customer demand, all within the confines of the infrastructure developed in the design phase. In solving this complex problem, a two-phase, multi-objective, deterministic supply chain model, comprised of a strategic submodel and a tactical submodel, is developed to provide a strategic/tactical-level planning tool for the design and operation of a multi-echelon supply chain over a given planning horizon. The strategic submodel, represented by a multi-period mixed integer linear program, is formulated to determine the following: (1) supplier selections for critical raw materials, (2) plant construction decisions, (3) plant and warehouse operating decisions, and (4) necessary production capacities (based on optimal production quantities). While determining these elements of the supply chain, the strategic submodel is designed to achieve two conflicting objectives: (1) maximize the overall profit for the supply chain and (2) ensure market deliveries do not exceed demand. Although the profit objective is pursued through an objective function, the limits on deliveries are in fact achieved through the inclusion of a set of straightforward demand constraints.

Using the critical raw material supplier selections and infrastructure design decisions made in the solution to the strategic submodel; newly available raw material and finished product transit times; newly available supplier-specific, noncritical raw material availability and cost information; higher resolution demand data; and higher resolution production, storage, and shipping costs as inputs; the tactical submodel is then formulated as a linear goal programming model and solved to select suppliers of non-critical raw materials and determine (revised) best compromise production, shipment, and inventory quantities while seeking to achieve the following conflicting objectives: (1) *exactly* meet customer/market demand, (2) meet or exceed a specified profit goal, and (3) minimize supply chain response time. Figure 4.1 depicts the inputs, outputs, and objectives of the strategic and tactical submodels and shows the interconnectivity of the two submodels.

The index sets used in this model are defined as

i	for raw materials ($i = 1, \ldots, I$);
k	for suppliers ($k = 1, \ldots, K$);
m	for plants ($m = 1, \ldots, M$);
n	for warehouses ($n = 1, \ldots, N$);
p	for markets ($p = 1, \ldots, P$);
t	for time periods ($t = 1, \ldots, T$).

The data used in this model are represented by

a_i	units of raw material i needed to produce one unit of finished product;
c_{ikt}^R	cost per unit of (critical) raw material i purchased from supplier k in period t;
avc_{it}^R	average cost per unit (across all potential suppliers) of (noncritical) raw material i purchased in period t;
c_{mt}^{CON}	cost to build a plant of capacity U_m at location m in period t;

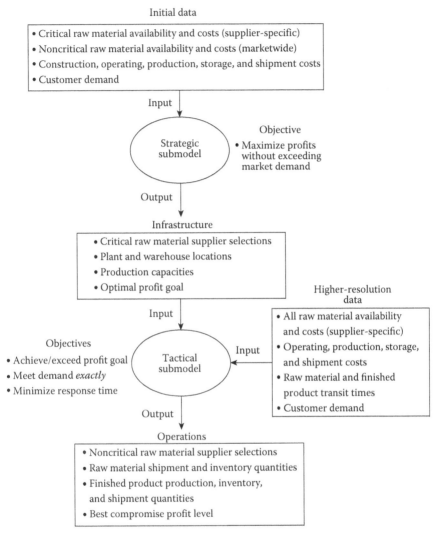

FIGURE 4.1
Inputs and outputs of strategic and tactical submodels.

c_{mt}^{FP} production cost per unit of finished product at plant m in period t;

c_{mt}^{PQ+} cost per unit of production quantity increase at plant m in period t;

c_{mt}^{PQ-} cost per unit of production quantity decrease at plant m in period t;

c_{ikmt}^{SRP} shipping cost per unit of (critical) raw material i from supplier k to plant m in period t;

avc_{imt}^{SRP} average shipping cost per unit (across all potential suppliers) of (noncritical) raw material i to plant m in period t;

c_{mnt}^{SFW} shipping cost per unit of finished product from plant m to warehouse n in period t;

c_{npt}^{SFM} shipping cost per unit of finished product from warehouse n to market p in period t;

c_{imt}^{HRP} holding cost per unit of raw material i held at plant m in period t;

c_{mt}^{HFP} holding cost per unit of finished product held at plant m in period t;

c_{nt}^{HFW} holding cost per unit of finished product held at warehouse n in period t;

f_{mt}^{P} fixed cost of operating plant m in period t;

f_{nt}^{W} fixed cost of operating warehouse n in period t;

C_{ikt}^{RS} availability (units) of (critical) raw material i from supplier k in period t;

C_{it}^{RS} total market availability (from all potential suppliers) of (noncritical) raw material i in period t;

U_m maximum possible production capacity (units) of finished product at plant m;

v_m minimum production quantity required for plant m to remain open in a given period;

q_n minimum number of units required in storage in a given period in order for warehouse n to remain open;

R_m^{PLANT} outbound shipping capacity at plant m in each period;

R_n^{INW} inbound shipping capacity at warehouse n in each period;

R_n^{OUTW} outbound shipping capacity at warehouse n in each period;

C_{imt}^{HRP} holding capacity (units) of raw material i at plant m in period t;

C_{mt}^{HFP} holding capacity (units) of finished product at plant m in period t;

C_{nt}^{HFW} holding capacity (units) of finished product at warehouse n in period t;

r_{im0} initial (known) inventory of raw material i at plant m;

g_{im0} initial (known) inventory of finished product at plant m;

h_{n0} initial (known) inventory of finished product at warehouse n;

h^{FIN} fraction of final period's total demand required in ending inventory;

x_{m0} initial production quantity at plant m;

d_{pt} demand for finished product in market p in period t;

S^{FP} sales price per unit of finished product.

The decision variables used in this model are

w_{ikmt} quantity of (critical) raw material i shipped from supplier k to plant m in period t;

w_{imt} quantity of (noncritical) raw material i shipped from all potential suppliers to plant m in period t;

x_{mt} quantity of finished product produced at plant m in period t;

e_{mt}	unrestricted production quantity change from period $t-1$ to period t;
e_{mt}^{+}	increase in production quantity from period $t-1$ to period t;
e_{mt}^{-}	decrease in production quantity from period $t-1$ to period t;
y_{mnt}	quantity of finished product shipped from plant m to warehouse n in period t;
z_{npt}	amount of finished product shipped from warehouse n to market p in period t;
r_{imt}	amount of raw material i held in inventory at plant m in period t;
g_{mt}	amount of finished product held in inventory at plant m in period t;
h_{nt}	amount of finished product held in inventory at warehouse n in period t;
α_{ikt}	$\begin{cases} 1 \text{ if supplier } k \text{ is selected to provide raw material } i \text{ in period } t \\ 0 \text{ otherwise} \end{cases}$;
β_{mt}	$\begin{cases} 1 \text{ if plant } m \text{ is in operation in period } t \\ 0 \text{ otherwise} \end{cases}$;
δ_{nt}	$\begin{cases} 1 \text{ if warehouse } n \text{ is open in period } t \\ 0 \text{ otherwise} \end{cases}$;
ϕ_{mt}	$\begin{cases} 1 \text{ if a plant of capacity } U_m \text{ is to be built at site } m \text{ in period } t \\ 0 \text{ otherwise} \end{cases}$.

The following sections describe the sequential development and solution of the strategic and tactical submodels.

4.3 Strategic Submodel

The strategic submodel, formulated as a mixed integer linear program, is developed as a tool to aid supply chain managers in designing the infrastructure of a multi-echelon manufacturing and distribution network. The solution to this submodel provides optimal selections of critical raw material suppliers, plant construction decisions, plant and warehouse operating locations, and optimal production quantities (to be used in the determination of production capacities for the tactical submodel). At the same time, supply chain profit is maximized while market deliveries are limited to forecasted demand. As a strategic model, this submodel applies to long-term planning and is appropriate for time periods in the one- to five-year range. In fact, supply chain managers might find it useful to run the strategic submodel once per year in order to validate the strategic-level decisions made in the design phase of the problem. However, this submodel is readily adaptable for shorter or longer periods.

A unique characteristic of this supply chain design and operation problem concerns the two-phase supplier selection process. Following the modern trend of establishing strategic partnerships with suppliers of critical materials, supply chain managers wish to make critical raw material supplier selections as soon as possible (i.e., during the supply chain design phase.) Because non-critical raw materials are assumed to be more readily available on the market, supplier selection decisions for these materials can be made more frequently and are deferred until supply chain operational decisions are considered. It is assumed that when first designing the supply chain infrastructure, supplier-specific information pertaining to raw material availability and costs is limited to those raw materials deemed as critical; for noncritical raw materials, only overall market availability is known in terms of the total availability of each raw material type across all potential suppliers (in each period). Furthermore, only estimated purchasing and shipping costs for each noncritical raw material type (across all potential suppliers) are assumed to be available during this phase. However, supply chain managers expect to obtain supplier-specific, noncritical raw material availability and cost data within a given amount of time, presumably once supply chain design decisions are made. Therefore, with such raw material availability and cost information, the strategic sub-model is used to determine the supply chain infrastructure and make criti-cal raw material supplier selection decisions, while the tactical submodel uses inputs from the solution to the strategic submodel, various higher resolution cost and demand data, newly acquired raw material and finished product transit times, and supplier-specific, noncritical raw material availability and cost data to determine best compromise supplier selections (for noncritical raw materials) and revised production, inventory, and shipping quantities.

4.3.1 Strategic Submodel Objective Function

Throughout the development of the overall model, profit is defined as total supply chain revenue (TR) minus total supply chain cost (TC). In the strategic submodel, profit is expressed as

$$\text{Profit}^{STR} = TR^{STR} - TC^{STR}. \tag{4.1}$$

Here, TR^{STR} is calculated by multiplying the finished product unit sales price by the total number of finished product units sent to all markets over the entire planning horizon. In other words,

$$TR^{STR} = s^{FP} \sum_{n=1}^{N} \sum_{p=1}^{P} \sum_{t=1}^{T} z_{npt}. \tag{4.2}$$

The costs associated with this supply chain include plant construction costs, plant and warehouse fixed operating costs, raw material costs, variable production costs, production quantity change costs, shipping costs, and holding costs. The total cost for a given planning horizon can then be expressed as the sum of these respective costs:

$$TC^{STR} = CN^{STR} + FC^{STR} + RM^{STR} + PC^{STR}$$
$$+ PQ^{STR} + SC^{STR} + HC^{STR}. \tag{4.3}$$

The following subsection describes the formulations of these various costs.

4.3.1.1 Strategic Submodel Costs

A one-time cost c_{mt}^{CON} is associated with the construction of a plant of capacity U_m at each location m. In fact, overall construction costs are expressed as

$$CN^{STR} = \sum_{m=1}^{M} \sum_{t=1}^{T} c_{mt}^{CON} \phi_{mt}, \tag{4.4}$$

where the binary variable ϕ_{mt} indicates whether or not a plant of capacity U_m is to be built at location m in period t.

In the strategic submodel, fixed operating costs, such as utility charges, are incurred in each period that plant m is used for production, and warehouse n is used to hold inventory. That is,

$$FC^{STR} = \sum_{m=1}^{M} \sum_{t=1}^{T} f_{mt}^{P} \beta_{mt} + \sum_{n=1}^{N} \sum_{t=1}^{T} f_{nt}^{W} \delta_{nt}. \tag{4.5}$$

In this scenario, it is assumed that a limited number of suppliers have the capability to provide critical raw materials, while numerous suppliers can provide noncritical raw materials. Moreover, each potential supplier of critical raw materials is capable of providing any/all of the necessary critical and noncritical raw materials, while each potential noncritical material supplier is capable of providing any/all of the required noncritical materials. Following the increasingly common business practice of developing strategic partnerships with suppliers of critical materials, suppliers who will provide critical components or materials (or both) are selected in the solution to the strategic submodel. In contrast, suppliers providing more common, less critical components or materials (or both) will be selected more frequently and only once more detailed supplier information becomes available. Hence, these supplier selections are made using the tactical submodel. For critical components/materials and their suppliers, the acquisition and shipping costs, as well as availability by supplier and period, are assumed to be known during formulation of the strategic submodel. On the other hand, the strategic submodel does not consider individual suppliers of noncritical components or materials (or both). Instead, acquisition and shipping costs, as well as availability, are assumed to be known only in the aggregate for noncritical materials. More precisely, for each type of noncritical component or material (or for both), it is assumed that only estimated acquisition and shipping costs (across all potential suppliers, for each time period) are known and that only the broad market availability (across all potential suppliers, for each time period) is known. Therefore, in the strategic submodel, total raw material costs are calculated as the sum of the supplier-specific costs for critical raw materials plus the marketwide estimated costs for noncritical raw materials purchased over the entire planning horizon. That is,

$$RM^{STR} = \sum_{i=1}^{I'}\sum_{k=1}^{K'}\sum_{m=1}^{M}\sum_{t=1}^{T} c_{ikt}^{R} w_{ikmt} + \sum_{i=I'+1}^{I}\sum_{m=1}^{M}\sum_{t=1}^{T} avc_{it}^{R} w_{imt}. \qquad (4.6)$$

Here, critical raw materials are designated by the index range 1 through I', while noncritical raw materials are represented by the index range $I' + 1$ through I. Likewise, potential suppliers of critical raw materials are designated by the index range 1 through K', while the index range $K' + 1$ through K designates those suppliers capable of providing only noncritical raw materials. (Recall that all suppliers 1 through K are capable of providing any of the noncritical raw materials.)

Variable production costs are calculated as the sum of the number of units of finished product produced at each plant during each period times the unit production cost. That is,

$$PC^{STR} = \sum_{m=1}^{M}\sum_{t=1}^{T} c_{mt}^{FP} x_{mt}. \qquad (4.7)$$

A production quantity change cost, related to workforce changes, the start-up or idling of production equipment (or both), and other production factors, is incurred (at each plant) in any period in which production quantity either increases or decreases from the previous period. This cost (incurred in period t) may be expressed as

$$PQ \text{ change cost} = (\text{per unit change cost}) \cdot |x_{mt} - x_{mt-1}|, \qquad (4.8)$$

where $|x_{mt} - x_{mt-1}|$ represents the change in production quantity at plant m from period $t - 1$ to period t. However, the use of the absolute value operator here introduces the undesirable characteristic of nonlinearity into the model and prevents the use of separate per unit costs for production quantity increases and decreases. In order to avoid this situation, an unrestricted variable is used in place of the difference $x_{mt} - x_{mt-1}$. That is,

$$x_{mt} - x_{mt-1} = e_{mt}, \quad m = 1, \dots, M; \quad t = 1, \dots, T. \tag{4.9}$$

Moreover, the unrestricted variable e_{mt} is further defined as the difference of two nonnegative deviational variables:

$$e_{mt} = e_{mt}^+ - e_{mt}^-, \quad m = 1, \dots, M; \quad t = 1, \dots, T. \tag{4.10}$$

Hence, e_{mt}^+ and e_{mt}^- represent, respectively, the increase and decrease in production quantity from period $t - 1$ to period t. When the costs per unit of production quantity change are known, the total production quantity change cost over the entire planning horizon can be expressed as

$$PQ^{STR} = \sum_{m=1}^{M} \sum_{t=1}^{T} (c_{mt}^{PQ+} e_{mt}^+ + c_{mt}^{PQ-} e_{mt}^-), \tag{4.11}$$

where c_{mt}^{PQ+} and c_{mt}^{PQ-} represent, respectively, the cost per unit of production quantity increase and decrease at plant m in period t. Because these costs are to be minimized in the objective function, only one of the deviational variables for each m and t will take on a positive value, with the other equal to zero. Furthermore, if production takes place at plant m in period 1, it is assumed that production increases from 0 to x_{m1} in the first period. Hence,

$$x_{m0} = 0, \quad m = 1, \dots, M. \tag{4.12}$$

Minimization of the aforementioned production quantity change costs results in the "smoothing" of production quantities (from period to period) over the entire planning horizon.

Shipping costs are calculated for the shipment of critical and noncritical raw materials from all suppliers to all plants, for the shipment of finished products from all plants to all warehouses, and for the shipment of finished products from all warehouses to all markets over the entire planning horizon. Recall, however, that shipping costs for noncritical raw materials are known only in the aggregate in the strategic submodel and are not associated with specific suppliers. Hence, overall shipping costs are calculated as

$$SC^{STR} = \sum_{i=1}^{I'} \sum_{k=1}^{K'} \sum_{m=1}^{M} \sum_{t=1}^{T} c_{ikmt}^{SRP} w_{ikmt} + \sum_{i=I'+1}^{I} \sum_{m=1}^{M} \sum_{t=1}^{T} avc_{imt}^{SRP} w_{imt}$$

$$+ \sum_{m=1}^{M} \sum_{n=1}^{N} \sum_{t=1}^{T} c_{mnt}^{SFW} y_{mnt} + \sum_{n=1}^{N} \sum_{p=1}^{P} \sum_{t=1}^{T} c_{npt}^{SFM} z_{npt}. \tag{4.13}$$

Holding costs for raw materials and finished products held in inventory at all production facilities and for finished products held in inventory at all warehouses are calculated as

$$HC^{STR} = \sum_{i=1}^{I}\sum_{m=1}^{M}\sum_{t=1}^{T} c_{imt}^{HRP} r_{imt} + \sum_{m=1}^{M}\sum_{t=1}^{T} c_{mt}^{HFP} g_{mt} + \sum_{n=1}^{N}\sum_{t=1}^{T} c_{nt}^{HFW} h_{nt}. \tag{4.14}$$

Because the strategic model seeks to maximize total supply chain profit, the objective function becomes

$$
\begin{aligned}
\text{Maximize } & s^{FP}\sum_{n=1}^{N}\sum_{p=1}^{P}\sum_{t=1}^{T} z_{npt} - \sum_{m=1}^{M}\sum_{t=1}^{T} c_{mt}^{CON}\phi_{mt} - \sum_{m=1}^{M}\sum_{t=1}^{T} f_{mt}^{P}\beta_{mt} \\
& - \sum_{n=1}^{N}\sum_{t=1}^{T} f_{nt}^{W}\delta_{nt} - \sum_{i=1}^{I'}\sum_{k=1}^{K'}\sum_{m=1}^{M}\sum_{t=1}^{T} c_{ikt}^{R}w_{ikmt} - \sum_{i=I'+1}^{I}\sum_{m=1}^{M}\sum_{t=1}^{T} avc_{it}^{R}w_{imt} \\
& - \sum_{m=1}^{T}\sum_{t=1}^{T} c_{mt}^{FP}x_{mt} - \sum_{m=1}^{M}\sum_{t=1}^{T}(c_{mt}^{PQ+}e_{mt}^{+} + c_{mt}^{PQ-}e_{mt}^{-}) \\
& - \sum_{i=1}^{I'}\sum_{k=1}^{K'}\sum_{m=1}^{M}\sum_{t=1}^{T} c_{ikmt}^{SRP}w_{ikmt} - \sum_{i=I'+1}^{I}\sum_{m=1}^{M}\sum_{t=1}^{T} avc_{imt}^{SRP}w_{imt} \\
& - \sum_{m=1}^{M}\sum_{n=1}^{N}\sum_{t=1}^{T} c_{mnt}^{SFW}y_{mnt} - \sum_{n=1}^{N}\sum_{p=1}^{P}\sum_{t=1}^{T} c_{npt}^{SFM}z_{npt} - \sum_{i=1}^{I}\sum_{m=1}^{M}\sum_{t=1}^{T} c_{imt}^{HRP}r_{imt} \\
& - \sum_{m=1}^{M}\sum_{t=1}^{T} c_{mt}^{HFP}g_{mt} - \sum_{n=1}^{N}\sum_{t=1}^{T} c_{nt}^{HFW}h_{nt}.
\end{aligned}
\tag{4.15}
$$

4.3.2 Strategic Submodel Constraints

Maximization of profit in the supply chain is subject to various constraints regarding suppliers' capacities to provide raw materials, plants' production capacities, warehouses' storage capacities, market demand, and to plant and warehouse flow conservation. Each of these constraint types is expressed as follows.

During the formulation of the strategic submodel, it is assumed that detailed supplier information (e.g., cost and availability) is available for critical raw materials. Hence, the total amount of critical raw materials purchased and shipped to all plants must be less than or equal to the critical raw material supply capacity at each corresponding supplier during each period.

Hence, the critical raw material availability and supplier selection constraints are expressed as

$$\sum_{m=1}^{M} w_{ikmt} \le C_{ikt}^{RS}\alpha_{ikt}, \quad i=1,...,I'; \ k=1,...,K'; \ t=1,...,T, \qquad (4.16)$$

where $I' \le I$ represents the number of critical raw material types, and $K' \le K$ represents the number of potential suppliers of critical raw materials. Furthermore, the model must reflect the fact that critical raw materials can only be purchased from those suppliers designated as potential sources of critical raw materials. In other words, critical raw materials may not be sought from "marketwide" sources and therefore are not purchased from suppliers $K' + 1$ through K. This restriction is imposed by declaring the decision variables w_{ikmt} and α_{ikt} as undefined over certain ranges in the overall formulation of the strategic submodel. (During numerical computation, this restriction may be addressed by assigning a value of zero to the appropriate supplier selection decision variables.) Additionally, because the selection of critical raw material suppliers during the supply chain design phase represents the establishment of strategic partnerships with suppliers of hard-to-find or sensitive materials, it is assumed that minimum purchase quantities are inherent to such supplier selections. Hence, the corresponding constraints are expressed as

$$\sum_{m=1}^{M} w_{ikmt} \ge w_{ik}^{\min}\alpha_{ikt}, \quad i=1,...,I'; \ k=1,...,K'; \ t=1,...,T, \qquad (4.17)$$

where $w_{ik}^{\min}$ represents the user-defined minimum purchase quantity of raw material i from supplier k when supplier k is selected to provide raw material i in any period. (It is assumed here that minimum purchase quantities are constant across time periods.)

For noncritical raw materials, only broad marketwide information is assumed to be available during the design phase. Therefore, the total quantity of each noncritical raw material purchased and shipped to all plants must be less than or equal to the overall market availability of each noncritical raw material during each period. Hence, the noncritical raw material availability constraints are expressed as

$$\sum_{m=1}^{M} w_{imt} \le C_{it}^{RS}, \quad i=I'+1, ..., I; \ t=1, ..., T. \qquad (4.18)$$

As with critical raw materials, the decision variable w_{imt} is declared as undefined over certain ranges to reflect that the strategic submodel may not attempt to make noncritical raw material purchases from specific suppliers.

As part of the design phase of the supply chain problem, the strategic submodel determines where and when to construct plants, based on the various cost and demand inputs. At each potential location m, at most one plant with production capacity U_m may be built. In other words,

$$\sum_{t=1}^{T} \phi_{mt} \leq 1, \quad m = 1, \ldots, M. \tag{4.19}$$

Obviously, a plant must have been constructed at location m in order for it to operate there. Hence, the following constraint is added:

$$\sum_{\tau=1}^{t} \phi_{m\tau} \geq \beta_{mt}, \quad m = 1, \ldots, M; \ t = 1, \ldots, T. \tag{4.20}$$

Notice that Equation 4.20 does not necessarily imply operation of a plant at location m in period t; instead, it simply requires plant operation to be preceded by or coincide with plant construction. In other words, if a plant is built at location m in period t, operation at plant m may commence in period t or later.

Each potential plant location m may accommodate a plant with maximum production capacity U_m. However, it is assumed that supply chain managers have chosen to limit plant capacity (in the design phase) to some fraction of maximum site capacity in order to allow for future capacity expansion. Hence, production at plant m in period t is limited as follows:

$$x_{mt} \leq uU_m\beta_{mt}, \quad m = 1, \ldots, M; \ t = 1, \ldots, T, \tag{4.21}$$

where u represents a user-defined production capacity factor, and the binary variable β_{mt} indicates whether or not plant m operates in period t. For instance, if supply chain managers wish to limit plant capacity to 90% of maximum site capacity at all potential plant locations, the production capacity factor is set to $u = 0.90$. Furthermore, in order to remain operational in period t, plant m must produce a minimum quantity v_m of finished product. That is,

$$x_{mt} \geq v_m\beta_{mt}, \quad m = 1, \ldots, M; \ t = 1, \ldots, T. \tag{4.22}$$

A function of the optimal production quantity at plant m in period t will be used to set production capacity for plant m over the same time span in the tactical submodel.

As in any supply chain scenario, this model requires the conservation of flow of raw materials (both critical and noncritical) through all plants. Hence, the following two constraints represent this conservation of flow for critical and noncritical raw materials, respectively:

$$r_{im(t-1)} + \sum_{k=1}^{K'} w_{ikmt} - a_i x_{mt} = r_{imt}, \quad i = 1, \ldots, I'; \ m = 1, \ldots, M; \ t = 1, \ldots, T; \tag{4.23}$$

$$r_{im(t-1)} + w_{imt} - a_i x_{mt} = r_{imt}, \quad i = I' + 1, \ldots, I; \ m = 1, \ldots, M; \ t = 1, \ldots, T. \tag{4.24}$$

It is assumed that a (known) amount r_{im0} of each raw material i is on hand at each plant m at the beginning of the initial period.

Although plants' required production capacities are not determined until after the strategic submodel is solved, their raw material storage capacities are assumed to be known with certainty. Hence, the amount of raw material i held in inventory at plant m during period t is limited to a known inventory capacity. Again, the use of the binary variable β_{mt} indicates whether or not plant m is utilized in period t:

$$r_{imt} \le C_{imt}^{HRP} \beta_{mt}, \quad i = 1,...,I; \; m = 1,...,M; \; t = 1,...,T. \tag{4.25}$$

As with raw materials, this model requires the conservation of flow of finished products through all plants. That is,

$$g_{m(t-1)} + x_{mt} - \sum_{n=1}^{N} y_{mnt} = g_{mt}, \quad m = 1,...,M; \; t = 1,...,T. \tag{4.26}$$

As with raw materials, it is assumed that an initial (known) inventory g_{m0} of finished product is on hand at each plant at the beginning of the initial period.

As is the case with raw material storage capacities at each plant, the finished product storage capacities are assumed to be known. Hence, the number of units of finished product held in inventory at plant m during period t is limited to a known inventory capacity. Again, a binary variable is used to indicate whether or not plant m is utilized in period t:

$$g_{mt} \le C_{mt}^{HFP} \beta_{mt}, \quad m = 1,...,M; \; t = 1,...,T. \tag{4.27}$$

Additionally, it is assumed that plant m must be in operation in period t in order for it to be able to ship finished products to the open warehouses in period t. Moreover, if plant m is operational in period t, it is assumed to have outbound shipment capacity R_m^{PLANT}. In other words,

$$\sum_{n=1}^{N} y_{mnt} \le R_m^{PLANT} \beta_{mt}, \quad m = 1,...,M; \; t = 1,...,T. \tag{4.28}$$

Similar to the previous conservation of flow requirements, the warehouse inventory of finished products must meet this requirement as follows:

$$h_{n(t-1)} + \sum_{m=1}^{M} y_{mnt} - \sum_{p=1}^{P} z_{npt} = h_{nt}, \quad n = 1,...,N; \; t = 1,...,T. \tag{4.29}$$

It is assumed that an initial (known) inventory h_{n0} of finished product is on hand at each warehouse at the beginning of the initial period.

Furthermore, warehouse n must be open in period t to receive shipments of finished products from the operational plants. Hence,

$$\sum_{m=1}^{M} y_{mnt} \leq R_n^{INW} \delta_{nt}, \quad n = 1,...,N; \ t = 1,...,T, \tag{4.30}$$

where R_n^{INW} represents the inbound shipping capacity of warehouse n in each period, and the binary variable δ_{nt} is used to indicate whether or not warehouse n is open during period t.

The number of units of finished product held in inventory at warehouse n during period t is limited to a known inventory capacity. Hence,

$$h_{nt} \leq C_{nt}^{HFW} \delta_{nt}, \quad n = 1,...,N; \ t = 1,...,T. \tag{4.31}$$

Furthermore, if warehouse n is open in period t, it must store at least q_n units of finished product in that period. That is,

$$h_{nt} \geq q_n \delta_{nt}, \quad n = 1, ..., N; \ t = 1, ..., T. \tag{4.32}$$

Note, however, that this minimum storage requirement may be set to zero to reflect "crossdocking" operations at the warehouses. Additionally, each open warehouse has a defined outbound shipping capacity R_n^{OUTW}. Hence,

$$\sum_{p=1}^{P} z_{npt} \leq R_n^{OUTW} \delta_{nt}, \quad n = 1,...,N; \ t = 1,...,T. \tag{4.33}$$

Because supply chain operations are expected to continue beyond the initial planning horizon considered in the model, a predefined finished product quantity is required to remain in inventory during the final time period. Specifically, the sum of the finished product inventory remaining in all plants and warehouses during the final period must be equal to or greater than some fraction of the final period's total demand. In other words,

$$\sum_{m=1}^{M} g_{mT} + \sum_{n=1}^{N} h_{nT} \geq h^{FIN} \sum_{p=1}^{P} d_{pT}, \tag{4.34}$$

where $0 \leq h^{FIN} \leq 1$.

During the design phase, managers seek to build a supply chain infrastructure that will fulfill but not exceed demand through deliveries to customer markets. In other words, the number of units of finished product shipped from all warehouses to market p during period t must be less than or equal to demand at market p in period t. That is,

$$\sum_{n=1}^{N} z_{npt} \leq d_{pt}, \quad p = 1,...,P; \ t = 1,...,T. \tag{4.35}$$

4.3.3 Strategic Submodel Summary

Now, the overall strategic submodel formulation becomes

$$
\text{Maximize } s^{FP}\sum_{n=1}^{N}\sum_{p=1}^{P}\sum_{t=1}^{T} z_{npt} - \sum_{m=1}^{M}\sum_{t=1}^{T} c_{mt}^{CON}\phi_{mt} - \sum_{m=1}^{M}\sum_{t=1}^{T} f_{mt}^{P}\beta_{mt}
$$

$$
- \sum_{n=1}^{N}\sum_{t=1}^{T} f_{nt}^{W}\delta_{nt} - \sum_{i=1}^{I'}\sum_{k=1}^{K'}\sum_{m=1}^{M}\sum_{t=1}^{T} c_{ikt}^{R}w_{ikmt} - \sum_{i=I'+1}^{I}\sum_{m=1}^{M}\sum_{t=1}^{T} avc_{it}^{R}w_{imt}
$$

$$
- \sum_{m=1}^{T}\sum_{t=1}^{T} c_{mt}^{FP}x_{mt} - \sum_{m=1}^{M}\sum_{t=1}^{T} (c_{mt}^{PQ+}e_{mt}^{+} + c_{mt}^{PQ-}e_{mt}^{-})
$$

$$
- \sum_{i=1}^{I'}\sum_{k=1}^{K'}\sum_{m=1}^{M}\sum_{t=1}^{T} c_{ikmt}^{SRP}w_{ikmt} - \sum_{i=I'+1}^{I}\sum_{m=1}^{M}\sum_{t=1}^{T} avc_{imt}^{SRP}w_{imt}
$$

$$
- \sum_{m=1}^{M}\sum_{n=1}^{N}\sum_{t=1}^{T} c_{mnt}^{SFW}y_{mnt} - \sum_{n=1}^{N}\sum_{p=1}^{P}\sum_{t=1}^{T} c_{npt}^{SFM}z_{npt} - \sum_{i=1}^{I}\sum_{m=1}^{M}\sum_{t=1}^{T} c_{imt}^{HRP}r_{imt}
$$

$$
- \sum_{m=1}^{M}\sum_{t=1}^{T} c_{mt}^{HFP}g_{mt} - \sum_{n=1}^{N}\sum_{t=1}^{T} c_{nt}^{HFW}h_{nt}
$$

Subject to: (4.36)

$$
\sum_{m=1}^{M} w_{ikmt} \le C_{ikt}^{RS}\alpha_{ikt}, \quad i = 1,\ldots,I'; \; k = 1,\ldots,K'; \, t = 1,\ldots,T;
$$

$$
\sum_{m=1}^{M} w_{ikmt} \ge w_{ik}^{\min}\alpha_{ikt}, \quad i = 1,\ldots,I'; \; k = 1,\ldots,K'; \, t = 1,\ldots,T;
$$

$$
\sum_{m=1}^{M} w_{imt} \le C_{it}^{RS}, \quad i = I'+1,\ldots,I; \, t = 1,\ldots,T;
$$

$$
\sum_{t=1}^{T} \phi_{mt} \le 1, \quad m = 1,\ldots,M;
$$

$$
\sum_{\tau=1}^{t} \phi_{m\tau} \ge \beta_{mt}, \quad m = 1,\ldots,M; \, t = 1,\ldots,T;
$$

$$
x_{mt} \le uU_m\beta_{mt}, \quad m = 1,\ldots,M; \, t = 1,\ldots,T;
$$

$$
x_{mt} \ge v_m\beta_{mt}, \quad m = 1,\ldots,M; \, t = 1,\ldots,T;
$$

$$x_{mt} - x_{mt-1} = e_{mt}, \quad m = 1, ..., M; \ t = 1, ..., T;$$

$$e_{mt} = e_{mt}^+ - e_{mt}^-, \quad m = 1, ..., M; \ t = 1, ..., T;$$

$$x_{m0} = 0, \quad m = 1, ..., M;$$

$$r_{im(t-1)} + \sum_{k=1}^{K'} w_{ikmt} - a_i x_{mt} = r_{imt}, \quad i = 1, ..., I'; \ m = 1, ..., M;$$

$$t = 1, ..., T;$$

$$r_{im(t-1)} + w_{imt} - a_i x_{mt} = r_{imt}, \quad i = I'+1, ..., I; \ m = 1, ..., M;$$

$$t = 1, ..., T;$$

$$r_{imt} \le C_{imt}^{HRP} \beta_{mt}, \quad i = 1, ..., I; \ m = 1, ..., M; \ t = 1, ..., T;$$

$$g_{m(t-1)} + x_{mt} - \sum_{n=1}^{N} y_{mnt} = g_{mt}, \quad m = 1, ..., M; \ t = 1, ..., T;$$

$$g_{mt} \le C_{mt}^{HFP} \beta_{mt}, \quad m = 1, ..., M; \ t = 1, ..., T;$$

$$\sum_{n=1}^{N} y_{mnt} \le R_m^{PLANT} \beta_{mt}, \quad m = 1, ..., M; \ t = 1, ..., T;$$

$$h_{n(t-1)} + \sum_{m=1}^{M} y_{mnt} - \sum_{p=1}^{P} z_{npt} = h_{nt}, \quad n = 1, ..., N; \ t = 1, ..., T;$$

$$\sum_{m=1}^{M} y_{mnt} \le R_n^{INW} \delta_{nt}, \quad n = 1, ..., N; \ t = 1, ..., T;$$

$$h_{nt} \le C_{nt}^{HFW} \delta_{nt}, \quad n = 1, ..., N; \ t = 1, ..., T;$$

$$h_{nt} \ge q_n \delta_{nt}, \quad n = 1, ..., N; \ t = 1, ..., T;$$

$$\sum_{p=1}^{P} z_{npt} \le R_n^{OUTW} \delta_{nt}, \quad n = 1, ..., N; \ t = 1, ..., T;$$

$$\sum_{m=1}^{M} g_{mT} + \sum_{n=1}^{N} h_{nT} \ge h^{FIN} \sum_{p=1}^{P} d_{pT};$$

$$\sum_{n=1}^{N} z_{npt} \le d_{pt}, \quad p = 1, ..., P; \ t = 1, ..., T;$$

$$w_{imt} \ge 0, \quad i = I'+1, ..., I; \ m = 1, ..., M; \ t = 1, ..., T;$$

$$w_{imt} \text{ undefined}, \quad i = 1, ..., I'; \ m = 1, ..., M; \ t = 1, ..., T;$$

$$w_{ikmt} \geq 0, \quad i = 1,\dots,I'; \ k = 1,\dots,K'; \ m = 1,\dots,M; \ t = 1,\dots,T;$$

$$w_{ikmt} \ \text{undefined}, \quad i = 1,\dots,I'; \ k = K'+1,\dots,K; \ m = 1,\dots,M;$$

$$t = 1,\dots,T;$$

$$w_{ikmt} \ \text{undefined}, \quad i = I'+1,\dots,I; \ k = 1,\dots,K; \ m = 1,\dots,M;$$

$$t = 1,\dots,T;$$

$$x_{mt}, e^{+}_{mt}, e^{-}_{mt}, y_{mnt}, z_{npt}, r_{imt}, g_{mt}, h_{nt} \geq 0, \quad \forall i,m,n,p,t;$$

$$e_{mt} \ \text{unrestricted}, \quad m = 1,\dots,M; \ t = 1,\dots,T;$$

$$\alpha_{ikt} \ \text{binary}, \quad i = 1,\dots,I'; \ k = 1,\dots,K'; \ t = 1,\dots,T;$$

$$\alpha_{ikt} \ \text{undefined}, \quad i = 1,\dots,I'; \ k = K'+1,\dots,K; \ t = 1,\dots,T;$$

$$\alpha_{ikt} \ \text{undefined}, \quad i = I'+1,\dots,I; \ k = 1,\dots,K; \ t = 1,\dots,T;$$

$$\beta_{mt}, \delta_{nt}, \phi_{mt} \ \text{binary}, \quad m = 1,\dots,M; \ n = 1,\dots,N; \ t = 1,\dots,T.$$

This submodel involves $T(2I'K' + 2IM + I - I' + 8M + 5N + P) + 2M + 1$ constraints and $T(7M + 2N + 2IM - I'M + I'K'M + MN + NP + I'K')$ decision variables, of which $T(I'K' + 2M + N)$ are integer (binary) variables. Clearly, the greatest impact to the size of the strategic submodel would result from a change in the number of time periods. For example, doubling the number of time periods would double the overall number of variables and nearly double the number of constraints. Depending on data availability and software limitations, care should be taken when considering any significant increase in the number of time periods considered in this submodel.

When data related to costs, capacities, and demand are available, this mixed integer linear program can be solved using a variety of commercially available solvers. Once solved, the strategic submodel provides managers with optimal figures for the following supply chain infrastructure planning elements: (1) critical raw material supplier selections, (2) plant construction decisions, (3) locations of operating plants and warehouses for each period, (4) input for production capacity requirements, and (5) a profit goal. The tactical submodel, whose formulation is described in the next section, uses these elements (along with revised cost and other data) as inputs and provides as outputs the following best compromise supply chain operational planning elements: (1) noncritical raw material supplier selections; (2) raw material shipments and inventory quantities; (3) finished product production, shipment, and inventory quantities; and (4) a profit figure. Even though optimal purchase, production, inventory, and shipment quantities for both raw materials and finished products are determined in the solution to the strategic submodel, these quantities are overridden by the solution to the tactical submodel.

4.4 Tactical Submodel

In the two-phase construct of the overall supply chain model, it is assumed that only limited information is available to supply chain managers during the design phase. Once supply chain infrastructure decisions have been made, however, higher resolution cost and demand data, supplier-specific noncritical raw material data, and inter-echelon transit times for raw materials and finished products become available to supply chain designers and operators. Therefore, once the solution to the strategic submodel has indicated the optimal critical raw material supplier selections and determined the general infrastructure of the supply chain, the tactical submodel is formulated and solved to select suppliers of noncritical raw materials and to determine (revised) best compromise production quantities and raw material and finished product shipment and inventory quantities. In order to connect the two submodels, the critical raw material supplier selections, plant and warehouse locations, and optimal production quantities determined in the strategic submodel are used as inputs to the tactical submodel, with user-defined functions of the optimal production quantities determined in the solution to the strategic submodel utilized as production capacity limits in the tactical submodel.

During the operational phase of this supply chain scenario, managers present the additional objective of minimizing the overall supply chain response time. This objective, interpreted here as minimizing total weighted transit time for raw material and finished product shipments, may be particularly important for perishable materials or products, such as foodstuffs and medicines. In order to achieve this objective, it is assumed that detailed raw material and finished product transportation times among the various echelons of the supply chain become available to planners once the infrastructure has been determined via the solution to the strategic submodel. Furthermore, it is assumed that supply chain managers now wish to *exactly* meet customer/ market demand in an effort to avoid shortages (i.e., customer dissatisfaction) and overproduction (i.e., wasted surplus). At the same time, managers are able to develop a profit target based on the optimal profit figure determined in the solution to the strategic submodel. As such, the tactical submodel is designed to reflect the desire of supply chain managers to minimize deviations from the profit, demand, and response time targets to the greatest extent possible. Therefore, because multiple, nonrigid objectives are considered in the tactical submodel, linear goal programming is adopted as an appropriate optimization technique for this problem. A significant advantage to this technique stems from the inclusion of goal constraints, which allow for deviations from the objectives' target values without rendering the entire solution infeasible. Hence, the three objectives of meeting or exceeding a certain profit level, *exactly* meeting customer demand, and minimizing total weighted transit time are expressed as traditional and nontraditional goal constraints in the tactical submodel. Because goal programming objective functions include the minimization of deviations from stated target values, the goal and regular constraints are presented here first, followed by the formulation of the deviation-minimizing objective function.

It is assumed in this supply chain scenario that inputs available to the tactical submodel include newly obtained supplier-specific, noncritical raw material information, higher resolution cost and demand information (based on shorter time periods than those used in the strategic submodel), and detailed raw material and finished product transportation times among the various supply chain elements. Because such a great amount of new and revised information is assumed to be available after the solution to the strategic submodel has been determined, the best compromise profit, raw material shipments and inventory levels, and finished product production, inventory, and shipment quantities determined in the solution to the tactical submodel override those of the strategic submodel's solution. Also, because the length of a time period differs between the two submodels, inputs to the tactical submodel derived from the solution to the strategic submodel must be converted/scaled appropriately. Finally, all notation in the tactical submodel is assumed to correspond to the shorter time periods, unless otherwise stated.

4.4.1 Additional Notation

In general, the tactical submodel uses the same notation and many of the same data and decision variables as the strategic submodel. However, because new information is assumed to be available to supply chain managers after infrastructure decisions have been made, additional notation is needed. The additional data variables are as follows:

b_{ikm}^{TRP} transportation time per unit of raw material I from supplier k to plant m;

b_{mn}^{TFW} transportation time per unit of finished product from plant m to warehouse n;

b_{np}^{TFM} transportation time per unit of finished product from warehouse n to market p;

C_{mt}^{FP} production capacity at plant m in period t;

t^{TAC} the number of time periods in the tactical submodel that comprise one time period in the strategic submodel;

Y profit goal as determined in the solution to the strategic submodel.

In addition to the data variables listed here, the following decision variables are added to the tactical submodel:

$d_{\text{dem-}pt}^{-}$ negative deviational variable related to fulfillment of demand at market p in period t;

d_{profit}^{+} positive deviational variable related to achievement of profit goal;

d^-_{profit} negative deviational variable related to achievement of profit goal;

d^+_{time} positive deviational variable related to achievement of weighted transit time goal;

d^-_{time} negative deviational variable related to achievement of weighted transit time goal.

4.4.2 Tactical Submodel Goal Constraints

As mentioned earlier, three goal constraints are formulated in the tactical submodel to reflect the objectives of meeting or exceeding a certain profit level, *exactly* meeting customer demand, and minimizing total weighted transit time. These goals' formulations are described as follows.

4.4.2.1 Profit Optimization Goal Constraint

Using the optimal profit figure that resulted from the solution to the strategic submodel, supply chain managers can set a specific profit target in the tactical submodel. Once again, total revenue is defined as

$$TR^{TAC} = s^{FP} \sum_{n=1}^{N} \sum_{p=1}^{P} \sum_{t=1}^{T} z_{npt}, \tag{4.37}$$

and total cost is defined as

$$TC^{TAC} = CN^{TAC} + FC^{TAC} + RM^{TAC} + PC^{TAC}$$
$$+ PQ^{TAC} + SC^{TAC} + HC^{TAC}. \tag{4.38}$$

Because several of the per unit costs may have changed since infrastructure decisions were made via the solution to the strategic submodel, these tactical submodel costs are recalculated as follows.

As in the strategic submodel, a one-time construction cost c^{CON}_{mt} is associated with the construction of a plant of capacity U_m at each location m. However, because construction decisions have already been made via the solution to the strategic submodel, the values of the binary variables ϕ_{mt} are known for each plant location m and each period t. Therefore, construction costs are again calculated as

$$CN^{STR} = \sum_{m=1}^{M} \sum_{t=1}^{T} c^{CON}_{mt} \phi_{mt}, \tag{4.39}$$

where the binary variables ϕ_{mt} are now known constants for all m and t. Here, it is assumed that a plant to be constructed in a given strategic submodel period is constructed in the first of the tactical submodel periods that combine to comprise the same time span as that of the given strategic submodel period.

In the tactical submodel, fixed costs are incurred in each period whenever plant m is used for production and warehouse n is used to hold inventory. Although these costs are recalculated in the tactical submodel to account for potential cost changes, the values of the binary variables β_{mt} and δ_{nt} are known for each plant m, each warehouse n, and each period t. Hence, fixed operating costs are recalculated as

$$FC^{TAC} = \sum_{m=1}^{M}\sum_{t=1}^{T} f_{mt}^{P}\beta_{mt} + \sum_{n=1}^{N}\sum_{t=1}^{T} f_{nt}^{W}\delta_{nt}, \tag{4.40}$$

where the binary variables β_{mt} and δ_{nt} are now known constants for all m, n, and t.

Because the solution to the strategic submodel determined the optimal critical raw material supplier selections, these "strategic partnerships" are assumed to endure throughout the operational phase of the supply chain. Furthermore, supplier-specific, noncritical raw material information is now assumed to be available at the beginning of the operational phase of the supply chain problem. Hence, overall raw material shipment amounts and costs may change in the solution to the tactical submodel, and shipment quantities of critical and noncritical raw materials from each supplier are used to determine overall raw material costs as follows:

$$RM^{TAC} = \sum_{i=1}^{I'}\sum_{k=1}^{K'}\sum_{m=1}^{M}\sum_{t=1}^{T} c_{ikt}^{R}w_{ikmt} + \sum_{i=I'+1}^{I}\sum_{k=1}^{K}\sum_{m=1}^{M}\sum_{t=1}^{T} c_{ikt}^{R}w_{ikmt}. \tag{4.41}$$

Production costs are calculated as the sum of the number of units of finished product produced times the finished product unit production cost. Hence, the following term is identical to the one used in the strategic submodel:

$$PC^{TAC} = \sum_{m=1}^{M}\sum_{t=1}^{T} c_{mt}^{FP}x_{mt}. \tag{4.42}$$

As in the strategic submodel, an attempt is made to "smooth" production from one period to the next. Again, nonlinearity through use of the absolute value operator is avoided by the introduction of an unrestricted variable and positive and negative deviational variables. Hence, the total production quantity change cost over the entire planning horizon is calculated as

$$PQ^{TAC} = \sum_{m=1}^{M}\sum_{t=1}^{T} (c_{mt}^{PQ+}e_{mt}^{+} + c_{mt}^{PQ-}e_{mt}^{-}). \tag{4.43}$$

As in the strategic submodel, constraints in the form of Equations 4.9, 4.10, and 4.12 are added to the tactical submodel.

In addition, as in the strategic submodel, shipping costs are calculated for the shipment of raw materials from all suppliers to all plants, for the shipment of finished products from all plants to all warehouses, and for the shipment of finished products from all warehouses to all markets over the entire planning horizon. However, the tactical submodel's inclusion of detailed costs regarding suppliers of noncritical raw materials is in contrast to the strategic submodel. Hence, overall shipping costs are calculated as

$$
SC^{TAC} = \sum_{i=1}^{I'} \sum_{k=1}^{K'} \sum_{m=1}^{M} \sum_{t=1}^{T} c_{ikmt}^{SRP} w_{ikmt} + \sum_{i=I'+1}^{I} \sum_{k=1}^{K} \sum_{m=1}^{M} \sum_{t=1}^{T} c_{ikmt}^{SRP} w_{ikmt}
$$
$$
+ \sum_{m=1}^{M} \sum_{n=1}^{N} \sum_{t=1}^{T} c_{mnt}^{SFW} y_{mnt} + \sum_{n=1}^{N} \sum_{p=1}^{P} \sum_{t=1}^{T} c_{npt}^{SFM} z_{npt}. \tag{4.44}
$$

As in the strategic submodel, holding costs are calculated for raw materials and finished products held at all production facilities and for finished products held at all warehouses. That is,

$$
HC^{TAC} = \sum_{i=1}^{I} \sum_{m=1}^{M} \sum_{t=1}^{T} c_{imt}^{HRP} r_{imt} + \sum_{m=1}^{M} \sum_{t=1}^{T} c_{mt}^{HFP} g_{mt} + \sum_{n=1}^{N} \sum_{t=1}^{T} c_{nt}^{HFW} h_{nt}. \tag{4.45}
$$

In formulating and solving the tactical submodel, managers may seek to earn at least as much overall profit as indicated in the solution to the strategic submodel. Given a profit goal of Y (based upon the optimal profit determined in the solution to the strategic submodel), the goal constraint corresponding to the optimization of profit becomes

$$
s^{FP} \sum_{n=1}^{N} \sum_{p=1}^{P} \sum_{t=1}^{T} z_{npt} - \sum_{m=1}^{M} \sum_{t=1}^{T} c_{mt}^{CON} \phi_{mt} - \sum_{m=1}^{M} \sum_{t=1}^{T} f_{mt}^{P} \beta_{mt} - \sum_{n=1}^{N} \sum_{t=1}^{T} f_{nt}^{W} \delta_{nt}
$$
$$
- \sum_{i=1}^{I'} \sum_{k=1}^{K'} \sum_{m=1}^{M} \sum_{t=1}^{T} c_{ikt}^{R} w_{ikmt} - \sum_{i=I'+1}^{I} \sum_{k=1}^{K} \sum_{m=1}^{M} \sum_{t=1}^{T} c_{ikt}^{R} w_{ikmt} - \sum_{m=1}^{T} \sum_{t=1}^{T} c_{mt}^{FP} x_{mt}
$$
$$
- \sum_{m=1}^{M} \sum_{t=1}^{T} (c_{mt}^{PQ+} e_{mt}^{+} + c_{mt}^{PQ-} e_{mt}^{-}) - \sum_{i=1}^{I'} \sum_{k=1}^{K'} \sum_{m=1}^{M} \sum_{t=1}^{T} c_{ikmt}^{SRP} w_{ikmt} \tag{4.46}
$$
$$
- \sum_{i=I'+1}^{I} \sum_{k=1}^{K} \sum_{m=1}^{M} \sum_{t=1}^{T} c_{ikmt}^{SRP} w_{ikmt} - \sum_{m=1}^{M} \sum_{n=1}^{N} \sum_{t=1}^{T} c_{mnt}^{SFW} y_{mnt} - \sum_{n=1}^{N} \sum_{p=1}^{P} \sum_{t=1}^{T} c_{npt}^{SFM} z_{npt}
$$
$$
- \sum_{i=1}^{I} \sum_{m=1}^{M} \sum_{t=1}^{T} c_{imt}^{HRP} r_{imt} - \sum_{m=1}^{M} \sum_{t=1}^{T} c_{mt}^{HFP} g_{mt} - \sum_{n=1}^{N} \sum_{t=1}^{T} c_{nt}^{HFW} h_{nt} + d_{profit}^{-} - d_{profit}^{+} = Y,
$$

where d_{profit}^- and d_{profit}^+ represent the under- and overachievement, respectively, of the profit goal Y. In order to achieve a profit that meets or exceeds Y, the negative deviational variable d_{profit}^- will be minimized in the objective function. It is important to note that while the tactical submodel seeks to achieve a profit greater than or equal to Y (presumably the optimal profit determined in the solution to the strategic submodel), the formulation of the profit objective as a goal constraint allows for the possibility of a best compromise profit that is less than Y without rendering the entire solution infeasible.

4.4.2.2 Total Weighted Transit Time Goal Constraint

In an effort to ensure a more responsive supply chain and achieve higher levels of customer satisfaction, supply chain managers often seek to minimize the time between order placement and finished product delivery (to the customer.) This requirement is addressed in the tactical submodel by including the additional objective of minimizing total weighted transit time, which is defined here as the time required to ship one unit of raw material/final product from one supply chain element to another multiplied by the number of units to be shipped, summed over all raw materials types, suppliers, plants, warehouses, markets, and time periods. Hence, the corresponding goal constraint is expressed as

$$
\begin{aligned}
&\sum_{i=1}^{I'}\sum_{k=1}^{K'}\sum_{m=1}^{M}\sum_{t=1}^{T} b_{ikm}^{TRP} w_{ikmt} + \sum_{i=I'+1}^{I}\sum_{k=1}^{K}\sum_{m=1}^{M}\sum_{t=1}^{T} b_{ikm}^{TRP} w_{ikmt} \\
&+ \sum_{m=1}^{M}\sum_{n=1}^{N}\sum_{t=1}^{T} b_{mn}^{TFW} y_{mnt} + \sum_{n=1}^{N}\sum_{p=1}^{P}\sum_{t=1}^{T} b_{np}^{TFM} z_{npt} + d_{\text{time}}^- - d_{\text{time}}^+ = 0,
\end{aligned}
\tag{4.47}
$$

where d_{time}^- and d_{time}^+ represent the under- and overachievement, respectively, of the total weighted transit time goal. Because the goal (unrealistically) is zero weighted transit time, the positive deviational variable d_{time}^+ will be minimized in the objective function to achieve the lowest possible total weighted transit time while still maintaining a feasible solution.

4.4.2.3 Customer Demand Nontraditional Goal Constraint

Whereas supply chain managers sought to meet but not exceed demand when planning the infrastructure of the production–distribution network, they now also wish to minimize the number of units of unsatisfied demand. This requirement is expressed here in the form of a nontraditional, one-sided goal constraint in which positive deviations (i.e., excess deliveries to customer markets) are not permitted. Hence, the constraint in the tactical submodel that seeks to meet demand *exactly* is expressed as

$$\sum_{n=1}^{N} z_{npt} + d^-_{\text{dem-}pt} = d_{pt}, \quad p = 1,...,P; \ t = 1,...,T, \tag{4.48}$$

where the negative deviational variable $d^-_{\text{dem-}pt}$ represents the underachievement of the customer demand goal at market p in period t. In an attempt to *exactly* meet the demand of market p in period t (represented by d_{pt}), $d^-_{\text{dem-}pt}$ is minimized in the objective function.

4.4.3 Tactical Submodel Regular Constraints

In addition to the traditional and nontraditional goal constraints described in the previous section, the tactical submodel requires several regular constraints that must be met for the overall solution to remain feasible. These constraints are formulated as follows.

Because supplier selections for critical raw materials have already been made via the solution to the strategic submodel, the only supplier selections necessary in the tactical submodel are those involving noncritical raw materials. As in the strategic submodel, the total amount of raw material i shipped from supplier k to all production facilities in period t must be less than or equal to the supply capacity of raw material i at supplier k during each period t. Hence,

$$\sum_{m=1}^{M} w_{ikmt} \leq C^{RS}_{ikt} \alpha_{ikt}, \quad i = 1,...,I'; \ k = 1,...,K'; \ t = 1,...,T; \tag{4.49}$$

$$\sum_{m=1}^{M} w_{ikmt} \leq C^{RS}_{ikt} \alpha_{ikt}, \quad i = I'+1,...,I; \ k = 1,...,K; \ t = 1,...,T. \tag{4.50}$$

Note that for $i = 1, ...I'$, the binary variables α_{ikt} (indicating whether or not supplier $k \leq K'$ has been selected to provide critical raw material i in period t) have already been assigned values via the solution to the strategic submodel and are therefore constants in this constraint. Therefore, only the binary variables α_{ikt} where $i = I' + 1, ..., I$ (indicating supplier selections for noncritical raw materials) are considered decision variables in the tactical submodel.

As discussed earlier, the critical raw material supplier selections made in the solution to the strategic submodel are accompanied by minimum purchase quantity requirements. It is assumed here that the tactical submodel requires the same minimum purchase quantities be made over the same time periods. Hence, in the tactical submodel, each period's minimum purchase quantity (when applicable) is equal to the corresponding strategic submodel minimum purchase requirement divided by the number of tactical submodel periods that comprise a single strategic model period. In other words,

$$\sum_{m=1}^{M} w_{ikmt} \geq \frac{w_{ik}^{\min}}{t^{TAC}} \alpha_{ikt}, \quad i = 1,...,I'; \; k = 1,...,K'; \; t = 1,...,T, \tag{4.51}$$

where α_{ikt} is known from the solution to the strategic submodel and are scaled appropriately for the tactical submodel (i.e., for shorter time periods.) As with the strategic submodel, an effort must be made to ensure the tactical submodel does not allow critical raw material purchases to be made from noncritical raw material suppliers. Once again, this restriction is imposed by declaring the appropriate variables as undefined over a certain range.

In the solution to the strategic submodel, (initial) optimal production quantities are determined for the operating plants. As stated earlier, functions of these optimal quantities are used as production capacities in the tactical submodel. This is done to reflect a supply chain manager's desire to maintain production capacities that are slightly higher than the previously planned optimal production quantities. This planning decision is made in anticipation of different cost and demand data than were available during the supply chain design phase. Recall that in the strategic submodel, production capacity at each plant m was limited to uU_m. Once the (initial) optimal production quantities are determined in the strategic submodel, it is assumed that supply chain managers wish to set the production capacity at each plant m (in the tactical submodel) to $1 + (1 - u) = 2 - u$ times the strategic submodel's optimal production quantity for plant m over the same time span. Of course, this capacity must be scaled to correspond to tactical submodel time periods. For example, suppose production capacity factors of 0.9- and 1-year time periods are used in the strategic submodel, while three-month time periods are used in the tactical submodel. (Hence, $u = 0.9$ and $t^{TAC} = 4$.) It follows that the (strategic submodel) production capacity at plant m in each period t is set to $0.9U_m$. If the optimal production quantity (from the solution to the strategic submodel) at plant m in period (year) 1 is 5,000 units, then the (tactical submodel) production capacity at plant m in each corresponding period (quarters 1, 2, 3, and 4) is $\dfrac{(2-0.9)5000}{4} = \dfrac{1.1(5000)}{4} = 1,375$ units. In the tactical submodel, this new production capacity for plant m in periods 1 through 4 is denoted as $C_{mt}^{FP} = 1,375$ for $t = 1,2,3,4$. Furthermore, in order to avoid confusion due to the mixing of time period lengths, this capacity calculation is done "offline" and is not included in the final mixed integer linear goal program. Hence, in order to limit tactical submodel production to the new plant capacities, the following constraint is added to the tactical submodel:

$$x_{mt} \leq C_{mt}^{FP} \beta_{mt}, \quad m = 1,...,M; \; t = 1,...,T, \tag{4.52}$$

where the constant β_{mt} (whose value is determined in the solution to the strategic submodel) indicates whether or not plant m is utilized in period t. Furthermore, in order to prevent open plants from sitting idle, each plant m that operates in period t must produce a minimum number of units of finished product in that period. That is,

$$x_{mt} \geq \frac{v_m}{t^{TAC}}\beta_{mt}, \quad m = 1,...,M; \ t = 1,...,T. \tag{4.53}$$

As in the strategic submodel, production quantity change costs are incurred in each period t in which production quantity changes from the previous period.

In the tactical submodel, raw material conservation of flow constraints are similar to those in the strategic submodel. Hence,

$$r_{im(t-1)} + \sum_{k=1}^{K'} w_{ikmt} - a_i x_{mt} = r_{imt}, \quad i = 1,...,I'; \ m = 1,...,M; \ t = 1,...,T; \tag{4.54}$$

$$r_{im(t-1)} + \sum_{k=1}^{K} w_{ikmt} - a_i x_{mt} = r_{imt}, \quad i = I'+1,...,I; \ m = 1,...,M; \ t = 1,...,T. \tag{4.55}$$

As in the strategic submodel, it is assumed that a reasonable (known) amount $\frac{r_{im0}}{t^{TAC}}$ of each raw material i is on hand at each plant m at the beginning of the initial period.

Although plants' operational production capacities are not determined until the strategic submodel is solved, their raw material storage capacities are assumed to be known with certainty. Hence, the amount of raw material i held in inventory at plant m during period t is limited to a known inventory capacity C_{imt}^{RP}. Because the values of the binary variables β_{mt} (indicating whether or not plant m is utilized in period t) were determined in the solution to the strategic submodel, they are included as constants in the following constraint:

$$r_{imt} \leq C_{imt}^{HRP}\beta_{mt}, \quad i = 1,...,I; \ m = 1,...,M; \ t = 1,...,T. \tag{4.56}$$

As in the strategic submodel, the number of units of finished product held in inventory at plant m during period t is equal to the number of units of finished product held in inventory in the previous period plus the number of units of finished product produced in the current period minus the total number of units of finished product shipped to all warehouses during period t. In other words,

$$g_{m(t-1)} + x_{mt} - \sum_{n=1}^{N} y_{mnt} = g_{mt}, \quad m = 1,...,M; \ t = 1,...,T. \tag{4.57}$$

As in the strategic submodel, it is assumed that an initial inventory $\frac{g_{m0}}{t^{TAC}}$ of finished product is on hand at each plant at the beginning of the initial period.

In addition, as in the strategic submodel, the number of units of finished product held in inventory at plant m during period t is limited to a known inventory capacity. Because the solution to the strategic submodel determined which production facilities should be used during which periods, the values of the indicator variables β_{mt} are constants and are used in the tactical submodel to indicate whether or not plant m is utilized in period t. Hence, the corresponding constraint is expressed as

$$g_{mt} \leq C_{mt}^{HFP}\beta_{mt}, \quad m = 1,...,M;\ t = 1,...,T. \tag{4.58}$$

Moreover, if plant m is operational in period t, it is assumed to have outbound shipment capacity $\frac{R_m^{PLANT}}{t^{TAC}}$. In other words,

$$\sum_{n=1}^{N} y_{mnt} \leq \frac{R_m^{PLANT}}{t^{TAC}}\beta_{mt}, \quad m = 1,...,M;\ t = 1,...,T. \tag{4.59}$$

Similar to the strategic submodel, the number of units of finished product held in inventory at warehouse n during period t is equal to the number of units of finished product held in inventory at warehouse n during the previous period plus the number of units of finished product shipped from all production plants to warehouse n during period t minus the number of units of finished product shipped from warehouse n to all markets during period t. That is,

$$h_{n(t-1)} + \sum_{m=1}^{M} y_{mnt} - \sum_{p=1}^{P} z_{npt} = h_{nt}, \quad n = 1,...,N;\ t = 1,...,T. \tag{4.60}$$

As in the strategic submodel, it is assumed that an initial inventory $\frac{h_{n0}}{t^{TAC}}$ of finished product is on hand at each warehouse at the beginning of the initial period. Furthermore, warehouse n must be open in period t to receive shipments of finished products from the operational plants. Hence,

$$\sum_{m=1}^{M} y_{mnt} \leq \frac{R_n^{INW}}{t^{TAC}}\delta_{nt}, \quad n = 1,...,N;\ t = 1,...,T, \tag{4.61}$$

where R_n^{INW} represents the inbound shipping capacity of warehouse n in each (strategic submodel) period, and the binary variable δ_{nt} (actually a constant here) is used to indicate whether or not warehouse n is open during period t.

Similar to the strategic submodel, the number of units of finished product held in inventory at warehouse n during period t is limited to a known inventory capacity. Because the solution to the strategic submodel determined which warehouses are used in which periods, the (known) values of the binary variables δ_{nt} are used here to indicate whether or not warehouse n is utilized during period t. Hence,

$$h_{nt} \leq C_{nt}^{HFW} \delta_{nt}, \quad n = 1,...,N; \ t = 1,...,T. \tag{4.62}$$

Furthermore, if warehouse n is open in period t, it must store a minimum number of units of finished product in that period. In other words,

$$h_{nt} \geq \frac{q_n}{t^{TAC}} \delta_{nt}, \quad n = 1,...,N; \ t = 1,...,T. \tag{4.63}$$

Each open warehouse has a defined capacity to ship units of finished product out to customer markets (as in the strategic submodel). Hence,

$$\sum_{p=1}^{P} z_{npt} \leq \frac{R_n^{OUTW}}{t^{TAC}} \delta_{nt}, \quad n = 1,...,N; \ t = 1,...,T, \tag{4.64}$$

where R_n^{OUTW} represents the outbound shipping capacity for warehouse n in each (strategic submodel) period.

As in the strategic submodel, a predefined finished product quantity is required to remain in inventory during the final time period. Specifically, the sum of the finished product inventory remaining in all plants and warehouses during the final period must be equal to or greater than some fraction of the final period's total demand. In other words,

$$\sum_{m=1}^{M} g_{mT} + \sum_{n=1}^{N} h_{nT} \geq h^{FIN} \sum_{p=1}^{P} d_{pT}, \tag{4.65}$$

where $0 \leq h^{FIN} \leq 1$.

4.4.4 Tactical Submodel Objective Function

Because the multiple objectives stated by supply chain managers are formulated as goal constraints with allowable deviations in the tactical submodel, the objective function is formulated to minimize some function of the deviations. Here, two different goal programming techniques are considered: preemptive and non-preemptive goal programming. With non-preemptive goal programming, decision makers assign weights to each goal, allowing for tradeoffs among goals. Using non-preemptive goal programming, and with the objectives in no particular order, the single objective function for the tactical submodel is formulated as

$$\text{Minimize } w_1 d_{\text{profit}}^- + w_2 \sum_{p=1}^{P} \sum_{t=1}^{T} d_{\text{dem-}pt}^- + w_3 d_{\text{time}}^+. \tag{4.66}$$

In order to determine the weight values for Equation 4.66, Ballestero (2005) suggests several techniques for eliciting the relative importance of multiple goals, including those detailed in Keeney and Raiffa (1976), Roy (1991), Brans and Vincke (1985), Mareschal (1988), and Saaty (1994). In addition, Masud and Ravindran (2008) summarize several other methods for determining weight values that help define the relative importance among goals, including weights from ranks, the rating method, and the ratio weighing method. Despite the existence of such techniques for determining weight values, however, it generally may be easier to elicit from decision makers a priority ranking among multiple goals. When preemptive goal programming is used, decision makers rank their goals from most to least important. The objective function is then formulated such that the solution technique first focuses on the most important goal, then the second-most important goal, and so on. Suppose here that supply chain managers have determined that achieving a minimum profit level is their top priority, followed by exactly meeting demand, and then minimizing total weighted transit time. First, a priority level P_r, $r = 1, 2, 3$ is assigned to each of these objectives. The objective function is then formulated as a linear combination of functions of the deviational variables as follows:

$$\text{Minimize } P_1 d_{\text{profit}}^- + P_2 \sum_{p=1}^{P} \sum_{t=1}^{T} d_{\text{dem-}pt}^- + P_3 d_{\text{time}}^+. \tag{4.67}$$

Besides involving the relatively straightforward task of eliciting priority rankings from decision makers, preemptive goal programming provides an additional advantage over its non-preemptive counterpart regarding the objective function. Because relative weights are used in a non-preemptive goal programming formulation, the deviational variables corresponding to different units (e.g., dollars versus years) must be scaled or normalized appropriately. With preemptive goal programming, the sequential optimization of each successively lower-priority goal obviates the need for such normalization. Because goals are often incommensurable with one another and can sometimes only be achieved at the expense of others, and because preemptive goal programming generally places less of a burden on decision makers in terms of prioritizing objectives, the formulation of Equation 4.67 will be used for the tactical submodel (Masud and Ravindran 2008).

4.4.5 Tactical Submodel Summary

The overall formulation is as follows. (Of course, the goals in the objective function may be reprioritized based on decision maker preferences.)

$$\text{Minimize } P_1 d^-_{\text{profit}} + P_2 \sum_{p=1}^{P} \sum_{t=1}^{T} d^-_{\text{dem-}pt} + P_3 d^+_{\text{time}}$$

Subject to:

$$s^{FP} \sum_{n=1}^{N} \sum_{p=1}^{P} \sum_{t=1}^{T} z_{npt} - \sum_{m=1}^{M} \sum_{t=1}^{T} c^{CON}_{mt} \phi_{mt} - \sum_{m=1}^{M} \sum_{t=1}^{T} f^{P}_{mt} \beta_{mt}$$

$$- \sum_{n=1}^{N} \sum_{t=1}^{T} f^{W}_{nt} \delta_{nt} - \sum_{i=1}^{I'} \sum_{k=1}^{K'} \sum_{m=1}^{M} \sum_{t=1}^{T} c^{R}_{ikt} w_{ikmt} - \sum_{i=I'+1}^{I} \sum_{k=1}^{K} \sum_{m=1}^{M} \sum_{t=1}^{T} c^{R}_{ikt} w_{ikmt}$$

$$- \sum_{m=1}^{T} \sum_{t=1}^{T} c^{FP}_{mt} x_{mt} - \sum_{m=1}^{M} \sum_{t=1}^{T} \left(c^{PQ+}_{mt} e^+_{mt} + c^{PQ-}_{mt} e^-_{mt} \right)$$

$$- \sum_{i=1}^{I'} \sum_{k=1}^{K'} \sum_{m=1}^{M} \sum_{t=1}^{T} c^{SRP}_{ikmt} w_{ikmt} - \sum_{i=I'+1}^{I} \sum_{k=1}^{K} \sum_{m=1}^{M} \sum_{t=1}^{T} c^{SRP}_{ikmt} w_{ikmt}$$

$$- \sum_{m=1}^{M} \sum_{n=1}^{N} \sum_{t=1}^{T} c^{SFW}_{mnt} y_{mnt} - \sum_{n=1}^{N} \sum_{p=1}^{P} \sum_{t=1}^{T} c^{SFM}_{npt} z_{npt} - \sum_{i=1}^{I} \sum_{m=1}^{M} \sum_{t=1}^{T} c^{HRP}_{imt} r_{imt} \quad (4.68)$$

$$- \sum_{m=1}^{M} \sum_{t=1}^{T} c^{HFP}_{mt} g_{mt} - \sum_{n=1}^{N} \sum_{t=1}^{T} c^{HFW}_{nt} h_{nt} + d^-_{\text{profit}} - d^+_{\text{profit}} = Y;$$

$$\sum_{n=1}^{N} z_{npt} + d^-_{\text{dem-}pt} = d_{pt}, \quad p = 1, \ldots, P; \; t = 1, \ldots, T;$$

$$\sum_{i=1}^{I'} \sum_{k=1}^{K'} \sum_{m=1}^{M} \sum_{t=1}^{T} b^{TRP}_{ikm} w_{ikmt} + \sum_{i=I'+1}^{I} \sum_{k=1}^{K} \sum_{m=1}^{M} \sum_{t=1}^{T} b^{TRP}_{ikm} w_{ikmt}$$

$$+ \sum_{m=1}^{M} \sum_{n=1}^{N} \sum_{t=1}^{T} b^{TFW}_{mn} y_{mnt} + \sum_{n=1}^{N} \sum_{p=1}^{P} \sum_{t=1}^{T} b^{TFM}_{np} z_{npt} + d^-_{\text{time}} - d^+_{\text{time}} = 0;$$

$$\sum_{m=1}^{M} w_{ikmt} \le C^{RS}_{ikt} \alpha_{ikt}, \quad i = 1, \ldots, I'; \; k = 1, \ldots, K'; \; t = 1, \ldots, T;$$

$$\sum_{m=1}^{M} w_{ikmt} \le C_{ikt}^{RS} \alpha_{ikt}, \quad i = I'+1, ..., I; \ k = 1, ..., K; \ t = 1, ..., T;$$

$$\sum_{m=1}^{M} w_{ikmt} \ge \frac{w_{ik}^{min}}{t^{TAC}} \alpha_{ikt}, \quad i = 1, ..., I'; \ k = 1, ..., K'; \ t = 1, ..., T;$$

$$x_{mt} \le C_{mt}^{FP} \beta_{mt}, \quad m = 1, ..., M; \ t = 1, ..., T;$$

$$x_{mt} \ge \frac{v_m}{t^{TAC}} \beta_{mt}, \quad m = 1, ..., M; \ t = 1, ..., T;$$

$$x_{mt} - x_{mt-1} = e_{mt}, \quad m = 1, ..., M; \ t = 1, ..., T;$$

$$e_{mt} = e_{mt}^{+} - e_{mt}^{-}, \quad m = 1, ..., M; \ t = 1, ..., T;$$

$$x_{m0} = 0, \quad m = 1, ..., M;$$

$$r_{im(t-1)} + \sum_{k=1}^{K'} w_{ikmt} - a_i x_{mt} = r_{imt}, \quad i = 1, ..., I'; \ m = 1, ..., M;$$

$$t = 1, ..., T;$$

$$r_{im(t-1)} + \sum_{k=1}^{K} w_{ikmt} - a_i x_{mt} = r_{imt}, \quad i = I'+1, ..., I; \ m = 1, ..., M;$$

$$t = 1, ..., T;$$

$$r_{imt} \le C_{imt}^{HRP} \beta_{mt}, \quad i = 1, ..., I; \ m = 1, ..., M; \ t = 1, ..., T;$$

$$g_{m(t-1)} + x_{mt} - \sum_{n=1}^{N} y_{mnt} = g_{mt}, \quad m = 1, ..., M; \ t = 1, ..., T;$$

$$g_{mt} \le C_{mt}^{HFP} \beta_{mt}, \quad m = 1, ..., M; \ t = 1, ..., T;$$

$$\sum_{n=1}^{N} y_{mnt} \le \frac{R_m^{PLANT}}{t^{TAC}} \beta_{mt}, \quad m = 1, ..., M; \ t = 1, ..., T;$$

$$h_{n(t-1)} + \sum_{m=1}^{M} y_{mnt} - \sum_{p=1}^{P} z_{npt} = h_{nt}, \quad n = 1, ..., N; \ t = 1, ..., T;$$

$$\sum_{m=1}^{M} y_{mnt} \le \frac{R_n^{INW}}{t^{TAC}} \delta_{nt}, \quad n = 1, ..., N; \ t = 1, ..., T;$$

$$h_{nt} \le C_{nt}^{HFW} \delta_{nt}, \quad n = 1, ..., N; \ t = 1, ..., T;$$

$$h_{nt} \geq \frac{q_n}{t^{TAC}} \delta_{nt}, \quad n = 1,...,N; \ t = 1,...,T;$$

$$\sum_{p=1}^{P} z_{npt} \leq \frac{R_n^{OUTW}}{t^{TAC}} \delta_{nt}, \quad n = 1,...,N; \ t = 1,...,T;$$

$$\sum_{m=1}^{M} g_{mT} + \sum_{n=1}^{N} h_{nT} \geq h^{FIN} \sum_{p=1}^{P} d_{pT};$$

$$w_{ikmt} \geq 0, \quad i = 1,...,I'; \ k = 1,...,K'; \ m = 1,...,M; \ t = 1,...,T;$$

$$w_{ikmt} \geq 0, \quad i = I'+1,...,I; \ k = 1,...,K; \ m = 1,...,M; \ t = 1,...,T;$$

$$w_{ikmt} \ \text{undefined}, \quad i = 1,...,I'; \ k = K'+1,...,K; \ m = 1,...,M;$$

$$t = 1,...,T;$$

$$x_{mt}, e_{mt}^+, e_{mt}^-, y_{mnt}, z_{npt}, r_{imt}, g_{mt}, h_{nt}, d_{\text{profit}}^-, d_{\text{profit}}^+, d_{\text{time}}^-, d_{\text{time}}^+,$$

$$d_{\text{dem-}pt}^- \geq 0, \quad \forall i, m, n, p, t;$$

$$e_{mt} \ \text{unrestricted}, \quad m = 1,...,M; \ t = 1,...,T;$$

$$\alpha_{ikt} \ \text{binary}, \quad i = I'+1,...,I; \ k = 1,...,K; \ t = 1,...,T;$$

$$\alpha_{ikt} \ \text{constants}, \quad i = 1,...,I'; \ k = 1,...,K'; \ t = 1,...,T;$$

$$\alpha_{ikt} \ \text{undefined}, \quad i = 1,...,I'; \ k = K'+1,...,K; \ t = 1,...,T;$$

$$\beta_{mt}, \delta_{nt}, \phi_{mt} \ \text{constants}, \quad m = 1,...,M; \ n = 1,...,N; \ t = 1,...,T.$$

This submodel involves $T(2I'K' + IK - I'K + 2IM + 7M + 5N + P) + M + 3$ constraints and $T(I'K'M + IKM - I'KM + 5M + MN + NP + IM + N + IK - I'K + P) + 4$ decision variables, of which $T(IK - I'K)$ are integer (binary) variables. Once again, a change in the number of time periods would have the most impact on the overall size of the submodel. Furthermore, if a sequential solution approach is used to solve this linear integer goal program, the number of decision variables will decrease with each successive optimization. However, the magnitude of the decrease in the number of decision variables, which results from the fixing of deviational variable values after each successive optimization, depends upon the priority order of the objectives.

The solution to the tactical submodel provides supply chain managers with a best compromise solution for (1) noncritical raw material supplier selections; (2) raw material shipment and inventory quantities; (3) finished product production, inventory, and shipment quantities; and (4) a profit figure.

For convenience, the following constraint is added during numerical computation:

$$
\begin{aligned}
PROFIT = {} & s^{FP} \sum_{n=1}^{N} \sum_{p=1}^{P} \sum_{t=1}^{T} z_{npt} - \sum_{m=1}^{M} \sum_{t=1}^{T} c_{mt}^{CON} \phi_{mt} - \sum_{m=1}^{M} \sum_{t=1}^{T} f_{mt}^{P} \beta_{mt} - \sum_{n=1}^{N} \sum_{t=1}^{T} f_{nt}^{W} \delta_{nt} \\
& - \sum_{i=1}^{I'} \sum_{k=1}^{K'} \sum_{m=1}^{M} \sum_{t=1}^{T} c_{ikt}^{R} w_{ikmt} - \sum_{i=I'+1}^{I} \sum_{k=1}^{K} \sum_{m=1}^{M} \sum_{t=1}^{T} c_{ikt}^{R} w_{ikmt} - \sum_{m=1}^{M} \sum_{t=1}^{T} c_{mt}^{FP} x_{mt} \\
& - \sum_{m=1}^{M} \sum_{t=1}^{T} (c_{mt}^{PQ+} e_{mt}^{+} + c_{mt}^{PQ-} e_{mt}^{-}) - \sum_{i=1}^{I'} \sum_{k=1}^{K'} \sum_{m=1}^{M} \sum_{t=1}^{T} c_{ikmt}^{SRP} w_{ikmt} \\
& - \sum_{i=I'+1}^{I} \sum_{k=1}^{K} \sum_{m=1}^{M} \sum_{t=1}^{T} c_{ikmt}^{SRP} w_{ikmt} - \sum_{m=1}^{M} \sum_{n=1}^{N} \sum_{t=1}^{T} c_{mnt}^{SFW} y_{mnt} - \sum_{n=1}^{N} \sum_{p=1}^{P} \sum_{t=1}^{T} c_{npt}^{SFM} z_{np_{i}} \\
& - \sum_{i=1}^{I} \sum_{m=1}^{M} \sum_{t=1}^{T} c_{imt}^{HRP} r_{imt} - \sum_{m=1}^{M} \sum_{t=1}^{T} c_{mt}^{HFP} g_{mt} - \sum_{n=1}^{N} \sum_{t=1}^{T} c_{nt}^{HFW} h_{nt},
\end{aligned}
\tag{4.69}
$$

where *PROFIT* is an unrestricted variable.

4.5 Case Study

To demonstrate its applicability, the two-phase model described in Sections 4.2 through 4.4 is now applied to the example supply chain scenario depicted in Figure 4.2. In this scenario, consisting of five suppliers (S1–S5), three manufacturing locations (P1–P3), four warehouses (WH1–WH4), and five customer markets (M1–M5), a single product is manufactured from two critical (i = 1, 2) and three noncritical (i = 3, 4, 5) raw materials. Specifically, raw material requirements for each unit of finished product are 5, 7, 7, 12, and 6 units each of raw materials 1, 2, 3, 4, and 5, respectively. Suppliers 1 and 2 are each capable of providing both of the critical raw materials as well as all of the noncritical raw materials, while suppliers 1 through 5 can each provide all of the noncritical raw materials (to varying degrees, that is.) The finished product may be produced at any of the three manufacturing sites (m = 1, 2, 3) and shipped to any of the four warehouses (w = 1, 2, 3, 4). Although the storage capacities for raw materials and finished products at each potential plant location are known, the production capacities initially are set to some fraction of the maximum site capacities. Given a five-year

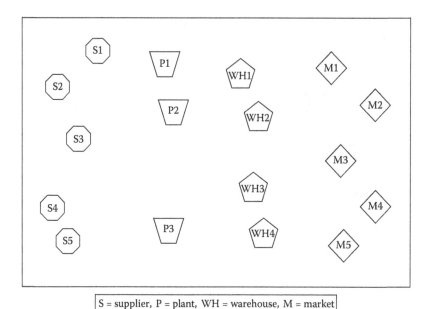

S = supplier, P = plant, WH = warehouse, M = market

FIGURE 4.2
An example of a supply chain scenario.

planning horizon, supply chain managers are charged with two tasks: (1) supply chain design—establishing the infrastructure of the supply chain by making critical raw material supplier selections, choosing the optimal set of plants and warehouses, and determining the necessary plant capacities, and (2) supply chain operation planning—determining best compromise noncritical supplier selections and production, inventory, and shipping quantities for each quarter over the five-year planning horizon. In this case, upper-level decision makers have chosen profit maximization as their top priority goal, followed by exactly meeting market demand, and then minimizing total weighted transit time in an effort to improve customer service.

4.5.1 Model Input

All data related to purchase, production, holding, and shipment costs for raw and finished materials; demand forecasts; and plant and warehouse capacities and costs are presented in Tables 4.1 through 4.4. Because raw material, production, holding, and shipping costs vary over periods, routes, and supply chain elements, Table 4.1 presents only the ranges of these costs. Data related to plant costs and capacities are shown in Table 4.2. Each unit of finished product has a sale price of $450, and managers have chosen to limit strategic submodel production to 99% of maximum site capacity. Other inputs

TABLE 4.1

Strategic Submodel Cost Ranges

Cost	Range ($)
Critical raw material	5.60–9.00/unit
Noncritical raw material	4.00–6.00/unit
Shipping—critical raw material	0.90–1.90/unit
Shipping—noncritical raw material	0.40–1.20/unit
Shipping—finished product	2.30–6.40/unit
Holding—raw material	0.20–0.60/unit/period
Holding—finished product	0.70–1.10/unit/period
Production	4.50–9.00/unit

TABLE 4.2

Plant Costs and Capacities

Plant	Year	Construction Cost ($)	Fixed Operating Cost ($)	Minimum Production Quantity (Units)	Maximum Production Capacity (Units)	Finished Product Storage Capacity (Units)	Outbound Shipping Capacity (Units)
1	1	1,000,000	300,000	1,000	5,500	1,000	150,000
	2	1,050,000	300,000	1,000	5,500	1,100	150,000
	3	1,100,000	350,000	1,000	5,500	1,200	150,000
	4	1,150,000	350,000	1,000	5,500	1,400	150,000
	5	1,200,000	400,000	1,000	5,500	1,500	150,000
2	1	1,000,000	400,000	1,000	6,000	2,000	150,000
	2	1,050,000	400,000	1,000	6,000	2,000	150,000
	3	1,100,000	450,000	1,000	6,000	2,000	150,000
	4	1,150,000	450,000	1,000	6,000	2,000	150,000
	5	1,200,000	500,000	1,000	6,000	2,000	150,000
3	1	800,000	300,000	1,000	4,000	3,000	150,000
	2	825,000	300,000	1,000	4,000	3,100	150,000
	3	850,000	350,000	1,000	4,000	3,200	150,000
	4	875,000	350,000	1,000	4,000	3,300	150,000
	5	900,000	400,000	1,000	4,000	3,400	150,000

used in the strategic submodel (but not shown here) include raw material availability, storage capacity (at plants), and minimum purchase data; raw material and finished product initial inventories; and production quantity change costs.

Data used here as input to the tactical submodel is generally proportional to that used in the strategic submodel. For example, although input to the strategic submodel reflects demand at Market 1 as 4,000 units in Year 1, demand at Market 1 in the tactical submodel is 1,000 units in each of quarters

TABLE 4.3

Warehouse Costs and Capacities

Warehouse	Year	Fixed Operating Cost ($)	Minimum Storage Quantity (Units)	Storage Capacity (Units)	Outbound Shipping Capacity (Units)
1	1	100,000	0	4,000	150,000
	2	100,000	0	4,000	150,000
	3	150,000	0	4,000	150,000
	4	150,000	0	4,000	150,000
	5	150,000	0	4,000	150,000
2	1	200,000	0	5,000	150,000
	2	200,000	0	5,000	150,000
	3	250,000	0	5,000	150,000
	4	250,000	0	5,000	150,000
	5	250,000	0	5,000	150,000
3	1	200,000	0	6,000	150,000
	2	200,000	0	6,000	150,000
	3	250,000	0	6,000	150,000
	4	250,000	0	6,000	150,000
	5	250,000	0	6,000	150,000
4	1	200,000	0	4,500	150,000
	2	200,000	0	4,500	150,000
	3	250,000	0	4,500	150,000
	4	250,000	0	4,500	150,000
	5	250,000	0	4,500	150,000

TABLE 4.4

Market Demand (Units)

Market	Year 1	2	3	4	5
1	4,000	4,200	5,000	5,300	6,000
2	3,500	3,600	3,700	3,800	3,900
3	2,000	2,000	2,300	2,400	2,500
4	3,000	3,100	3,200	3,300	3,400
5	2,500	2,500	2,500	2,500	2,500

one through four. Furthermore, although not shown here, transportation times for raw materials and finished products among different elements in the supply chain range from one to five days. Additionally, in an effort to explicitly demonstrate the results of changing the priority order of the three objectives, a disruption in one of the transportation routes is simulated in the tactical submodel. Specifically, the cost of delivering finished products to Market 1 is made prohibitively expensive.

4.5.2 Model Outputs and Results

This numerical example was formulated and solved using Extended LINGO 9.0 optimization software. The solution to the strategic submodel (which took nearly zero processing time) provides an optimal profit target of $5,643,366, along with the supply chain infrastructure plan. In this example, plants 1, 2, and 3 should be constructed in year 1, corresponding to quarter 1 in the tactical submodel. Results related to supplier selections for critical raw materials, warehouse operating schedules, optimal production quantities, and production capacities to be used as input to the tactical submodel are presented in Tables 4.5–4.7. Based upon the optimal production quantities for each of

TABLE 4.5

Critical Raw Material Supplier Selections

	Year									
	Critical Raw Material #1					Critical Raw Material #2				
Supplier	1	2	3	4	5	1	2	3	4	5
#1		✓				✓	✓	✓	✓	✓
#2	✓	✓	✓	✓	✓	✓	✓	✓		✓

TABLE 4.6

Warehouse Operating Schedule

	Warehouse			
Year	1	2	3	4
1	✓	✓	✓	✓
2	✓			
3	✓			
4	✓			
5	✓			

TABLE 4.7

Strategic Submodel Optimal Production Quantities (Units)

	Plant		
Year	1	2	3
1	4,950	5,400	3,600
2	4,950	5,400	3,600
3	4,950	5,400	3,600
4	4,950	5,400	3,600
5	4,950	5,400	3,600

the operating plants over the five-year planning horizon, and a user-defined production capacity factor of $u = 0.99$, production capacities for input to the tactical submodel are shown in Table 4.8.

Using the infrastructure and supplier selection decisions made in the solution to the strategic submodel, along with higher resolution data (omitted here for brevity), the tactical submodel was solved using the preemptive goal programming technique to determine noncritical raw material supplier selections and best compromise purchasing, production, inventory, and shipment quantity decisions. Using Extended LINGO 9.0, each of the three sequential optimizations of the tactical submodel required three or fewer seconds of processing time. When the profit goal has top priority, followed by the demand goal, and then the response time goal, a best compromise profit level of $3,131,097 is achieved. When meeting demand is given the highest priority, followed by meeting or exceeding the profit goal, and then minimizing response time, the solution indicates a profit of $1,353,256 over the five-year planning horizon. This lower profit figure can be attributed to the tactical submodel attempting to first minimize unsatisfied demand, despite the prohibitively high costs associated with the disrupted transportation routes to Market 1. Indeed, this case resulted in only 6,145 units of unsatisfied demand, compared to the 24,500 units of unsatisfied demand in the profit-first case.

Table 4.9 summarizes the best compromise production quantities resulting from this implementation of the tactical submodel. Due to the disruption in the transportation routes leading to Market 1 (and the associated prohibitively high shipping costs), none of the demand for Market 1 was met in an effort to maximize overall profits. However, this situation frees up the necessary resources to satisfy all other demand over the five-year planning horizon. Figure 4.3 compares the profit goal achievement levels for the profit-first and demand-first cases. Although both profit goal achievement

TABLE 4.8

Tactical Submodel Production Capacities (Units)

| Quarter | Plant | | | Quarter | Plant | | |
	1	2	3		1	2	3
1	1,362	1,485	990	11	1,362	1,485	990
2	1,362	1,485	990	12	1,362	1,485	990
3	1,362	1,485	990	13	1,362	1,485	990
4	1,362	1,485	990	14	1,362	1,485	990
5	1,362	1,485	990	15	1,362	1,485	990
6	1,362	1,485	990	16	1,362	1,485	990
7	1,362	1,485	990	17	1,362	1,485	990
8	1,362	1,485	990	18	1,362	1,485	990
9	1,362	1,485	990	19	1,362	1,485	990
10	1,362	1,485	990	20	1,362	1,485	990

TABLE 4.9

Tactical Submodel Optimal Production (Profit First)

	Plant (Units)				Plant (Units)		
Quarter	1	2	3	Quarter	1	2	3
1	1,362	1,009	250	11	1,362	1,388	250
2	1,362	1,246	250	12	1,362	1,388	250
3	1,362	1,485	250	13	1,362	1,313	250
4	1,362	1,485	250	14	1,362	1,238	250
5	1,362	1,485	250	15	1,362	1,238	250
6	1,362	1,485	250	16	1,362	1,189	250
7	1,362	1,485	250	17	1,362	1,189	250
8	1,362	1,485	250	18	1,362	1,040	250
9	1,362	1,241	250	19	1,362	1,040	250
10	1,362	1,288	250	20	1,362	1,040	250

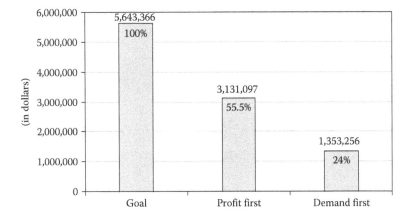

FIGURE 4.3
Profit goal achievement as a percentage of goal target.

levels fall well short of the original profit goal due to the prohibitively high shipping costs corresponding to transportation routes leading to Market 1, this example is meant to demonstrate the ability to conduct tradeoff analysis using the deterministic tactical submodel. Table 4.10 summarizes the best compromise production quantities resulting from this implementation of the tactical submodel, while Table 4.11 shows the quarterly change in production at each plant as the demand goal replaces the profit goal as the top priority. Clearly, Plant 3, which operates at its minimum production rate when profit achievement takes top priority, provides most of the additional production necessary to fulfill demand when the minimization

TABLE 4.10

Tactical Submodel Optimal Production (Demand First)

Quarter	Plant (Units)			Quarter	Plant (Units)		
	1	2	3		1	2	3
1	1,362	1,485	990	11	1,362	1,485	990
2	1,362	1,485	990	12	1,362	1,485	990
3	1,362	1,485	990	13	1,362	1,485	975
4	1,362	1,485	990	14	1,362	1,485	868
5	1,362	1,485	990	15	1,362	1,485	863
6	1,362	1,485	990	16	1,362	1,485	863
7	1,362	1,485	990	17	1,362	1,485	990
8	1,362	1,485	990	18	1,362	1,485	990
9	1,362	1,485	990	19	1,362	1,485	990
10	1,362	1,485	990	20	1,362	1,485	990

TABLE 4.11

Production Change as Demand Goal Replaces Profit Goal as Top Priority

Quarter	Plant			Quarter	Plant		
	1	2	3		1	2	3
1	0	+476	+740	11	0	+97	+740
2	0	+239	+740	12	0	+97	+740
3	0	0	+740	13	0	+172	+725
4	0	0	+740	14	0	+247	+618
5	0	0	+740	15	0	+247	+613
6	0	0	+740	16	0	+296	+613
7	0	0	+740	17	0	+296	+740
8	0	0	+740	18	0	+445	+740
9	0	+244	+740	19	0	+445	+740
10	0	+197	+740	20	0	+445	+740

of unsatisfied demand is set as the top priority goal. Table 4.12 presents the distribution of unsatisfied demand over all markets and periods in both the profit-first and demand-first cases. As expected, the achievement level for the demand satisfaction goal increases when it is assigned top priority (see Figure 4.4). However, because demand alone is not affected by the prohibitively high shipping costs assigned to all shipping routes leading to Market 1, the change in the achievement level as the demand satisfaction goal moves from first to second or second to first priority is not as drastic as that of the profit goal.

TABLE 4.12

Demand Shortages (Profit First/Demand First)

Quarter	Market									
	1		2		3		4		5	
	Profit	Demand	Profit	Demand	Profit	Demand	Profit	Demand	Profit	Demand
1	1,000	0	0	0	0	0	0	0	0	0
2	1,000	0	0	0	0	0	0	0	0	0
3	1,000	0	0	0	0	0	0	0	0	0
4	1,000	0	0	0	0	0	0	0	0	0
5	1,050	0	0	0	0	0	0	0	0	0
6	1,050	0	0	0	0	0	0	0	0	0
7	1,050	0	0	0	0	0	0	0	0	0
8	1,050	0	0	0	0	0	0	0	0	0
9	1,250	0	0	0	0	0	0	0	0	0
10	1,250	0	0	0	0	0	0	0	0	0
11	1,250	0	0	0	0	0	0	0	0	0
12	1,250	369	0	0	0	0	0	0	0	0
13	1,325	354	0	0	0	0	0	0	0	0
14	1,325	461	0	0	0	0	0	0	0	0
15	1,325	565	0	0	0	0	0	0	0	0
16	1,325	965	0	0	0	0	0	0	0	0
17	1,500	664	0	0	0	0	0	0	0	0
18	1,500	664	0	0	0	0	0	0	0	0
19	1,500	664	0	0	0	0	0	0	0	0
20	1,500	1444	0	0	0	0	0	0	0	0
Total	24,500	6,150	0	0	0	0	0	0	0	0

Note: Overall shortage: profit first = 24,500 units; demand first = 6,150 units.

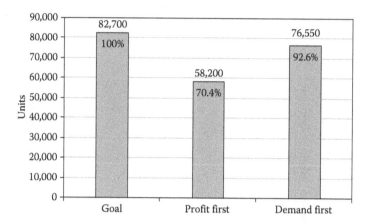

FIGURE 4.4
Demand goal achievement as a percentage of goal target.

4.6 Managerial and Planning Implications

The two-phase model formulated here provides a tool for supply chain designers and operators to determine the best supplier selection, purchasing, production, shipping, and inventory decisions for a single product manufacturing and distribution network. The strategic submodel first gives supply chain designers an opportunity to establish the initial supply chain infrastructure for the overall manufacturing and distribution network that will maximize overall profit. With detailed information pertaining to noncritical raw material costs and availability, transportation times, and customer demand, supply chain operators can use this newly obtained information, along with the results of the strategic submodel, as input to the tactical submodel to determine best compromise noncritical raw material supplier selections and (revised) production, inventory, and shipment quantities.

References

Al-Mutawah, K., V. Lee, and Y. Cheung. (2006). Modeling supply chain complexity using a distributed multi-objective genetic algorithm. In M. Gavrilova, O. Gervasi, V. Kumar, C.K. Tan, and D. Taniar (Eds.), *Computational Science and Its Applications – ICCSA 2006*, Vol. 3980 (pp. 586–595). Berlin, Germany: Springer.

Altiparmak, F., M. Gen, L. Lin, and T. Paksoy. (2006). A genetic algorithm approach for multi-objective optimization of supply chain networks. *Computers & Industrial Engineering*, **51** (1), 196–215.

Ashayeri, J. and J. Rongen. (1997). Central distribution in Europe: A multi-criteria approach to location selection. *International Journal of Logistics Management*, **8** (1), 97–109.

Attai, T.D. (2003). *A Multiple Objective Approach to Global Supply Chain Design.* Unpublished master's thesis, Penn State University, University Park, PA.

Ballestero, E. (2005). Using stochastic goal programming: Some applications to management and a case of industrial production. *INFOR*, **43** (2), 63–77.

Beamon, B.M. (1998). Supply chain design and analysis: Models and methods. *International Journal of Production Economics*, **55**, 281–294.

Bilsel, R.U. and A. Ravindran. (2011). A multi-objective chance constrained programming model for supplier selection under uncertainty. *Transportation Research Part B*, **45**, 1284–1300.

Bilsel, R.U. and A. Ravindran. (2012). Modeling disruption risk in supply chain risk management. *International Journal of Operations Research and Information Systems*, **3** (3), 15–39.

Brans, J.P. and P. Vincke. (1985). A preference ranking organisation method: The PROMETHEE method for MCDM. *Management Science*, **31** (6), 647–656.

Cintron, A., A.R. Ravindran, and J. Ventura. (2010). Multi-criteria mathematical model for designing the distribution network of a consumer goods company. *Computers and Industrial Engineering*, **58**, 584–593.

Keeney, R.L. and H. Raiffa. (1976). *Decisions with Multiple Objectives: Preferences and Value Trade-Offs.* New York: Wiley.

Mareschal, B. (1988). Geometrical representations for MCDA: The GAIA procedure. *European Journal of Operational Research*, **34**, 69–77.

Masud, A.S.M. and A.R. Ravindran. (2008). Multiple criteria decision making. In A.R. Ravindran (Ed.), *Operations Research and Management Science Handbook* (pp. 5–1 – 5–41). Boca Raton, FL: CRC Press.

Melachrinoudis, E. (1999). Bicriteria location of a semi-obnoxious facility. *Computers & Industrial Engineering*, **37**, 581–593.

Melachrinoudis, E. and H. Min. (2000). The dynamic relocation and phase-out of a hybrid, two-echelon plant/warehousing facility: A multiple objective approach. *European Journal of Operational Research*, **123**, 1–15.

Melachrinoudis, E., H. Min, and A. Messac. (2000). The relocation of a manufacturing/distribution facility from supply chain perspectives: A physical programming approach. *Advances in Management Science*, **10**, 15–39.

Min, H. and G. Zhou. (2002). Supply chain modeling: Past, present and future. *Computers & Industrial Engineering*, **43**, 231–249.

Ravindran, A.R., R. Ufuk Bilsel, V. Wadhwa, and T. Yang. (2010). Risk adjusted multicriteria supplier selection models with applications. *International Journal of Production Research*, **48** (2), 405–424.

Ravindran, A.R. and D.P. Warsing, Jr. (2013). *Supply Chain Engineering: Models and Applications.* Boca Raton, FL: CRC Press.

Rienkhemaniyom, K. and A.R. Ravindran. (2014). Global supply chain network design incorporating disruption risk. *International Journal of Business Analytics*, **1** (3), 39–64.

Roy, B. (1991). The outranking approach and the foundations of ELECTRE methods. *Theory and Decision*, **31**, 49–73.

Saaty, T. (1994). How to make a decision: The analytic hierarchy process. *Interfaces*, **24**, 19–43.

Sabri, E.H. and B.M. Beamon (2000). A multi-objective approach to simultaneous strategic and operational planning in supply chain design. *Omega*, **28**, 581–598.

5

Multi-Criteria Distribution Planning Model for a Consumer Goods Company

Aixa L. Cintrón

Supply Chain Manager, San Juan, Puerto Rico

CONTENTS

5.1 Introduction

The optimization model presented in this chapter was developed to design a supply chain distribution network for a consumer goods company located on a Caribbean island. This company is a major global competitor in its area, selling approximately \$20 billion per year worldwide. The company has markets in more than 150 countries, and its brands are in first or second position in most of these markets. The country analyzed in this case study has sales of approximately \$86 million per year. Its market includes 71 customers (66 retailers and 5 independent distributors), and it receives products from four manufacturing plants (all outside this country). To distribute the demand in this region, the company owns one distribution center located on this island.

The integrated supply chain model presented in this chapter was developed to help the company reduce their distribution costs in this region. The results of this model will help the company in making several decisions, such as evaluating the location of their distribution center (DC) and its capacity or whether more than one DC is needed and the optimal locations to consider. Also, the model will identify the best source (i.e., the manufacturing plants, the DC, or an independent distributor) to serve the demand of each retailer. The costs may be reduced by decreasing the customer demand supplied from the regional DC (because there will be less handling costs) and hence supplying more from independent distributors or directly from the plants' warehouses. An independent distributor, who is also considered a customer, stores and distributes the merchandise to smaller clients but does not sell it directly as a retailer. The model includes several manufacturing plants, where each plant manufactures several products. It is assumed that a mixture of products can be sent directly from a plant to a customer as long as all the products in the container are manufactured at the same plant.

Most researchers, such as Ambrosino et al. (2009) and Rabbani et al. (2008), consider an optimal design as one that minimizes the distribution costs or that maximizes profit. However, other criteria that are important in distribution network design are also considered in this study: *customer response time, power, credit performance,* and *distributor reputation*. Profit is the most commonly used criterion for decision making. It includes revenue from sales minus the distribution costs. Profit is considered, instead of just minimizing the distribution costs, because the revenue obtained from sales depends on the way a customer is supplied (e.g., discounts apply to some distribution options, such as receiving a full container directly from the manufacturing plant). The terms used to calculate the profit will be discussed in a later section. Response time is the time between the order entry and order's proof-of-delivery at the customer. The response time determines the ability to satisfy the customer's demand in a reasonable time. The power criterion is a rating (from 1 to 10) given by the sales team, reflecting their desire to keep a customer. A preference for specific customers may be due to their growth potential or their relationship with the company. The credit performance criterion is a rating (from 1 to 10) dependent on the customer's credit history. Clearly, clients with a good credit history will be preferred. This rating is given by a decision maker from the credit department. The distributor's reputation rating is based on the distributor's experience and service to the clients. This criterion ranges from 1 to 10 and considers the distributor's responsiveness, their skills, and their relationship with the clients/company. Higher rating values are preferred for all three criteria—credit performance, power, and distributor's reputation.

The problem presented here integrates strategic and tactical decisions to obtain a better supply chain performance. Integrated supply chains consider more than one decision level when modeling: strategic, tactical, or operational decisions (or any combination thereof). Strategic decisions are those that are typically made for the long term (e.g., years) and that are very expensive to alter at short notice. Tactical decisions are those decisions made quarterly/yearly, and the decisions that are made weekly or daily are considered as operational decisions. The integrated supply chain model presented in this chapter provides optimal DC locations to use and the capacities of the DCs as well as the flow of products in the distribution network. The optimal locations and capacities of the DCs are considered strategic decisions because contracts are required for leasing the DCs, and companies do not want to change locations frequently due to the high relocation costs. The actual distribution of the products to the customers in each period impacts the tactical decisions.

This chapter presents a mathematical model to select the best way of configuring the existing customers so that profit is maximized (and hence, distribution costs are reduced) while meeting other key criteria. A strategic-tactical model will be discussed in the next sections. Section 5.2 contains a detailed description of the deterministic strategic-tactical model, and Section 5.3 summarizes the applicability of this model using the case study described.

5.2 Literature Review

Designing a distribution network involves making a large number of decisions. Different researchers, such as Bachlaus et al. (2008), Portillo-Bollat (2008), and Solo (2009), among others, have already considered many of these aspects in the distribution network design process, mostly based on the number of warehouses and plants needed and their locations, production and inventory levels, and optimal routing plans. Supply chain optimization or distribution network optimization is the term used for most models that pretend to solve these decision-making problems. The research in supply chain optimization is very broad nowadays, but a small review on research related to this chapter is presented in this section.

Simchi-Levi et al. (2008) define supply chain management as a set of approaches used to integrate all the supply chain components efficiently, so that goods are produced and distributed at the right quantities, to the right locations, and at the right time, in order to minimize system-wide costs while satisfying service level requirements. In line with this definition is the research of Rabbani et al. (2008), where a distribution network design problem is presented in a multi-product supply chain system that locates production plants and warehouses and that determines the best distribution strategy from plants to warehouses and from warehouses to customers. Similarly, Wang et al. (2005) formulated a multi-echelon distribution network design problem with transportation and inventory considerations, in addition to the facility location problem.

Most supply chain models tend to minimize cost or to minimize cost while maximizing service level, but nowadays it is getting more common to include other criteria in the models. Portillo-Bollat (2008) modeled a multi-echelon supply chain design process, including facilities' location and allocation, capacity requirements, production and distribution network planning, and other international issues (such as currency changes), using multi-criteria selection techniques to integrate the following objectives in the model: financial, customer service, risk, and strategic factors. Bachlaus et al. (2008) integrated production, distribution, and logistics activities when designing a multi-echelon supply chain network aiming to minimize costs and to maximize plant flexibility and volume flexibility. Later, Bachlaus et al. (2009) integrated tangible and intangible factors into the design consideration of a resource assignment problem for a product-driven supply chain, formulating a multi-objective optimization model to maximize profit—ahead of time of delivery, quality, and volume flexibility. In addition, Solo (2009) developed a stochastic programming model integrating manufacturing and distribution decisions to maximize profit while fulfilling uncertain demand and minimizing supply chain response time.

The model presented in this chapter was developed by Cintrón et al. (2010) and Cintrón (2010), where a multi-criteria mixed-integer linear model was created to determine the optimal configuration of manufacturing plants, distributors, and customers in a distribution network based on several criteria: profit, lead time, power, credit performance, and distributors' reputation. Moreover, Cintrón (2010) also integrated a more operational model that makes the distribution decisions of supplying the customer demands and making the replenishment orders for the DCs while meeting the following criteria: maximize profit, minimize customer response time for filled orders, and minimize the number of stock-outs. This chapter will describe in detail the development of the supply chain integrated model that makes the strategic-tactical decisions of the DC locations and product flow from the plants to the customers.

5.3 Integrated Supply Chain Model

This chapter presents a mathematical model for designing the best distribution network so that profit is maximized while optimizing the other key criteria discussed in Section 5.1. The model also considers multiple time periods. This allows the company to plan for actions to be taken in future periods. That is, the model results show the time period when a DC should be used, its location, and its capacity. It also allows for expanding the capacity of an already opened DC in the future. Adding this type of dynamic decision makes the model more realistic and useful for companies.

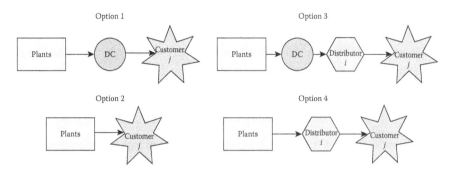

FIGURE 5.1
Distribution options in the supply chain.

The model considers four options that may occur when supplying a customer. These four options are illustrated in Figure 5.1. Let $S = \{1, 2, ..., n_S\}$ be the set of manufacturing sites, $R = \{1, 2, ..., n_R\}$ be the set of DC locations (already built DCs), $J = \{1, 2, ..., n_J\}$ be the set of customers or retailers, and $I = \{1, 2, ..., n_I\}$ be the set of independent distributors. The first option represents the situation when plant s sends the order to a regional DC r, and from there, it is then sent to customer j. Option 2 represents a direct shipment from manufacturing plant s to customer j. A direct shipment goes directly from the manufacturing plant to the customer, skipping the regional DC. In option 3, customer j is supplied by distributor i, and distributor i receives the products from regional DC r, which is supplied by manufacturing plant s. Option 4 represents the scenario when customer j is supplied by distributor i, and distributor i receives direct shipments from manufacturing plant s. Also, a set $K = \{1, 2, ..., n_K\}$ is introduced to identify the different vehicle types (e.g., van or trucks with different container sizes) that can be used to ship products from the DC to the customers and distributors. Each vehicle has a different cost and capacity (in pallets). The relationship between the vehicles' cost and capacities is discussed in Section 5.3.4. Finally, let $C = \{1, 2, ..., n_C\}$ be the set of possible DC capacities (in pallets) and $P = \{1, 2, ..., n_P\}$ be the set of time periods. The next subsections present the notations, the constraints, and the objective functions used in the strategic-tactical model.

5.3.1 Notations

5.3.1.1 Model Parameters

N_j	set of independent distributors that can supply customer j
M	very large number
cd_{sjp}	demand of customer j from plant s in period p (in pallets)
dd_{sip}	demand of independent distributor i from plant s in period p (in pallets)

D_{min} minimum demand necessary for direct shipments (in pallets)—if demand is less than D_{min}, a direct shipment is not possible

CAP_{rc} capacity c of DC r (in pallets)

$LTCC_{krj}$ transportation cost per trip to deliver from DC r to customer j when using vehicle type k

$LTCD_{kri}$ transportation cost per trip to supply from DC r to distributor i when using vehicle type k

vc_k capacity of vehicle type k (in pallets)

CC capacity of the containers sent from the plants to DCs (in pallets)

TCC_{sjp} transportation cost for delivering the demand of customer j directly from plant s in period p

TCD_{sip} transportation cost for delivering the demand of independent distributor i directly from plant s in period p

VCM_{sjp} variable contribution margin (selling price—product landed cost) of customer j for the demand from plant s in period p

VCM_{sip} variable contribution margin (selling price—product landed cost) of distributor i for the demand from plant s in period p

STC cost per customer incurred by the sales department (total salaries paid for merchandisers and sales representatives divided by the number of customers)

HCC_{sjp} inventory holding cost per pallet at the DC of the demand of customer j from plant s in period p

HCD_{sip} inventory holding cost per pallet at the DC of the demand of independent distributor i from plant s in period p

CPP cost per pallet position (DC storage costs divided by the DC capacity in pallets, fixed for all periods)

$WLOC_{rcp}$ fixed cost of operating a DC at location r with capacity c in period p

ILF inventory level factor; represents the fraction of demand (rate) withheld as average inventory

RC utilization level at which the DC is intended to be run ($0 < RC \leq 1$)

$DCLT_{rj}$ lead time from the DC r to customer j (in periods)

SLT_{sj} lead time from plant s to customer j (in periods)

DLT_{ij} lead time from distributor i to customer j (in periods)

P_j power rating for customer j, where $P_j \in \{1, 2, ..., 10\}$

CP_j credit performance rating for customer j, where $CP_j \in \{1, 2, ..., 10\}$

DR_i reputation rating for distributor i, where $DR_i \in \{1, 2, ..., 10\}$

5.3.1.2 Decision Variables

y_{srjp} 1 if option 1 is selected for customer j when receiving from plant s via DC r in period p, and 0 otherwise

t_{sjp} 1 if option 2 is selected for customer j when receiving from plant s in period p, and 0 otherwise

x_{srijp} 1 if option 3 is selected for customer j when receiving from plant s via distributor i, who is distributed from DC r in period p, and 0 otherwise

m_{sijp} 1 if option 4 is selected for customer j when receiving from plant s via distributor i in period p, and 0 otherwise

λ_j 1 if customer j receives product from a DC or the plants, and 0 if it receives it from a distributor

β_{sip} 1 if distributor i is supplied directly from plant s in period p, and 0 if it is supplied from a DC

α_{ij} 1 if distributor i supplies customer j, and 0 otherwise

γ_{krjp} number of vehicles type k (or number of trips) needed to supply the demand of customer j from DC r in period p, assuming that there is an unlimited number of vehicles

δ_{krip} number of vehicles type k (or number of trips) needed to supply the demand of distributor i from DC r in period p, assuming that there is an unlimited number of vehicles

IC_{sip} number of containers to be sent from plant s to distributor i in period p, assuming that there is an unlimited of containers

τ_{srip} 1 if distributor i receives the demand from plant s through DC r in period p, and 0 otherwise

ω_{rcp} 1 if DC r with capacity c is opened during period p, and 0 otherwise

5.3.2 Relevant Costs and Revenue Factors

One of the objectives or criteria considered in this model is to maximize profit. In this model, the profit is calculated by subtracting the distribution costs from the sales revenue. The revenue can be obtained by multiplying the variable contribution margin (VCM) of an option times the binary variable for that option. The VCM is the revenue obtained from the sales according to how the product is supplied (which option is selected for each customer per plant). If the product is sent directly from the plant or if the product is sold to the independent distributors, the VCM for these demands will have some discount. This is to encourage customers to receive direct shipments and to reward the distributors for storing and distributing the products of several customers.

The distribution costs include transportation costs, inventory holding costs, storage costs, and "customer service" costs. The transportation costs vary according to the option selected and the demand. If the product is sent directly from the plant, it will be sent only in containers and the costs will depend on the distance from the plant to the customer's city. On the other hand, when the product is supplied locally from the DC, there exist several transportation vehicles (e.g., a van that holds up to three pallets or a container truck that holds up to 30 pallets, among others). Hence, the transportation cost will depend on the type of vehicle used, according to the customer's demand, and on the travel distance between the DC and the customer location. This model assumes that orders from different customers are not consolidated when delivering orders because the model is used only for tactical decisions. The optimal arrangement of vehicles and routes for customer deliveries would require the development of another optimization model for operational decisions.

It is also important to consider other costs that are only incurred when the demand is supplied locally from the DC, such as the inventory holding costs and storage costs. These costs are considered in order to allow the model to select direct shipment whenever possible; that is, it is costs more to store products in the DC for distribution than to ship them directly from a plant. Because the VCM is lower when supplied directly, it is important to show in the model that, when demand is high, the profit is still higher when supplying directly rather than locally due to storage and inventory holding costs incurred at the DC. Another storage cost considered is the cost per pallet position. This is to "charge" for storing the product at the DC. The cost per pallet position is equal to the sum of warehouse storage costs (e.g., rent, salaries, pallets, and wrapping paper) divided by the maximum number of pallets that fit in the DC. Even though costs such as the rent and salaries are constant every month, independent of the size of the demand supplied from the DC, these costs are considered to force the model to use direct shipments. That is, in the future, if less demand is supplied locally, the DC can be replaced by a smaller warehouse in order to lower rental and labor cost.

Finally, the cost of "customer service" is considered. This cost is incurred when customers are supplied from the company, directly or locally, and not from the independent distributors. This is due to the fact that a company merchandiser has to go regularly to the customer stores to provide service. In addition, a sales representative is needed to negotiate with these customers and to prepare customers' orders. Hence, this cost is represented as that incurred per customer in the sales team, which is the sum of the salaries of the merchandisers and sales representatives divided by the total number of customers currently supplied by the company, including the distributors. This cost was included in the model to encourage low-demand customers to move to distributors. When a customer has low demand, its revenue or VCM is lower than the distribution costs (including the "customer service" cost); hence, it will be moved to the aggregated demand of distributors.

With the aforementioned revenues and costs, a profit function can be obtained. However, this is not an exact accounting profit but a representation of a profit according to the costs and revenue factors that affect the decisions to be made by the model presented in this study. This function is only used to obtain the best arrangement of customers and distributors in the supply chain so that "profit" can be maximized.

5.3.3 Shipping Considerations

The distribution to the customers in this region can be performed in three different ways: directly from the manufacturing plant, from the DC in the island (regional DC), or from an independent distributor. The shipping considerations for the different distribution options are as follows:

- *Manufacturing plant:* The manufacturing plants are located in North, South, and Central America. For customers to receive their merchandise directly from the manufacturing plant, they must order full container loads (in this case study, containers are assumed to be 53 feet long). These containers are all shipped by ocean because the region in this study is an island.

- *Regional distribution center (DC):* To serve the customers from the DC in the island, several ground vehicles can be used. The different vehicles used are vans, 12- to 26-foot-long trucks, and 40- to 53-foot-long containers. The smallest vehicle that is used would be a van, which can carry up to three pallets, and the largest vehicle would be a 53-foot-long container, which holds up to 30 pallets.

- *Independent distributors:* These distributors are all located in the island and deliver to smaller customers. The distributors all use the same ground transportation options that are used at the company's regional DC.

Figure 5.2 illustrates the different shipping options.

The vehicles at the manufacturing plants and at the regional DC are all loaded with pallets. The pallets may carry only one product or may have a mix of products. Figure 5.3 shows an example of a pallet load. In this case study, the demand is measured in pallets, and the individual product stock keeping units (SKUs) were not considered in order to reduce

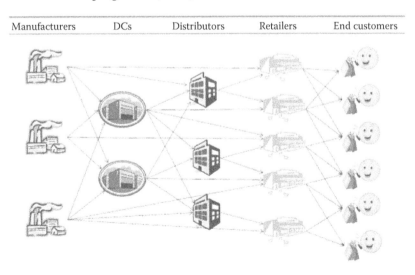

| Manufacturers | DCs | Distributors | Retailers | End customers |

FIGURE 5.2
Illustrative distribution/shipping options.

FIGURE 5.3
Pallet load examples.

the complexity of the model. (There are more than 300 SKUs, which would increase the model size too much.) Hence, the demand in pallets was calculated from the demand in cases before running the model, using the cases per pallet from the company's database.

5.3.4 Model Constraints

The model is formulated under the assumption that only one option may be selected per customer per plant for each period. Set N_j is introduced for each customer, which includes all the independent distributors that can supply customer j. Equation 5.1 summarizes the set of constraints that considers this assumption:

$$\sum_{r\in R} y_{srjp} + t_{sjp} + \sum_{r\in R}\sum_{i\in N_j} x_{srijp} + \sum_{i\in N_j} m_{sijp} = 1, \quad s\in S, j\in J, p\in P. \quad (5.1)$$

Another important assumption is that a customer may be distributed either from the company (i.e., a manufacturing plant or a DC) or from an independent distributor but not from both. Therefore, for each customer, options 3 and 4 may not be selected if option 1 or 2 is selected for a plant. This set of constraints is shown in Equations 5.2 and 5.3:

$$\sum_{s\in S}\sum_{r\in R}\sum_{p\in P} y_{srjp} + \sum_{s\in S}\sum_{p\in P} t_{sjp} \le M\lambda_j, \quad j\in J, \quad (5.2)$$

$$\sum_{s\in S}\sum_{r\in R}\sum_{i\in I}\sum_{p\in P} x_{srijp} + \sum_{s\in S}\sum_{i\in I}\sum_{p\in P} m_{sijp} \le M(1-\lambda_j), \quad j\in J, \quad (5.3)$$

where λ_j is a binary variable introduced to allow exactly one of the constraints (option 2 or 3) to be true for each customer $j\in J$.

In each period, each independent distributor may be supplied either directly from the plant or locally from a DC. Hence, only one of the options

(3 or 4) may be selected per distributor for each plant in each period. Equations 5.4 and 5.5 represent these constraints. The set of binary variables β_{sip} is introduced in these constraints, so that when $\beta_{sip} = 1$, distributor i is supplied directly from plant s in period p, and when β_{sip} is 0, it is supplied from one of the regional DCs.

$$\sum_{r \in R} \sum_{j \in J} x_{srijp} \leq M\left(1 - \beta_{sip}\right), \quad s \in S, i \in I, p \in P, \tag{5.4}$$

$$\sum_{j \in J} m_{sijp} \leq M\beta_{sip}, \quad s \in S, i \in I, p \in P. \tag{5.5}$$

In addition, a variable τ_{srip} is introduced to identify when a distributor is supplied from a DC. When $\tau_{srip} = 1$, it means that distributor i receives the demand from plant s via DC r in period p. Equation 5.6 indicates that only one τ_{srip} and β_{sip} can be equal to 1 for each period, plant, and distributor because, at each period, a distributor may receive the demand from a specific plant either directly from the plant or from only one of the DCs.

$$\sum_{r \in R} \tau_{srip} + \beta_{sip} = 1, \quad s \in S, i \in I, p \in P. \tag{5.6}$$

After identifying from which DC a distributor is being supplied, a constraint has to be introduced to relate this variable to the one related with option 3 (x_{srijp}). That is, Equation 5.7 makes the r value in the index the same in both x and τ.

$$\sum_{s \in S} \sum_{j \in J} x_{srijp} \leq M \sum_{s \in S} \tau_{srip}, \quad r \in R, i \in I, p \in P. \tag{5.7}$$

Another important assumption is that, in all periods, only one distributor may be selected per customer. This is because the decision of moving a customer to an independent distributor is a strategic decision. This means that if a customer is to be given to an independent distributor, the customer will stay with that independent distributor for the entire time horizon and cannot be a direct customer of the company anymore or be moved to another distributor. To represent this, binary variable α_{ij} is introduced, where $\alpha_{ij} = 1$ implies that customer j is supplied by distributor i. Equations 5.8 and 5.9 denote these constraints.

$$\left(\sum_{s \in S} \sum_{r \in R} \sum_{p \in P} x_{srijp} + \sum_{s \in S} \sum_{p \in P} m_{sijp} \right) \leq M\alpha_{ij}, \quad i \in N_j, j \in J, \tag{5.8}$$

$$\sum_{i \in N_j} \alpha_{ij} \leq 1, \quad j \in J. \tag{5.9}$$

The next set of constraints considers the minimum demand needed for a customer or a distributor to receive direct shipments from the plants.

Customers/distributors must have a demand larger than MD pallets for the specific plant. These sets of constraints are shown in Equations 5.10 and 5.11.

$$cd_{sjp} \geq MDt_{sjp}, \quad s \in S, j \in J, p \in P, \tag{5.10}$$

$$dd_{sip} + \sum_{j \in J} cd_{sjp} m_{sijp} \geq D_{min} \beta_{sip}, \quad s \in S, i \in I, p \in P. \tag{5.11}$$

The next set of constraints selects the best vehicle types from each DC fir each customer and distributor for each period so that the transportation costs are minimized. The transportation cost when the customers and distributors are supplied locally depends on the demand size; that is, different vehicles can be used with different capacities and costs. This means that the transportation cost for local supply is a step function. Figure 5.4 illustrates an example of the local transportation cost function, where the LTC_ks are the costs of using vehicle k and the vc_ks are the vehicle capacities. The model assumes that partial loads are charged at the full load capacity of the vehicle.

Equations 5.12 and 5.13 represent the set of constraints for vehicle arrangements.

$$\sum_{s \in S} cd_{sjp} y_{srjp} \leq \sum_{k \in K} \gamma_{krjp} vc_k, \quad r \in R, \ j \in J, p \in P, \tag{5.12}$$

$$\sum_{s \in S} dd_{sip} \tau_{srip} + \sum_{s \in S} \sum_{j \in J} cd_{sjp} x_{srijp} \leq \sum_{k \in K} \delta_{krip} vc_k, \quad r \in R, \ i \in I, p \in P. \tag{5.13}$$

For the distributors that receive their demand directly from a plant, two sets of constraints (Equations 5.14 and 5.15) must be introduced. These constraints determine the number of containers to be sent from each plant to each distributor in each period. A constraint in this set is only true if a distributor receives its demand directly from a plant (option 4). An integer variable

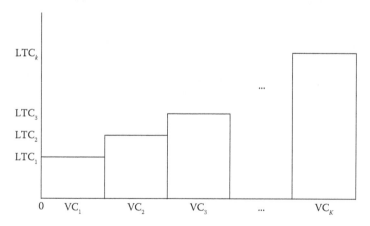

FIGURE 5.4
Step-wise transportation cost function.

is introduced to obtain the demand in containers by rounding up the division of the demand in pallets over the number of pallets per container (CC).

$$\frac{\left(dd_{sip}\beta_{sip} + \sum_{j} cd_{sip}m_{sijp} \right)}{CC} \leq IC_{sip}, \quad s \in S, i \in I, p \in P, \tag{5.14}$$

$$\frac{\left(dd_{sip}\beta_{sip} + \sum_{j} cd_{sip}m_{sijp} \right)}{CC} + 1 \geq IC_{sip}, \quad s \in S, i \in I, p \in P. \tag{5.15}$$

Finally, to have the DCs opened, additional constraints are introduced. First, two sets of constraints are used to show that, for a customer or a distributor to receive a shipment from a DC, this DC must be open. Variable ω_{rcp} is introduced in Equations 5.16 and 5.17 to activate τ_{srip} or y_{srjp} only if the corresponding ω_{rcp} is equal to 1 for each location and period:

$$\sum_{s \in S} \sum_{i \in I} \tau_{srip} \leq M \sum_{c \in C} \omega_{rcp}, \quad r \in R, p \in P, \tag{5.16}$$

$$\sum_{s \in S} \sum_{j \in J} y_{srjp} \leq M \sum_{c \in C} \omega_{rcp}, \quad r \in R, p \in P. \tag{5.17}$$

Then, a set of constraints is introduced to select the capacity needed for each DC. If a DC with capacity CAP_{rc} is opened, capacity CAP_{rc} must be greater than or equal to the average inventory at that DC divided by the capacity at which the DC is run. The average amount stored in inventory at a DC can be expressed as the inventory level factor (*ILF*) times the demand in that period. The *ILF* is the fraction of a period that is planned to be the average inventory level in the inventory review policy. This model assumes that the average inventory level used in the inventory review policy will remain the same throughout the entire time horizon. If the average inventory or *ILF* is changed, especially if it is increased, the model results may change. The other factor considered at the moment of selecting the size of a DC is the capacity at which it will be run (the running capacity, or *RC*). A DC should not be run at 100% because, if changes in demand occur, some space should be available to take care of those sudden changes. For this reason, the average inventory is divided by a factor *RC* in the capacity equation to make sure that the size of the DC considers the capacity at which it will be run. Equations 5.18 and 5.19 denote the capacity constraints for each DC location, allowing only one capacity or less to be opened for each location at each period:

$$\frac{ILF}{RC} \left(\sum_{s \in S} \sum_{j \in J} cd_{sjp}y_{srjp} + \sum_{s \in S} \sum_{i \in I} dd_{sip}\tau_{srip} + \sum_{s \in S} \sum_{j \in J} cd_{sjp} \sum_{i \in I} x_{srijp} \right) \tag{5.18}$$

$$\leq \sum_{c \in C} CAP_{rc}\,\omega_{rcp}, r \in R, \, p \in P,$$

$$\sum_{c \in C} \omega_{rcp} \leq 1 \quad r \in R, p \in P. \tag{5.19}$$

Finally, it is important to consider that after a DC at a specific location is opened, it must remain open or be expanded during the remaining time horizon or planning period considered in the model, but it cannot be closed. Equation 5.20 forces a DC to remain open or be expanded at period p if it was already opened during the previous period:

$$\sum_{c \in C} CAP_{rc} \omega_{rcp} \geq \sum_{c \in C} CAP_{rc} \omega_{rcp-1} \quad r \in R, p \in P\{1\}. \tag{5.20}$$

5.3.5 Objective Functions

This model considers multiple objectives. The criteria modeled are: profit, customer response time, power, customer's credit performance, and distributor's reputation. Equations 5.21 through 5.25 represent the five objectives for the integrated supply chain model.

- Maximize profit:

$$\sum_{s \in S} \sum_{j \in J} \sum_{p \in P} VCM_{sjp} \sum_{r \in R} y_{srjp} + \sum_{s \in S} \sum_{j \in J} \sum_{p \in P} VCM_{sjp} t_{sjp}$$

$$+ \sum_{s \in S} \sum_{i \in I} \sum_{p \in P} \left[VCM_{sip} * \left(1 - \beta_{sip} \right) + \sum_{j \in J} VCM_{sijp} \sum_{r \in R} x_{srijp} \right]$$

$$+ \sum_{s \in S} \sum_{i \in I} \sum_{p \in P} \left[VCM_{sip} \beta_{sip} + \sum_{j \in J} VCM_{sijp} m_{sijp} \right] - \sum_{k \in K} \sum_{r \in R} \sum_{j \in J} LTCC_{krj} \sum_{p \in P} \gamma_{krjp}$$

$$- \sum_{s \in S} \sum_{j \in J} \sum_{p \in P} TCC_{sjp} t_{sjp} - \sum_{k \in K} \sum_{r \in R} \sum_{i \in I} LTCD_{kri} \sum_{p \in P} \delta_{krip} - \sum_{s \in S} \sum_{i \in I} TCD_{si} \sum_{p \in P} IC_{sip} \tag{5.21}$$

$$- STC \left(\sum_{j \in J} \lambda_j + n_I \right) - \sum_{s \in S} \sum_{j \in J} \sum_{p \in P} ILF * HC_{sjp} \sum_{r \in R} y_{srjp} - \sum_{r \in R} \sum_{c \in C} \sum_{p \in P} WLOC_{rcp} \omega_{rcp}$$

$$- \sum_{s \in S} \sum_{i \in I} \sum_{p \in P} \left[ILF * HC_{sip} \left(1 - \beta_{sip} \right) + \sum_{j \in J} ILF * HC_{sijp} \sum_{r \in R} x_{srijp} \right]$$

$$- CPP \left(\sum_{s \in S} \sum_{j \in J} \sum_{p \in P} cd_{sjp} \sum_{r \in R} y_{srjp} + \sum_{s \in S} \sum_{i \in I} \sum_{p \in P} \left[dd_{sip} \left(1 - \beta_{sip} \right) + \sum_{j \in J} cd_{sijp} x_{sijp} \right] \right),$$

- Minimize response time:

$$
\left[\sum_{r\in R} \sum_{j\in J} DCLT_{rj} \sum_{s\in S} \sum_{p\in P} y_{srjp} + \sum_{s\in S} \sum_{j\in J} SLT_{sj} \sum_{p\in P} t_{sjp} \right.
$$

$$
\left. + DLT \left(\sum_{s\in S} \sum_{i\in I} \sum_{j\in J} \sum_{r\in R} \sum_{p\in P} x_{srijp} + \sum_{s\in S} \sum_{i\in I} \sum_{j\in J} \sum_{p\in P} m_{sijp} \right) \right],
$$

(5.22)

- Maximize power:

$$
\sum_{j\in J} P_j \lambda_j + \sum_{j\in J} (10 - P_j)(1 - \lambda_j),
$$

(5.23)

- Maximize credit performance:

$$
\sum_{j\in J} CP_j \lambda_j + \sum_{j\in J} (10 - CP_j)(1 - \lambda_j),
$$

(5.24)

- Maximize distributor's reputation:

$$
\frac{\left(\sum_{s\in S} \sum_{r\in R} \sum_{i\in N_j} \sum_{j\in J} \sum_{p\in P} DR_i x_{srijp} + \sum_{s\in S} \sum_{i\in N_j} \sum_{j\in J} \sum_{p\in P} DR_i m_{sijp} \right)}{MDR}.
$$

(5.25)

5.3.5.1 Non-Preemptive Goal Programming

Non-preemptive or weighted goal programming is used to solve the multi-criteria model by modeling the objective functions presented earlier as goals. Each goal uses a target value that can be set by the company. Non-preemptive goal programming allows for tradeoffs between goals or objectives and allows the decision makers to change their preferences easily (i.e., the decision makers' preferences can be easily changed by just changing the weights). In this chapter, the ideal values are used as the targets. To get the ideal value of each objective, a single objective model is solved, ignoring the other objectives (e.g., maximum profit, minimum response time, maximum power, etc.). Equations 5.26 through 5.30 represent the goal constraints of the multi-period deterministic strategic-tactical model. The goal constraints are scaled using their ideal values.

- Profit goal:

$$
\left(\sum_{s \in S} \sum_{j \in J} \sum_{p \in P} VCM_{sjp} \sum_{r \in R} y_{srjp} + \sum_{s \in S} \sum_{j \in J} \sum_{p \in P} VCM_{sjp} t_{sjp} \right.
$$

$$
+ \sum_{s \in S} \sum_{i \in I} \sum_{p \in P} \left[VCM_{sip} * (1 - \beta_{sip}) + \sum_{j \in J} VCM_{sijp} \sum_{r \in R} x_{srijp} \right]
$$

$$
+ \sum_{s \in S} \sum_{i \in I} \sum_{p \in P} \left[VCM_{sip} \beta_{sip} + \sum_{j \in J} VCM_{sijp} m_{sijp} \right] - \sum_{k \in K} \sum_{r \in R} \sum_{j \in J} LTCC_{krj} \sum_{p \in P} \gamma_{krjp}
$$

$$
- \sum_{s \in S} \sum_{j \in J} \sum_{p \in P} TCC_{sjp} t_{sjp} - \sum_{k \in K} \sum_{r \in R} \sum_{i \in I} LTCD_{kri} \sum_{p \in P} \delta_{krip}
$$

$$
- \sum_{s \in S} \sum_{i \in I} TCD_{si} \sum_{p \in P} IC_{sip} - STC \left(\sum_{j \in J} \lambda_j + n_I \right) - \sum_{s \in S} \sum_{j \in J} \sum_{p \in P} ILF * HC_{sjp} \sum_{r \in R} y_{srjp}
$$

$$
- \sum_{r \in R} \sum_{c \in C} \sum_{p \in P} WLOC_{rcp} \omega_{rcp}
$$

$$
- \sum_{s \in S} \sum_{i \in I} \sum_{p \in P} \left[ILF * HC_{sip} (1 - \beta_{sip}) + \sum_{j \in J} ILF * HC_{sijp} \sum_{r \in R} x_{srijp} \right]
$$

$$
- CPP \left(\sum_{s \in S} \sum_{j \in J} \sum_{p \in P} cd_{sjp} \sum_{r \in R} y_{srjp} \right.
$$

$$
\left. \left. \left. + \sum_{s \in S} \sum_{i \in I} \sum_{p \in P} \left[dd_{sip} (1 - \beta_{sip}) + \sum_{j \in J} cd_{sijp} x_{sijp} \right] \right) \right) \right)
$$

$$
\Big/ MP \tag{5.26}
$$

$$
+ \, d_1^- - d_1^+ = 1,
$$

where MP is the maximum profit (ideal value).

- Response time goal:

$$
\left[\sum_{r \in R} \sum_{j \in J} DCLT_{rj} \sum_{s \in S} \sum_{p \in P} y_{srjp} + \sum_{s \in S} \sum_{j \in J} SLT_{sj} \sum_{p \in P} t_{sjp} \right.
$$

$$
\left. + DLT \left(\sum_{s \in S} \sum_{i \in I} \sum_{j \in J} \sum_{r \in R} \sum_{p \in P} x_{srijp} + \sum_{s \in S} \sum_{i \in I} \sum_{j \in J} \sum_{p \in P} m_{sijp} \right) \right] \Big/ MRT + d_2^- - d_2^+ = 1, \tag{5.27}
$$

where MRT is the minimum response time (ideal value).

- Power goal:

$$\left(\sum_{j\in J}P_j\lambda_j + \sum_{j\in J}(10-P_j)(1-\lambda_j)\right)\Big/MW + d_3^- - d_3^+ = 1, \qquad (5.28)$$

where MW is maximum power value (ideal value).

- Credit performance goal:

$$\left(\sum_{j\in J}CP_j\lambda_j + \sum_{j\in J}(10-CP_j)(1-\lambda_j)\right)\Big/MCP + d_4^- - d_4^+ = 1, \qquad (5.29)$$

where MCP is the maximum credit performance value (ideal value).

- Distributor's reputation goal:

$$\frac{\left(\sum_{s\in S}\sum_{r\in R}\sum_{i\in N_j}\sum_{j\in J}\sum_{p\in P}DR_i x_{srijp} + \sum_{s\in S}\sum_{i\in N_j}\sum_{j\in J}\sum_{p\in P}DR_i m_{sijp}\right)}{MDR} + d_5^- - d_5^+ = 1, \quad (5.30)$$

where MDR is the maximum distributors' reputation value (ideal value).

With non-preemptive goal programming, the model minimizes the objective function (Equation 5.31), which is a weighted sum of the deviations of the goals. The ws in this equation are the weights for each criterion,

$$z = w_1 d_1^- + w_2 d_2^+ + w_3 d_3^- + w_4 d_4^- + w_5 d_5^-. \qquad (5.31)$$

Finally, the strategic-tactical non-preemptive goal programming model minimizes Equation 5.31 subject to Equations 5.1 through 5.20 and Equations 5.26 through 5.30. The goals are normalized using the ideal values obtained from solving the model with each criterion as a single objective.

5.4 Case Study: Results and Discussion

Real data from the case study described in Section 5.1 was used to list the applicability of the integrated supply chain model (Additional material is available from the CRC Press website: http://www.crcpress.com/product/isbn/9781498708586). The case study considered 24 periods, and each period was one month. The demand data used for this model were approximate monthly forecasts. The average inventory to be kept in the DCs is for two weeks; hence, the *ILF* is equal to 0.5 in this model. Also, each DC is to be run at 85% (i.e., *RC* = 0.85) of its capacity to keep a 15% of capacity available for emergencies.

Three DC locations were considered and three different sizes (capacities) were possible at each location. The three different capacities considered at each location were: 500; 1,000; and 2,000 pallets. The DC costs according to its location and size are shown in Table 5.1. The costs shown in this table are a sum of the general overhead costs and labor costs. The general overhead costs include: rent (or mortgage), property taxes, utilities, equipment (e.g., pallets, racks, material handling equipment, etc.), and security devices, among others.

This case study was run with General Algebraic Modeling System (GAMS) optimization software. Table 5.2 displays the model statistics (e.g., number of equations and different variables) to show the problem size. It took approximately six hours to run this model with an Intel Pentium Dual Core, 2 GHz processor with 4 GB memory, when using the actual data from the company. However, some parameters were changed for validating the model (e.g., weights, DC capacities and costs, and demand data), and the running time may vary according to the data. Depending on the data used when running the model, it could take from 15 minutes to up to 8 hours to run this model. The next section summarizes the results obtained from the case study.

TABLE 5.1

Cost of Each Distribution Center

	Capacity (Pallets)		
Location	500 (Small)	1,000 (Medium)	2,000 (Large)
1	$210,000	$250,000	$300,000
2	$200,000	$240,000	$290,000
3	$180,000	$210,000	$250,000

TABLE 5.2

Problem Size

Model Statistics	
Equations	21,915
Objective Function	1
Goal Constraints	5
Hard Constraints	21,909
Variables	180,647
Continuous	11
Discrete	180,636
Binary	156,036
Integer	24,600

Several scenarios were evaluated by varying the non-preemptive weights to show the multiple results to the decision makers. Tables 5.3 and 5.4 present the solutions of the different scenarios with their weights, goal achievements, and DC locations and their size. These results are shown to the decision makers so that they can decide which scenario represents the best strategy for implementation. Table 5.3 shows the results from the single objective models with 100% weight in one objective and zeros in the others (the highlighted cells are the ideal or optimal values for the respective objectives). Table 5.4 presents four more scenarios with different weights on the objectives.

It can be observed in these tables that changes to the weights affect the results. In Scenario 1, where profit is the only goal considered, the power and credit performance goals are close to the ideal values, but the response time and distributor reputation goals are not. This happens because only four out of 66 customers had power and credit performance ratings lower than 5 (two for power and two for credit performance), and no customers were moved to

TABLE 5.3

Results of the Single Objective Models and Their Impact on All Criteria

	Weights (Profit, Power, Credit Performance, Response Time, Distributor's Reputation)				
	Scenario 1 (1,0,0,0,0)	Scenario 2 (0,1,0,0,0)	Scenario 3 (0,0,1,0,0)	Scenario 4 (0,0,0,1,0)	Scenario 5 (0,0,0,0,1)
Profit Goal	$52,680,802	$43,388,000	$42,087,000	$34,439,240	$38,771,000
Power Goal	624	630	610	624	566
Credit Perf. Goal	502	496	506	502	476
Response Time Goal	30,334	30,320	28,839	6,375	26,755
Dist. Rep. Goal	0	1,920	1,920	0	12,480
DC 1 Size	500 for periods 23 and 24	500 for periods 1–5 1,000 for periods 6–8 2,000 for periods 9–24	500 for periods 1–3 1,000 for periods 4–6 2,000 for periods 7–24	2,000 for all periods	500 for period 1 1,000 for periods 2–3 2,000 for periods 4–24
DC 2 Size	500 for all periods	500 for periods 1–12 1,000 for periods 13–24	500 for periods 1–14 1,000 for periods 15–24	2,000 for all periods	500 for period 1 2,000 for periods 2–24
DC 3 Size	500 for all periods	500 for periods 1–5 2,000 for periods 6–24	500 for period 1 1,000 for periods 2–8 2,000 for periods 9–24	500 for periods 1–12 2,000 for periods 13–24	500 for periods 1–5 2,000 for periods 6–24

TABLE 5.4

Results of the Multi-Criteria Model for Some Scenarios

	Weights (Profit, Power, Credit Performance, Response Time, Distributor's Reputation)			
	Scenario 6 (0.45,0.2,0.19,0.13,0.03)	Scenario 7 (0.63,0.05,0.05,0.25,0.02)	Scenario 8 (0.72,0.05,0.05,0.15,0.03)	Scenario 9 (0.62,0.05,0.05,0.15,0.15,0.03)
Profit Goal	$46,043,021	$41,249,068	$51,416,463	$45,990,340
Power Goal	618	620	618	612
Credit Perf. Goal	425	504	425	498
Response Time Goal	9,148	7,223	11,883	9,051
Dist. Rep. Goal	1,920	1,920	1,920	1,920
DC 1 Size	1,000 for period 1 2,000 for periods 2–24	2,000 for all periods	1,000 for all periods	2,000 for all periods
DC 2 Size	500 for all periods	500 for all periods	500 for periods 1–4 1,000 for periods 5–24	500 for period 24
DC 3 Size	500 for period 24	500 for all periods	0	0

an independent distributor. Hence, the solution does not affect the power and credit performance goals significantly but makes the value of the distributors' reputation goal zero. On the other hand, the customer response time is drastically affected in Scenario 1 because every direct shipment from the plant that is possible and profitable is selected and each has really large lead times. In Scenarios 2 and 3, where power and credit performance are the only goals considered, all the goals, except for those of credit performance and power, seem to be affected. This is because when the other goals are not taken into account, the model selects the distribution randomly as long as the customers with power and credit performance ratings lower than 5 are moved to an independent distributor. When response time is the only objective considered (Scenario 4), it can be observed that profit and distributors' reputation are the most affected goals. This is attributed to the fact that everything is being supplied by the DC closest to each customer. Scenario 5, in Table 5.3, considers only the distributors' reputation goal. In this situation, the model selects all the customers that can receive from a distributor (e.g., customers in the N_j sets) and moves them to an independent distributor. This affects all the other goals—even the power and credit performance goals—due to the fact that customers with high ratings are moved to independent distributors only because they are allowed to receive from them.

In Table 5.4, it can be observed that, even though all the criteria are considered, the weight distribution affects the different goal achievements significantly. Scenario 6 represents the weights given by the decision makers initially. These weights were changed in Scenarios 7, 8, and 9, so that the impact of weights can be demonstrated to the decision makers in terms of the actual solutions. Figure 5.5 is a value path graph that shows the achievements of each goal under Scenarios 6, 7, 8, and 9 and allows a graphic view of the trade-off among objectives (a graphical illustration of Table 5.4 results). To construct this graph, the objective function values from Table 5.4 were scaled using the ideal values. That is, for the maximization goals (e.g., profit, power, credit performance, and distributors' reputation), the objective function values were divided by the ideal ones, and for the minimization goal (e.g., customer response time), the ideal value was divided by the objective function result. This converts all the values to numbers between 0 and 1 (with 1 being the ideal value); hence, the higher the number, the closer the solution is to achieving the ideal value (even for the minimization goals). These values were plotted in the graph and then connected by lines (for clarity) representing each scenario.

This graph helps to identify whether one scenario dominates another. That is, if one line has all its values higher than another line, it means that first line (solution or scenario) dominates the other. In Figure 5.4, no scenario dominates another because all the lines intersect with each other. Also, it can be observed that the five criteria are conflicting, especially profit and response time. The conflict between profit and customer response time can be easily identified by seeing that Scenario 8 has the highest profit but the

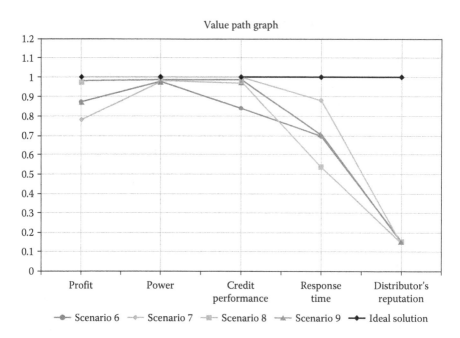

FIGURE 5.5
Value path graph of the scenarios in Table 5.4.

lowest customer response time achievement, whereas Scenario 7 has the lowest profit but the highest response time achievement.

In addition, more detailed results and comparisons can be obtained about each scenario's goal achievements from Table 5.4 and Figure 5.5. In Scenario 6, the profit weight is higher than those of the other criteria, the power and credit performance weights are almost the same, and the customer response time weight is not too far from the latter. The distributors' reputation goal has a significantly lower weight in all the scenarios, based on the decision makers' preferences. Scenario 7 has slightly higher weights for profit and customer response time but lower weights for power and credit performance. Scenario 8 includes a significantly higher weight for profit, a somewhat lower weight for response time, and significantly lower weights for profit, credit performance, and distributors' reputation. Finally, Scenario 9 is similar to Scenario 7, but it reduces the response time weight and increases the credit performance weight. From these scenarios, it can be observed that if the profit weight is not significantly high, the profit goal will be notably affected. The profit decreases by 10.5% from Scenario 8 to Scenarios 6 and 9 and by 20% compared to Scenario 7. In Scenario 7, the profit was also affected by the weight increase in the customer response time. Similarly, Scenario 7 shows the best customer response time among the four scenarios, but it affects the profit the most. It seems that these two criteria (profit and response time) are the most conflicting with each other. The power and credit performance criteria were never highly affected because in all the cases one of the two customers with low ratings for each criterion was selected. The distributors' reputation obtained the same value in all scenarios, which was that of moving two customers to an independent distributor. This criterion does not make any difference in this case study because the reputation ratings were the same for all distributors. Thus, the value path graph is a good way for the decision makers to visualize the trade-off among the conflicting criteria.

Scenarios 1, 6, and 8 were selected for detailed discussion in order to compare their solutions. Scenario 1 represents the model that most companies use—where only profit is considered as the objective function. Scenario 6 uses the weights that were selected by the decision makers when solving the model initially. Scenario 8 is also discussed because it shows a "most likely to be selected" solution where the profit is close to the ideal although the response time does not increase that much compared to Scenario 1. When the decision makers selected the weights used in Scenario 6, they were looking only at the criteria and their relative importance without knowing how these criteria would impact the final solution. However, when looking at the results of Scenarios 6 and 8, Scenario 8 will most likely be selected by the decision makers because they would probably not want to give up as much in profit for a small increase in response time.

The distribution plans obtained from the (profit maximizing) single objective model (Scenario 1) and the multi-criteria models in Scenarios 6 and 8 are shown in Figures 5.6, 5.7, and 5.8, respectively. The results shown in the figures are the averages (in percentages) for each distribution among all periods. Each customer may have a different distribution option in every period. To construct these figures, the total demand in pallets from all

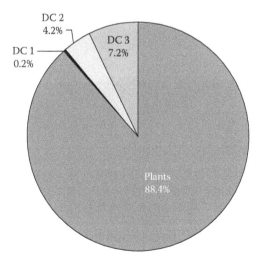

FIGURE 5.6
Scenario 1 model results (weights = 1,0,0,0,0).

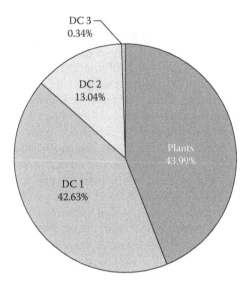

FIGURE 5.7
Scenario 6 model results (weights = 0.45,0.2,0.19,0.13,0.03).

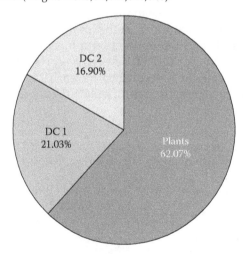

FIGURE 5.8
Scenario 8 model results (weights = 0.72,0.05,0.05,0.15,0.03).

customers was obtained for each period as well as the corresponding distribution option. Then, the average demand of all periods for each distribution option was obtained, and the four averages (for four different distribution options) were converted to percentages.

Some interesting results can be observed from these figures. First, looking at Figure 5.7, we see that, on average, only 44% of the demand is to be sent directly from the plants to the customers each month, while the profit maximizing single objective model (Figure 5.6) indicates that 88% of demand is directly shipped from the plants. On the other hand, the direct shipments from the plants suggested in Scenario 8 (Figure 5.8) are closer to the profit maximizing model results (Scenario 1). In Scenario 8, the DC at location 3 is always closed, and the DC at location 1 never expands to the largest size (see Table 5.5). This is explained by the fact that more direct shipments from the plants are recommended; hence, there is no need to have so much storage space at the DCs. However, because of the larger amounts of direct shipments from the plant, Scenario 8 has a higher profit than Scenario 6 at the expense of higher response time.

A comparison of the optimal distribution plans for Scenarios 1, 6, and 8 is shown in Table 5.5. In the model with profit as the only objective (Scenario 1), the results suggest opening only two DCs with the lowest cost at the beginning (locations 2 and 3 at the lowest capacity) and to open the location with the highest cost (location 1 at the lowest capacity) for the last two periods. On the other hand, the multi-criteria model for Scenario 6 opens DCs at locations 1 and 2 from the beginning (location 1 at the second capacity for the first period and the highest capacity for the rest and location 2 at the lowest capacity) and a DC at location 3 during the last period (at the lowest capacity). Similarly, the model for Scenario 8 opens DCs at locations 1 and 2 (location 1 at medium capacity for all periods and location 2 at the lowest capacity in the first four periods and at the medium capacity for the rest) and does not suggest opening a DC at location 3 at all. This difference in results occurs because the multi-criteria models consider customer response time as another objective,

TABLE 5.5

Comparison of Scenarios 1, 6, and 8

	Scenario 1 (1,0,0,0,0)	Scenario 6 (0.45,0.2,0.19,0.13,0.03)	Scenario 8 (0.72,0.05,0.05,0.15,0.03)
Profit Goal	$52,680,802	$46,043,021	$51,416,463
Power Goal	624	618	618
Credit Perf. Goal	502	425	425
Response Time Goal	30,334	9,148	11,883
Dist. Rep. Goal	0	1,920	1,920
DC 1 Size	500 for periods 23 and 24	1,000 for period 1 2,000 for periods 2–24	1,000 for all periods
DC 2 Size	500 for all periods	500 for all periods	500 for periods 1–4 1,000 for periods 5–24
DC 3 Size	500 for all periods	500 for period 24	0
Distribution from plants	88.4%	43.41%	62.07%
Distribution from DC 1	0.2%	43.21%	21.03%
Distribution from DC 2	4.2%	13.04%	16.90%
Distribution from DC 3	7.2%	0.34%	0%
# of customers moved to distributors	0	2	2

whereas the profit maximizing single objective model does not. Direct shipments from the plants have significantly larger lead times compared to those from a DC. Hence, when response times (and the other criteria) are included, the multi-criteria models seem to obtain a better objective function value (weighted sum of the deviations) by opening the DCs that are closer to the high demand points and delivering less from the plants as compared to opening the less costly DCs and also supplying more product directly from the plants. This makes the profit in Scenario 6 decrease by 13% (representing about $6.6 million) and the profit in Scenario 8 reduce by 2% (representing $1.3 million). Note that the profit calculated from this model is not an actual accounting profit but an approximate representation of the revenues and costs that affect the supply chain. In other words, the profit numbers obtained from this model are not the ones reported in the profit and loss statements.

Another difference, observed from Table 5.5, is that the single objective model does not recommend moving any customers to a distributor, whereas the multi-criteria models suggest doing this for two customers. This difference is attributed to the power and credit performance criteria. These two criteria have the second and third highest weights, giving them a higher chance to have an impact on the results.

The objectives considered in the multi-criteria model conflicted with one another. Non-preemptive goal programming with ideal values as targets was used to obtain the best possible solution that represented the decision makers' preferences. Because the criteria were conflicting, it was not possible to achieve any of the ideal values. Table 5.6 shows how much of each criterion was achieved and the percent difference from the ideal values for Scenarios 6 and 8. As can be observed, in both scenarios, the power objective was almost fully met but the credit performance was not met very much at all. This happened because very few customers had low ratings (two customers had power ratings below 5 out of 10 and two had credit performance ratings below 5 as well) and two of them were selected.

The profit goal in Scenario 6 did not seem to have such a high percentage of difference but, in dollar terms, it was a large amount. Even though the profit criterion had the largest weight in this scenario, the profit values

TABLE 5.6

Goal Achievements for Scenario 6

Goal	Ideal	Scenario 6		Scenario 8	
		Achieved	% Difference	Achieved	% Difference
Profit	$52,680,802	$46,043,021	13	$51,416,463	2
Power	630	618	2	618	2
Cred. Perf.	506	425	16	425	16
Resp. Time	6,375	9,148	43	11,883	86
Dist. Rep.	12,480	1,920	85	1,920	85

were significantly larger in magnitude than the other criteria's values—hence the large difference in the amounts. Also, in order to consider other objectives, the model recommended opening more expensive DCs and supplying less from the plants, which resulted in a large drop in profit. On the other hand, Scenario 8 used a much higher weight for profit; hence, the difference from the ideal profit value was not significant.

The customer response time criterion was affected by those customers receiving direct shipments from the plant. The ideal value for response time would be achieved if every customer receives everything from their closest DC. However, the profit objective forces some direct shipments from the plant, which increases the response time to customers. In Scenario 6, the response time goal was not affected too much (compared to Scenario 8) because the model suggested opening more or larger DCs (or both) to supply more demands from the DCs than from the plants. However, Scenario 8 recommended using more direct shipments from the plants and opening less or smaller DCs (or both); hence, the response time goal was affected more.

Finally, the distributor's reputation goal was not close to being satisfied in either Scenario 6 or 8 because the ideal assumed that all customers would be supplied by a distributor. Because this goal had a significantly lower weight, it did not have much impact on the multi-criteria model results. If the weights were to be changed, these results might change as well.

The discussion of the results of Scenario 6 with weights (0.45, 0.20, 0.19, 0.13, and 0.03 for profit, power, credit performance, customer response time, and distributors' reputation, respectively) is primarily for comparison. These weights are not necessarily the preferred solution for all decision makers, but they represented the initial preferences of the company's decision makers. Most likely, decision makers might not sacrifice so much profit ($6.6 million) and might pick one of the solutions with higher profit, such as the one for Scenario 8 with the (0.72, 0.05, 0.05, 0.15, 0.03) weight vector (see Table 5.4). It is clear that the customer response time objective affects the profit significantly. However, in this case study, the company is interested in maintaining good customer responsiveness; therefore, this plays an important role in the model as an objective. In some cases, different weights could also be applied, where the criteria weights could be different for customers. With this method, responsiveness could be considered as important as profit for major customers and not as important for minor customers.

5.5 Conclusions

The model developed in this chapter integrates strategic and tactical decisions when designing a supply chain distribution network. The strategic decisions are what distribution options and DC locations to use and the size of the DCs to be opened in specific time periods. The tactical decisions are the selection or planning of the distribution options to be used for each customer in each period. The integrated model considers conflicting criteria—such as profit, customer response time, power, credit performance, and distributor's reputation. In addition, this model also considers multiple time periods in order to make decisions for a given planning horizon.

The case study involving a consumer goods company, described in Section 5.1, was used to show the applicability of this model. The model was run in GAMS and took approximately six to eight hours to obtain optimal results with an Intel Pentium Dual Core, 2 GHz processor with 4 GB memory. It was shown that, when multiple criteria are considered in long-term decision-making models, direct shipments from the plant are not always the best supplying option even if the demand is sufficient. However, this will depend on the importance of each criterion. In Scenario 6, the profit criterion weight was not high enough to manipulate the decision of increasing the number of direct shipments from the plants. It could be observed that the multi-criteria model suggested that only 44% (on average) of the monthly demand should be supplied directly from the plants; whereas the model that only considered profit (Scenario 1), recommended direct shipments from the plants for 88% of the monthly demand. On the other hand, Scenario 8 used a significantly higher profit weight, resulting in supplying 62% of the demand directly from the plants. Also, the model considering only the profit does not propose moving any customers to the distributors—whereas the multi-criteria models do it for two customers. The latter decision in the multi-criteria models is influenced by the power, credit performance, and customer responsiveness criteria.

The different results obtained from this case study showed the importance of considering multiple criteria when designing and analyzing supply chains. To have an effective supply chain, several factors and criteria must be considered. Many researchers consider cost or profit as their only objective and fail to consider that response time and other factors (e.g., dealing with irresponsible customers that represent problems and implicit costs to the company). Also, using weighted non-preemptive goal programming allows changing the priorities of each objective according to the situation at the moment (e.g., in most cases, profit has a significantly higher weight, but in case of an emergency, customer response time may end up as the most important criterion). The criteria weights can also be adjusted by customer. For example, for important customers, response time could be as important as profit.

One weakness or concern in having a multi-period model is that profit and the other criteria values are considered only for a specific number of periods, and that the decisions to be made depend on the demands of each period. To take care of this, a demand sensitivity analysis should be used, such as a procedure to evaluate different demand patterns. This is necessary because the DC opening decisions are very dependent on when the large demands occur. Also, a scenario approach that deals with the demand uncertainty (e.g., actual changes in demand not changes in the demand pattern) should be used, such as discrete economic scenarios.

The multi-criteria deterministic model showed how effective it can be when making practical decisions in the marketplace. The model was developed to generate realistic planning decisions that consider the decision makers' preferences. Based on the results obtained for the case study, this model can be very helpful when designing a supply chain distribution network. The model serves as a support tool for the managers to make the important strategic decisions of opening new DCs and giving up customers to distributors. The model makes the strategic decisions of opening DCs, but these decisions can also be considered tactical because, for the opening of DCs in future periods, the model should be run again before that period to make sure that it is still optimal to open a DC at that moment.

References

Ambrosino, D., A. Sciomachen, and M. Grazia Scutellá. (2009). A heuristic based on multi-exchange techniques for a regional fleet assignment location-routing problem. *Computers and Operations Research*, **36**(2), 442–460.

Bachlaus, M., M. K. Pandey, C. Mahajan, R. Shankar, and M. K. Tiwari. (2008). Designing an integrated multi-echelon agile supply chain network: A hybrid Taguchi-particle swarm optimization approach. *Journal of Intelligent Manufacturing*, **19**(6), 747–761.

Bachlaus, M., M. K. Tiwari, and F. T. S. Chan. (2009). Multi-objective resource assignment problem in a product-driven supply chain using a Taguchi-based DNA algorithm. *International Journal of Production Research*, **47**(9), 2345–2371.

Cintrón, A. (2010). *Optimizing an integrated supply chain*. PhD dissertation, The Pennsylvania State University, University Park, PA.

Cintrón, A., A. R. Ravindran, and J. A. Ventura. (2010). Multi-criteria mathematical model for designing the distribution network of a consumer goods company. *Computers and Industrial Engineering*, **58**(4), 584–593.

Portillo-Bollat, R. C. (2008). *Resilient global supply chain network design optimization*. PhD dissertation, The Pennsylvania State University, University Park, PA.

Rabbani, M., R. Tavakkoli-Moghaddam, and H. Parsa. (2008). A new mathematical model for a distribution network problem in a multi-product supply chain system: A real-case study. *International Journal of Manufacturing Technology and Management*, **15**(1), 1–11.

Simchi-Levi, D., P. Kaminsky, and E. Simchi-Levi. (2008). *Designing and Managing the Supply Chain: Concepts, Strategies and Case Studies*. 3rd edition. McGraw Hill, New York.

Solo, C. J. (2009). *Multi-objective, integrated supply chain design and operation under uncertainty.* Unpublished doctoral dissertation. The Pennsylvania State University, University Park, PA.

Wang, X., X. Sun, and F. Yang. (2005). A two-level distribution network design based on inventory optimization. *Proceedings of the International Conference on Services Systems and Services Management,* **1**(1), 291–296.

6

Multi-Criteria Network Design in Health and Humanitarian Logistics

Nathaniel D. Bastian
The Pennsylvania State University, University Park, Pennsylvania

Paul M. Griffin
Georgia Institute of Technology, Atlanta, Georgia

CONTENTS

6.1 Introduction

Within the applications of health and humanitarian logistics, there are often multiple conflicting objectives or criteria that are important to the decision makers. Examples include designing a logistics network that serves the maximum number of people, responds in the shortest time possible, and targets those in need. There may also be objectives that are unique to health and humanitarian applications such as ensuring that there are not disparities in the outcomes (i.e., the solution is equitable for the population).

In this chapter, we present two examples of multi-criteria network design optimization models for health and humanitarian logistics. The first example is a model to optimize the design of a humanitarian assistance and disaster relief (HA/DR) supply chain network for military aerial delivery operations under uncertainty. In addition to optimizing the logistics costs, staging locations, procurement amounts, and inventory levels across a wide range of real-world, probabilistic scenarios, the proposed model enables decision makers to explore the trade-offs between military HA/DR aerial delivery supply chain efficiency and responsiveness. The second example is a model to optimize the network design for community health centers to serve at-risk populations in Pennsylvania. Additional details about both models may be found in Bastian et al. (2015) and Griffin et al. (2014), respectively.

The layout of the chapter is as follows. We first provide the background and literature review for the two applications. The HA/DR network design optimization model is then presented and applied to US military aerial delivery operations. The community health center network design model is then presented and applied to the state of Pennsylvania. Results are discussed for each example. Conclusions and future work are discussed in Section 6.4.

6.2 Background and Literature Review

In this section, we provide a brief review of the literature on humanitarian and health logistics, with special emphasis on network design.

6.2.1 Network Design in Humanitarian Logistics

Supply chain management (SCM) for HA/DR delivery operations is the process of planning, implementing, and controlling the efficient, cost-effective flow and storage of goods and materials, as well as related information, from the point of origin to the point of consumption for the purpose of alleviating the suffering of vulnerable people (Thomas and Kopczak 2005). Logistics in the HA/DR sector encompass several traditional activities such as the procurement, transportation, and warehousing of goods and services, as well as other specific activities such as disaster preparedness and planning (Van Wassenhove 2006). Network design emphasizes the optimal design of the HA/DR supply chain using mathematical models and methods to determine optimal strategies and policies for managing the supply chain (Ravindran and Warsing 2013). Important performance criteria include supply chain efficiency, responsiveness, and risk.

Characteristics that bring additional complexity and unique challenges to HA/DR delivery supply chain design and management include: unpredictability of demand in terms of timing, geographic location, type of commodity, and quantity of commodity; suddenly occurring demand in very large amounts and short lead times for a wide variety of supplies; high importance associated with response time; and lack of initial resources (supplies, people, technology, transportation capacity, and money) (Balcik and Beamon 2008). The flow of resources coincides with four main phases of disaster relief: assessment (minimal resources are required to identify what is needed), deployment (resource requirements ramp up to meet the needs), sustainment (operations are sustained for a period of time), and reconfiguration (operations are reduced, then terminated).

Given that HA/DR delivery supply chains usually operate in highly uncertain environments, they must be engineered and executed in shorter periods of time so as to provide relief to the affected population as soon as possible (Ratliff 2007). Further, inventory management in HA/DR delivery supply chains is affected by unreliable, incomplete, or nonexistent information about lead times, demand levels, and locations (Beamon 2004). In terms of distribution network configuration, the number and location of distribution centers is uncertain. This makes cost assessment difficult in terms of planning financial flows.

For the HA/DR supply chain network, there are three dominating costs: supply costs, distribution costs, and inventory holding costs. Unpredictable demand patterns increase the complexity of relief organization–supplier relationships, making them more difficult to foster than in the relatively stable demand environment of the commercial supply chain (Beamon and Balcik 2008). Further, supply procurement options generally cannot be evaluated before a disaster occurs. Thus, it may be difficult to control the cost of supplies. Distribution costs stem from the need to transport massive amounts of materials in a very short amount of time. Varied disaster locations lead to varied modes of transportation. The types of inventory costs include inventory investment, inventory obsolescence (and spoilage), order/setup costs, and holding (carrying) costs. Inventory control for supply warehouses in the relief chain is challenging due to the higher variations in lead times, demands, and demand locations (Beamon and Balcik 2008). Coordinating activities among various agencies for HA/DR is also a challenging issue (Duran et al. 2012; Ergun et al. 2014).

Relatively few studies have been conducted to optimize HA/DR delivery operations in terms of distribution center pre-positioning and inventory staging. Akkihal (2006) solves an array of mixed-integer linear program formulations to examine the strategic impact of inventory pre-positioning on delivery lead time of HA/DR operations. The model determines optimal locations for warehousing nonconsumable inventories required for initial deployment of aid. The objective of the model is to minimize the average global distance from the nearest warehouse to a forecasted homeless person.

Demand patterns, along with correlated variables such as population and hazard frequency, offer views of regional vulnerability to natural disasters. Similarly, Balcik and Beamon (2008) consider facility location decisions for a humanitarian relief chain responding to quick-onset disasters, where they develop an optimization model that determines the number and locations of distribution centers in a relief network and the amount of relief supplies to be stocked at each distribution center to meet the needs of the affected population. The model integrates facility location and inventory decisions, while considering multiple item types and capturing budgetary constraints and capacity restrictions.

Duran et al. (2011) develop a mixed-integer programming inventory location model to evaluate the effect that pre-positioning relief items would have on average relief-aid emergency response time. They find the optimal number and location of pre-positioning warehouses given that demand for relief supplies can be met from both pre-positioned warehouses and suppliers. They allow multiple HA/DR events to occur within a replenishment period, thus capturing the adverse effect of warehouse replenishment lead time. They also allowed the probability of need for each item to depend on both local conditions and natural hazard type. Salmeron and Apte (2010) developed a two-stage stochastic optimization model with the goal of minimizing casualties by determining location and expansion decisions of assets such as warehouses and shelters in the first stage and then determining the best supporting logistics decisions in the second stage. The second stage decisions classify the population in those that need emergency evacuation (critical), those that need commodities (stay-back), and those that are displaced (transfer). The stochastic optimization formulation helps model the inherent uncertainty.

Mogilevsky (2013) developed the Disaster Relief Airlift Planner (DRAP), which is an optimization-based decision support tool that determines optimal routes to deliver material given certain data such as disaster location and available airports, aircraft, and supply stockpiles. DRAP is formulated to minimize disaster material shortages while preferring to choose routes that reduce transportation costs (and delivery times) based on decision maker constraints and priorities. The model is also useful for helping determine the optimal aircraft allocation and positioning for HA/DR operations. DRAP can be used by logistics planners and decision makers to conduct trade-off analysis among routes with respect to transportation costs and demand shortages in very short time horizon logistics planning.

Relatively few studies have used multiple criteria optimization approaches for improving HA/DR delivery operations and logistics planning. As an exception, Park (2007) develops a multi-objective decision making model to incorporate the decision maker(s) value trade-offs in the disaster relief resource allocation problem. The decision window for resource allocation is the critical first 72 hours after the initial damage assessment has been made. Value-focused thinking was used to capture the value trade-offs, and the resulting value hierarchy is optimized via a mathematical programming model to solve the multi-objective resource allocation problem. In another study, Vitoriano et al. (2011) propose a goal programming model to provide decision support to solve the multi-criteria humanitarian logistics aid distribution problem, attempting to minimize costs and time of response while maximizing equity of distribution or reliability and security of the operation routes.

In addition, Bozorgi-Amiri et al. (2013) develop a multi-objective robust stochastic programming approach for HA/DR logistics under uncertain demand, supply, and costs (procurement and transportation). Further, the model considers uncertainty for the locations where those demands might arise and the possibility that some of the pre-positioned supplies in the relief distribution center or the supplier might be partially destroyed by the disaster. The multi-objective model attempts to minimize the sum of the expected value and the variance of the total cost of the relief chain while penalizing the solution's infeasibility due to parameter uncertainty. The model also aims to maximize the affected areas' satisfaction levels through minimizing the sum of the maximum shortages in the affected areas. To solve this bi-criteria problem, they formulated a compromise programming model and solve it to obtain a Pareto-efficient (non-dominated) compromise solution. The purpose of the model is to provide decision support on both facility location and resource allocation in cases of HA/DR efforts.

Recent developments in social media have been useful in facilitating humanitarian relief. For example, emergency response times can be reduced through the use of Twitter data (Schnebele et al. 2013; Tapia et al. 2013). Further, web-based mapping services such as Ushahidi and Crisis Mapping have taken advantage of crowdsourcing to get information to relief agencies in a more timely way (Zook et al. 2010).

Despite these recent studies, a critical gap in the literature remains in assessing the trade-offs between supply chain efficiency (i.e., total logistics costs) and supply chain responsiveness (i.e., supply delivery time, demand fulfillment) for aerial delivery operations in the entire military HA/DR supply chain network. None of these previous studies considered the delivery of HA/DR consumable aid via aerial delivery mechanisms. Further, none of these previous studies considered the trade-offs of response time, total cost, and amount of demand satisfied. Therefore, we seek to fill the gap in the literature while providing military HA/DR decision makers with strategic decision support using a multiple criteria decision analysis (MCDA) framework.

6.2.2 Network Design in Public Health

Providing comprehensive health care services to all the members in a community is important for the achievement of health equity and for increasing a community member's quality of life. However, there are many disparities that exist in health care services that affect not only individuals but also the entire community. Two important measures of disparity are not having a primary source of care (or lack of access) and a persistent lack of insurance coverage.

It is well known that having a source of primary care has many health benefits (Blumenthal et al. 1995) including improvements in health status (Shi 1992; Shi and Starfield 2001), fewer hospitalizations (Freeman et al. 1982), more physician visits (Okada and Wan 1982), more control over treatable diseases (Fihn and Wicher 1988; Lurie et al. 1984), and fewer preventable hospitalizations (Deprez et al. 1987; O'Connor et al. 1990). However, there are many persons who do not have a main source of primary care. This may be due to a lack of insurance coverage over a significant period of time, the fact that not all doctors take Medicaid patients, or because of a limited supply of primary care physicians where they live. According to "Kaiser Health Facts," the percentage of population in primary care shortage areas is 11.8% in the United States (Kaiser Family Foundation 2012). One of the specific goals of the Healthy People 2020 initiative is to "increase the proportion of persons who have a specific source of ongoing care" (HHS 2012a).

The number of persons without health insurance across the nation is significant. In 2011, 48.6 million Americans were uninsured for more than at least one calendar year, which is roughly 16% of the US population (Kaiser Family Foundation 2012). A persistent lack of adequate coverage makes it difficult for people to obtain the health care they need and, when they do get care, it typically leads to a financial burden on the individual.

Current policy efforts focus on the provision of access to health care and insurance coverage. Two examples include expanding federally qualified health centers (FQHCs) and relaxing eligibility requirements for Medicaid. Health care reform will provide $11 billion to expand FQHCs over the next five years (2013–2018), and beginning in 2014, Medicaid rules will be modified so that more people will be eligible for the program (Clemens-Cope et al. 2012; Dievler and Giovannini 1998; HHS, 2012b; Sommers et al. 2012). It is estimated that Medicaid enrollment increases under full implementation of the Affordable Care Act (ACA) will be roughly 37%; nationally, total enrollments will rise from 48.3 million persons to 66.4 million (Blavin et al. 2012; HRSA 2013a).

The FQHC Initiative is one program designed to improve access of primary care, particularly for needy populations (Adashi et al. 2010). These centers provide primary and preventive health care, outreach, dental care, some mental health and substance abuse treatments, and prenatal care, especially for people living in rural and urban medically underserved communities. More than 90% of FQHC patients live with incomes below 200% of the federal poverty limits, and more than 40% of FQHC patients are uninsured.

Expanding FQHCs increases access to primary care for those who currently do not have it. In addition, it can increase the availability of free or lower cost services for those who remain uninsured, which has the same effect as expanding coverage. Another alternative to improve coverage is expanding Medicaid by relaxing eligibility requirements. Medicaid is a state-administered health insurance program for low-income people—families and children, the elderly, and people with disabilities. Although it does not improve access, it is an effective form of coverage. For the state of Pennsylvania, the composition of users for FQHCs in 2010 was as follows: 26.5% were uninsured, 43.0% had Medicaid coverage, 9.3% had Medicare coverage, and 21.2% were privately insured (HRSA 2013b).

By many measures, FQHCs are improving the health care of the community. Research has found that they reduced hospitalizations, reduced mortality, reduced usage of emergency rooms, and increased visits to physicians (Dievler and Giovannini 1998; Okada and Wan 1982). It has also been found that FQHCs' quality of service is comparable to other types of primary care (Shi and Stevens 2007), and they may be cost-effective for Medicaid patients compared to some other sources of care (Dor et al. 2008; Stuart and Steinwachs 1993). Although 75% of uninsured persons in the United States report that they have a source of primary care, approximately 99% of FQHC users actually do have a source of primary care (Carlson et al. 2001). In addition, with the implementation of health care reform, the importance of FQHCs grows (Adashi et al. 2010).

There are a few studies that explicitly consider how delivering care through FQHCs compares to other alternatives. Griffin et al. (2008) developed an optimization model to determine the FQHC locations, the services to offer at each, and the capacity level of the services and facility. Okada and Wan (1982) tried to determine the effect of FQHCs and Medicaid service on health care through surveys, and Cunningham and Hadley (2004) used data from the Community Tracking Study and FQHC reports to compare the impact of expanding FQHCs on increased insurance coverage. Shi and Stevens (2007) also compared the primary care experiences of FQHC uninsured and Medicaid insured. Using three aspects of primary care experience: access, longitudinality, and comprehensiveness, they found that FQHCs could fill an important gap in primary care for Medicaid and uninsured patients. They also report that Medicaid insurance remains important for high quality primary care, even with the presence of FQHCs.

These comparisons of delivery alternatives, however, do not take into account the specific location of FQHCs to improve a particular measure based on geographic and demographic differences in communities. We develop an integrated model to examine the impact of increasing the current government budget for FQHCs in Pennsylvania and expanding Medicaid through relaxing the income eligibility limits. We consider the geographic and demographic differences in our model to consider the trade-offs between these two policies. The objective of this study is to find a balanced investment between FQHC expansion and relaxing Medicaid eligibility to improve both access (by increasing the number of FQHCs) and coverage (by FQHC and Medicaid expansion). The comparison is achieved by integrating mathematical models with several data sets that allow for specific estimations of health care need.

6.3 Multi-Criteria Network Design Optimization Models

In this section, we discuss the multiple objective mathematical programming formulations and results for network design optimization in health and humanitarian logistics.

6.3.1 Humanitarian Logistics Network Design—Military Aerial Delivery Operations

In the event of a natural disaster, military HA/DR aerial delivery planners and policymakers must make a series of quick decisions in an effort to provide humanitarian aid to the affected population as soon as possible. In order to facilitate this tactical- and operational-level decision making, strategic planners must fully understand the process flow of consumable aid for military HA/DR aerial delivery operations. Figure 6.1 depicts the military HA/DR aerial delivery process flow.

In this aerial delivery process flow depicted in Figure 6.1, HA/DR consumable aid is purchased from the vendor(s) and transported to HA/DR supply depot(s) (typically located in the United States). Next, the consumable aid is transported from the depot(s) to be pre-positioned at HA/DR staging locations around the world, where the consumable aid is stored. The consumable aid consists of food bars and water, both of which have extremely long shelf lives; hence, perishability is not a concern. In the event that a natural disaster occurs requiring HA/DR aerial delivery operations, the aerial delivery capability is immediately prepared for mission execution, and the consumable aid is transported and airdropped to the affected population.

In addition to the process flow, Figure 6.2 depicts the military HA/DR aerial delivery supply chain network. Upon examining the four stages of the

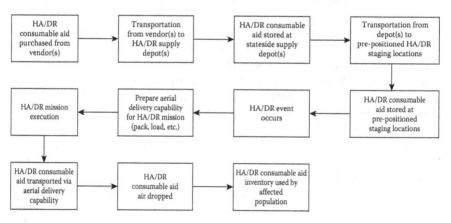

FIGURE 6.1
Military humanitarian assistance and disaster relief (HA/DR) aerial delivery process flow.

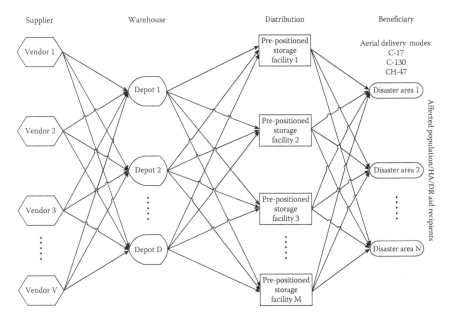

FIGURE 6.2
Military humanitarian assistance and disaster relief (HA/DR) aerial delivery supply chain network.

supply chain network, the vendors represent the suppliers, the depots represent the warehouses, the pre-positioned storage facilities represent the distribution centers, and the disaster areas represent the customers. We use this multi-stage supply chain network representation in Figure 6.2 to develop the stochastic, mixed-integer, weighted goal programming optimization model. This MCDA framework is used as a strategic-level planning tool for optimizing the military HA/DR aerial delivery supply chain network design.

In the MCDA framework, we incorporate several modeling methodologies to provide a robust decision support tool. First, we use goal programming to allow decision makers to systematically explore and examine different optimization problem criteria. The decision maker defines goals for each of the criteria considered and then evaluates the effects each of these criteria have on the global optimal solution. This methodology is particularly useful for strategic planning when incorporated with goal priority weights determined by the decision maker(s) (Bastian 2010). Second, we use design of experiments (DOE) to estimate the impact of the underlying factors causing uncertainty within the system. We use a 2^3 full-factorial DOE to model the interactive effects among experimental design factors; this approach helps identify robust alternatives over the set of probabilistic scenarios (Bastian 2010). Third, we use stochastic optimization to incorporate random elements into the model objective function and data parameters; this method provides more robust solutions to aid decision makers when optimizing under uncertainty (Bastian 2010). In this model, we optimize the expected value of the objective function (due to the probabilistic scenarios) and calculate many of the data parameters stochastically.

In this model, we assume that each delivery mode transports its maximum allowable capacity each trip and that all consumable aid onboard is delivered. We assume that each aerial delivery mode is capable of traveling the full distance required each trip in terms of flight crew and fuel (i.e., fuel is available en route, if necessary). We also assume that there is no limit on the number of hours flown for each aerial delivery mode. Finally, we assume that all pre-positioned aerial delivery assets are available to be used (if necessary, but number of trips may vary) to deliver consumable aid to the disaster area (aircraft will fly in parallel, as opposed to each aircraft waiting for the prior vehicle to return before departing with aid).

In the model, there are three goals: (i) meet a target total aerial delivery response time (in trip-hours), (ii) spend no more on total supply chain cost than a target budget, and (iii) ensure that the amount of consumable aid demanded and the amount actually delivered (i.e., shortage) be no more than a specified target. The disaster planning scenarios generated from the DOE are related to the impact of disaster; they are represented by expected consumable aid demand, days of food required, and supply chain disruption. Further, the model iterations refer to the affected area hit by the disaster (i.e., one iteration per each disaster area).

6.3.1.1 Humanitarian Logistics Network Design Model

The following are the sets, parameters, and decision variables used in the model.

Model Sets

V	set of consumable aid vendors (suppliers) with $v \in V$
D	set of consumable aid depots (warehouses) with $d \in D$
J	set of candidate storage facilities (distribution centers) with $j \in J$
N	set of high-risk disaster areas (beneficiaries) with $i \in N$
K	set of aerial delivery modes (aircraft types) with $k \in K$
S	set of disaster planning scenarios (based on impact factors) with $s \in S$
B	set of model iterations (mapped to disaster area affected) with $b \in B$
G	set of decision maker goals with $g \in G$

Model Parameters

p_{sb}	probability of occurrence of disaster planning scenario s in iteration b

w_g	decision maker weight for goal g
$Disrupt_{sb}$	supply chain disruption effect on supply chain costs in scenario s and iteration b
$Food_{sb}$	number of days worth of food to provide in scenario s and iteration b
Imp_{sb}	disaster impact above or below estimated demand in scenario s and iteration b
Dem_{isb}	expected consumable aid demand (pounds) per day at disaster area i in scenario s and iteration b
ds_{ij}	geodesic distance (nautical miles) from storage facility j to disaster area i
l_{dj}	geodesic distance (nautical miles) from depot d to storage facility j
Spd_k	average speed of aerial delivery mode k
$LoadDelay_k$	load time for aid (per trip) of aerial delivery mode k
t_{ijk}	travel time (per trip) from facility j to disaster area i via delivery mode k
r_{dj}	travel time (per trip) from depot d to storage facility j
OMF_k	operation and maintenance and fuel cost ($\$$ per hour) of aerial delivery mode k
$TDcost_{dj}$	transportation cost (per trip) from depot d to storage facility j
$TScost_{ijk}$	transportation cost (per trip) from facility j to disaster area i via delivery mode k
Atd	amount of aid (lbs) transported (per trip) (between each depot and storage facility)
Ats_k	amount of aid (lbs) transported (per trip) via mode k (between each facility and disaster area)
$IHDcost_d$	inventory holding cost (per lb) at depot d
$IHScost_j$	inventory holding cost (per lb) at storage facility j
$Pcost_v$	procurement cost (per lb) of consumable aid from vendor v
Cap_j	inventory holding capacity (lbs) at storage facility j
Cp_d	inventory holding capacity (lbs) at depot d
$Fcost_j$	fixed cost of opening storage facility j
Ntd_{dj}	maximum number of trips with consumable aid from depot d to storage facility j
Nts_{ijk}	maximum number of trips with consumable aid from storage facility j to disaster area i via aerial delivery mode k
ADM_{jk}	number of aerial delivery modes k pre-positioned at storage facility j
$TG1_{sb}$	target goal for the total aerial delivery response time in scenario s and iteration b
$TG2_{sb}$	target goal for total supply chain cost in scenario s and iteration b
$TG3_{sb}$	target goal for unmet demand in scenario s and iteration b

Model Decision and Goal Deviation Variables

X_j equals 1 if open storage facility j or 0 otherwise

Y_{ij} equals 1 if disaster area i is served by storage facility j or 0 otherwise

Z_{ijksb} number of trips with consumable aid from storage facility j to disaster area i via aerial delivery mode k in scenario s and iteration b

H_{djsb} number of trips with consumable aid from depot d to storage facility j in scenario s and iteration b

Q_{dv} amount of aid (lbs) purchased from vendor v for storage at depot d

Inv_j amount of aid (lbs) to store in inventory at storage facility j

In_d amount of aid (lbs) to store in inventory at depot d

pos_{gsb} positive deviation for goal g in scenario s and iteration b

neg_{gsb} negative deviation for goal g in scenario s and iteration b

Model Formulation

$$\min \sum_b \sum_s p_{sb}(w_1 pos_{1,sb} + w_2 pos_{2,sb} + w_3 pos_{3,sb}) \tag{6.1}$$

Subject to:

$$\sum_i \sum_j \sum_k t_{ijk} Z_{ijksb} + \sum_d \sum_j r_{dj} H_{djsb} + neg_{1,sb} - pos_{1,sb} = TG1_{sb} \quad \forall s \in S, b \in B \tag{6.2}$$

$$Disrupt_{sb}\left(\sum_d \sum_j TDcost_{dj} H_{djsb} + \sum_i \sum_j \sum_k TScost_{ijk} Z_{ijksb} \right.$$

$$\left. + \sum_j (Fcost_j X_j + IHScost_j Inv_j) + \sum_d IHDcost_d In_d + \sum_v \sum_d Pcost_v Q_{dv} \right)$$

$$+ neg_{2,sb} - pos_{2,sb} = TG2_{sb} \quad \forall s \in S, b \in B \tag{6.3}$$

$$\sum_i Dem_{isb} Imp_{sb} Food_{sb} - \sum_i \sum_j \sum_k Ats_k Z_{ijksb} ADM_{jk} + neg_{3,sb} - pos_{3,sb} = TG3_{sb} \tag{6.4}$$

$$\forall s \in S, b \in B$$

$$\sum_j Y_{ij} = 1 \quad \forall i \in N \tag{6.5}$$

$$\sum_i Y_{ij} = X_j \quad \forall j \in J \tag{6.6}$$

$$\sum_i \sum_k Ats_k Z_{ijksb} ADM_{jk} \le Inv_j \quad \forall j \in J, s \in S, b \in B \tag{6.7}$$

$$Inv_j \le Cap_j X_j \quad \forall j \in J \tag{6.8}$$

$$Inv_j \ge X_j \quad \forall j \in J \tag{6.9}$$

$$Atd \sum_j H_{djsb} \le In_d \quad \forall d \in D, s \in S, b \in B \tag{6.10}$$

$$In_d \le Cp_d \quad \forall d \in D \tag{6.11}$$

$$\sum_v Q_{dv} \le In_d \quad \forall d \in D \tag{6.12}$$

$$H_{djsb} \le Ntd_{dj} X_j \quad \forall d \in D, j \in J, s \in S, b \in B \tag{6.13}$$

$$Z_{ijksb} \le Nts_{ijk} Y_{ij} \quad \forall i \in N, j \in J, k \in K, s \in S, b \in B \tag{6.14}$$

$$Atd \sum_d H_{djsb} \ge \sum_i \sum_k Ats_k Z_{ijksb} ADM_{jk} \quad \forall j \in J, s \in S, b \in B \tag{6.15}$$

$$\sum_d Q_{dv} \ge Atd \sum_d \sum_j H_{djsb} \quad \forall v \in V, s \in S, b \in B \tag{6.16}$$

$$
\begin{aligned}
&X_j \in \{0,1\} \quad \forall j \in J \\
&Y_{ij} \in \{0,1\} \quad \forall i \in N, j \in J \\
&Z_{ijksb} \ge 0, \text{integer} \quad \forall i \in N, j \in J, k \in K, s \in S, b \in B \\
&H_{djsb} \ge 0, \text{integer} \quad \forall d \in D, j \in J, s \in S, b \in B \\
&Inv_j \ge 0 \quad \forall j \in J \\
&In_d \ge 0 \quad \forall d \in D \\
&Q_{dv} \ge 0 \quad \forall d \in d, v \in V \\
&pos_{gsb} \ge 0 \quad \forall g \in G, s \in S, b \in B \\
&neg_{gsb} \ge 0 \quad \forall g \in G, s \in S, b \in B
\end{aligned}
\tag{6.17}
$$

The objective function in Equation 6.1 seeks to minimize the sum of the three expected weighted goal deviations for target response time, target budget, and target demand met across all probabilistic disaster planning scenarios s and iterations b. The weights allow the planner to prioritize the targets. Goal constraints (Equation 6.2) ensure target $TG1_{sb}$ is met for the total aerial delivery response time (in trip-hours) for each scenario s and iteration b. The amount by which the first target is not met, $pos_{1,sb}$, is minimized in Equation 6.1. Note that $TG1_{sb}$ is set to 0 for all s and b because the decision maker wishes to minimize total aerial delivery time, which is a function of replenishment time between depots and storage facilities as well as the final disaster response time between storage facilities and affected areas.

Goal constraints (Equation 6.3) ensure the target for total supply chain cost ($TG2_{sb}$) with supply chain disruption factor is met for each scenario s and iteration b; target deviation is captured in $pos_{2,sb}$. The amount by which the second target is not met, $pos_{2,sb}$, is minimized in Equation 6.1. Note that $TG2_{sb}$ is set to 0 for all s and b because the decision maker wishes to minimize total supply chain cost. Goal constraints (Equation 6.4) ensure that the amount of delivered consumable aid shortage to the affected population including disaster impact and food factors for each scenario s and iteration b does not exceed the target $TG3_{sb}$; the amount of shortage above the target is captured in $pos_{3,sb}$. Again, the amount by which the third target is not met, $pos_{3,sb}$, is minimized in Equation 6.1. Note that $TG3_{sb}$ is set to 0 for all s and b because the decision maker wishes for the estimated demand to be met.

Constraints (Equation 6.5) ensure that each disaster area i is served by exactly one storage facility j. Constraints (Equation 6.6) ensure that if disaster area i is served by storage facility j, then storage facility j must be opened for pre-positioning inventory and assets, and that each storage facility j can only serve one disaster area i. Note that Equation 6.5 and Equation 6.6 are set partitioning constraints. From Equation 6.7, the amount of inventory to store at storage facility j must be greater than or equal to the sum of the product of the number of trips, the amount of consumable aid transported per trip, and the number of assets pre-positioned for every scenario s and iteration b. From Equation 6.8, the inventory is held only at opened storage facilities, and the amount of inventory kept at the storage facility j must not exceed its capacity. Constraints (Equation 6.9) enforce that if a storage facility j is opened, then inventory must be stored there.

Constraints (Equation 6.10) ensure that the amount of inventory to store at each depot d must be greater than or equal to the sum of the product of the number of trips (of a single C-17 aircraft) and the amount of consumable aid transported per trip for every scenario s and iteration b. In Equation 6.11, all depots are assumed to be open, but the amount of inventory kept at depot d must not exceed its capacity. In Equation 6.12, if consumable aid is purchased from the vendors for storage at depot d, then there is inventory for storage at depot d. Constraints (Equation 6.13) ensure that the number of trips with consumable aid from each depot d to each storage facility j must not exceed a specified maximum; note that this maximum is a function of a target total flight time budget value set by the decision maker.

In Equation 6.14, the number of trips with consumable aid from each storage facility j to each disaster area i via each delivery mode k must not exceed a specified maximum number; again, this maximum is a function of a target total flight time budget value by the decision maker. Constraints (Equation 6.15) ensure that the total amount of consumable aid shipped from the depots d to each storage facility j must appropriately backfill the total amount of aid delivered to the disaster areas i for each scenario s and iteration b. From Equation 6.16, the amount procured from each of the vendors v for storage at all of the depots d must be greater than or equal to the total amount of aid shipped out of depot d for each scenario s and iteration b. In Equation 6.17, we have the binary, integer, and nonnegativity decision variable constraints.

As part of the MCDA framework, we incorporated a 2^3 full-factorial experimental design as a mechanism to help mitigate uncertainty associated with consumable aid demand as well as the effects of supply chain disruption on total supply chain costs. By exploring three different design factors (each at two levels), we generate eight different disaster planning scenarios that are combinatorially applied to each of the disaster areas in the military HA/DR supply chain network. Note that each of these disaster areas represents a unique model iteration, making sb scenario-iteration pairs.

6.3.1.2 Military Humanitarian Logistics Network Design for Aerial Delivery Operations

In this example, clustering methods were used to determine eight foreign disaster areas (beneficiaries): Haiti, Indonesia, Mexico, Tanzania, India, China, Australia, and Peru. In addition, there are 10 possible servicing storage facilities (distribution centers) at pre-positioned US Air Force bases around the world: Ramstein, Charlotte, McChord, Hickam, Yokata, Incirlik, Osan, Ali Al Salem, Soto Cano, and MacDill. Two consumable aid depots (warehouses) are considered at pre-positioned, stateside US Marine Corps bases: Albany and Barstow. These depots procure from three consumable aid vendors (suppliers) located in the United States. Finally, three air transportation modes for consumable aid aerial delivery are considered: C-17s, C-130s, and CH-47s. Ordinary least squares multiple regression was used to estimate the total number of affected people per year. Additional details on the data and methods used to populate the network design optimization model may be found in Bastian et al. (2015).

The three factors included in the 2^3 full-factorial DOE were Imp_{sb}, $Food_{sb}$, and $Disrupt_{sb}$. Imp_{sb} represents a disaster impact factor that adjusts the estimated expected consumable aid demand in each scenario s and iteration b up or down by 25% to account for the deviation from expected impact. $Food_{sb}$ represents a days of food factor that adjusts the estimated expected consumable aid demand in scenario s and iteration b by the number of days worth of food to provide for each affected person; this factor is also varied at two levels (7 or 14 days' worth of food). Note that these first two DOE factors address uncertainty involving the amount of beneficiary demand, affecting both supply chain efficiency and responsiveness. $Disrupt_{sb}$ represents a supply chain disruption impact factor to better account for uncertainty in supply chain costs for each scenario s and iteration b, while also increasing the robustness of the supply chain network design. We assume that supply chain disruptions (such as aerial delivery weather delays and maintenance issues) will affect supply chain processes associated with transportation and storage of consumable aid, which is reflected in the overall supply chain costs. Therefore, this factor increases the total supply chain costs by 0% (low risk) and 11% (high risk).

To implement the MCDA framework for solving the multi-criteria military HA/DR aerial delivery supply chain network design optimization problem under uncertainty, we leveraged the General Algebraic Modeling System (GAMS), Microsoft Excel, and Microsoft Visual Basic for Applications (VBA) platforms. In particular, we used GAMS v.23.9.3 with IBM ILOG Cplex 12.4.0.1 to solve the stochastic, mixed-integer weighted goal programming model, and we used Excel/VBA to create an automatic, user-friendly interface with the decision maker for model input and analysis of model output. The following best compromise solution to the computational experiment was solved in 0.499 seconds on a Lenovo Thinkpad W510 laptop with an Intel i7 CPU (1.6 GHz) and 8.00 GB of RAM.

In the following solution, the decision maker heavily weighted the third goal to place significant priority on meeting the estimated expected consumable aid demand across all high-risk disaster areas. Note that the solution depends upon the pseudo-random number generator seed in GAMS. Table 6.1 highlights which storage facilities were opened, the amount of pre-positioned inventory to store, and the number of required trips by each aerial delivery mode.

Given that each storage facility must serve exactly one disaster area, the results in Table 6.1 indicate that eight of the ten candidate storage facilities are opened for pre-positioning both aerial assets and consumable aid inventory; note that the US Air Force bases in Kuwait and Honduras should not be opened as part the optimal supply chain network design. Table 6.2 shows the amount of inventory to store at each of the stateside Marine Corps logistics bases as well as the breakdown of the amount procured from each of the three consumable aid vendors.

These results in Table 6.2 indicate that both depots in the supply chain network are used to store inventory stateside, but it is clear that the depot in Albany is utilized more heavily. Further, only one of the three vendors supplies consumable aid to both depots.

Table 6.3 depicts which global disaster areas (representing high-risk geographic regions) are served by which opened storage facilities.

TABLE 6.1

Results for Storage Facility Locations, Inventory, and Trips

Storage Facility Name	Opened	Inventory	Number of Trips		
Ramstein Air Base (Germany)	1	665,600	4	2	0
Charlotte Air National Guard Base (North Carolina, USA)	1	832,000	3	5	0
McChord Air Force Base (Washington, USA)	1	896,000	4	5	0
Hickam Air Force Base (Hawaii, USA)	1	769,600	3	2	1
Yokota Air Base (Japan)	1	640,000	3	5	0
Incirlik Air Base (Turkey)	1	588,800	3	4	0
Osan Air Base (South Korea)	1	563,200	2	4	0
Ali Al Salem Air Base (Kuwait)	0	0	0	0	0
Soto Cano Air Base (Honduras)	0	0	0	0	0
MacDill Air Force Base (Florida, USA)	1	435,200	5	7	0
			C-17	*C-130*	*CH-47*

TABLE 6.2

Results for Depot Inventory and Vendor Procurement

Depot Name	Inventory	Amount Procured from Vendors		
Marine Corps Logistics Base Albany	14,208,000	3,072,000	5,568,000	5,568,000
Marine Corps Logistics Base Barstow	2,496,000	2,496,000	0	0
		V1	*V2*	*V3*

TABLE 6.3

Results for Disaster Area and Storage Facility Assignments

Disaster Area (Geographic Region)	Servicing Storage Facility
Haiti (Caribbean)	MacDill Air Force Base (Florida, USA)
Indonesia (South-Eastern Asia)	Osan Air Base (South Korea)
Mexico (Central America)	McChord Air Force Base (Washington, USA)
Tanzania (Eastern Africa)	Ramstein Air Base (Germany)
India (Southern Asia)	Incirlik Air Base (Turkey)
China (Eastern Asia)	Yokota Air Base (Japan)
Australia (Australia and New Zealand)	Hickam Air Force Base (Hawaii, USA)
Peru (South America)	Charlotte Air National Guard Base (North Carolina, USA)

From these best compromise solution results, Figure 6.3 provides a visual illustration of the optimal military HA/DR aerial delivery supply chain network design. Upon investigating the trade-offs of supply chain efficiency versus responsiveness for this best compromise solution to the multiple criteria problem, the goal deviation variables provided critical information about response time, cost, and demand unmet for every scenario *s* and iteration *b*. In particular, this supply chain network design provided an average total aerial delivery response time (across all disaster areas) of roughly six days, an average total supply chain cost (across all stages of the supply chain network) of roughly $153 billion, and an average total demand shortage (across all disaster areas) of roughly 47 million pounds. Moreover, this supply chain network design provided identical median values for the response time and cost, but the median total demand shortage equaled 0; in fact, there were only eight of the 64 scenario-iteration combinations (13%) where the demand was unmet.

Although not presented here, we leveraged the sample average approximation (SAA) method within the MCDA framework to better estimate the optimal solution to the stochastic goal program, given that many of the parameters were computed by randomly sampling from a prior probability distribution. In particular, the decision maker uses the MCDA framework to run the optimization model for 30 separate instances to obtain 30 optimal solutions; the average of these solutions provides an unbiased estimate of the true optimal solution. The MCDA framework uses the results of the SAA method to construct statistical lower and upper bounds.

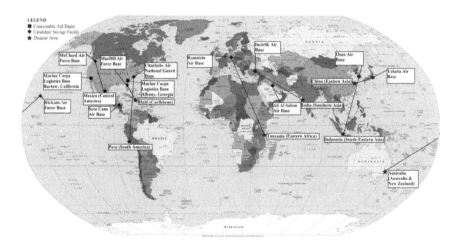

FIGURE 6.3
Optimal military humanitarian assistance and disaster relief (HA/DR) aerial delivery supply chain network design.

This approach served as strategic decision support by helping the decision maker to better understand the range of possible best compromise solutions to the multi-criteria military HA/DR aerial delivery supply chain network design problem.

6.3.2 Public Health Network Design—Federally Qualified Health Centers

Health status disparities can be addressed better if the population is prioritized according to current access and coverage status. Table 6.4 shows six population groups according to their current access status (served and underserved) and coverage status (private, public, and persistent lack of insurance [uninsured]).

We define an individual as being underserved if they live in a health professional shortage area (HPSA) as defined by the HRSA (2013a). Several studies have found that persons who live in an HPSA have poorer health outcomes compared to their counterparts (Brown et al. 2011; Kohrs and Mainous 1995; Liu 2007), even after controlling for sociodemographic factors. On the other hand, some studies have found no difference in health outcomes between these two groups (Kohrs and Mainous 1996). Further, because there are many different sources of health care, not all persons in the region that is an HPSA will have limited access. However, by its very definition, on average an individual living in an HPSA will have access to fewer health professionals than those that do not. We therefore use HPSA designation as a proxy for being underserved.

An individual is defined as having a persistent lack of insurance if they have been uninsured for at least one year. From this point on, we simply use the term uninsured. The primary components of public insurance are Medicaid and Medicare.

We introduce a multi-objective model to decide the optimal FQHC locations considering population groups with different priorities. Demand is estimated based on current access and coverage status. Details of demand estimate are given in Griffin et al. (2014).

TABLE 6.4

Population Groups by Access and Coverage

	Coverage		
Access	**No Insurance**	**Public Insurance**	**Private Insurance**
Underserved	①	②	③
Served	④	⑤	⑥

6.3.2.1 Public Health Network Design Model

The following are the indices, parameters, and decision variables used in the model.

Model Indices

i	FQHC location
z	Population location
j	Service type (General, OBGyn, Dental, Mental)
k	Capacity (Small, Medium, Large)
l	Distance level (0, 10 miles, 20 miles, 30 miles)
g_1	Insurance group (Private, Public, Uninsured)
g_2	Access (Access, No access)

Model Parameters

FL	Fixed cost per location
FS_k	Fixed cost per capacity level
VS_j	Variable cost per service
RB_{g1}	Reimbursement rate
CAP_{jk}	Number of patients of service type j that can be served at level k
w_i	Weight by service type j
P_l	Maximum percentage of z's population that can be served at distance level l
$n_{zjg_1g_2}$	Demand for service j in county z of insurance and access group
$m_{izjg_1g_2}$	Maximum demand of county z can be served CHC located county i ($=P_l n_{zjg_1g_2}$, if the distance between i and z corresponds to level l, 0 otherwise)
I_{izl}	Binary parameter equal to 1 if the distance level between i and z is greater than l, 0 otherwise

Model Decision Variables

y_{izj}	Number of encounters from county z served by FQHC in county i for service j
s_{ijk}	Binary variable equal to 1 if county i has FQHC with service j at capacity k
c_i	Number of FQHC centers in location i
$y_{izjg_1g_2}$	Number of encounters by insurance group g_1 and access group g_2 in county z served by FQHC in county i for service j

We categorize demand by insurance and access group, which makes it possible to use multiple objectives based on the groups. We set the first priority to maximize insurance coverage (Equation 6.18), which is the sum of encounters of the uninsured population ($g_1 = 3$). The second priority is to maximize access (Equation 6.19), which is from the underserved population ($g_2 = 2$). Finally, we maximize the utilization of FQHCs by providing the most weighted services (Equation 6.20). These weights were based on the odds ratios from a logistic regression performed on National Health and

Nutrition Examination Survey (NHANES) data, where self-reported general health (poor, fair, good, excellent) was used as the dependent variable. The weights used are shown in Table 6.5, and the details of the regression are provided in Griffin et al. (2008).

Model Formulation
  Objective:

$$\text{1st objective (Max Coverage): max} \sum_{i,z,j,g_2,g_1=3} w_j y_{izjg_1g_2} \tag{6.18}$$

$$\text{2nd objective (Max Access): max} \sum_{i,z,j,g_1,g_2=2} w_j y_{izjg_1g_2} \tag{6.19}$$

$$\text{3rd objective (Max Utilization): max} \sum_{i,z,j,g_1,g_2} w_j y_{izjg_1g_2} \tag{6.20}$$

Subject to:

$$y_{izjg_1g_2} = y_{izj} \times \frac{n_{zjg_1g_2}}{\sum_{g_1g_2} n_{zjg_1g_2}} \quad \text{for} \quad i,z,j,g_1,g_2 \tag{6.21}$$

$$\sum_i FLc_i + \sum_{ijk} FS_k s_{ijk} + \sum_{izjg_1g_2} VS_j\, RB_{g_1}\, y_{izjg_1g_2} \leq B \tag{6.22}$$

$$\sum_z y_{izj} \leq \sum_k CAP_{jk} s_{ijk} \quad \text{for} \quad i,j \tag{6.23}$$

$$\sum_k s_{ijk} \leq c_i \quad \text{for} \quad i,j \tag{6.24}$$

$$\sum_i I_{izl} y_{izj} \leq P_l \sum_{g_1,g_2} n_{zjg_1g_2} \quad \text{for} \quad l,z,j \tag{6.25}$$

TABLE 6.5

Adjusted Weights for the Four Service Types

	Primary (w_1)	OBGyN (w_2)	Dental (w_3)	Mental (w_4)	Total
Weights	0.88	1.20	0.07	0.05	2.20
Normalized weights	0.40	0.55	0.03	0.02	1.00

Source: Griffin PM, et al. *IIE Transactions*, 40(9), 880–892, 2008.

$$y_{izj} \leq \sum_{g_1, g_2} m_{izjg_1g_2} \quad \text{for only } i, z, j \tag{6.26}$$

To define decision variable $Y_{izjg_1g_2}$, we assume that the proportion of each group in FQHC encounters will follow the same rate of estimated demand at the population location (Equation 6.21). This variable is defined by the ratio of each group in the estimated demand ($n_{zjg_1g_2}$) at the location to the total number of encounters (y_{izj}). Constraint (Equation 6.22) restricts the total spending on fixed costs for locating FQHCs, fixed costs for capacity, and variable costs for services to be no greater than a given budget B. Constraint (Equation 6.23) ensures that for each service type (General, OBGyn, Dental, and Mental) the number of patients served does not exceed the capacity for that service. Constraint (Equation 6.24) ensures that services can only be provided at a location if there is capacity established at the location for that service. Constraint (Equation 6.25) ensures that service is provided to a patient only if they are eligible for that service and live close enough to the facility to access it. It is implied in this constraint that the likelihood a patient visits an FQHC decreases linearly in distance from the facility. Finally, constraint (Equation 6.26) ensures that the number of patients served in a county for each service type does not exceed the number of persons that require that service.

6.3.2.2 Public Health Network Design for Pennsylvania

We apply the model for data for the state of Pennsylvania and use a preemptive optimization approach based on the order given for the objective functions. The optimal locations given for the FQHCs for Pennsylvania from this example are shown in Figure 6.4. In this example, the budget is $300M, and the resulting served population is 1,456,641 persons. The "•" locations are from the multi-objective solution and the "x" solutions are for the case where only the single objective of utilization (Equation 6.20) was used. In Figure 6.4a, access status is shown by county. The darker the shading, the poorer is the access for an average person in the county. Similarly, Figure 6.4b shows coverage; darker shaded counties have poorer coverage status. As can be seen from the figure, the optimal solution using the multi-objective tends to place FQHCs in darker shaded regions and clearly outperforms the single objective solution, showing the value of a multi-criteria framework.

6.3.2.3 Discussion

The optimization framework presented here can be used by policymakers to estimate the impact of certain changes. For example, the Medicaid expansion from the ACA that started in 2014 will significantly increase demand for FQHC services. One estimate is that the number of Medicaid beneficiaries being served by FQHCs in the United States will increase from 7.5 million in 2010

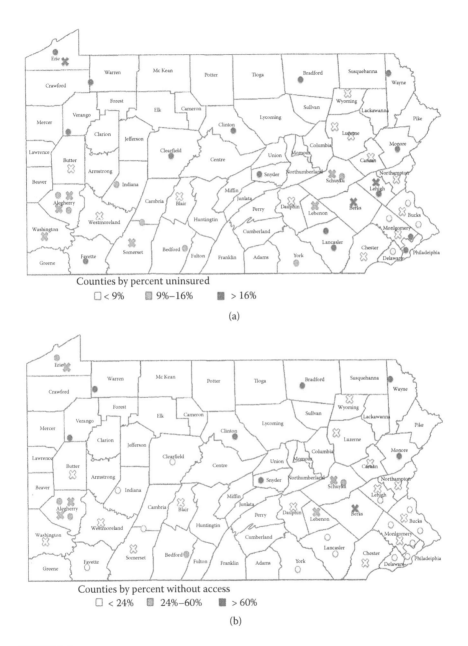

Counties by percent uninsured

☐ < 9%   ▨ 9%–16%   ■ > 16%

(a)

Counties by percent without access

☐ < 24%   ▨ 24%–60%   ■ > 60%

(b)

FIGURE 6.4
Federally qualified health center (FQHC) optimal locations comparing (a) current access status and (b) current coverage status.

to more than 18 million in 2015 (NACHC 2012). The optimization model could be solved directly to determine the impact on the current FQHC network and how to best expand that network to meet the demand. The payment scheme for FQHCs by Medicaid will also change (HHS 2012c). In 2014, state Medicaid agencies will reimburse FQHCs for services based on a per visit rate based on a prospective payment system (PPS). Further, if an FQHC contracts with a managed care organization (MCO) to serve Medicaid patients, the FQHC must be paid by the MCO at the same rate that it pays other providers. If the MCO rate is less than the PPS rate, then the state must provide a "wrap around" payment up to the PPS rate. This provides significant revenue opportunities for FQHCs, which is particularly important because grants will likely decrease in the near future. The variable cost component used in the optimization model can be easily modified to account for these changes in order to model FQHC expansion.

6.4 Conclusions

In this chapter, we have shown two examples of multi-criteria network design optimization in health and humanitarian logistics applications. Because neither of these areas is profit-based, the use of multiple objectives is extremely important. Although cost could be used as a key driver, in practice it is typically the case for both of these areas that there is a budget provided and the goal is to effectively deliver services. Multi-criteria optimization methods help the decision maker to more effectively consider the trade-offs. We have illustrated two ways that these trade-offs can be considered. For the humanitarian logistics case, targets are set by the decision maker, and the importance of each target is defined by a corresponding weight. The decision maker can adjust either the targets or the weights (or both), depending on their preference. In the second case, the decision maker adjusts the importance of each objective by their order. In this case, the decision maker is not required to set targets or weights if they do not have that information. However, the key limitation of this preemptive approach is that it assumes there are alternative optima at the earlier stages. If there is a unique optima in the first solution, then none of the remaining objectives have any importance.

When applying network design models to the applications of humanitarian and health logistics, there are many unknowns. Getting accurate estimates for these parameters can be quite difficult. The proper quantification of the uncertainty of the model parameters as well as the framework for incorporating the uncertainty into the model is therefore extremely important. For the military humanitarian logistics example, a stochastic optimization approach was used to incorporate probabilistic scenarios. However, additional work is needed in both examples presented, particularly on estimating the "demand"-related parameters. For example, in the health application, there are many national data sets that can be used to estimate overall demand in the form of prevalence of conditions (and corresponding standard errors). However, there is very little data for local geographic regions; hence, some type of local estimation technique typically must be developed—such as the use of synthetic estimates. There is opportunity for refining these estimates through the use of spatial statistics models as well if there is some correlation structure among local regions that can be exploited.

Another important factor that was not considered in the models presented that is important for the decision maker to consider is how the network is built over time. In the two models presented here, the assumption is that the entire networks would be designed at the same instant. In many cases, however, the entire budget is not available from the start of the project, and so the network may be built up over a number of years. For this reason, some of the initial locations may be "suboptimal" in the short term in order to achieve good overall performance as the network evolves. Adding a temporal component is therefore an important extension for what is presented here.

References

Adashi EY, Geiger HJ, Fine MD. (2010). Health care reform and primary care—The growing importance of the community health center. *New England Journal of Medicine*, 362(22): 2047–2050.

Akkihal A. (2006). *Inventory Pre-positioning for Humanitarian Operations*. Unpublished master's thesis, Massachusetts Institute of Technology.

Balcik B, Beamon B. (2008). Facility location in humanitarian relief. *International Journal of Logistics: Research and Applications*, 11(2), 101–121.

Bastian N. (2010). A robust, multi-criteria modeling approach for optimizing aeromedical evacuation asset emplacement. *Journal of Defense Modeling and Simulation*, 7(1): 5–23.

Bastian ND, Griffin PM, Spero S, Fulton LV. (2015). Multi-criteria logistics modeling for military humanitarian assistance and disaster relieve aerial delivery operations. *Optimization Letters*. DOI: 10.1007/s11590-015-0888-1.

Beamon B, Balcik B. (2008). Performance measurement in humanitarian relief chains. *International Journal of Public Sector Management*, 21(1): 4–25.

Beamon BM. (2004). Humanitarian relief chains: Issues and challenges. *Proceedings of International Conference on Computers and Industrial Engineering*, Seattle, WA: University of Washington, 34: 77–82.

Blavin F, Buettgens M, Roth J. (2012). *State Progress Toward Health Reform Implementation: Slower Moving States Have Much to Gain*. Washington, DC: The Urban Institute.

Blumenthal D, Mort E, Edward J. (1995). The efficacy of primary care for vulnerable population groups. *Health Services Research*, 30(1): 253–273.

Bozorgi-Amiri A, Jabalameli M, Mirzapour Al-e-Hashem S. (2013). A multi-objective robust stochastic programming model for disaster relief logistics under uncertainty. *OR Spectrum*, 35(4): 905–933.

Brown TM, Parmar G, Durant RW, Halanych JH, Hovater M, Muntner P, Prineas RJ, Roth DL, Samdarshi TE, Safford MM. (2011). Health professional shortage areas, insurance status, and cardiovascular disease prevention in the reasons for geographic and racial differences in stroke (REGARDS) study. *Journal of Health Care for the Poor and Underserved*, 22(4): 1179–1189.

Carlson BL, Eden J, O'Connor D, Jerrilynn R. (2001). Primary care of patients without insurance by community health centers. *Journal of Ambulatory Care Management*, 24(2): 47–53.

Central Intelligence Agency. (2013). *The World Factbook 2013–14*. Washington, DC: Central Intelligence Agency.

Clemens-Cope L, Kenney GM, Buettgens M, Carroll C, Blavin F. (2012). The Affordable Care Act's coverage expansions will reduce differences in uninsurance rates by race and ethnicity. *Health Affairs*, 31: 920–930.

Cunningham P, Hadley J. (2004). Expanding care versus expanding coverage: How to improve access to care. *Health Affairs*, 23(4): 234–235.

Deprez R, Pennel B, Libby M. (1987). The substitutability of outpatient primary care in rural community health centers for inpatient hospital care. *Health Services Research*, 22(2): 207–233.

Dievler A, Giovannini T. (1998). Community health centers: Promise and performance. *Medical Care Research and Review*, 55(4): 405–431.

Dor A, Pylypchuck Y, Shin P, Rosenbaum S. (2008). *Uninsured and Medicaid Patients' Access to Preventive Care: Comparison of Health Centers and Other Primary Care Providers*, The George Washington University, Washington, DC. Research Brief #4. RCHN Community Health Foundation Research Collaborative.

Duran S, Ergun O, Keskinocak P, Swann JL. (2012). Humanitarian logistics: Advanced purchasing and pre-positioning of relief items. In *Handbook of Global Logistics: Transportation in International Supply Chains*, Vol. 181, J.H. Bookbinder (Ed.). Springer, New York, pp. 447–462.

Duran S, Gutierrez M, Keskinocak P. (2011). Pre-positioning of emergency items for CARE international. *Interfaces*, 41(3), 223–237.

Ergun O, Guyi L, Heier-Stamm J, Keskinocak P, Swann JL. (2014). Improving humanitarian operations through collaboration. *Production and Operations Management*, 23(6): 1002–1014.

Fihn S, Wicher J. (1988). Withdrawing routine outpatient medical services. *Journal of General Internal Medicine*, 3(4): 356–362.

Freeman HE, Kiecolt KJ, Allen HM. (1982). Community health centers: An initiative of enduring utility. *The Milbank Memorial Fund Quarterly/Health and Society*, 60(2): 245–267.

Griffin PM, Lee H, Scherrer C, Swann JL. (2014). Balancing investments in federally qualified health centers and Medicaid for improved access and coverage in Pennsylvania. *Health Care Management Science*, 17(4): 348–364.

Griffin PM, Scherrer CR, Swann JL. (2008). Optimization of community health center locations and service offerings with statistical need estimation. *IIE Transactions*, 40(9): 880–892.

HHS (U.S. Department of Health and Human Services). (2012a). Healthy People 2020 [Internet]. http://www.healthypeople.gov/2020/ (accessed November 15, 2015).

HHS (U.S. Department of Health and Human Services). (2012b). HealthCare.gov [Internet]. http://www.healthcare.gov/news/ (accessed November 15, 2015)

HHS (U.S. Department of Health and Human Services). (2012c). Medicaid program; eligibility changes under the Affordable Care Act of 2010. *Federal Register,* **77**(57 Part III): 17144–17217.

HRSA (Health Resources and Services Administration). (2013a). Find shortage areas: HPSA by state & country [Internet]. http://hpsafind.hrsa.gov/ (accessed November 15, 2015)

HRSA (Health Resources and Services Administration). (2013b). Health center data: 2010 Pennsylvania data [Internet]. http://bphc.hrsa.gov/uds/view.aspx?year=2010&state=PA (accessed November 15, 2015)

Kaiser Family Foundation. (2012). State Health Facts [Internet]. http://www.state-healthfacts.org/ (accessed November 15, 2015)

Kohrs FP, Mainous AG. (1995). The relationship of health professional shortage areas to health status. Implications for health manpower policy. *Archives of Family Medicine,* 4(8): 681–685.

Kohrs FP, Mainous AG. (1996). Is health status related to residence in medically underserved areas? Evidence and implications for policy. *Journal of Rural Health,* 12(3): 218–224.

Liu JJ. (2007). Health professional shortage and health status and health care access. *Journal of Health Care for the Poor and Underserved,* 18(3): 590–598.

Lurie EE, Robinson BC, Barbaccia JC. (1984). Helping hospitalized elderly: Discharge planning and informal support. *Home Health Care Services Quarterly,* 5(2): 25–43.

Mogilevsky P. (2013). *Optimizing Transportation of Disaster Relief Material to Support U.S. Pacific Command Foreign Humanitarian Assistance Operations.* Unpublished master's thesis, Naval Postgraduate School.

O'Connor P, Wagner E, Strogatz D. (1990). Hypertension control in a rural community: An assessment of community-oriented primary care. *Journal of Family Practice,* 30(4): 420–424.

Okada LM, Wan TTH. (1982). Impact of community health centers and Medicaid on the use of health services [findings of surveys conducted in ten urban and two rural areas; United States]. *Public Health Reports,* 95: 520–534.

Park S. (2007). *A Multi-Objective Decision-Making Model for Resource Allocation in Humanitarian Relief.* Unpublished master's thesis, Air Force Institute of Technology.

Ratliff HD. (2007). The challenge of humanitarian relief logistics. *OR-MS Today,* 34(6): 31.

Ravindran AR, Warsing DP. (2013). *Supply Chain Engineering: Models and Applications.* Boca Raton, FL: Taylor and Francis Group, LLC.

Salmeron J, Apte A. (2010). Stochastic optimization for natural disaster asset prepositioning. *Production and Operations Management,* 19(5): 561–574.

Schnebele E, Cervone G, Waters N. (2013). Road assessment after flood events using non-authoritative data. *Natural Hazards and Earth Systems Discussions,* 1(4): 4155–4179.

Shi L. (1992). The relationship between primary care and life chances. *Journal of Health Care for the Poor and Underserved,* 3(2): 321–335.

Shi L, Starfield B. (2001). The effect of primary care physician supply and income inequality on mortality among blacks and whites in US metropolitan areas. *American Journal of Public Health,* 91(8): 1246–1250.

Shi L, Stevens GD. (2007). The role of community health centers in delivering primary care to the underserved: Experiences of the uninsured and Medicaid insured. *The Journal of Ambulatory Care Management,* 30(2): 159–170.

Sommers BD, Tomasi MR, Swartz K, Epstein AM. (2012). Reasons for the wide varia-tion in Medicaid participation rates among states hold lessons for coverage expansion in 2014. *Health Affairs*, 31: 909–919.

Stuart ME, Steinwachs DM. (1993). Patient-mix differences among ambulatory pro-viders and their effects on utilization and payments for Maryland Medicaid users. *Medical Care*, 31(12): 1119–1137.

Tapia A, Moore K, Johnson N. (2013). Beyond the trustworthy tweet: A deeper under-standing of microblogged data use by disaster response and humanitarian relief organizations. *Proceedings of the 10th International ISCRAM Conference*, Baden-Baden, Germany, August 5, 2013, pp. 770–778.

Thomas A, Kopczak L. (2005). *From Logistics to Supply Chain Management: The Path Forward in the Humanitarian Sector*. San Francisco, CA: Fritz Institute.

Van Wassenhove L. (2006). Humanitarian aid logistics: Supply chain management in high gear. *Journal of the Operational Research Society*, 57(5): 475–489.

Vitoriano B, Ortuno M, Tirado G, Montero J. (2011). A multi-criteria optimization model for humanitarian aid distribution. *Journal of Global Optimization*, 51, 189–208.

Zook M, Graham M, Shelton T, Gorman S. (2010). Volunteered geographic informa-tion and crowdsourcing disaster relief: A case study of the Haitian earthquake. *World Medical and Health Policy*, 2(2): 7–33.

7

Incorporating Disruption Risk in a Supply Chain Network Design Model

Kanokporn Rienkhemaniyom

King Mongkut's University of Technology Thonburi, Bangkok, Thailand

CONTENTS

7.1 Introduction

Globalization and outsourcing have enabled companies to focus on their core competencies and to increase their efficiency (Ravindran et al. 2010). However, the increase in lead time and uncertainties due to globalization and outsourcing has also made supply chains susceptible to disruptions.

A small incident may lead to the disruption of the entire supply chain network. Companies must understand both the risks and the vulnerability of their supply chain components to balance business efficiency and risk (Asbjørnslett 2009; Craighead et al. 2007; Fahimnia et al. 2015; Hohenstein et al. 2015; Jüttner 2005; Kungwalsong 2013).

7.1.1 Supply Chain Disruption

Supply chain disruptions are unplanned events that affect the flow of materials and result in adverse ability to satisfy customers' needs and a company's performance (Blackhurst et al. 2008). Supply chain disruptions can be provoked by an accident at a local company, such as a small fire at Nokia and Ericsson's supplier plant in 2000, or by a global catastrophe, such as the Japanese earthquake and tsunami and the massive floods in Thailand in 2011 (Ravindran and Warsing 2013; Stecke and Kumar 2009). The unexpected events could be internal to supply chain, such as equipment breakdown, labor dispute, quality issue, and poor information system management, which occur frequently (Chopra and Sodhi 2004) or external to supply chain, such as natural disasters, technological disasters, financial crisis, terrorist attacks. Even though many of these external risks are rare, the financial losses due to events such as natural disasters are usually enormous. Of the top ten costliest natural disasters reported in *The Economist* (2012), half of them have occurred since 2008. The majority of these disasters occurred in Asia, which is the manufacturing and supply base for several global supply chains. This observation is consistent with the disaster trend noted by the International Disaster Database, which found that Asia has had the highest number of disasters among five regions, based on the total number of disasters reported from 2003 to 2012. The top three most costly natural disasters that occurred in Asia are geophysical (e.g., earthquakes, volcano eruptions, and landslides), hydrological (e.g., floods and landslides), and meteorological (e.g., storms) (Guha-Sapir 2014).

　　Due to the large number and the variety of disasters, companies should proactively identify, assess, and mitigate the risks to help avoid possible disruptions or, at the very least, to minimize their impact.

7.1.2 Supply Chain Network Vulnerability

For global supply chain networks in which the entities (suppliers, manufacturers, warehouses, distribution centers, and retailers) are located in different regions, the geographical locations, government regulations, and the country risk of those entities could contribute to supply chain vulnerability (Kungwalsong 2013). Country risk refers to political, financial, and economic conditions of a country. For instance, Thailand is susceptible to meteorological hazards—such as intense rainfall, tropical storms, and cyclones, and many industrial parks are located in flood-prone areas. Another example is the Netherlands. Almost two-thirds of that country is flood-prone because its proximity to the North Sea and the Rhine and Meuse Rivers (The Economist 2012). Additionally, a country's political, financial, and economic conditions could also provoke disruptions. When goods are shipped between facilities through several countries using multiple transportation modes, increased handling and transfers could make supply chains more susceptible to disruptions. The higher the number of transshipment activities, the more chances there are of disruptions due to mishandling, pilferage, spoilage, and accidents. Thus, the conditions of facilities and transportation links are therefore important to the vulnerability of supply chains.

7.1.3 Risk Management Practice

Hazards and the vulnerability of facilities and transportation links are difficult to change; therefore, supply chain risks cannot be completely eliminated, especially those external risks for which the occurrence and impact are difficult to predict. However, supply chain risks must be managed in order to reduce the chance of occurrence or the impacts. The availability of supply chain risk management practices, including monitoring and mitigation, are important for alleviating the impacts of disruptions and for faster recovery. In the Netherlands, the 1953 North Sea flood was a major disaster that motivated that country to undertake the Delta Works project to prevent future flooding. With effective risk mitigation and a good monitoring system, the Netherlands has never experienced this type of disaster again, and the area between Amsterdam and Rotterdam is home to most of the country's supply chain activities (Chakravarty 2014). During Thailand's massive floods in 2011, many companies underestimated the situation and relied on the government. Water rose overnight before many plants could move their equipment; the floods damaged infrastructure and equipment and forced plants to shut down all operations. More than 800 companies in seven industrial parks were inundated. As of June 2012, 75% of them had resumed operations, but only 40% of those had returned to their pre-flood conditions (Haraguchi and Lall 2014).

The benefits of risk management practices can also be illustrated by the reactions of Nokia and Ericsson to the March 2000 fire at their supplier, a Phillips electronics semi-conductor plant in New Mexico. Nokia quickly responded to the potential disruption by shifting to a backup supplier, and production returned to normal in three weeks (Ravindran and Warsing 2013). Nokia's extraordinary efforts and collaborations with its suppliers enabled the company to avoid disrupting its customers (Sheffi 2005). Ericsson, however, underestimated the situation and had no backup plan. By the time Ericsson realized the magnitude of the problem, it was too late; the company endured partial shortages and lost $640 million in business in the

North American mobile phone market (Ravindran and Warsing 2013; Sheffi 2005). A survey by Aon plc (2013) revealed that companies' risk readiness in 2013 has decreased by 7% due to inefficient risk management planning.

In this chapter, we present a disruption risk assessment procedure for determining the disruption risk scores of facilities and transportation links in a supply chain network. Disruption risk score is calculated from three factors: hazard, vulnerability, and risk management practice. We also present the use of disruption risk scores as a risk parameter in a mathematical model.

The remainder of this chapter is organized as follows: Section 7.2 gives a review of the literature on risk assessment approaches. Section 7.3 provides a summary of the disruption risk assessment method. Section 7.4 provides a multi-criteria mathematical model for a supply chain design considering disruption risk and discusses solution methods. Section 7.5 outlines a numerical example. Section 7.6 presents conclusions and directions for future work.

7.2 Literature Review

A general framework of supply chain risk management includes risk identification, risk assessment, and risk mitigation. Risk assessment in the supply chain risk management literature focuses on estimating the occurrence of a risk event and its potential impact. The assessment techniques include qualitative assessment by risk rating (Knemeyer et al. 2009; Stecke and Kumar 2009), risk prioritization using risk priority number (RPN) and risk mapping (Ravindran and Warsing 2013; Yosha 2012), simulation (Vilko and Hallikas 2012), stochastic model (Goh et al. 2007), disruption analysis network (Wu et al. 2007), failure mode and effect analysis (Chen and Wu 2013; Tuncel and Alpan 2010), the multi-criteria scoring approach (Blackhurst et al. 2008), and bow-tie analysis (Aqlan and Lam 2015).

Other risk assessment studies focus on evaluating the vulnerability of a supply chain that is susceptible to disruptions (Asbjørnslett 2009). Craighead et al. (2007) studies the design characteristics (e.g., supply chain density, supply chain complexity, and node criticality) and mitigation capabilities (e.g., recovery and warning). Stecke and Kumar (2009) have identified that an increase in number of exposure points (e.g., transportation routes, transportation modes, geographical factors, socioeconomic factors, additional security check points), an increase in distance or time, a decrease in flexibility due to sole sourcing, and a decrease in redundancy through just-in-time or lean policies are all drivers for vulnerability. Chaudhuri et al. (2013) determined the vulnerability score during a new product development considering group decision making and linguistic data. The authors considered the degree of supplier involvement, process complexity, logistical complexity, and manufacturing capacity as the vulnerability drivers. Kim et al. (2015) evaluated the structural relationships among network entities using graph theory.

7.3 A Disruption Risk Assessment Framework

7.3.1 Disruption Risk Assessment

In this section, we present a framework for calculating the disruption risk score of each facility and each transportation link based on three main factors: *hazard*, *vulnerability*, and *risk management practice*, and their attributes, as shown in Figure 7.1. Interested readers can refer to Kungwalsong (2013) for more detail on disruption risk assessment.

Hazard refers to possible threats, such as natural disasters and technological (man-made) disasters that could harm supply chain entities. The level of harm to a supply chain due to a hazard can be assessed from three attributes: predictability, occurrence, and impact.

Vulnerability refers to the sensitivity of each facility and transportation link to disruptions. The facility's vulnerability is assessed from its geographical location and the country risk (political, financial, and economic conditions). The transportation link's vulnerability is assessed from mode of transportation, transportation route, logistics performance index (LPI)—developed by the World Bank for the country of origin as well as the country of destination, and the number of transshipments.

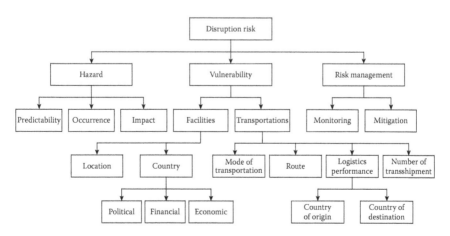

FIGURE 7.1
Disruption risk factors and their attributes. (From Kungwalsong K. Managing Disruption Risks in Global Supply Chains. Unpublished PhD dissertation, Pennsylvania State University, 2013.)

Risk management practice refers to the availability of actions for coping with hazards or vulnerability. Risk management practice consists of two attributes: risk monitoring and risk mitigation.

To determine the disruption risk of facilities and transportation links, a decision maker first rates each attribute on a three-point scale (1, 2, 3: the higher number indicates the higher level for disruption risk). The description of disruption risk factors and their attributes for a facility and a transportation link are given in Table 7.1. The guidelines for attribute rating are provided in Table 7.2. Once the attributes are rated, the hazard score,

TABLE 7.1

Disruption Risk Assessment of a Facility and a Transportation Link

Term	Description
Hazard	A possible risk event that may cause facility disruptions. The events could be natural or man-made disasters.
• Predictability	• Is the location and time of the risk event predictable?
• Occurrence	• How often does the hazard occur?
• Impact	• How long does the hazard take to disrupt a facility (or a transportation link)?
Vulnerability of a facility	Condition of a facility and its country
• Location	• The physical location of a facility compared to the location of the hazard
• Political	• The political instability of a country where the facility is located
• Financial	• The financial instability of a country where the facility is located
• Economic	• The economic instability of a country where the facility is located
Vulnerability of a transportation link	Characteristics of the transportation link that are relevant to disruption
• Mode	• A main transportation mode that is used to ship items among facilities
• Route	• A shipping path and duration from an original facility to a destination (including number of countries, key chokepoints)
• LPI	• Logistics performance index of the countries of origin and destinations
• Number of transshipments	• Number of transshipments during the transportation, including inspections, ports of call, etc.
Risk management practice	The availability of actions or strategies to manage a hazard or vulnerability
• Monitoring	• Does a facility (or a transportation link) have actions or strategies in place to monitor a hazard or its vulnerability (e.g., business continuity standard, warning system, etc.)?
• Mitigation	• Does a facility (or a transportation link) have actions or strategies in placed to prevent or respond to a hazard?

Source: From Kungwalsong K. *Managing Disruption Risks in Global Supply Chains.* Unpublished PhD dissertation, Pennsylvania State University, 2013.

TABLE 7.2

Attribute Rating Guidelines

Hazard		
Predictability	**Risk Level**	**Risk Score**
Location and time of the hazard are predictable.	Low	1
Location and time of the hazard are somewhat predictable.	Moderate	2
Both location and time of the hazard are unpredictable.	High	3
Impact		
A hazard may take a longer time to disrupt a facility/ transportation link.	Low	1
A hazard may take a short time to disrupt a facility/ transportation link.	Moderate	2
A hazard could disrupt a facility/transportation link immediately.	High	3
Occurrence		
A hazard rarely occurs (e.g., once in 5 years).	Low	1
A hazard occurs every other year.	Moderate	2
A hazard occurs every year.	High	3
Vulnerability of a facility		
Location		
A facility seldom has direct impact from a risk event.	Low	1
A facility may have direct impact from a risk event.	Moderate	2
A facility always has a direct impact from a risk event.	High	3
Financial Condition of a Country		
Financial condition of the country is very good.	Low	1
Financial condition of the country is moderate.	Moderate	2
Financial condition of the country is very poor.	High	3
Political Condition of a Country		
Political condition of the country is very good.	Low	1
Political condition of the country is moderate.	Moderate	2
Political condition of the country is very poor.	High	3
Economic Condition of a Country		
Economic condition of the country is very good.	Low	1
Economic condition of the country is moderate.	Moderate	2
Economic condition of the country is very poor.	High	3
Vulnerability of a transportation link		
Transportation Mode		
Surface transportation only (truck)	Low	1
Air	Moderate	2
Ship	High	3

(Continued)

TABLE 7.2 *(Continued)*

Attribute Rating Guidelines

Transportation Route	Risk Level	Risk Score
Shipping path is in a domestic route or of short duration.	Low	1
Shipping path is within a region or of moderate duration.	Moderate	2
Shipping path is across continents or of long duration.	High	3
Logistics Performance Index/LPI (World Bank)		
LPI of the country is high.	Low	1
LPI of the country is moderate.	Moderate	2
LPI of the country is low.	High	3
Numbers of Transshipments		
The number of transshipments is low.	Low	1
The number of transshipments is moderate.	Moderate	2
The number of transshipments is high.	High	3
Risk Management Practice		
Monitoring		
Risk monitoring is available.	Low	1
Risk monitoring is under preparation.	Moderate	2
Risk monitoring is not available.	High	3
Mitigation		
Risk mitigation is available.	Low	1
Risk mitigation is under preparation.	Moderate	2
Risk mitigation is not available.	High	3

Source: From Kungwalsong K. *Managing Disruption Risks in Global Supply Chains.* Unpublished PhD dissertation, Pennsylvania State University, 2013.

the vulnerability score, and the risk management practice score are calculated using Equations 7.1 through 7.4. Finally, the disruption risk score for each facility and transportation link is determined using Equation 7.5.

$$\text{Hazard score} = (\text{Predictability} \times \text{Occurrence} \times \text{Impact})^{1/3} \quad (7.1)$$

$$\text{Facility's vulnerability score} = (\text{Location} \times \text{Political} \times \text{Financial} \times \text{Economic})^{1/4} \quad (7.2)$$

$$\text{Transportation's vulnerability score} = (\text{Mode} \times \text{Route} \times \text{LPI}_O \times \text{LPI}_D \times \text{Transshipments})^{1/5} \quad (7.3)$$

$$\text{Risk management practice score} = (\text{Monitoring} \times \text{Mitigation})^{1/2} \quad (7.4)$$

$$\text{Disruption risk score} = \text{Hazard score} \times \text{Vulnerability score} \times \text{Risk management practice score} \quad (7.5)$$

7.4 A Multi-Criteria Mathematical Model

This section illustrates the use of the disruption risk scores in a multi-criteria mathematical model. We consider disruption risk as one of the objective functions, along with profit and customer responsiveness, in a supply chain optimization model for designing the supply chain network. A supply chain network solution that has higher value of risk objective would imply a higher potential of disruption due to high-disruption risk facilities or transportation links. Therefore, a supply chain network that consists of low-disruption risk supply chain components should be more robust and preferable. To handle the multiple conflicting objectives, we apply goal programming (GP) techniques and an interactive method, which allow for a trade-off between benefits and risks among various design solutions in order to design a robust supply chain network.

7.4.1 Supply Chain Network Design Criteria and Model Assumptions

Consider that a global supply chain consists of suppliers, manufacturing plants, distribution centers (DCs), and customer zones that are located in different locations. There are multiple transportation links available between each pair of facilities. Raw materials are shipped from suppliers to plants in order to produce finished products. Finished products are then shipped to DCs to support customer demand. A physical representation of a global supply chain is shown in Figure 7.2.

We formulate a multi-criteria optimization model to make the following decisions: (i) supply chain network structure, including which suppliers, manufacturing plants, and DCs to use; (ii) production and distribution planning, including which plants should produce which finished products, and which plants or DCs should distribute finished products to which customers;

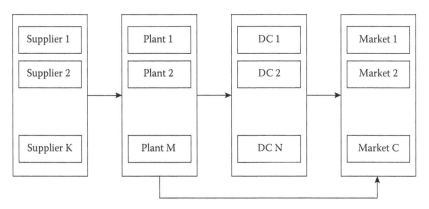

FIGURE 7.2
A physical representation of a global supply chain.

and (iii) transportation selection, including which transportation links should be used to ship items among facilities. These decisions will be made to satisfy the following objectives: maximize profit (Z1), maximize demand fulfillment or minimize unfulfilled demand (Z2), minimize delivery time to customer (Z3), minimize facility disruption risk (Z4), and minimize disruption risk to transportation links (Z5). The supply chain network criteria are shown in Figure 7.3.

The strategic supply chain network design is based on the following assumptions:

- A multi-national company wants to design a supply chain network for new products. A set of potential suppliers, plant locations, DCs, and transportation links are available; hence, the decisions focus on network structure and distribution planning.

- When items (raw materials or finished products) are shipped internationally, additional costs are incurred (e.g., tariffs and import fees, export tax, etc.) that must be determined. In this study, import fees apply to raw materials that arrive at the plants because suppliers and plants are located in different countries. It is expressed as a percentage of total raw material cost. Tariffs do not apply when finished products are shipped from plants to the company-owned DCs; however, export fees apply to finished products that are shipped directly from plants to customers in different countries. Export fees are calculated as a percentage of the total revenue at the plants.

- Products can be shipped directly from the plants to the demand zones if demand meets a minimum level.

- Business environments are deterministic. In addition, all relevant prices and costs are given in a standard currency (USD).

- Disruption risk scores for facilities (suppliers, plants, and DCs) and transportation links are pre-determined by the company and may vary based on facility location.

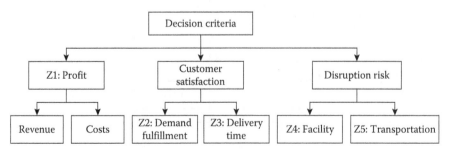

FIGURE 7.3
Supply chain network design criteria.

7.4.2 Mathematical Formulation

Notations:
Indices

i	For raw materials, $i \in I$
j	For finished products, $j \in J$
k	For raw materials suppliers, $k \in K$
m	For manufacturing plants, $m \in M$
n	For distribution centers, $n \in N$
c	For customer zones, $c \in C$
f	For origin facilities, $f \in K \cup M \cup N$
d	For destination facilities, $d \in M \cup N \cup C$
u	For transportation links connecting between facilities $(u \in U_{fd})$

Parameters

D_{jc}	Forecasted demand of product j to customer c (units)
f_{jc}	Fraction of demand of product j to customer c that a company desires to satisfy
b_{ij}	Quantity of raw material i needed to produce one unit of product j (units)
RMD_i	Quantity of raw material i required based on the forecasted demand (units) (*Note*: $RMD_i = \sum_j b_{ij} \sum_c D_{jc}$)
FSK_k	Fixed cost of selecting supplier k
FSM_m	Fixed cost of selecting plant m
FSN_n	Fixed cost of selecting DC n
FOK_{ik}	Fixed operating cost when assigning raw material i to supplier k
FOM_{jm}	Fixed operating cost when assigning product j to plant m
FON_{jn}	Fixed operating cost when assigning product j to DC n
$FAKM_{ikm}$	Fixed cost when assigning raw material i between supplier k and plant m
$FAMN_{jmn}$	Fixed cost when assigning product j between plant m and DC n
$FAMC_{jmc}$	Fixed cost when assigning product j between plant m and customer c
$FANC_{jnc}$	Fixed cost when assigning product j between DC n and customer c
S_j	Space required at a distribution center to store one unit of product j
SPM_{jmc}	Selling price of product j from plant m to customer c

SPN_{jnc}	Selling price of product j from DC n to customer c
MC_{ik}	Cost per unit of raw material j shipped from supplier k
PC_{jm}	Unit production cost of producing product j at plant m
SC_{jn}	Storage cost per space unit of product j at DC n
$FTKM_{ukm}$	Fixed transportation cost of link u if used between supplier k and plant m
$FTMN_{umn}$	Fixed transportation cost of link u if used between plant m and DC n
$FTMC_{umc}$	Fixed transportation cost of link u if used between plant m and customer c
$FTNC_{unc}$	Fixed transportation cost of link u if used between DC n and customer c
$TCKM_{iukm}$	Unit shipping cost of raw material i via link u from supplier k to plant m
$TCMN_{jumn}$	Unit shipping cost of product j via link u from plant m to DC n
$TCMC_{jumc}$	Unit shipping cost of product j via link u from plant m to customer c
$TCNC_{junc}$	Unit shipping cost of product j via link u from DC n to customer c
$LTKM_{ukm}$	Average lead time when using link u between supplier k and plant m
$LTMN_{umn}$	Average lead time when using link u between plant m and DC n
$LTMC_{umc}$	Average lead time when using link u between plant m and customer c
$LTNC_{unc}$	Average lead time when using link u between DC n and customer c
$CAPm_{m}$	Capacity of plant m
$CAPn_{n}$	Capacity of DC n
$CAPik_{ik}$	Capacity of raw material i at supplier k
$CAPjm_{jm}$	Capacity of product j at plant m
$MINik_{ik}$	Minimum order quantity to purchase raw material i at supplier k
$MINjm_{jm}$	Minimum production quantity to produce product j at plant m
$MIND$	Minimum order to allow direct shipment between a plant and a customer (cumulative over all products)
$CAPkm_{ukm}$	Capacity of transportation link u from supplier k to plant m
$CAPmn_{umn}$	Capacity of transportation link u from plant m to DC n
$CAPmc_{umc}$	Capacity of transportation link u from plant m to customer c

$CAPnc_{unc}$	Capacity of transportation link u from DC n to customer c
$mCAPkm_{ukm}$	Minimum quantity required for transportation link u from supplier k to plant m
$mCAPmn_{umn}$	Minimum quantity required for transportation link u from plant m to DC n
$mCAPmc_{umc}$	Minimum quantity required for transportation link u from plant m to customer c
$mCAPnc_{unc}$	Minimum quantity required for transportation link u from DC n to customer c
$VarK_k$	Disruption risk scores of supplier k
$VarM_m$	Disruption risk scores of plant m
$VarN_n$	Disruption risk scores of DC n
$VarKM_{ukm}$	Disruption risk score of transportation link u between supplier k and plant m
$VarMN_{umn}$	Disruption risk score of transportation link u between plant m and DC n
$VarMC_{umc}$	Disruption risk score of transportation link u between plant m and customer c
$VarNC_{unc}$	Disruption risk score of transportation link u between DC n and customer c
$\varnothing_m$	Percentage of import fees applied to the variable purchasing cost at plant m
∂_m	Percentage of export fees applied to the revenue of plant m

Decision Variables

Xk_k	Binary variable equals to 1 if supplier k is selected; 0 otherwise
Xm_m	Binary variable equals to 1 if plant m is selected; 0 otherwise
Xn_n	Binary variable equals to 1 if DC n is selected; 0 otherwise
Xik_{ik}	Binary variable equals to 1 if raw material i is assigned to supplier k; 0 otherwise
Xjm_{jm}	Binary variable equals to 1 if product j is assigned to plant m; 0 otherwise
Xjn_{jn}	Binary variable equals to 1 if product j is assigned to DC n; 0 otherwise
$Xikm_{ikm}$	Binary variable equals to 1 if raw material i is shipped from supplier k to plant m; 0 otherwise
$Xjmn_{jmn}$	Binary variable equals to 1 if product j is shipped from plant m to DC n; 0 otherwise
$Xjmc_{jmc}$	Binary variable equals to 1 if product j is shipped from plant m to customer c; 0 otherwise

$Xjnc_{jnc}$	Binary variable equals to 1 if product j is shipped from DC n to customer c; 0 otherwise
Xkm_{ukm}	Binary variable equals to 1 if link u is used to ship raw material between supplier k and plant m; 0 otherwise
Xmn_{umn}	Binary variable equals to 1 if link u is used to ship product between plant m and DC n; 0 otherwise
Xmc_{umc}	Binary variable equals to 1 if link u is used to ship product between plant m and customer c; 0 otherwise
Xnc_{unc}	Binary variable equals to 1 if link u is used to ship product between DC n and customer c; 0 otherwise
Qkm_{iukm}	Quantity of material i shipped via transportation link u from supplier k to plant m
Qmn_{jumn}	Quantity of product j shipped via transportation link u from plant m to DC n
Qmc_{jumc}	Quantity of product j shipped via transportation link u from plant m to customer c
Qnc_{junc}	Quantity of product j shipped via transportation link u from DC n to customer c
Y_{jm}	Quantity of product j produced at plant m
W_{jc}	Quantity of unfulfilled demand of product j to customer c
σk_{k}	Fraction of raw materials handled by supplier k
σm_{m}	Fraction of products handled by plant m
σn_{n}	Fraction of products handled by DC n
δkm_{ukm}	Fraction of raw materials handled by link u connecting supplier k and plant m
δmn_{umn}	Fraction of products handled by link u connecting plant m and DC n
δmc_{umc}	Fraction of products handled by link u connecting plant m and customer c
δnc_{unc}	Fraction of products handled by link u connecting DC n and customer c

7.4.2.1 Objective Functions

- *Objective 1: Maximize Profit of the Supply Chain (Z_1)* Profit is the difference between revenue and total cost. The first component represents the revenues from plants and DCs. Next are the facility location cost, the raw material purchasing cost (which consists of the fixed purchasing cost and variable cost), the production cost (which consists of the fixed cost of producing a specific product at a specific plant and the variable production cost), the distribution center cost (which consists of the fixed operating cost and the variable cost calculated based on the space used), the transportation cost (which consists of the fixed transportation cost and the variable cost based on shipping quantities), the additional fixed administration cost that may occur when assigning an item between facilities, and the cross-sourcing cost incurred at plants when raw materials are imported from suppliers and finished products are exported to customers. Before tax profit of a supply chain can be determined using Equation 7.6.

$$
\begin{aligned}
Max\ Z1 = &\left[\sum_{c \in C} \sum_{j \in J} \sum_{u \in U_{mc}} \sum_{m \in M} SPM_{jmc} Qmc_{jumc} + \sum_{c \in C} \sum_{j \in J} \sum_{u \in U_{nc}} \sum_{n \in N} SPN_{jnc} Qnc_{junc} \right] \\[6pt]
&- \left[\sum_{k \in K} FSK_k Xk_k + \sum_{m \in M} FSM_m Xm_m + \sum_{n \in N} FSN_n Xn_n \right] \\[6pt]
&- \left[\sum_{k \in K} \sum_{i \in I} FOK_{ik} Xik_{ik} + \sum_{k \in K} \sum_{i \in I} MC_{ik} \left(\sum_{m \in M} \sum_{u \in U_{km}} Qkm_{iukm} \right) \right] \\[6pt]
&- \left[\left(\sum_{m \in M} \sum_{j \in J} FOM_{jm} Xjm_{jm} \right) + \left(\sum_{m \in M} \sum_{j \in J} PC_{jm} Y_{jm} \right) \right] \\[6pt]
&- \left[\left(\sum_{m \in M} \sum_{j \in J} FON_{jn} Xjn_{jn} \right) + \left(\sum_{n \in N} \sum_{j \in J} SC_{jn} S_j \left(\sum_{m \in M} \sum_{u \in U_{km}} Qmn_{jumn} \right) \right) \right] \\[6pt]
&- \left[\left(\sum_{m \in M} \sum_{k \in K} \sum_{u \in U_{km}} FTKM_{ukm} Xkm_{ukm} + \sum_{n \in N} \sum_{m \in M} \sum_{u \in U_{mn}} FTMN_{umn} Xmn_{umn} \right. \right. \\[6pt]
&\left. \left. + \sum_{c \in C} \sum_{m \in M} \sum_{u \in U_{mc}} FTMC_{umc} Xmc_{umc} + \sum_{c \in C} \sum_{n \in N} \sum_{u \in U_{nc}} FTNC_{unc} Xnc_{unc} \right) \right] \\[6pt]
&+ \left[\sum_{m \in M} \sum_{k \in K} \sum_{u \in U_{km}} \sum_{i \in I} TCKM_{iukm} Qkm_{iukm} + \sum_{n \in N} \sum_{m \in M} \sum_{u \in U_{mn}} \sum_{j \in J} TCMN_{jumn} Qmn_{jumn} \right. \\[6pt]
&\left. + \sum_{c \in C} \sum_{m \in M} \sum_{u \in U_{mc}} \sum_{j \in J} TCMC_{jumc} Qmc_{jumc} + \sum_{c \in C} \sum_{n \in N} \sum_{u \in U_{nc}} \sum_{j \in J} TCNC_{junc} Qnc_{junc} \right]
\end{aligned}
$$

$$-\left[\sum_{m \in M}\sum_{k \in K}\sum_{i \in I}FAKM_{ikm}Xikm_{ikm} + \sum_{n \in N}\sum_{m \in M}\sum_{j \in J}FAMN_{jmn}Xjmn_{jmn}\right.$$

$$\left. + \sum_{c \in C}\sum_{m \in M}\sum_{j \in J}FAMC_{jmc}Xjmc_{jmc} + \sum_{c \in C}\sum_{n \in N}\sum_{j \in J}FANC_{jnc}Xjnc_{jnc}\right]$$

$$-\left[\sum_{m \in M}\emptyset_m\sum_{k \in K}\sum_{i \in I}MC_{ik}\left(\sum_{u \in U_{km}}Qkm_{iukm}\right) + \sum_{m \in M}\partial_m\sum_{c \in C}\sum_{j \in J}SP_{jc}\left(\sum_{u \in U_{mc}}Qmc_{jumc}\right)\right]\right] \quad (7.6)$$

- *Objective 2: Minimize Unfulfilled Demand (or Maximize Demand Fulfillment)* (Z_2) Because the first objective is to maximize profit, it is possible that some customer demands may not be fully met. This objective is introduced to achieve customer responsiveness by maximizing customer demand fulfillment—in other words, minimizing the unfulfilled demand or shortages, as shown in Equation 7.7.

$$\text{Min } Z_2 = \sum_{c \in C}\sum_{j \in J}W_{jc} \quad (7.7)$$

- *Objective 3: Minimize Delivery Time to Customer* (Z_3) Besides the demand fulfillment, the delivery time to customer is another customer responsiveness measure. Given the estimated lead times between plants and customers and between DCs and customers based on the transportation links used, we multiply these values with the amount of customer demand that is fulfilled by plants and DCs. Even though this value does not represent the true delivery time to customers, it provides a useful measure of responsiveness in terms of volume-weighted lead time. If a link with a long travel time carries a huge amount of demand, then the volume-weighted delivery time value will be high. Hence, the customer demand should be allocated to each link in such a way that the total volume-weighted delivery time is minimal. In Equation 7.8, the first component represents the delivery time from plants to customers, while the second one represents the delivery time from DCs to customers.

$$\text{Min } Z_3 = \sum_{c \in C}\sum_{m \in M}\sum_{u \in U_{mc}}LTMC_{umc} \times \left(\sum_j Qmc_{jumc}\right)$$

$$+ \sum_{c \in C}\sum_{n \in N}\sum_{u \in U_{nc}}LTNC_{unc} \times \left(\sum_j Qnc_{junc}\right) \quad (7.8)$$

7.4.2.1.1 Disruption Risks

Supply chain disruption could come from either a disruption to a facility or a disruption to the transportation network. In addition, it depends upon the quantity (flow) handled by a particular node (link). If a node (link) with high-disruption risk value accounts for a large amount of flow, the disruption risk to the supply chain will be high. Hence, items should be allocated to each node and link in such a way that the "flow weighted" disruption risk value of the whole supply chain is minimal. In this study, we consider two types of disruption risk: facility disruption risk and transportation disruption risk.

- *Objective 4: Minimize Disruption Risk of Facility* (Z_4) Equation 7.9 presents the facility disruption risk, which is the summation of disruption risk of all individual facilities in the supply chain network, which includes suppliers, manufacturing plants, and DCs.

$$\text{Min } Z_4 = \left(\sum_{k \in K} \sigma k_k VarK_k + \sum_{m \in M} \sigma m_m VarM_m + \sum_{n \in N} \sigma n_n VarN_n \right) \tag{7.9}$$

where variables σk_k, σm_m, and σn_n can be determined using Equations 7.10 through 7.12.

$$\sigma k_k = \frac{\sum_{m \in M} \sum_{u \in U_{km}} \sum_{i \in I} Qkm_{iukm}}{\sum_{i \in I} \sum_{j \in J} b_{ij} \left(\sum_{c \in C} D_{jc} \right)} \tag{7.10}$$

$$\sigma m_m = \frac{\sum_{j \in J} Y_{jm}}{\sum_{c \in C} \sum_{j \in J} D_{jc}} \tag{7.11}$$

$$\sigma n_n = \frac{\sum_{c \in C} \sum_{u \in U_{nc}} \sum_{j \in J} Qnc_{junc}}{\sum_{c \in C} \sum_{j \in J} D_{jc}} \tag{7.12}$$

- *Objective 5: Minimize Disruption Risk of Transportation* (Z_5) Equation 7.13 represents the transportation disruption risk, which is the summation of disruption risks of all transportation links among facilities in the supply chain network.

$$\text{Min } Z_5 = \left(\sum_{m \in M} \sum_{k \in K} \sum_{u \in U_{km}} \delta km_{ukm} VarKM_{ukm} + \sum_{n \in N} \sum_{m \in M} \sum_{u \in U_{mn}} \delta mn_{umn} VarMN_{umn} \right.$$

$$\left. + \sum_{c \in C} \sum_{m \in M} \sum_{u \in U_{mc}} \delta mc_{umc} VarMC_{umc} + \sum_{c \in C} \sum_{n \in N} \sum_{u \in U_{nc}} \delta nc_{unc} VarNC_{unc} \right) \tag{7.13}$$

where variables δkm_{ukm}, δmn_{umn}, δmc_{umc}, and δnc_{unc} can be determined using Equations 7.14 through 7.17.

$$\delta km_{ukm} = \frac{\sum_{i \in I} Qkm_{iukm}}{\sum_{i \in I} \sum_{j \in J} b_{ij} \left(\sum_{c \in C} D_{jc} \right)} \tag{7.14}$$

$$\delta mn_{umn} = \frac{\sum_{j \in J} Qmn_{jumn}}{\sum_{c \in C} \sum_{j \in J} D_{jc}} \tag{7.15}$$

$$\delta mc_{umc} = \frac{\sum_{j \in J} Qmc_{jumc}}{\sum_{c \in C} \sum_{j \in J} D_{jc}} \tag{7.16}$$

$$\delta nc_{unc} = \frac{\sum_{j \in J} Qnc_{junc}}{\sum_{c \in C} \sum_{j \in J} D_{jc}} \tag{7.17}$$

7.4.2.2 Model Constraints

7.4.2.2.1 Demand Fulfillment Constraints

Equation 7.18 represents the demand fulfillment constraint, which ensures that customer demands are satisfied to the extent desired by the company.

$$\left(\sum_{m \in M} \sum_{u \in U_{mc}} Qmc_{jumc} + \sum_{n \in N} \sum_{u \in U_{nc}} Qnc_{junc} \right) + W_{jc} = D_{jc} \quad \forall j \in J, c \in C \tag{7.18}$$

Equation 7.19 represents the constraint that allows the company to specify different levels of customer responsiveness, especially when shortages occur due to disruptions. The right side of the equation represents the maximum shortage allowed.

$$W_{jc} \leq (1 - f_{jc})D_{jc} \quad \forall j \in J, c \in C \tag{7.19}$$

7.4.2.2.2 Supplier Selection and Capacity Constraints

Equation 7.20 ensures that raw material i can be purchased from supplier k if supplier k is selected:

$$Xik_{ik} \leq Xk_k \quad \forall i \in I, k \in K \tag{7.20}$$

Equation 7.21 ensures that plant m can purchase raw material i from supplier k if supplier k is selected:

$$Xikm_{ikm} \le Xik_{ik} \quad \forall i \in I, k \in K, m \in M \tag{7.21}$$

Equation 7.22 ensures that quantity of raw material i must be sufficient to meet forecasted demand:

$$\sum_{m \in M} \sum_{k \in K} \sum_{u \in U_{km}} Qkm_{iukm} \ge RMD_i \quad \forall i \in I \tag{7.22}$$

where $RMD_i = \sum_{j \in J} b_{ij} \sum_{c \in C} D_{jc}$.

Equation 7.23 ensures that the total amount of raw material purchased and shipped from a supplier to plants cannot exceed its capacity and must meet minimum order quantity:

$$MINik_{ik} Xik_{ik} \le \sum_{m \in M} \sum_{u \in U_{km}} Qkm_{iukm} \le CAPik_{ik} Xik_{ik} \quad \forall i \in I, k \in K \tag{7.23}$$

7.4.2.2.3 Plant Selection and Production Capacity

Equation 7.24 ensures that finished product j can be produced at plant m if plant m is selected:

$$Xjm_{jm} \le Xm_m \quad \forall j \in J, m \in M \tag{7.24}$$

Equations 7.25 and 7.26 ensure that DC n can receive a finished product j from plant m if plant m produces product j and DC n is opened for product j:

$$Xjmn_{jmn} \le Xjm_{jm} \quad \forall j \in J, m \in M, n \in N \tag{7.25}$$

$$Xjmn_{jmn} \le Xjn_{jn} \quad \forall j \in J, m \in M, n \in N \tag{7.26}$$

Equation 7.27 ensures that plant m can ship product j directly to customer c if product j is produced at plant m:

$$Xjmc_{jmc} \le Xjm_{jm} \quad \forall j \in J, m \in M, c \in C \tag{7.27}$$

Equation 7.28 ensures that the quantity of product j produced at plant m meets the minimum production requirement and does not exceed its capacity:

$$MINjm_{jm} Xjm_{jm} \le Y_{jm} \le CAPm_{jm} Xjm_{jm} \quad \forall j \in J, m \in M \tag{7.28}$$

Equation 7.29 ensures that the production quantities are limited by the received raw material:

$$\sum_{j\in J} b_{ij} Y_{jm} \leq \sum_{k\in K} \sum_{u\in U_{km}} Qkm_{iukm} \quad \forall i \in I, m \in M \tag{7.29}$$

Equation 7.30 ensures that the use of raw material i cannot exceed the amount of the material purchased from suppliers:

$$\sum_{j\in J} b_{ij} \sum_{m\in M} Y_{jm} \leq \sum_{m\in M} \sum_{k\in K} \sum_{u\in U_{km}} Qkm_{iukm} \quad \forall i \in I \tag{7.30}$$

Equations 7.31 and 7.32 ensure that the production quantity must meet the minimum demand fulfillment target but that more than the forecasted demand will not be produced:

$$\sum_{m\in M} Y_{jm} \geq \sum_{c\in C} f_{jc} D_{jc} \quad \forall j \in J \tag{7.31}$$

$$\sum_{m\in M} Y_{jm} \leq \sum_{c\in C} D_{jc} \quad \forall j \in J \tag{7.32}$$

Equation 7.33 ensures that the total quantity of product j shipped from plant m to the customers and DCs cannot exceed the amount that is produced at the plant:

$$\sum_{u\in U_{mn}} \sum_{n\in N} Qmn_{jumn} + \sum_{u\in U_{mc}} \sum_{c\in C} Qmc_{jumc} \leq Y_{jm} \quad \forall j \in J, m \in M \tag{7.33}$$

7.4.2.2.4 DC Selection and Storage Capacity

Equation 7.34 ensures that a finished product j can be stored at the DC if the DC is selected:

$$Xjn_{jn} \leq Xn_{n} \quad \forall j \in J, n \in N \tag{7.34}$$

Equation 7.35 ensures that DC n can respond to a demand of product j from a customer c if the product is stored at the DC:

$$Xjnc_{jnc} \leq Xjn_{jn} \quad \forall j \in J, c \in C, n \in N \tag{7.35}$$

Equation 7.36 ensures that total space used by all products cannot exceed the capacity of the DC:

$$\sum_{j\in J} S_j \left(\sum_{m\in M} \sum_{u\in U_{mn}} Qmn_{jumn} \right) \leq CAPN_n Xn_n \quad \forall n \in N \tag{7.36}$$

Equation 7.37 ensures that quantity of product j shipped out of DC n to customers cannot exceed the available quantity that is received from the plants:

$$\sum_{u\in U_{nc}}\sum_{c\in C}Qnc_{junc} \leq \sum_{u\in U_{mn}}\sum_{m\in M}Qmn_{jumn} \quad \forall j\in J, n\in N \tag{7.37}$$

7.4.2.2.5 Transportation Link Operation

Equations 7.38 through 7.41 ensure that transportation link u can be used if items are assigned among the facilities:

$$Xkm_{ukm} \leq \sum_{i\in I}Xikm_{ikm} \quad \forall u\in U_{km}, k\in K, m\in M \tag{7.38}$$

$$Xmn_{umn} \leq \sum_{j\in J}Xjmn_{jmn} \quad \forall u\in U_{mn}, m\in M, n\in N \tag{7.39}$$

$$Xmc_{umc} \leq \sum_{j\in J}Xjmc_{jmc} \quad \forall u\in U_{mc}, m\in M, c\in C \tag{7.40}$$

$$Xnc_{unc} \leq \sum_{j\in J}Xjnc_{jnc} \quad \forall u\in U_{nc}, n\in N, c\in C \tag{7.41}$$

7.4.2.2.6 Transportation Capacity

Equation 7.42 ensures that the quantity shipped by each transportation link must be larger than the minimum requirement of the transportation link but that it cannot exceed its capacity:

$$mCAPkm_{ukm}Xkm_{ukm} \leq \sum_{i\in I}Qkm_{iukm} \leq CAPkm_{ukm}Xkm_{ukm}$$

$$\forall u\in U_{km}, i\in I, k\in K, m\in M \tag{7.42}$$

Equation 7.43 ensures that a direct shipment between plant m and customer c is allowed if the minimum order quantity is met (*MIND*):

$$Qmc_{jumc} \geq MIND\times Xmc_{umc} \quad \forall j\in J, u\in U_{mc}, m\in M, c\in C \tag{7.43}$$

Equations 7.44 through 7.52 represent binary and nonnegativity constraints:

$$Xk_{k,}\, Xm_m,\, Xn_n \in \{0,1\} \quad \forall k\in K, m\cup M, n\cup N \tag{7.44}$$

$$Xik_{ik},\, Xjm_{jm},\, Xjn_{jn} \in \{0,1\} \quad \forall i\in I, j\in\cup J, k\in K, m\cup M, n\cup N \tag{7.45}$$

$$Xikm_{ikm},\, Xjmn_{jmn},\, Xjmc_{jmc},\, Xjnc_{jnc} \in \{0,1\}$$

$$\forall i\in I, j\in\cup J, k\in K, m\cup M, n\cup N, c\cup C \tag{7.46}$$

$$Xukm_{ukm}, Xumn_{umn}, Xumc_{umc}, Xunc_{unc} \in \{0,1\}$$
$$\forall u \in U_{km}, u \in U_{mn}, u \in U_{mc}, u \in U_{nc} \tag{7.47}$$

$$Qkm_{iukm}, Qmn_{iumn}, Qmc_{jumc}, Qnc_{junc} \geq 0$$
$$\forall u \in U_{km}, u \in U_{mn}, u \in U_{mc}, u \in U_{nc}, i \in I, j \in J \tag{7.48}$$

$$Y_{jm} \geq 0 \quad \forall j \in J, m \in M \tag{7.49}$$

$$W_{jc} \geq 0 \quad \forall j \in J, c \in C \tag{7.50}$$

$$\sigma k_k, \sigma m_m, \sigma n_n \geq 0 \quad \forall k \in K, m \cup M, n \cup N \tag{7.51}$$

$$\delta km_{ukm}, \delta mn_{umn}, \delta mc_{umc}, \delta nc_{unc} \geq 0 \quad \forall u \in U_{km}, u \in U_{mn}, u \in U_{mc}, u \in U_{nc} \tag{7.52}$$

7.4.3 Solution Techniques

This section discusses the solution techniques for solving the proposed multi-criteria optimization model. To solve the multiple and conflicting objectives model, we use preemptive goal programming (P-GP), non-preemptive goal programming (NP-GP), and the interactive method.

The P-GP and NP-GP techniques are two of the four GP approaches. GP requires a complete knowledge of decision makers' preferences. However, they are different in the way the objective functions are prioritized and in the way deviations from targets are handled. The interactive method, however, requires partial information about decision makers' preferences (Masud and Ravindran 2008).

Additional Parameters

P_i Priority of goal i for the preemptive GP formulation ($i = 1, 2, 3, 4, 5$)

Z_i Objective functions denoting profit, demand fulfillment, delivery time, and disruption risk

$IDEAL_i$ Ideal value of objective i. The ideal value of objective i can be obtained by solving a single objective optimization problem (ignoring other objectives). For example, the ideal value of profit is obtained by solving the problem to maximize profit ignoring the other objectives.

$TARG_i$ Target value of objective i. This value is set by the decision maker based on the ideal value and whether the objective is to maximize or minimize. For example, a profit target may be set at 95% of the ideal profit, while a delivery time target may be set at 110% of the ideal value.

Additional Variables

d_i^+ Positive deviation from target value of objective i

d_i^- Negative deviation from target value of objective i

7.4.3.1 Preemptive Goal Programming Model

In our model, it is assumed that the decision maker ranks the priorities (from high to low) as P1: profit, P2: delivery time, P3: facility disruption risk, P4: transportation link disruption risk, and P5: unfulfilled demand. Hence, the objective function for the goal programming model is to minimize the deviations from the target values defined for each objective. For instance, minimize the negative deviation of the profit (d_1^-), minimize the positive deviation of the delivery lead time (d_3^+), minimize the positive deviation of the facility disruption risk (d_4^+), minimize the positive deviation of the transportation disruption risk (d_5^+), and minimize the positive deviation of the unfulfilled demand (d_2^+). The preemptive goal programming formulation would be as follows.

  P-GP Objective Function

$$\text{Min} \quad P_1 d_1^- + P_2 d_3^+ + P_3 d_4^+ + P_4 d_5^+ + P_5 d_2^+ \tag{7.53}$$

$$\text{Subject to:} \qquad Z_1 - d_1^+ + d_1^- = TARG_1 \tag{7.54}$$

$$Z_2 - d_2^+ + d_2^- = TARG_2 \tag{7.55}$$

$$Z_3 - d_3^+ + d_3^- = TARG_3 \tag{7.56}$$

$$Z_4 - d_4^+ + d_4^- = TARG_4 \tag{7.57}$$

$$Z_5 - d_5^+ + d_5^- = TARG_5 \tag{7.58}$$

$$d_i^+, d_i^- \geq 0 \quad i = 1, \ldots, 5 \tag{7.59}$$

including the other real constraints in Equations 7.18 through 7.52 given in Section 7.4.2.2.

7.4.3.2 Non-Preemptive Goal Programming Model

The NP-GP formulation for the supply chain network design problem is

$$\text{Min} \quad W_1 d_1^- + W_2 d_2^+ + W_3 d_3^+ + W_4 d_4^+ + W_5 d_5^+ \tag{7.60}$$

$$\text{Subject to:} \qquad \frac{Z_1}{TARG_1} - d_1^+ + d_1^- = 1 \tag{7.61}$$

$$\frac{Z_2}{TARG_2} - d_2^+ + d_2^- = 1 \tag{7.62}$$

$$\frac{Z_3}{TARG_3} - d_3^+ + d_3^- = 1 \qquad (7.63)$$

$$\frac{Z_4}{TARG_4} - d_4^+ + d_4^- = 1 \qquad (7.64)$$

$$\frac{Z_5}{TARG_5} - d_5^+ + d_5^- = 1 \qquad (7.65)$$

$$d_i^+, d_i^- \geq 0 \quad i = 1, \ldots, 5 \qquad (7.66)$$

including the other real constraints in Equations 7.18 through 7.52 given in Section 7.4.2.2, where W_i are the cardinal weight of goal i.

7.4.3.3 Interactive Method

Goal programming techniques used in Sections 7.4.3.1 and 7.4.3.2 require completely prespecified preference from a decision maker. In addition, the NP-GP assumes that a decision maker's utility function is linear. In practice, defining preference numerically could be difficult. Another MCMP approach, called an interactive method, can be used to overcome this issue. An interactive method does not require prespecified preference but relies on the progressive articulation of preferences by a decision maker (Masud and Ravindran 2008). The steps for an interactive method are as follows:

- **Step 1:** *Find an efficient solution.*
- **Step 2:** *Interact with the decision maker to choose the most preferable solution.*
- **Step 3:** *Repeat steps 1 and 2 until satisfaction is achieved or until a termination criterion is met.*

7.5 Numerical Example

Consider a global supply chain that consists of three suppliers (K1, K2, K3), two manufacturing plants (M1, M2), two DCs (N1, N2), and three customer zones (C1, C2, C3), which are located in different locations. There are two transportation links (U1, U2) available between each pair of facilities. There are two types of raw materials (*i*1, *i*2) and two types of finished products (*j*1, *j*2). A representation of the global supply chain is shown in Figure 7.4.

To solve the proposed P-GP model, we assume that preemptive priority is available. For the NP-GP model, we use criteria weights from a simple rating

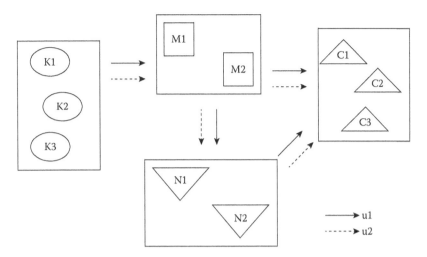

FIGURE 7.4
Supply chain problem for a numerical example.

TABLE 7.3

Priorities and Weights Used in the P-GP and NP-GP Models

Criteria	Preemptive Priority	Weights (Rating Method)	Weights (AHP Method)
Z1: Profit	#1	0.45	0.572
Z2: Unfilled demand	#5	0.10	0.056
Z3: Delivery time	#2	0.25	0.260
Z4: Facility risk	#3	0.10	0.056
Z5: Transportation risk	#4	0.10	0.056

and AHP methods. The priorities and weights are summarized in Table 7.3. The target value for each objective is set at 0.5% away from the ideal value, as shown in Table 7.4.

For an interactive method, in this study, we use six different weight sets, as shown in Table 7.5, to generate a set of efficient solutions. Note that the first five weight sets correspond to individual optimization of each objective, ignoring other objectives. The sixth weight set gives equal weights to all objectives. The objective function values and the corresponding network design for each weight set are presented in Tables 7.6 and 7.7.

- **Step 1:** *Find an efficient solution.*

  From Table 7.6, we obtain three different efficient designs. The first design is from the weight set 1, which provides the highest profit ($100,442,000), but it also provides the highest disruption risks (29.64 and 31.93). The second design is from the weight sets 4 and 5, which

TABLE 7.4

Ideal Values and Target Values

Objective	Ideal Values	Target Values (0.5% from Ideal Value)
Z1: Profit ($)	101,046,500	100,541,267.5
Z2: Unfilled demand (%)	0	0.5
Z3: Delivery time (days)	240,000	241,200
Z4: Facility risk	22.16	22.27
Z5: Transportation risk	17.92	19.82

TABLE 7.5

Weight Sets to Generate Efficient Solutions

Criteria	Weight Set 1	Weight Set 2	Weight Set 3	Weight Set 4	Weight Set 5	Weight Set 6
Z1: Profit	0.96	0.01	0.01	0.01	0.01	0.2
Z2: Unfilled demand	0.01	0.96	0.01	0.01	0.01	0.2
Z3: Delivery time	0.01	0.01	0.96	0.01	0.01	0.2
Z4: Facility risk	0.01	0.01	0.01	0.96	0.01	0.2
Z5: Transportation risk	0.01	0.01	0.01	0.01	0.96	0.2
Sum	1.00	1.00	1.00	1.00	1.00	1.00

TABLE 7.6

Objective Function Values Corresponding to Each Weight Set

Criteria	Weight Set 1	Weight Set 2	Weight Set 3	Weight Set 4	Weight Set 5	Weight Set 6
Z1: Profit ($\times 10^6$ $)	100.442	95.538	95.538	88.058	88.058	95.538
Z2: Unfilled demand (%)	0	0	0	0	0	0
Z3: Delivery time (days)	241,200	240,000	240,000	480,000	480,000	240,000
Z4: Facility risk	29.64	25.47	25.47	22.16	22.16	25.47
Z5: Transportation risk	31.93	24.36	24.36	19.72	19.72	24.36

TABLE 7.7

Network Design Corresponding to Each Weight Set

Supply Chain Component	Weight Set 1	Weight Set 2	Weight Set 3	Weight Set 4	Weight Set 5	Weight Set 6
Suppliers	K3	K1, K3	K1, K3	K1, K3	K1, K3	K1, K3
Plants	M1, M2	M1, M2	M1, M2	M1, M2	M1, M2	M1, M2
DCs	N1	N2	N2	–	–	N2
Transportation links	U1, U2	U1	U1	U1	U1	U1
Direct shipment from plants to customers	No	No	No	No	No	No

provide the lowest disruption risks (22.16 and 19.72), but they also provide the lowest profit ($88,058,517). The third design is from the weight sets 2, 3, and 6, which has a profit of $95,538,900 and disruption risk values of 25.47 and 24.36. Their objective function values lie between those of designs 1 and 2.

- **Step 2:** *Interact with the decision maker to choose the most preferable solution.*

For an illustrative purpose, suppose a decision maker prefers the third design solution (from the weight sets 2, 3, and 6).

- **Step 3:** *Repeat Steps 1 and 2 until satisfaction is achieved.*

We generate a new set of efficient solutions around the second design solution. Based on the weight sets 2, 3, and 6, we vary the weight values as shown in Table 7.8 and re-optimize the NP-GP model. The results are summarized in Table 7.9.

From Table 7.9, there are two efficient design solutions. The first solution is from the weight sets 2_1 and 3_1. The profit is $100,230,100; unfilled demand is 0%; delivery time is 240,000; facility disruption risk is 30.05; and transportation link risk is 30.65. The supply chain network configuration is the same as the design from weight set 1. Another solution is from weight set 6_1, which is the same as the solution from weight set 6. Next, we repeat Step 2.

- **Repeat Step 2:** *Interact with the decision maker to choose the preferred solution.*

Suppose the decision maker chooses the design from weight set 6_1 and is satisfied with this solution. We stop the interaction process.

TABLE 7.8

Weight Sets to Generate Efficient Solutions

Criteria	Weight Set 2_1	Weight Set 3_1	Weight Set 6_1
Z1: Profit	0.21	0.21	0.4
Z2: Unfilled demand	0.76	0.01	0.1
Z3: Delivery time	0.01	0.76	0.1
Z4: Facility risk	0.01	0.01	0.2
Z5: Transportation risk	0.01	0.01	0.2

TABLE 7.9

Objective Function Values Corresponding to Each Weight Set

Criteria	Weight Set 2_1	Weight Set 3_1	Weight Set 6_1
Z1: Profit ($\times 10^6$ $)	100.23	100.23	95.538
Z2: Unfilled demand (%)	0	0	0
Z3: Delivery time (days)	240,000	240,000	240,000
Z4: Facility risk	30.05	30.05	25.47
Z5: Transportation risk	30.65	30.65	24.36

7.5.1 Comparison of the Supply Chain Network Design Results

The supply chain network design decisions and their performances from the multi-criteria model solved by P-GP, NP-GP, and the interactive method are summarized in Tables 7.10 and 7.11.

From Tables 7.10 and 7.11, the P-GP solution suggests choosing supplier K3, plants M1 and M2, distribution center N1, using transportation link U2 (to ship items among suppliers, plants, and DC facilities), and using transportation link U1 (to ship items from DC to customer zones). The profit and the unfulfilled demand objectives are achieved. However, the delivery time to customers, the facility disruption risk, and the transportation disruption risk objectives are not achieved, differing by 16.7%, 33.1%, and 65.1% from the target values, respectively. Because profit is the most important, this supply chain network design solution includes inexpensive facilities and transportation links. Raw materials are purchased from supplier K3, which has the lowest cost among the three suppliers. Most of the finished products are produced at plant M1 because its production costs are lower than those at plant M2. Similarly, DC N1 is selected because it is less expensive to operate than DC N2. Transportation link U2 carries a higher quantity of raw materials and finished products than the link U1. There is no direct shipment from plants to customers.

The decisions from the NP-GP model (with weights from the simple rating method) and the interactive method provide the same results. They choose suppliers K1 and K3, plants M1 and M2, distribution center N2, and transportation link U1. Direct shipment from plants to customers is not allowed. Finished products are distributed to customers via DC N2. For this solution, the unfulfilled demand and delivery time to customer are achieved.

TABLE 7.10

Supply Chain Network Decisions

Supply Chain Network Components		P-GP Model	NP-GP Model (Weights from Rating Method)	NP-GP Model (Weights from AHP)	Interactive Method
Suppliers	K1	No	Select	No	Select
	K2	No	No	No	No
	K3	Select	Select	Select	Select
Plants	M1	Select	Select	Select	Select
	M2	Select	Select	Select	Select
DCs	N1	Select	No	Select	No
	N2	No	Select	No	Select
Transportation links	U1	Select	Select	Select	Select
	U2	Select	No	No	No

TABLE 7.11

Supply Chain Network Performances

Objective Function	Ideal Value	Target Value	Supply Chain Performance			
			P-GP Model	NP-GP Model (Weights from Rating Method)	NP-GP Model (Weights from AHP)	Interactive Model
Z1	101,046,500	100,541,267.5	100,541,267.5 (Achieved)	95,538,900 (Underachieved by 4.98%)	98,168,900 (Underachieved by 2.36%)	95,538,900 (Underachieved by 4.98%)
Z2	0	0.5	0 (Achieved)	0 (Achieved)	0 (Achieved)	0 (Achieved)
Z3	240,000	241,200	281,507 (Underachieved by 16.7%)	240,000 (Achieved)	240,000 (Achieved)	240,000 (Achieved)
Z4	22.16	22.27	29.64 (Underachieved by 33.1%)	25.47 (Underachieved by 14.36%)	29.03 (Underachieved by 30.35%)	25.47 (Underachieved by 14.36%)
Z5	19.72	19.82	32.71 (Underachieved by 65.1%)	24.36 (Underachieved by 22.9%)	25.25 (Underachieved by 27.4%)	24.36 (Underachieved by 22.9%)

However, profit, facility disruption risk, and transportation disruption risk objectives are not achieved, differing by 4.98%, 14.36%, and 22.9% from the target values, respectively. Notice that this solution has lower facility and transportation disruption risk values than the P-GP solution. However, the profit value is decreased.

The NP-GP model (with weights from AHP) selects supplier K3, plants M1 and M2, distribution center N1, and transportation link U1. Direct shipment from plant to customers is not allowed. Finished products are distributed to customers via DC N1. For this network design, the unfulfilled demand and delivery time to customers are achieved. However, profit, the facility disruption risk, and the transportation disruption risk goals are not achieved, differing by 2.36%, 30.35%, and 27.4% from the target values, respectively.

From the numerical example, we observe the following:

1. The NP-GP solution has lower disruption risk objective values than the P-GP solution. This is because P-GP is a sequential optimization model. The problem is solved sequentially with respect to the decision maker's order of preference. Because the profit objective is the most important, the model selects facilities and transportation links that are inexpensive (e.g., facilities K3, N1, and link U2), resulting in high-disruption risks. On the other hand, NP-GP is a single objective optimization model, and all criteria are solved simultaneously with relative weights assigned to them. The NP-GP solutions contain low-disruption risk facilities and transportation links (e.g., facilities K1, N2, and link U1). Thus, it is likely that the company will spend some resources to prepare and mitigate potential disruptions but at a loss in profit. From the numerical example, the NP-GP solution (weights from rating method) has 4.97% lower profit than the P-GP solution. However, the loss in profit results in a decrease in facility disruption risk and transportation disruption risk values by 14.07% and 25.53%, respectively. Similarly, the NP-GP solution (weights from AHP) has 2.36% lower profit than the P-GP solution, which results in a decrease in facility disruption risk and transportation disruption risk values by 2.06% and 22.81%, respectively.

2. Between the two NP-GP solutions, the NP-GP solution (weights from rating method) has lower disruption risk values than the other. This is because the disruption risk weight values from the simple rating method are higher than the values from AHP.

3. None of the solutions could achieve all the target values. In other words, a decision maker has to consider the trade-offs between different solutions. A decision maker can evaluate how much profit the company is willing to compromise in order to reduce the disruption risk values or to improve the robustness of the supply chain network.

4. We can study the impact of the supply chain disruption on each network design by examining the disruption risk scores. In the P-GP solution, supplier K3 and plant M1 have very high-disruption risk values compared to the other facilities due to a high occurrence of risk events and a lack of risk monitoring and risk mitigation practices at these two locations. Hence, the company should closely monitor supplier K3 and plant M1 and prepare mitigation strategies. Supplier K3 is prone to floods, which is quite predictable. However, this occurs frequently. Supplier K3's suppliers are located in a disaster prone area. In addition, the supplier is located in a developing country where economic instability is high and risk management practices are not fully implemented. A company should establish risk mitigation strategies by having a backup supplier or by carrying extra inventory at plants to cope with the supply disruption. Plant M1 is also prone to flooding, which occurs almost every year. The facility is located in a disaster prone area, and the country is politically unstable. Disaster preparedness and a recovery plan are not yet implemented. The company may develop a contingency plan to relocate its production to other plant facilities in order to reduce risk from a possible plant disruption. Furthermore, the company should also pay attention to the transportation link U2 from supplier K3 to all plants. Risk mitigation strategies, such as choosing alternate transportation links and risk monitoring, should help address plausible disruptions from unpredictable events, long transportation lead times, and a large number of transshipments.

In this section, we compare the supply chain design alternatives and their trade-offs using the *value path approach* (VPA) proposed by Schilling et al. (1983) in order to display the trade-offs among objective function values of different solutions and levels of goal achievement.

From the solutions obtained from the P-GP, NP-GP, and interactive models, the VPA starts with determining the best value corresponding to each objective function. The best value corresponding to a maximization objective is the highest value among all alternatives, while the best value corresponding to a minimization objective is the lowest value among all alternatives. Next, the best value is scaled to 1, while others are scaled to a value greater than 1. The larger the scaled value, the worse a method performs on that objective. A scaled value corresponding to a maximization objective is determined by dividing the best value by the achieved value, while a scaled value corresponding to a minimization objective is determined by dividing the achieved value by the best value.

From Table 7.12, the best values for profit and demand fulfillment (which are maximization objectives) are 100,541,267.5 and 100. The best values for delivery time to customers, facility disruption risk, and transportation

TABLE 7.12

Summary of the Objective Function Values and the Scaled Values

Objective Function Value	P-GP Method	NP-GP Method (Weights from Rating Method)	NP-GP Method (Weights from AHP)	Interactive Method	Best Value
Z1: Profit ($)	100,541,267.5	95,538,900	98,168,500	95,538,900	100,541,267.5
	(1.00)	(1.05)	(1.02)	(1.05)	(1.00)
Z2: Demand fulfillment (%)	100	100	100	100	100
	(1.00)	(1.00)	(1.00)	(1.00)	(1.00)
Z3: Delivery time	281,507	240,000	240,000	240,000	240,000
	(1.17)	(1.00)	(1.00)	(1.00)	(1.00)
Z4: Facility disruption risk	29.64	25.47	29.03	25.47	25.47
	(1.16)	(1.00)	(1.14)	(1.00)	(1.00)
Z5: Transportation disruption risk	32.71	24.36	25.25	24.36	24.36
	(1.34)	(1.00)	(1.05)	(1.00)	(1.00)

disruption risk (which are minimization objectives) are 240,000, 25.47, and 24.36, respectively. Note that we replace the unfulfilled demand objective with the demand fulfillment to avoid a computational error. For the P-GP method, the achieved values for profit, demand fulfillment, delivery time to customers, facility disruption risk, and transportation disruption risk are 100,541,267.5, 100, 281,507, 29.64, and 32.71, respectively. Hence, the scaled objective values corresponding to the P-GP solution will be (100,541,267.5/100,541,267.5), (100/100), (281,507/240,000), (29.64/25.47), and (32.71/24.36), respectively. Table 7.12 summarizes the objective values with their ratios in parentheses for the solutions obtained from the GP methods and the interactive method. Figure 7.5 shows the value path of supply chain network design alternatives. The horizontal axis represents profit, demand fulfillment, delivery time to customers, facility disruption risk, and transportation disruption risk. The vertical axis represents the ratios of the objective values.

The output of the VPA can be used to determine dominated and non-dominated solutions. If the value path of one solution is above another, then the solution is a dominated solution. If the value paths of two solutions cross each other, then these solutions do not dominate each other. As shown in Figure 7.5, none of the three solutions are dominated. VPA can be used to perform a visual trade-off analysis among the different solutions. For example, the NP-GP solution (with weights from the rating method) does 17% better than the P-GP solution on delivery time to customers, 16% better on the facility disruption risk, and 34% better on the transportation disruption risk—but with a 5% lower profit.

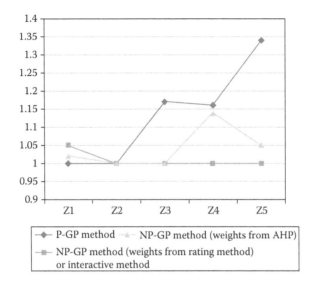

FIGURE 7.5
The value path comparison for supply chain network design solution.

7.6 Conclusions and Future Research

This chapter presented a disruption risk assessment method for managing the supply disruptions in a global supply chain. The assessment can help practitioners to quantify risks in their supply chains based on hazards, vulnerability, and risk management practices. The disruption risk scores of suppliers' facilities and transportation links can lead a company to proactively manage its suppliers. They then can use the disruption risk matrix to visualize the relative risk of all identified hazards. We presented a case study of a global distribution company to illustrate the application of this framework in assessing disruption risks for facilities and transportation links. This framework can be used to develop a company disruption risk profile, which in turn can be used to identify the critical network components that are prone to disruptions and to prioritize the risk mitigation activities.

This work can be extended in several directions. The qualitative assessment scores for hazards and vulnerability can be improved by using the more elaborate quantitative models of risk developed by Bilsel and Ravindran (2012) for major disruptive events. For rare events, such as earthquakes and floods, Bilsel and Ravindran have used extreme value distributions to determine the financial impacts of disruptions. For other events, such as transportation failures, they use Taguchi's loss functions. Efforts can be taken to extend the risk assessment to consider multiple decision makers. Fuzzy logic can also be used to handle ambiguity in the scores.

References

Aon plc. Global Risk Management Survey. http://www.aon.com/2013GlobalRisk/ (accessed April 22, 2013).

Aqlan, Faisal, and Sarah S. Lam. Supply Chain Risk Modelling and Mitigation. *International Journal of Production Research* 53 (2015): 5640–5656.

Asbjørnslett, Bjørn E. Assessing the Vulnerability of Supply Chains. In *Supply Chain Risk: A Handbook of Assessment, Management, and Performance*, eds. George A. Zsidisin and Bob Ritchie, 15–33. New York: Springer, 2009.

Bilsel, Ragip U., and A. Ravi Ravindran. Modeling Disruption Risk in Supply Chain Risk Management. *International Journal of Operations Research and Information Systems* 3, no. 3 (2012): 15–39.

Blackhurst, Jennifer V., Kevin P. Scheibe, and Danny J. Johnson. Supplier Risk Assessment and Monitoring for the Automotive Industry. *International Journal of Physical Distribution & Logistics Management* 38, no. 2 (2008): 143–165.

Chakravarty, Amiya K. *Supply Chain Transformation: Evolving with Emerging Business Paradigms*. Heidelberg: Springer, 2014.

Chaudhuri, Atanu, Bhaba K. Mohanty, and Kashi N. Singh. Supply Chain Risk Assessment during New Product Development: A Group Decision Making Approach using Numeric and Linguistic Data. *International Journal of Production Research* 51, no. 10 (2013): 2790–2804.

Chen, Ping-Shun, and Ming-Tsung Wu. A Modified Failure Mode and Effects Analysis Method for Supplier Selection Problems in the Supply Chain Risk Environment: A Case Study. *Computers & Industrial Engineering* 66, no. 4 (2013): 634–642.

Chopra, Sunil, and ManMohan S. Sodhi. Managing Risk to Avoid Supply-Chain Breakdown. *MIT Sloan Management Review* 46, no. 1 (2004): 52–61.

Craighead, Christopher W., Jennifer Blackhurst, M. Johnny Rungtusanatham, and Robert B. Handfield. The Severity of Supply Chain Disruptions: Design Characteristics and Mitigation Capabilities. *Decision Sciences* 38, no. 1 (2007): 131–156.

Fahimnia, Behnam, Christopher S. Tang, Hoda Davarzani, and Joseph Sarkis. Quantitative Models for Managing Supply Chain Risks: A Review. *European Journal of Operational Research* 247 (2015): 1–15.

Goh, Mark, Joseph Y. S. Lim, and Fanwen Meng. A Stochastic Model for Risk Management in Global Supply Chain Networks. *European Journal of Operational Research* 182, no. 1 (2007): 164–173.

Guha-Sapir, Debarati, R. Below, Ph. Hoyois. *EM-DAT: International Disaster Database*. Brussels, Belgium: Université Catholique de Louvain. www.emdat.be (accessed March 15, 2014).

Haraguchi, Masahiko, and Upmanu Lall. Flood Risks and Impacts: A Case Study of Thailand's Floods in 2011 and Research Questions for Supply Chain Decision Making. *International Journal of Disaster Risk Reduction* 14, part 3 (2014): 256–272.

Hohenstein, Nils-Ole, Edda Feisel, Evi Hartmann, and Larry Giunipero. Research on the Phenomenon of Supply Chain Resilience: A Systematic Review and Paths for Further investigation. *International Journal of Physical Distribution & Logistics Management* 45, no. 1/2 (2015): 90–117.

Jüttner, Uta. Supply Chain Risk Management: Understanding the Business Requirements from a Practitioner Perspective. *The International Journal of Logistics Management* 16, no. 1 (2005): 120–141.

Kim, Yusoon, Yi-Su Chen, and Kevin Lindermand. Supply Network Disruption and Resilience: A Network Structural Perspective. *Journal of Operations Management* 33–34 (2015): 43–59.

Knemeyer, Michael A., Walter Zinn, and Cuneyt Eroglu. Proactive Planning for Catastrophic Events in Supply Chains. *Journal of Operations Management* 27, no. 2 (2009): 141–153.

Kungwalsong, Kanokporn. *Managing Disruption Risks in Global Supply Chains.* Unpublished PhD dissertation, Pennsylvania State University, 2013.

Masud, Abu SM, and A. Ravi Ravindran. Multiple Criteria Decision Making. In *Operations Research and Management Science Handbook*, ed. A. Ravi Ravindran, Chapter 5. Boca Raton, FL: CRC Press, 2008.

Ravindran, A. Ravi, Ragip U. Bilsel, Vijay Wadhwa, and Tao Yang. Risk Adjusted Multicriteria Supplier Selection Models with Applications. *International Journal of Production Research* 48, no. 2 (2010): 405–424.

Ravindran, A. Ravi, and Donald P. Warsing Jr. *Supply Chain Engineering: Models and Applications.* Boca Raton, FL: CRC Press, 2013.

Schilling, David A., Charles Revelle, and Jared Cohon. An approach to the display and analysis of multi-objective problems. *Socio-Economic Planning Sciences* 17, no. 2 (1983): 57–63.

Sheffi, Yossi. *The Resilient Enterprise: Overcoming Vulnerability for Competitive Advantage.* Cambridge, MA: The MIT Press, 2005.

Stecke, Kathryn E., and Sanjay Kumar. Sources of Supply Chain Disruptions, Factors that Breed Vulnerability, and Mitigating Strategies. *Journal of Marketing Channels* 16, no. 3 (2009): 193–226.

The Economist. Natural Disasters: Counting the Cost of Calamities. http://www.economist.com/node/21542755 (accessed January 14, 2012).

Tuncel, Gonca, and Gülgün Alpan. Risk Assessment and Management for Supply Chain Networks: A Case Study. *Computers in Industry* 61, no. 3 (2010): 250–259.

Vilko, Jyri P. P., and Jukka M. Hallikas. Risk Assessment in Multimodal Supply Chains. *International Journal of Production Economics* 140, no. 2 (2012): 586–595.

Wu, Teresa, J. Blackhurst, and P. O'Grady. Methodology for Supply Chain Disruption Analysis. *International Journal of Production Research* 45, no. 7 (2007): 1665–1682.

Yosha, Refael. Make It Not Go Wrong. *Industrial Engineer* 44, no. 6 (2012): 36–41.

8

A Bi-Criteria Model for Closed-Loop Supply Chain Network Design Incorporating Customer Behavior

Subramanian Pazhani

Senior Engineer – Manufacturing Operations, Malta, New York

CONTENTS

8.1 Introduction

Environmental concerns today include the rapid depletion of natural resources and minerals, adverse impacts of transportation and manufacturing processes on the environment, and the insurmountable amount of waste generated by used and condemned products. Due to rapid advances in technology, low initial costs, and planned obsolescence, a surplus of computers and other electronic components is growing around the globe. According to the US Environmental Protection Agency (USEPA), around 30–40 million surplus computers are expected to be available for end-of-life management in the next few years (Morgan 2006). In the United States, more than 12 million computers are discarded every year, out of which fewer than 10% are remanufactured or recycled, while the others are sent to landfills (Platt and Hyde 1997). In 2007, the USEPA declared that more than 63 million computers in the United States were traded in for replacements or discarded, out of which only 15% of electronic devices and equipment were recycled. The estimated landfill space available in the United States is 10 or more years' worth in 29 states, between 5 and 10 years' worth in 15 states, and less than 5 years' worth in 6 states (Knemeyer et al. 2002). Landfill capacities have reduced considerably in recent years and are expected to fall at a much higher rate in the future (Akcalı et al. 2009). The hazardous materials from disposed electrical and electronic equipment, such as lead polybrominated diphenyl ether, mercury, cadmium, and hexavalent chromium, cause serious damage to the environment and affect the sustainability of the ecosystem. In this situation, the recycling, repair, remanufacture, and reuse of used products are all strategies that can contribute to the sustainability of manufacturing supply chains. With increasing concerns over environmental degradation, legislative compliance, diminishing supplies of raw materials, and consumer demands for eco-friendly products, companies have begun modifying traditional supply chain paths to form a *closed loop* to facilitate the recycling and reuse of product returns. The benefits of extracting and using the remaining value from old and reusable goods are being recognized by many developed countries such as Germany, Japan, the United States, France, and Australia. Japanese firms have started reclaiming rare minerals from used electronics (*New York Times* 2010). Efficient recycling processes will reduce disposal waste, thereby benefiting society as a whole (Visich et al. 2005).

Customers return products with which they are not satisfied, items that are defective or damaged, items that were leased, and items whose evaluations are complete. The concept of reuse, in order to reduce waste, has produced an opportunity for material flow from the users back to the manufacturers. The management of this material flow in the opposite direction of the conventional supply chain flow is defined as *reverse logistics* or *reverse supply chain management* (Stock 1992). The term reverse supply chain encompasses all the activities involved in collecting used products from consumers and distributing them to the upstream supply chain (recycling centers, manufacturers) for reprocessing them to either recover their leftover market value or to dispose of them (Pochampally et al. 2009). If returned products are not handled efficiently, then manufacturers will incur larger costs, and this could increase the cost of the final product (Mutha and Pokharel 2009). *Commercial returns* are the products returned by consumers in the initial period after the purchase, say, within 90 days. The annual estimate of such commercial returns in the United States is more than $100 billion due to the presence of liberal policies that facilitate easy return of used goods by consumers. In this chapter, we primarily focus on these types of returns.

The characteristics of forward and reverse supply chains differ in many aspects (Visich et al. 2005). A *forward supply chain* has a demand-driven flow where products move from a few entities (manufacturers) to many entities (customers). A *reverse supply chain* has a supply-driven flow where products move from many entities (customers) to a few entities (refurbishing plants). The supply of returned products is outside the direct control of the company. Also, uncertain product quantities and quality add complexity to the design of reverse supply chains (Thierry et al. 1995). The integration of forward and reverse supply chains is important because their independent operation and management lead to reductions in the efficiency of the supply chain as a whole. Fleischmann et al. (2001), Uster et al. (2007), and Pishvaee et al. (2010) discuss the importance of addressing forward and reverse supply chains in an integrated manner, considering the impact of returns in the network. A closed-loop supply chain (CLSC) is the integration of forward and reverse supply chains. Integration and management of CLSCs has proven to be a challenging task due to the differences in the nature of the activities that make up the forward and reverse flows (Visich et al. 2005).

In this chapter, an integrated four-stage supply chain network is considered with forward and reverse product flows with *commercial returns*, which could be potentially recovered by *light repair operations* or by *refurbishing*. Further to the literature in CLSC network design models, classification of the product returns in the supply chain based on their quality and customer behavior toward buying refurbished products are considered in the model.

Objectives of supply chain management have expanded from minimizing total costs and maximizing customer service to including minimizing adverse impact on the environment (Subramanian et al. 2013a). Two major objectives of a supply chain, maximizing profit and customer responsiveness, have resulted in globalization in search of cost minimization, access to new markets, and economies of scale. This is also coupled with time-based competition, driven by customers demanding a variety of products with minimum delivery time. This, in turn, has led to the increased complexity of supply chain functions and increased disruptions in supply chains. Reputational risks are one among them that may cause substantial, unanticipated additional costs in a supply chain (Geary et al. 2006; Halldórsson and Kovács 2010). Minimizing energy usage and thereby reducing emissions of carbon and greenhouse gases (GHGs) can help firms mitigate the reputational hazards (Palmbeck 2012). Along with minimizing reputational risks, rising energy prices, governmental regulations and incentives, increases in corporate environmental responsibility, and customers' increasing ecological awareness have forced companies to minimize their energy usage and carbon emissions in their supply chain operations. Thus, improving energy efficiency has become a significant concern for corporations around the globe.

In the literature, there is no publication that considers the objectives of minimizing energy usage at the facilities and during transportation, the classification of returns, and the buying behavior of customers toward refurbished products in designing a CLSC network.

In this chapter, the objectives of maximizing profit and minimizing energy usage are considered, and a bi-criteria network design model is developed for the CLSC network. The focus is on reducing energy usage at the warehousing facilities and the energy consumed during transportation in the supply chain. An interactive optimization algorithm is proposed to systematically solve the bi-criteria problem that poses less cognitive burden on the decision maker and converges faster to the best compromise solution.

This chapter is organized as follows: Section 8.2 provides a review of the literature. Section 8.3 describes the problem and the formulation of the objectives and presents a bi-criteria network design model for the CLSC network. In Section 8.4, we describe a bi-criteria interactive optimization algorithm for solving the model by involving the decision maker (DM) in the process. In Section 8.5, we present an illustrative example to show the applicability of the proposed approach. Section 8.6 presents some conclusions on the work and future research directions.

8.2 Literature Review

Network design in supply chains deals with the selection of the best location for the facilities in the supply chain network and optimal product flows through the selected set of facilities. Literature on CLSC network design primarily considers minimizing the cost of operating the network (Fleischmann et al. 2001; Salema et al. 2006, 2007; Uster et al. 2007; Easwaran and Uster 2009, 2010; Pishvaee et al. 2009; Subramanian et al. 2010, 2013a; Pishvaee et al. 2011; Hasani et al. 2012; De Rosa et al. 2013; Subramanian and Ravindran 2014).

Given the intrinsic multi-criteria nature of the network design problem, some studies have considered multiple objectives for designing CLSC networks. Tables 8.1, 8.2, and 8.3 show the supply chain characteristics, return network characteristics, and model characteristics for the multi-objective CLSC network design articles discussed in this section.

Krikke et al. (2003) considered a single period CLSC network for refrigerators of a Japanese consumer electronics company. A multi-objective mixed integer linear programming (MILP) model was developed to minimize cost, energy, and waste, and a weighted goal programming approach was used to solve the problem. Pishvaee and Torabi (2010) considered a single-product, multi-time period CLSC network with manufacturing plants, distributors, retailers, return product collection centers, and recycling centers. Uncertainty in the input parameters can arise in two ways: **(1) Aleatoric uncertainty** is due to intrinsic randomness of the model parameters, and *probability theory* is used to solve it, whereas **(2) epistemic uncertainty** occurs due to unavailability, incompleteness, or imprecise nature of data and is solved using *possibility theory*. In Pishvaee and Torabi's (2010) paper, uncertain parameters

TABLE 8.1

Supply Chain Characteristics of the Multi-Objective Network Design Models

	Supply Chain Characteristics			
Author (Year)	Planning Horizon	Number of Stages	Capacity at the Facilities	Location of the Facilities [Facility (K/NK)]
Krikke et al. (2003)	Single	4 (Forward) 4 (Reverse)	Uncapacitated facilities	Manufacturer (K), Warehouse (K), Disassembly (K), Inspection center (K), Recycling center (K), Rebuild center (K)
Pishvaee and Torabi (2010)	Multiple	2 (Forward) 5 (Reverse)	Capacitated facilities	Plants (K), Distribution centers (NK), Collection centers (NK), Recovery centers (NK), Recycling centers (NK)
Amin and Zhang (2012)	Single	3 (Forward) 4 (Reverse)	Capacitated facilities	Manufacturer (K), Warehouse (K), Refurbishing site (NK), Disassembly site (NK)
Pishvaee and Razmi (2012)	Single	1 (Forward) 4 (Reverse)	Capacitated facilities	Production centers (NK), Collection centers (NK), Steel recycling centers (K), Plastic recycling centers (K), Incineration centers (K)
Mehrbod et al. (2012)	Multiple	3 (Forward) 4 (Reverse)	Capacitated facilities	Plants (K), Distribution center (NK), Collection centers (NK), Recovery center (NK), Recycling center (NK)
Amin and Zhang (2013a)	Single	3 (Forward) 6 (Reverse)	Capacitated facilities	Manufacturer (K), Warehouse (K), Refurbishing site (NK), Disassembly site (NK), Subcontractor (NK)
Amin and Zhang (2013b)	Single	1 (Forward) 3 (Reverse)	Capacitated facilities	Manufacturer (NK), Collection center (NK), Disposal center (K)
Subramanian et al. (2013b)	Multiple	3 (Forward) 2 (Reverse)	Capacitated facilities	Plant (NK), Hybrid facility (NK), Warehouse (K)

Note: K, facility location is known; NK, facility location is not known.

were assumed to be epistemic and to follow a possibility distribution. A bi-criteria possibilistic MILP model was developed to minimize cost and delivery tardiness, and an interactive fuzzy solution approach was developed to solve the problem. An aggregation method was used to convert the bi-criteria problem into a single objective problem, and the problem was solved iteratively.

Amin and Zhang (2012) considered a CLSC network design problem with three objectives: profit maximization, defect rate minimization, and maximization of the importance of external suppliers. A fuzzy model was used to determine the importance scores of the suppliers, and scores were used in the maximization of the importance of the external suppliers' objective.

TABLE 8.2

Return Network Characteristics of the Multi-Objective Network Design Models

	Return Network Characteristics			
Author (Year)	Nature of Returns	Return Quantity	Return Location	Recovery Location
Krikke et al. (2003)	End-of-use/ end-of-life	Deterministic	Disassembly center	Rebuild center
Pishvaee and Torabi (2010)	End-of-use	Stochastic	Collection center	Recovery center/ recycling center
Amin and Zhang (2012)	End-of-use	Deterministic	Disassembly site	Refurbishing site
Pishvaee and Razmi (2012)	End-of-use	Stochastic	Collection center	Recycling center
Mehrbod et al. (2012)	End-of-use	Deterministic	Collection center	Recovery center/ recycling center
Amin and Zhang (2013a)	End-of-use	Deterministic	Collection center	Recovery center/ recycling center/ subcontractor
Amin and Zhang (2013b)	End-of-use	Deterministic	Collection center	Recovery center/ recycling center
Subramanian et al. (2013b)	End-of-use	Deterministic	Hybrid facilities	Manufacturing plant

The multi-objective MILP model was solved using the compromise programming method with $p = 1$. Pishvaee and Razmi (2012) considered a CLSC network of a firm manufacturing single-use medical needles and syringes. It dealt with end-of-life operations of the needles and the syringes (either incineration or recycling). In their study, uncertain parameters were assumed to be epistemic and to follow a possibility distribution. The problem was modeled as a bi-criteria possibilistic MILP with cost minimization and environmental impact minimization as objectives, and an interactive fuzzy solution method with ε-constraint was proposed to solve the bi-criteria model. The ε-constraint was used to convert the problem into a single objective problem for iterative solution.

Mehrbod et al. (2012) considered a multi-product, multi-time period CLSC network with manufacturing plants, distributors, retailers, return product collection centers, and recycling centers. The authors developed a bi-criteria mixed integer nonlinear program for the problem to minimize supply chain costs, delivery time of new products, and collection time of returned products. An interactive fuzzy goal programming method was used to solve the problem.

Amin and Zhang (2013a) considered a CLSC network with external suppliers, manufacturing plants, wholesalers, retailers, collection centers, disassembly sites, disposal sites, refurbishing sites, and remanufacturing subcontractors. The authors proposed a three stage model: Stage 1 used a fuzzy quality function

TABLE 8.3

Model Characteristics of the Multi-Objective Network Design Models

Author (Year)	Objective Function	Solution Methodology	Strategic/ Tactical
Krikke et al. (2003)	Minimize cost, minimize energy use, minimize waste	MILP, solved using non-preemptive goal programming	Tactical
Pishvaee and Torabi (2010)	Minimize cost, minimize total delivery tardiness	Possibilistic MILP, solved using interactive optimization approach	Strategic
Amin and Zhang (2012)	Maximize total profit, minimizes defect rates, maximizes importance of external suppliers	MILP, solved using compromise programming	Strategic
Pishvaee and Razmi (2012)	Minimize cost, minimize environmental impact	MILP, solved using interactive optimization approach	Strategic
Mehrbod et al. (2012)	Minimize cost, minimize delivery and collection time	MILP, solved using interactive fuzzy goal programming	Strategic
Amin and Zhang (2013a)	Minimize costs, minimize defect rates, maximize weights of selected facilities, maximize on-time delivery	MILP, solved using compromise programming	Strategic
Amin and Zhang (2013b)	Minimize costs, minimize environmental impact	MILP, solved using ε-constraint method	Strategic
Subramanian et al. (2013b)	Minimize costs, maximize service efficiency	MILP, solved using goal programming and compromise programming	Strategic

deployment model to evaluate suppliers, remanufacturing subcontractors, and refurbishing; Stage 2 used a stochastic programming model to configure the supply chain with uncertain demand and with the objective of maximizing the expected profit; and Stage 3 used a multi-objective model to solve the network design and the order allocation problem in the CLSC. The model considered four objectives: minimize cost; maximize the importance of suppliers, refurbishing sites, and remanufacturing subcontractors (the importance scores are obtained from stage 1); minimize defect rate; and maximize on-time delivery. Compromise programming and weighted goal programming methods were used to solve the multi-objective problem.

Amin and Zhang (2013b) considered a simple CLSC network comprising of manufacturing plants, retailers, return product collection centers, and disposal centers with cost minimization and environmental objectives. Under the environmental objective, the authors considered the use of environmentally friendly materials for production of new products at the plants and clean technology to process the returns at the collection centers. They developed a MILP model and solved the bi-criteria model using a weighted goal programming approach. Weights for the objectives were varied to generate different efficient solutions. An ε-constraint method was also used to generate different efficient points for the problem. The authors also considered uncertainty in demand of the product and quantity of return products. A scenario approach, analogous to Salema et al. (2007), was used to solve the problem. Finally, Subramanian et al. (2013b) considered a CLSC network with suppliers, manufacturing plants, warehouses, hybrid facilities, and retailers with cost minimization and service efficiency maximization objectives. They developed a bi-objective MILP model and solved it using goal programming and compromise programming. The efficient solutions from the different models are presented to the DM using the value path approach.

Based on the detailed review of literature on the multi-objective network design models in CLSC, some observations are presented here:

- Almost every study in the multi-objective network design models uses an interactive approach to solve the problem. Multiple efficient solutions are generated and presented to the DM. The DM guides the procedure until a best compromise solution is reached.

- Most of the studies use the ε-constraint method, the Torabi and Hassini aggregation method (Torabi and Hassini 2008), or the weighted goal programming method in their interactive approach. With these methods, the number of efficient solutions to be generated for reaching the best compromise solution is large. There is also a chance of missing the best compromise solution in the process.

- Minimization of energy due to transportation and warehousing, which is one of the important focuses of many businesses, has not been addressed in any of these studies.

- Quality of returns and customer behavior toward buying refurbished products have not been considered in the models in the literature.

This chapter addresses the problem of designing a network for a four-stage CLSC with forward and reverse product flows. A bi-criteria MILP model is proposed with two objectives: maximizing profit and minimizing energy usage. Categories of product returns based on their quality and on the buying behavior of customers toward refurbished products are incorporated in the model. An interactive bi-criteria optimization algorithm is developed for the problem based on the paired comparison method (PCM) of Sadagopan and Ravindran (1982). We show that the interactive algorithm poses less cognitive burden on the DM and converges faster to the best compromise solution.

The bi-criteria model is an extension of the single objective model developed by Subramanian and Ravindran (2014). Table 8.4 gives a classification of the recent key publications in multi-objective CLSC network design that are directly relevant to this study. The extensions carried out in this chapter are also indicated.

TABLE 8.4

Classification of Recent Key Publications in Multi-Objective CLSC Network Design Models

Paper	Categories of Product Returns Based on Quality	Customer Behavior for Refurbished Products	Objectives			
			Cost	Energy Use	Environmental Impact	Service Efficiency
Pishvaee and Torabi (2010)			✓			
Amin and Zhang (2012)			✓			
Pishvaee and Razmi (2012)			✓		✓	
Mehrbod et al. (2012)			✓			
Amin and Zhang (2013a)			✓			
Amin and Zhang (2013b)			✓		✓	
Subramanian et al. (2013b)			✓			✓
This chapter	✓	✓	✓	✓		

8.3 Bi-Criteria CLSC Network Design Model

In this chapter, a strategic-level decision-making problem of optimally designing a four-stage CLSC network is studied. Consider a CLSC network that produces and distributes a single product and recycles the return products in the return flow path. Let $S = \{1, 2 ..., n_S\}$ be the set of suppliers, $M = \{1, 2 ..., n_M\}$ be the set of manufacturing plants, $W = \{1, 2 ..., n_W\}$ be the set of warehouses, $H = \{1, 2 ..., n_H\}$ be the set of hybrid facilities, $C = \{1, 2, ..., n_C\}$ be the set of retailers, $R = \{1, 2, ..., n_R\}$ be the set of recovery centers, and $L = \{1, 2, ..., n_L\}$ be the set of capacity levels at each of the warehouse and hybrid facility locations. Figure 8.1 shows the CLSC network considered in the chapter.

The CLSC is comprised of a forward channel and a return channel. The forward channel includes suppliers, manufacturing plants, warehouses, hybrid facilities, and retailers. The return channel includes the retailers, hybrid

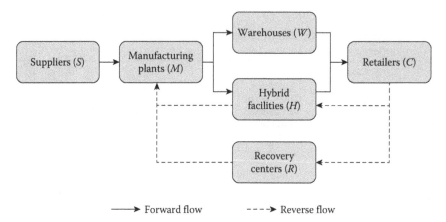

FIGURE 8.1
Structure of the CLSC network.

facilities, recovery centers, and plants. The suppliers provide raw materials for manufacturing new products. The plants perform two functions: (1) produce new products using the raw materials procured from the suppliers and (2) refurbish the returned products from the customers. The warehouses are used to distribute both new products and refurbished products in the forward channel.

Recovery centers function as inspection centers in the reverse channel. These centers collect the return products from the retailers, then inspect them and distribute them to the plants. Hybrid facilities act as warehouses in the forward channel and as recovery centers in the reverse channel. Hybrid facilities are preferred in practice due to economies of scale, with substantial savings in infrastructure, equipment, and human resources (Easwaran and Uster 2010). The retailers satisfy the demand in the forward channel and collect the products that are returned by the customers.

The retailers' demand is satisfied by using new products and refurbished products. The manufacturing plant procures the raw material required for production of new products from a set of suppliers. Customers return used or defective products to the retailers. In this chapter, we consider commercial returns. Once the customer buys the product from the retailer, he has a 90-day period to return the product for any of the reasons shown in Table 8.5.

8.3.1 Categorization of Product Returns

In this section, the categorization of the product returns based on return quality is discussed. Commercial returns initiate the reverse flow in the network (see Table 8.5). For instance, assume a customer buys a product (A) from retailer 1. In a week, he finds a different product (B) with specifications

TABLE 8.5

Reasons for Commercial Product Returns

Nature of Returns	Reason for Product Returns	Description	Length of Time Before Return
Commercial returns (less than 90 days from date of sale)	Customer satisfaction	The quality of product does not meet the customer's expectation. This category also includes miscellaneous reasons such as customers cannot use products, found a better price, over-ordered, or feel remorse.	Return period varies between 14 days and 90 days
	Evaluation product	Products that were reviewed and tested by editors or vendors.	Evaluation period (~30 days)
	Shipping damage	Products cannot be sold as new when their containers are damaged.	Shipping period (<7 days)
	Defective	Incompatible performance with user needs.	Return period varies between 14 days and 90 days

Sources: Vorasayan, J., and Ryan, S. M., *Production and Operations Management* 15, 369–383, 2009; Guide, V. D. R., and Wassenhove, L. V. N., *Operations Research* 57, 10–18, 2009.

that are the same as A but for a better price. He decides to return product A at retailer 1 and purchase product B. Subramanian and Ravindran (2014) assume only one category of returns and an average cost associated with refurbishing these returned products. But, in practice, the quality of product returns are bound to vary depending upon how long the product has been put to use, the nature of defects and shipping damages, and so on. Ovchinnikov (2011) classifies returns into four tiers based on the cost involved in refurbishing them.

- Tier 1 returns do not meet customers' expectations for some reason. The customers might have found the same product at a better price, or the customers might have experienced remorse for other reasons.

- Tier 2 returns have some shipping damages or minor product defects.

- Tier 3 and Tier 4 returns have major product defects. Even though we classify Tier 3 and Tier 4 returns as having major product defects, the refurbishing cost for Tier 4 returns is higher than that of Tier 3 returns. We consider this split explicitly in the optimization model.

In practice, the cost associated with refurbishing is comprised of the cost of inspecting the returned product (to determine to which tier it belongs and to plan appropriate refurbishing activities) and the actual refurbishing cost itself. The two cost components for refurbishing the return product are denoted as *inspection cost* and *refurbishing cost*. They vary depending on the type of returns. Tier 1 returns are typically products that are fully functional but have an opened package. These returns have the lowest refurbishing cost because they do not comprise any replacement of raw materials or components. Tier 2 returns have some shipping damages, cosmetic blemishes, or some minor defects (or a combination thereof). Tier 3 and 4 returns have major product defects, and the proportion of these returns is small. The cost of refurbishing Tier 3 and 4 returns is the highest. Table 8.6 shows the details of the inspection and refurbishing cost components for the different tiers of product returns.

According to an *Accenture Report* (Douthit et al. 2011), 95% of returns are Tier 1 returns, and only 5% can be attributed to actual defects in the product

TABLE 8.6

Components of the Inspection and Refurbishing Cost Based on the Reason for Return (Commercial Returns)

Nature of Returns	Reason for Product Returns	Tier	Components in Inspection Cost	Components in Refurbishing Cost
Commercial returns (less than 90 days from date of sale)	Customer satisfaction	Tier 1	Collection cost, storage cost, visual inspection for cosmetic defects (labor)	Cleaning and cosmetic repairs, repackaging and restocking cost
	Evaluation product	Tier 2	Collection cost, storage cost, visual inspection for cosmetic defects (labor)	Cleaning and cosmetic repairs, repackaging and restocking cost
	Shipping damage	Tier 2	Collection cost, storage cost, inspection for part damages during shipping, visual inspection for cosmetic defects (labor)	Damaged part cost, labor cost involved in replacing the damaged part, cleaning and cosmetic repairs, repackaging and restocking cost
	Defective	Tier 2, 3, and 4	Collection cost, storage cost, inspecting the product for electrical/mechanical faults, visual inspection for cosmetic defects (labor)	Defective part cost, labor cost involved in replacing the defective part, cleaning and cosmetic repairs, repackaging and restocking cost

(i.e., Tier 2, 3, and 4). Based on the case study published by Ovchinnikov (2011) for a major wireless carrier in North America, Tier 1 returns accounted for 60% of the total. Together, Tier 1 and Tier 2 returns accounted for more than 90% of all returns. The quantity of the returns under each tier may differ for various industries. The refurbishing cost also depends on its tier of return. Hence, it is imperative to distinguish the returns based on the tiers they belong to in the model. This chapter considers the four tiers of returns in the model.

Let rc_k and in_k be the refurbishing cost and inspection cost for tier k returns, respectively, $\forall k \in \{1,2,3,4\}$. Without loss of generality, we will assume that the inspection and refurbishing costs for lower tier returns will be less than those of the higher tier returns. Hence, $rc_1 < rc_2 < rc_3 < rc_4$ and $in_1 < in_2 < in_3 < in_4$. We will also assume that there is no difference among the refurbished products based on the tier of return; that is, all refurbished products are priced the same.

8.3.2 Customer Behavior in Buying Refurbished Products

Ovchinnikov (2011) categorizes customers as quality sensitive high-end customers and price-sensitive low-end customers. High-end customers prefer not to trade-off the quality of the product for a lower price. Low-end customers are willing to trade-off quality for lower product prices. Ovchinnikov (2011) conducted an empirical study and showed that both high-end and low-end customers exist. Buying behavior of the customers differs with respect to the refurbished products. Low-end customers are price sensitive and are more willing to buy refurbished items because of their lower price. Ovchinnikov (2011) assumes that the low-end consumers will buy refurbished items (if they are available) owing to their lower price. Guide and Li (2010) showed empirically that customer acceptance rate is influenced by preconceived impressions about quality, performance, and durability. A negative experience will keep customers from buying refurbished products. In general, a low-end customer tries to maximize his own utility based on his perceived value of the quality of the refurbished product. Lee (2011) refers to this concept as risk aversion—where consumers face critical uncertainties and ambiguities with regard to product quality. Risk aversion is a way to avoid potential future regrets in a natural decision-making mechanism when DMs in a CLSC perceive uncertainties and ambiguities. A low-end customer will buy the refurbished product if it is priced no more than his/her perceived value. Okada (2010) characterizes the perceived value using a concave curve with respect to a product's quality.

High-end customers are quality sensitive and often more inclined toward purchasing new products. Ovchinnikov (2011) finds that only a fraction of high-end consumers will switch from new to refurbished products because of the price. His analyses show that a fraction of high-end consumers who switch from new to refurbished products follow an inverted U-shaped curve. At very low discount levels, high-end customers stick to new products and are not willing to trade-off quality for the small savings in price. At moderate discount levels, a fraction of high-end customers (not all) switch to refurbished products due to their price. At large discount levels, high-end customers suspect that the product quality of refurbished products is very low and decide to buy the new product instead. The market has both high-end and low-end customers, and discounts offered for refurbished products directly affect the acceptance of the refurbished products. Thus, optimal discount levels have to be set, considering customer behavior.

The model presented in Subramanian and Ravindran (2014) does not consider customer categories. In this chapter, two customer categories (low-end and high-end) are considered. It is assumed that only a proportion of low-end customers will buy the refurbished products based on their perceived value and price. The perceived value is modeled as a function of the quality perception for the low-end customer. The acceptance rate of high-end customers is modeled using a U-shaped function.

8.3.2.1 Modeling Low-End Customer Acceptance Rate

Let rp be the price offered for refurbished products. As noted earlier, there are quality sensitive high-end customers and price-sensitive low-end customers. A low-end customer will buy the refurbished product only if his own utility is positive, that is, if the refurbished product price is less than or equal to his perceived value. Let q be the quality of the product and $v(q)$ be the perceived value for quality level q, where q and $v(q)$ are scaled between 0 and 1. Here, $q = 0$ implies that customers' quality perception for the product is zero and $v(q) = 0$. When $q = 1$, $v(q) = 1$, and customers value new and refurbished products the same. Figure 8.2 shows an example of the perceived value curve with respect to its product quality.

Given the new product price np and perceived value $v(q)$, a customer's perceived value for a refurbished product can be calculated as $(v(q) \times np)$. A low-end customer will purchase the refurbished product as long as he/she pays a price that is less than $(v(q) \times np)$. Thus, the customer gets a positive surplus $(v(q) \times np) - rp$. In the market, a customer's perception of product quality is uncertain and can be characterized to fall between $[q - i, q + i]$, where i is the uncertainty range. The corresponding perceived value of the product falls between $[v(q - i), v(q + i)]$. The distribution of perceived value (also referred to as a customer's willingness to pay) is assumed to follow a uniform distribution in the literature (Mitra 2007; Atasu et al. 2008; Ferguson 2009). We will also assume a uniform distribution to model the customer's perceived value. Note that the customer's perceived value for a refurbished product is always less than or equal to a new product price, that is, $(v(q) \times np) < np$.

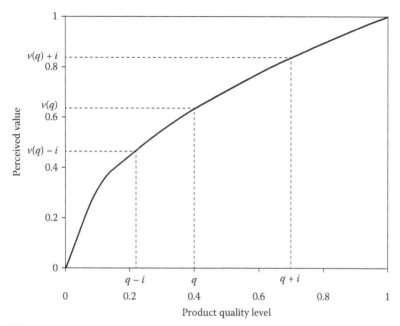

FIGURE 8.2
Perceived value curve. (From Okada, E. M., *Marketing Science*, 29, 75–84, 2010.)

Let $v(x)$ be the perceived value function uniformly distributed between $[v(q - i), v(q + i)]$. The fraction of customers whose perceived value is greater than rp, or simply the customer acceptance rate for refurbished products, can be calculated as follows:

$$P\left(np.v(x) > rp\right) = P\left(v(x) > \frac{rp}{np}\right),$$

where $v(x)$ is uniformly distributed between $[v(q - i), v(q + i)]$.
By solving the above equation, we get

$$P\left(np.v(x) > rp\right) = \left(\frac{v\left(q+i\right) - \dfrac{rp}{np}}{v\left(q+i\right) - v\left(q-i\right)}\right) \tag{8.1}$$

when $\dfrac{rp}{np} = v\left(q+i\right)$, $P(np.v(x) > rp) = 0$ and when $\dfrac{rp}{np} = v\left(q-i\right)$, $P(np.v(x) > rp) = 1$.
When the interval of uncertainty in product quality increases, that is, an increase in $[q - i, q + i]$, the interval of perceived value of the product increases because perceived value is a monotonically increasing curve with respect to q. Based on Equation 8.1, when the interval of perceived value of

the product increases, customer acceptance rate decreases. This is consistent with the fact that, as the uncertainty in product quality increases, the customer acceptance rate decreases.

The customer acceptance rate is illustrated using the following example. Table 8.7 shows data on product quality and its corresponding perceived value.

As an example, consider the case that the product quality in the market is uncertain and falls between $[q - i = 0.30, q + i = 0.7]$. The corresponding perceived value falls between $[v(q - i) = 0.55, v(q + i) = 0.84]$. We will assume that the perceived value is assumed to be uniformly distributed between $[0.55, 0.84]$. Let the new product price (np) be \$1,000 and refurbished product price (rp) be \$750.

$$\text{Customer acceptance rate, } P(np.v(x) > rp) = \left(\frac{v(q+i) - \dfrac{rp}{np}}{v(q+i) - v(q-i)} \right)$$

$$= \left(\frac{0.84 - \left(\dfrac{750}{1000} \right)}{0.84 - 0.55} \right) = 0.3103,$$

implying that 31.03% of low-end customers are willing to accept refurbished products for a price of \$750, that is, at a 25% discount.

Figure 8.3 shows the plot of the customer acceptance rate under varying levels of discounts offered for refurbished products. We observe that the customer acceptance rate is linear with respect to the discount offered. Using Equation 8.1, at discount rate 16%, $\frac{rp}{np} = 0.84$ and the acceptance rate is zero. When $\frac{rp}{np} = 0.55$, that is, at 45% discount, the acceptance rate is one.

TABLE 8.7

Product Quality vs. Perceived Value

Product Quality, q	Perceived Value, $v(q)$
0.00	0.00
0.10	0.32
0.20	0.45
0.30	0.55
0.40	0.63
0.50	0.71
0.60	0.77
0.70	0.84
0.80	0.89
0.90	0.95
1.00	1.00

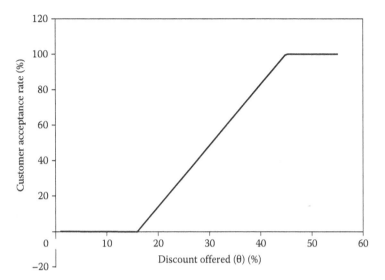

FIGURE 8.3
Discount versus customer acceptance rate (low-end customers).

8.3.2.2 Modeling High-End Customer Acceptance Rate

In this chapter, we will assume that a fraction of high-end customers will switch from new to refurbished products because of the discounts. The switching behavior of the high-end customers is modeled using an inverted U-shaped curve, as a function of the refurbished product price (Ovchinnikov 2011). This is illustrated here using the example that follows. Table 8.8 shows the data on the percentage of high-end customers willing to purchase refurbished products under different discount levels. The data in Table 8.8 is based on the empirical survey presented in Ovchinnikov (2011), where θ is the rate of discount offered for refurbished products.

NOTE: $\theta = \left(1 - \dfrac{rp}{np}\right)$.

The relationship between discount level and customer acceptance is shown in Figure 8.4.

Usually, customer surveys are done using a discrete set of discount values. The dots in the graph are the actual data collected from customer surveys. In order to study the behavior of the customers over a continuous scale of discount values, we fit a quadratic function on the data (Equation 8.2).

$$\text{Customer acceptance rate (High-end customers)}$$
$$= 0.008 - (1.227 \times \theta) + (13.45 \times \theta^2) - (31.12 \times \theta^3) + (20.68 \times \theta^4) \qquad (8.2)$$

This function is used to calculate the acceptance rate of high-end customers based on the discount offered for the refurbished products.

TABLE 8.8

Discounts vs. Customer Acceptance
Rate (High-End Customers)

Discount Offered for Refurbished Products ($\theta \times 100$) (%)	High-End Customers Accepting (%)
0.00	0.00
5.00	0.00
10.00	0.00
15.00	0.00
20.00	6.00
23.00	12.00
25.00	15.00
30.00	20.00
35.00	25.00
40.00	19.00
45.00	16.00
50.00	14.00
55.00	12.00
60.00	10.00
65.00	5.00
70.00	2.00

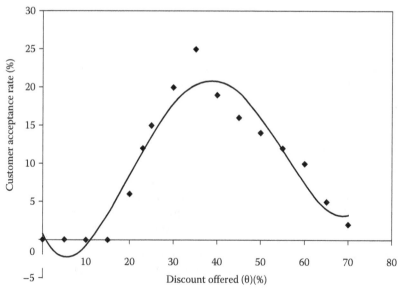

FIGURE 8.4

Plot of discount offered versus customer acceptance rate (high-end customers).

8.3.3 Objectives in the Model

In this chapter, the CLSC network is designed considering the objectives of maximizing profit and minimizing energy usage in the supply chain.

Under the profit objective, we maximize the profit of the entire supply chain. Different components considered under this objective are revenue generated from the sales of new and refurbished products, purchasing cost, production cost, refurbishing cost, transportation cost, inspection cost, and the fixed cost for opening facilities.

Under the energy usage objective, minimizing energy usage at the warehousing facilities and the energy consumed during transportation in the CLSC network is considered. The annual energy usage in warehouses in the United States ranges between 33 and 64 kBtu/sq.ft.[*] This range will be used for generating energy usage data in our model illustration. Commercial trucks deployed in road transportation use diesel fuel as the source of energy. According to the US Energy Information Administration (2007), a diesel-powered vehicle emits 10.15 kg/gallon of carbon into the environment. Burning a gallon of diesel produces 128.7 kBtu of energy. The average mileage for commercial trucks carrying weights between 20,000 pounds and 80,000 pounds ranges from 7.9 to 9.5 miles/gallon (Oscar 2011). This energy and mileage data will be used to calculate the energy consumed during transportation in our model illustration. The focus of this chapter is on reducing the energy footprint due to warehousing and distribution of products in the supply chain.

The profit objective is measured in US dollars. Energy use at the warehousing facilities and during transportation is typically measured in kBtu units. Hence, we can combine the two together into one energy objective.

In summary, Table 8.9 provides some observations about the existing literature, gaps, and motivation for this chapter.

8.3.4 The Bi-Criteria MILP Model

The proposed bi-criteria network design model for a CLSC is presented in this section. The list of input parameters, cost components, and decision variables for the model is given as follows:

Input Parameters

cap_m	Production capacity at manufacturing plant m
cap_w^l	Capacity of warehouse w of capacity level l
cap_h^l	Capacity of hybrid facility h of capacity level l
cap_r	Capacity of recovery center r
cap_s	Capacity of supplier s
d_c	Demand for products at retailer c

---

[*] kBtu/sq.ft = Kilo British thermal unit/square foot.

TABLE 8.9

Motivation for the Chapter

	Current State of Literature	Literature Gap or Motivation	Considered in This Research
Returns	Models in the literature do not consider different categories of returns and their corresponding refurbishing costs	Product returns can be categorized into different categories based on their quality level. The cost for refurbishing them differs	In this chapter, four tiers of product returns are considered with different refurbishing cost
Customers	Models in the literature do not consider different customer categories and their buying behavior for refurbished products	In the market, there exist quality sensitive high-end and price-sensitive low-end customers. Buying behavior of these customer categories varies with respect to refurbished products	The two customer categories are considered, and their buying behavior is modeled
Energy	Models in the literature have not considered energy usage objectives in their models	Minimizing energy usage and thereby reducing greenhouse gases is one of the important objectives in industries	In this chapter, we develop a bi-criteria model with profit and energy objectives

θ	Rate of discount offered for refurbished products
q	Quality of the product
$v(q)$	Perceived value for quality level q
$[q - i, q + i]$	Customer's perception range on product quality in the market
$[v(q - i), v(q + i)]$	Perceived value of the product for customer's perception range $[q - i, q + i]$
γ	Fraction of demand returned at retailer
β_k	Fraction of tier k returns
α_1	Fraction of low-end customers willing to buy refurbished items (calculated as discussed in Section 8.4.2.1)
α_2	Fraction of high-end customers willing to buy refurbished items (calculated as discussed in Section 8.4.2.2)

NOTE: $\alpha_1, \alpha_2 \in [0, 1]$

ω_1, ω_2	Fraction of low-end and high-end customers
sqf_r, ei_r	Square foot and energy usage/sq.ft used by recovery center r
sqf_w^l, ei_w^l	Square foot and energy usage/sq.ft used by warehouse w of capacity l
sqf_h^l, ei_h^l	Square foot and energy usage/sq.ft used by hybrid facility h of capacity l
eu_r	Energy usage at recovery center r
eu_w^l	Energy usage at warehouse w of capacity l
eu_h^l	Energy usage at hybrid facility h of capacity l

te	Energy produced by burning one gallon of diesel
dis_{ij}	Distance (in miles) between facilities in stage i and stage j, $i \in \{S, M, W, H, R, C\}$ and $j \in \{M, W, H, R, C\}$
teu_{ij}	Total energy used per unit of product between facilities i and j
mpg	Miles per gallon of vehicles
$vcap$	Carrying capacity of a vehicle (in units of products)

Cost Function Components

p_{sm}	Purchasing cost of raw material from supplier s by plant m
tr_{mw}	Transportation cost per unit from plant m to warehouse w
tr_{mh}	Transportation cost per unit from plant m to hybrid facility h
tr_{hc}	Transportation cost per unit from hybrid facility h to retailer c
tr_{wc}	Transportation cost per unit from warehouse w to retailer c
tr_{cr}	Transportation cost per unit from retailer c to recovery center r
tr_{rm}	Transportation cost per unit from recovery center r to plant m
pc_m	Production cost for a new product at plant m
rc_{km}	Refurbishing cost for a returned product in tier k at plant m
Np	Price of a new product
Rp	Price of a refurbished product
in_{kr}	Inspection cost of returned product in tier k at recovery center r
in_{kh}	Inspection cost of returned product in tier k at hybrid facility h
f_w^l	Fixed cost of opening a warehouse w of capacity level l
f_h^l	Fixed cost of opening a hybrid facility h of capacity level l
f_r	Fixed cost of opening a recovery center r

Decision Variables

QSM_{sm}	Quantity of raw materials purchased from supplier s by plant m
QMW_{mw}	Quantity of new products transported from plant m to warehouse w
$RQMW_{mw}$	Quantity of refurbished products transported from plant m to warehouse w
QMH_{mh}	Quantity of new products transported from plant m to hybrid facility h
$RQMH_{mh}$	Quantity of refurbished products transported from plant m to hybrid facility h
QWC_{wc}	Quantity of new products transported from warehouse w to retailer c
$RQWC_{wc}$	Quantity of refurbished products transported from warehouse w to retailer c
QHC_{hc}	Quantity of new products transported from hybrid facility h to retailer c
$RQHC_{hc}$	Quantity of refurbished products transported from hybrid facility h to retailer c
$RQCH_{kch}$	Quantity of returned products in tier k transported from retailer c to hybrid facility h

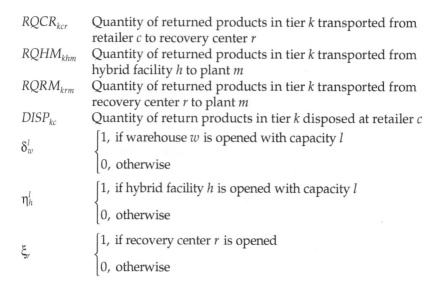

$RQCR_{kcr}$	Quantity of returned products in tier k transported from retailer c to recovery center r
$RQHM_{khm}$	Quantity of returned products in tier k transported from hybrid facility h to plant m
$RQRM_{krm}$	Quantity of returned products in tier k transported from recovery center r to plant m
$DISP_{kc}$	Quantity of return products in tier k disposed at retailer c
δ_w^l	$\begin{cases} 1, \text{ if warehouse } w \text{ is opened with capacity } l \\ 0, \text{ otherwise} \end{cases}$
η_h^l	$\begin{cases} 1, \text{ if hybrid facility } h \text{ is opened with capacity } l \\ 0, \text{ otherwise} \end{cases}$
ξ_r	$\begin{cases} 1, \text{ if recovery center } r \text{ is opened} \\ 0, \text{ otherwise} \end{cases}$

The following are the assumptions considered in this research:

1. Retailers' demands are deterministic. This assumption is reasonable given that the proposed model is at the strategic level.
2. Customer demands must be satisfied either by new or refurbished products. No shortages are allowed.
3. The refurbished products are assumed to be available for sale in the planning horizon.
4. The production process could produce defective products, which is indicative of the product return rate at the retailer.
5. Only a portion of customers are willing to purchase refurbished products.
6. If the demand for refurbished products exceeds their supply, then these units are allocated on a first-come, first-served basis. The remaining customers continue shopping and purchase the new product.
7. The transportation cost of raw material from the supplier to the manufacturing plant is included in the raw material purchasing cost.
8. The facilities in the entire supply chain (suppliers, manufacturing plants, warehouses, hybrid facilities, recovery centers) have capacity restrictions.
9. Vehicles have homogeneous capacities and are in similar conditions. Thus, all the vehicles in the supply chain have the same miles per gallon (MPG) values.
10. We assume that the product weight does not vary between stages.

The bi-criteria network design model for the CLSC network is formulated as follows:

- *Objective 1:* Maximize the total profit of the supply chain (Z_1):

Maximize Z_1

$$
\begin{aligned}
= &\left\{ np \left(\sum_{w \in W} \sum_{c \in C} QWC_{wc} + \sum_{h \in H} \sum_{c \in C} QHC_{hc} \right) + rp \left(\sum_{w \in W} \sum_{c \in C} RQWC_{wc} + \sum_{h \in H} \sum_{c \in C} RQHC_{hc} \right) \right] \\
&- \left\{ \sum_{s \in S} \sum_{m \in M} p_{sm} QSM_{sm} + \sum_{m \in M} \left(pc_m \left(\sum_{w \in W} QMW_{mw} + \sum_{h \in H} QMH_{mh} \right) \right) \right. \\
&+ \sum_{k \in K} \sum_{m \in M} \left(rc_{km} \left(\sum_{r \in R} RQRM_{krm} + \sum_{h \in H} RQHM_{khm} \right) \right) \\
&+ \sum_{m \in M} \sum_{w \in W} tr_{mw} \left(QMW_{mw} + RQMW_{mw} \right) \\
&+ \sum_{m \in M} \sum_{h \in H} tr_{mh} \left(QMH_{mh} + RQMH_{mh} + \sum_{k \in K} RQHM_{khm} \right) \\
&+ \sum_{w \in W} \sum_{c \in C} tr_{wc} \left(QWC_{wc} + RQWC_{wc} \right) \\
&+ \sum_{h \in H} \sum_{c \in C} tr_{hc} \left(QHC_{hc} + RQHC_{hc} + \sum_{k \in K} RQCH_{kch} \right) \\
&+ \sum_{k \in K} \sum_{c \in C} \sum_{r \in R} tr_{cr} RQCR_{kcr} + \sum_{k \in K} \sum_{r \in R} \sum_{m \in M} tr_{rm} RQRM_{krm} \\
&+ \sum_{k \in K} \sum_{r \in R} \left(in_{kr} \left(\sum_{c \in C} RQCR_{kcr} \right) \right) + \sum_{k \in K} \sum_{h \in H} \left(in_{kh} \left(\sum_{c \in C} RQCH_{kch} \right) \right) \\
&\left. + \sum_{l \in L} \sum_{w \in W} f_w^l \delta_w^l + \sum_{l \in L} \sum_{h \in H} f_h^l \eta_h^l + \sum_{r \in R} f_r \xi_r \right\}
\end{aligned}
$$

The objective function of the model consists of revenue generated from the sales of new products and refurbished products, purchasing cost of raw materials, production cost, refurbishing cost, transportation cost in the forward and return channel, inspection cost for the return products, and fixed cost for opening facilities. The terms in the objective function Z_1 are described as follows: The first and second term refer to the revenue generated from the sales of new and refurbished products. The third term refers to the cost of purchasing raw materials for the production of new products. The fourth term represents the production cost, which is the cost of producing new products, and the fifth term represents the cost of refurbishing the return products in the plant. The sixth through eleventh terms represent the costs incurred in the distribution of the new and refurbished products among the stages of the supply chain. The fourteenth and fifteenth terms represent the cost incurred in inspecting the return products to determine their usability. The last three terms are the fixed costs invested in opening warehouses, hybrid facilities, and recovery centers.

- *Objective 2:* Minimize the energy usage at the warehousing facilities and energy consumed during transportation in the supply chain (Z_2):

  Energy consumed during transportation between facilities i and j is calculated as follows:

  Number of gallons of diesel used per vehicle $= \dfrac{dis_{ij}}{mpg}$, and total energy used per vehicle $= \dfrac{dis_{ij}}{mpg} \times te$. Total energy used per unit of product (assuming that the vehicles are trucked at full capacity), between i and

  j (teu_{ij}) $= \dfrac{\left(\dfrac{dis_{ij}}{mpg} \times te\right)}{vcap}$. Thus, if Q is the quantity of shipments between i

  and j, the total energy consumed due to transportation $= teu_{ij} \times Q$.

Total energy used during transportation in the CLSC network is given by Equation 8.3:

$$\sum_{s \in S}\sum_{m \in M} teu_{sm}\, QSM_{sm} + \sum_{m \in M}\sum_{w \in W} teu_{mw}\left(QMW_{mw} + RQMW_{mw}\right)$$

$$+ \sum_{m \in M}\sum_{h \in H} teu_{mh}\left(QMH_{mh} + RQMH_{mh} + \sum_{k \in K} RQHM_{khm}\right)$$

$$+ \sum_{w \in W}\sum_{c \in C} teu_{wc}\left(QWC_{wc} + RQWC_{wc}\right) \qquad (8.3)$$

$$+ \sum_{h \in H}\sum_{c \in C} teu_{hc}\left(QHC_{hc} + RQHC_{hc} + \sum_{k \in K} RQCH_{kch}\right)$$

$$+ \sum_{c \in C}\sum_{r \in R} teu_{cr}\left(\sum_{k \in K} RQCR_{kcr}\right) + \sum_{r \in R}\sum_{m \in M} teu_{rm}\left(\sum_{k \in K} RQRM_{krm}\right)$$

Energy usages at the warehousing facilities (warehouses, hybrid facilities, and recovery centers) are calculated as follows:

- Energy usage at recovery center r $(eu_r) = sqf_r \times ei_r$
- Energy usage at warehouse w of capacity l $\left(eu_w^l\right) = sqf_w^l \times ei_w^l$
- Energy usage at hybrid facility h of capacity level l $\left(eu_h^l\right) = sqf_h^l \times ei_h^l$

Total energy usage at the warehousing facilities in the CLSC network is given by Equation 8.4:

$$\sum_{l\in L}\sum_{w\in W} eu_w^l\, \delta_w^l + \sum_{l\in L}\sum_{h\in H} eu_h^l\, \eta_h^l + \sum_{r\in R} eu_r \xi_r \tag{8.4}$$

Based on Equations 8.3 and 8.4, the energy objective is formulated as follows:

$$
\begin{aligned}
\text{Minimize } Z_2 = &\left(\sum_{s\in S}\sum_{m\in M} teu_{sm}\, QSM_{sm} + \sum_{m\in M}\sum_{w\in W} teu_{mw}\left(QMW_{mw} + RQMW_{mw}\right) \right. \\
&+ \sum_{m\in M}\sum_{h\in H} teu_{mh}\left(QMH_{mh} + RQMH_{mh} + \sum_{k\in K} RQHM_{khm} \right) \\
&+ \sum_{w\in W}\sum_{c\in C} teu_{wc}\left(QWC_{wc} + RQWC_{wc}\right) \\
&+ \sum_{h\in H}\sum_{c\in C} teu_{hc}\left(QHC_{hc} + RQHC_{hc} + \sum_{k\in K} RQCH_{kch} \right) \\
&\left. + \sum_{c\in C}\sum_{r\in R} teu_{cr}\left(\sum_{k\in K} RQCR_{kcr} \right) + \sum_{r\in R}\sum_{m\in M} teu_{rm}\left(\sum_{k\in K} RQRM_{krm} \right) \right) \\
&+ \left(\sum_{l\in L}\sum_{w\in W} eu_w^l\, \delta_w^l + \sum_{l\in L}\sum_{h\in H} eu_h^l\, \eta_h^l + \sum_{r\in R} eu_r \xi_r \right)
\end{aligned}
$$

Following are the set of constraints of the model, subject to the fact that each supplier s has a finite supply capacity.

Equation 8.5 ensures that the quantity of raw materials supplied by supplier s to all the manufacturing plants should be less than or equal to its capacity.

$$\sum_{m\in M} QSM_{sm} \leq cap_s \quad \forall s \in S \tag{8.5}$$

Equation 8.6 is the set of production capacity constraints at the plants. The left side term of the constraint represents the sum of new and refurbished products transported to warehouses and hybrid facilities from plant m, which should be less than or equal to its capacity.

$$\sum_{w \in W}(QMW_{mw} + RQMW_{mw}) + \sum_{h \in H}(QMH_{mh} + RQMH_{mh}) \le cap_m \quad \forall m \in M \quad (8.6)$$

Equation 8.7 ensures that the quantity of raw material flowing into plant m is equal to the quantity of new products flowing out of that plant to the warehouses and hybrid facilities. The left side term of the constraint represents the sum of products flowing into manufacturer m. The right side term of the constraint is the sum of products flowing out of manufacturer m to warehouses and hybrid facilities.

$$\sum_{s \in S}QSM_{sm} = \sum_{w \in W}QMW_{mw} + \sum_{h \in H}QMH_{mh} \quad \forall m \in M \quad (8.7)$$

Equation 8.8 ensures that the quantity of returned products under all tiers flowing into plant m is equal to the quantity of refurbished products flowing out of that plant to the warehouses and hybrid facilities.

$$\sum_{k \in K}\sum_{h \in H}RQHM_{khm} + \sum_{k \in K}\sum_{r \in R}RQRM_{krm} = \sum_{h \in H}RQMH_{mh} + \sum_{w \in W}RQMW_{mw} \quad \forall m \in M$$
$$(8.8)$$

Equation 8.9 ensures that the quantity of new products and refurbished products flowing into warehouse w does not exceed its storage capacity, if the warehouse is selected for operation. The left side term of the constraint is the sum of new and refurbished products flowing into warehouse w, and the right side term is the capacity of the selected warehouse. If a warehouse w is opened, Equation 8.10 ensures that only one of the capacity levels is selected.

$$\sum_{m \in M}(QMW_{mw} + RQMW_{mw}) \le \sum_{l \in L}cap_w^l \, \delta_w^l \quad \forall w \in W \quad (8.9)$$

$$\sum_{l \in L}\delta_w^l \le 1 \quad \forall w \in W \quad (8.10)$$

Equation 8.11 ensures that the quantity of new products flowing into warehouse w is equal to the quantity of new products flowing out of that warehouse. Similarly, Equation 8.12 is the flow constraint for the refurbished products at warehouse w.

$$\sum_{m\in M} QMW_{mw} = \sum_{c\in C} QWC_{wc} \quad \forall w \in W \tag{8.11}$$

$$\sum_{m\in M} RQMW_{mw} = \sum_{c\in C} RQWC_{wc} \quad \forall w \in W \tag{8.12}$$

Equation 8.13 ensures that the quantity of new products and refurbished products flowing in the forward channel and returned products flowing in the return channel into a hybrid facility h does not exceed its storage capacity, if the hybrid facility is selected for operation. If hybrid facility h is opened, Equation 8.14 ensures that only one of the capacity levels is selected.

$$\sum_{m\in M} (QMH_{mh} + RQMH_{mh}) + \sum_{k\in K}\sum_{c\in C} RQCH_{kch} \leq \sum_{l\in L} cap_h^l \, \eta_h^l \quad \forall h \in H \tag{8.13}$$

$$\sum_{l\in L} \eta_h^l \leq 1 \quad \forall h \in H \tag{8.14}$$

Equations 8.15 and 8.16 represent the flow constraints for the new and refurbished products, respectively, at hybrid facility h in the forward channel.

$$\sum_{m\in M} QMH_{mh} = \sum_{c\in C} QHC_{hc} \quad \forall h \in H \tag{8.15}$$

$$\sum_{m\in M} RQMH_{mh} = \sum_{c\in C} RQHC_{hc} \quad \forall h \in H \tag{8.16}$$

Equation 8.17 ensures that the quantity of return products, under all tiers, flowing into the hybrid facility h is equal to the quantity flowing out of that hybrid facility in the return channel.

$$\sum_{c\in C} RQCH_{kch} = \sum_{m\in M} RQHM_{khm} \quad \forall h \in H, \forall k \in K \tag{8.17}$$

Equation 8.18 deals with the capacity and operation constraints for recovery center r. This constraint ensures that the quantity of return products, under all tiers, flowing into recovery center r should be less than or equal to its storage capacity, if recovery center r is opened.

$$\sum_{k\in K}\sum_{c\in C} RQCR_{kcr} \leq cap_r \, \xi_r \quad \forall r \in R \tag{8.18}$$

Equation 8.19 represents the flow balance constraints for recovery center r.

$$\sum_{c \in C} RQCR_{kcr} = \sum_{m \in M} RQRM_{krm} \quad \forall r \in R, \forall k \in K \qquad (8.19)$$

Equation 8.20 represents the demand satisfaction constraints. The total quantity of products (new and refurbished) flowing into retailer c should be less than or equal to the demand at that retailer.

$$\sum_{w \in W} \left(QWC_{wc} + RQWC_{wc} \right) + \sum_{h \in H} \left(QHC_{hc} + RQHC_{hc} \right) = d_c \quad \forall c \in C \qquad (8.20)$$

Equation 8.21 ensures that the total quantity of refurbished products flowing into retailer c should be less than or equal to the sum of customer acceptance rate of low-end and high-end customers to buy refurbished products.

$$\sum_{w \in W} RQWC_{wc} + \sum_{h \in H} RQHC_{hc} \leq \left\lfloor \left(\alpha_1 . \omega_1 . d_c \right) + \left(\alpha_2 . \omega_2 . d_c \right) \right\rfloor \quad \forall c \in C \qquad (8.21)$$

Equation 8.22 represents the flow balance constraints for the return products in each tier at the retailers. The return products are either sent to refurbishing through recovery centers and hybrid facilities or are disposed at the retailer.

$$\sum_{h \in H} RQCH_{kch} + \sum_{r \in R} RQCR_{kcr} + DISP_{kc} = \left\lfloor \gamma . \beta_k . d_c \right\rfloor \quad \forall c \in C, \forall k \in K \qquad (8.22)$$

Equations 8.23 and 8.24 describe nonnegativity and binary conditions of the decision variables.

$$QSM_{sm}, QMW_{mw}, RQMW_{mw}, QMH_{mh}, RQMH_{mh}, QWC_{wc}, RQWC_{wc},$$
$$QHC_{hc}, RQHC_{hc}, RQCH_{kch}, RQCR_{kcr}, RQHM_{khm}, RQRM_{krm}, DISP_{kc} \geq 0 \qquad (8.23)$$

$$\delta_w^l, \eta_h^l, \xi_r \in \{0, 1\} \qquad (8.24)$$

8.4 Interactive Optimization Algorithm

In this section, we describe the PCM for solving bi-criteria optimization problems (Sadagopan and Ravindran 1982). PCM is an interactive method and has been successfully applied to solve bi-criteria mathematical programming problems in health planning and quality control. PCM eliminates a certain portion of the objective space at each iteration through interactions with the DM, using the golden section search (Masud and Ravindran 2008). This method poses lesser cognitive burden to the DM and converges faster to the best compromise solution. We will use this method to solve the bi-criteria network design model for the CLSC network.

The bi-criteria mathematical programming model in this study is stated in general as follows:

$$\text{Max } f_1(x)$$

$$\text{Min } f_2(x)$$

$$\text{Subject to: } g_i(x) \leq 0 \quad i = 1, \ldots, m$$

where x is an n-dimensional vector of decision variables, f_1 and f_2 represent the profit and energy objectives, and g_is are the set of constraints, representing Equations 8.5 through 8.24. Let $S = \{x \mid g_i(x) \leq 0\}$ denote the feasible region. Let $U[f_1(x), f_2(x)]$ be the *unknown* DM's utility function defined over the criterion values, such that for any two feasible solutions, $x^{(1)}$ and $x^{(2)}$, $U[f_1(x^{(1)}), f_2(x^{(1)})] > U[f_1(x^{(2)}), f_2(x^{(2)})]$, if DM prefers solution $x^{(1)}$ to $x^{(2)}$. The objective is to find the best compromise solution that maximizes the unknown utility function.

The steps of the proposed method are summarized as follows (see Figure 8.5):

Step 1:

$$\text{Solve (P1): Max } f_1(x), \quad \text{subject to } x \in S$$

$$\text{Set max } f_1(x) = v^*$$

$$\text{Solve (P2): Min } f_2(x), \quad \text{subject to } x \in S$$

$$\text{Set min } f_2(x) = w^*$$

Step 2:

$$\text{Solve } (P_v): \text{Min } f_2(x), \quad \text{subject to } x \in S \text{ and } f_1(x) \geq v^*$$

Set min $f_2(x) = w_u$. The optimal value of $f_2(x)$ lies between w^* and w_u. Set $w^* = w_1$.

Let the initial length of the interval $I_0 = w_u - w_1$.

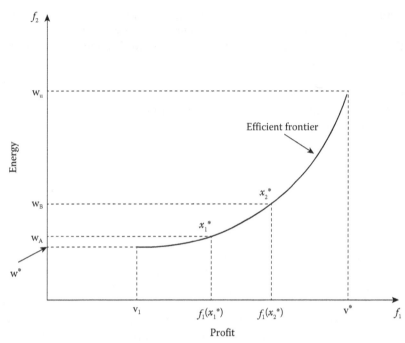

FIGURE 8.5
Illustration of the paired comparison method.

Step 3:
Choose two values w_A and w_B, such that $w_1 < w_A < w_B < w_u$. Golden section search is used to generate w_A and w_B. Solve the problem,

P_w: Max $f_1(x)$, subject to $x \in S$ and $f_2(x) \leq w$ for $w = w_A$ and $w = w_B$;

Let $g(w) = $ Max $f_1(x)$ for P_w.

Step 4:

Let $y^{(1)}$ and $y^{(2)}$ be the two feasible solutions in the objective space.

$$y^{(1)} = [g(w_A), w_A] \text{ and } y^{(2)} = [g(w_B), w_B]$$

DM is asked to specify his preference between the two solutions $y^{(1)}$ and $y^{(2)}$.

If $y^{(1)}$ is preferred to $y^{(2)}$, then $U[y^{(1)}] > U[y^{(2)}]$, and the optimal value of f_2 will not lie in the interval (w_B, w_u). Set $w_u = w_B$.

If $y^{(2)}$ is preferred to $y^{(1)}$, then $U[y^{(2)}] > U[y^{(1)}]$, and the optimal value of f_2 will not lie in the interval (w_1, w_A). Set $w_1 = w_A$.

Step 5:

We define the interval of uncertainty as $\left(\dfrac{(w_1 - w_u)}{I_0} \times 100 \right)$.

If the interval of uncertainty $< \varepsilon$ (chosen small value) or if the DM is satisfied with the current solution, stop; else return to Step 3.

At each iteration, we maximize $f_1(x)$ with a constraint on $f_2(x)$. The problem can also be solved by minimizing $f_2(x)$ with a constraint on $f_1(x)$.

8.5 Illustrative Example

In this section, we present an illustrative example and solve it using the proposed interactive optimization algorithm. The supply chain network consists of the following entities:

- Twenty potential suppliers provide the raw materials required to manufacture new products.
- Five manufacturing plants produce new products as well as refurbish the product returns.
- Sixteen potential warehousing facilities distribute new and refurbished products to the retailers in the forward channel.
- Five potential recovery centers collect product returns from the retailers and then inspect and distribute them to the manufacturing plants in the return channel.
- Nine potential hybrid facilities can act as warehouses in the forward channel and recovery centers in the return channel.
- One hundred retailers face demand from the customers.

The cost parameters are modeled as a function of the new product price. Refurbishing cost and inspection cost of returned products are set based on their tier of return; that is, the higher the tier of return, the higher is the cost of refurbishing and inspection. Initially, we assume a mix of 70% low-end and 30% high-end customers ($\omega_1 = 0.7$, $\omega_2 = 0.3$). Other cost parameters are shown in Table 8.10.

The capacities of the suppliers and plants, production cost and refurbishing cost at the plants, and the purchasing cost of raw materials are the same as given in the Appendix (see Table A1; available on the CRC Press website: http://www.crcpress.com/product/isbn/9781498708586). Three possible capacity levels (sizes) of warehouses and hybrid facilities could be built in their respective potential locations. The capacities and fixed cost of the warehouses, hybrid facilities, and the recovery centers are also given in

TABLE 8.10

Cost Parameters (Illustrative Example)

Parameter	Variable	Setting
Total cost of a new product	pp	$750
Profit margin		20%
Price of new product	np	$900
Purchasing cost of raw material	p_{sm}	~ Unif (70%, 80%) * pp
Production cost for a new product	pc_m	~ Unif (8%, 12%) * pp
Refurbishing cost for a returned product	rc_{1m}	~ Unif (6%, 8%) * pp
	rc_{2m}	~ Unif (14%, 18%) * pp
	rc_{3m}	~ Unif (25%, 35%) * pp
	rc_{4m}	~ Unif (45%, 55%) * pp
Transportation cost per unit between plant and warehouse/ hybrid facility/recovery center	$tr_{mw}, tr_{mh}, tr_{rm}$	~ Unif (5.5%, 6.5%) * pp
Transportation cost per unit between retailer and warehouse/ hybrid facility/recovery center	$tr_{wc}, tr_{hc}, tr_{cr}$	~ Unif (8.5%, 9.5%) * pp
Inspection cost of returned product at recovery center/ hybrid facility	in_{kr}, in_{kh}	~ Unif (8%, 12%) * rc_{km}
Price of a refurbished product	$rp < np$	75% of the new product price

the Appendix (see Tables A2, A3, and A4; available on the CRC Press website: http://www.crcpress.com/product/isbn/9781498708586). The demand values at the retailers are drawn from a uniform distribution between 500 and 700 units. New products are sold at a price of $1,000 per unit. The refurbished products are assumed to be sold at three-fourths of the new product price ($750 per unit). Product return percentage of 30% ($\gamma = 0.3$) is considered in this example. Out of the product returns, 50% are Tier 1 returns ($\beta_1 = 0.5$), 30% are Tier 2 returns ($\beta_2 = 0.3$), 10% are Tier 3 returns ($\beta_3 = 0.1$), and 10% are Tier 4 returns ($\beta_4 = 0.1$). Tier 1 and Tier 2 returns account for more than 90% of the total returns based on a case study published in Ovchinnikov (2011) for a major wireless carrier in North America. We assume 80% Tier 1 and Tier 2 returns. Tier 3 and Tier 4 returns are assumed to be 10% each in order to discuss their effect on the supply chain network design.

Vehicle capacity ($vcap$) is 40,000 units per vehicle. The energy produced by burning one gallon of diesel (te) is 128 kBtu, and the MPG of vehicles is 8.5. The distances between the stages in the supply chain are generated randomly using the settings shown in Table 8.11. The square footage and the energy used at the warehouses, hybrid facilities, and the recovery centers are given in the Appendix (see Tables A5, A6, and A7; available on the CRC Press website: http://www.crcpress.com/product/isbn/9781498708586).

We assume that the refurbished product quality in the market is uncertain and falls between [$q - i = 0.30, q + i = 0.7$]. The corresponding perceived

TABLE 8.11

Distance Settings (Illustrative Example)

Facilities in (Stage *i*—Stage *j*)	Distance Setting (in Miles)
(supplier – manufacturer)	~ Unif (100, 300) * 5
(manufacturer – warehouse), (manufacturer – hybrid facility), (recovery center – manufacturer)	~ Unif (100, 500) * 5
(warehouse – retailer), (hybrid facility – retailer), (retailer – recovery center)	~ Unif (200, 800) * 5

value falls between $[v(q–i) = 0.55, v(q+i) = 0.84]$ (see data in Table 8.7). The acceptance rate of low-end customers is calculated using Equation 8.1 and that of high-end customers is modeled using an inverted U-shaped function, given in Equation 8.2. In this example, the discount offered for refurbished products is initially set at 25% ($\theta = 0.25$). Customer acceptance rate for low-end customers (α_1) is calculated (using Equation 8.1) as 0.3103 (31.03%); for high-end customers (α_2), it is calculated (using Equation 8.2) as 0.1364 (13.64%).

The example is coded in Microsoft Visual C++ 6.0 and solved using ILOG Concert Technology with CPLEX 12.1 on a PC with INTEL(R) Core (TM) 2 Duo Processor at 2.8 GHz and 2.0 GB RAM. First, we solve and analyze the model with the profit objective. We will compare this solution with the Subramanian and Ravindran (2014) model solution to show the importance of incorporating the different tiers of returns in the model. We will then illustrate the utility of the proposed PCM using the example.

8.5.1 Profit Maximization Model

In this section, the model is first solved with the profit maximization objective. The model for this example has 11,723 variables (11,643 continuous variables and 80 binary variables) and 808 constraints. The model took approximately 12 seconds to solve for optimality. The optimal profit achieved by the model for this example is $12,295,957.

The total demand at the retailers is 60,028. Retailer returns in the model are calculated as follows:

$$\sum_{c \in C} \sum_{k \in K} \left\lfloor (\gamma.\beta_k.d_c) \right\rfloor = \underbrace{\sum_{c \in C} \left\lfloor 0.3 \times 0.5 \times d_c \right\rfloor}_{\text{Tier 1 returns}} + \underbrace{\sum_{c \in C} \left\lfloor 0.3 \times 0.3 \times d_c \right\rfloor}_{\text{Tier 2 returns}} + \underbrace{\sum_{c \in C} \left\lfloor 0.3 \times 0.1 \times d_c \right\rfloor}_{\text{Tier 3 returns}}$$

$$+ \underbrace{\sum_{c \in C} \left\lfloor 0.3 \times 0.1 \times d_c \right\rfloor}_{\text{Tier 4 returns}}.$$

Thus, retailer returns are 17,837, out of which 8,958 (50%) are Tier 1; 5,363 (30%) are Tier 2; 1,758 (10%) are Tier 3; and 1,758 (10%) are Tier 4 returns. Total acceptance for refurbished items is calculated as follows:

$$\sum_{c \in C} \left| \underbrace{(\alpha_1.\xi_1.d_c)}_{\substack{\text{low-end customer}\\\text{acceptance rate}}} + \underbrace{(\alpha_2.\xi_2.d_c)}_{\substack{\text{high-end customer}\\\text{acceptance rate}}} \right| = \sum_{c \in C} \left| \underbrace{(0.7 \times 0.3103 \times d_c)}_{\substack{\text{low-end customer}\\\text{acceptance rate}}} + \underbrace{(0.3 \times 0.1364 \times d_c)}_{\substack{\text{high-end customer}\\\text{acceptance rate}}} \right|.$$

Thus, the total acceptance for refurbished items is 15,449 based on the acceptance rates of low-end and high-end customers. Because the acceptance rate is less than the returns, some products are disposed of at the retailers. In the optimal solution, all the Tier 1 and Tier 2 returns are refurbished; 630 units of Tier 3 and 1,758 units of Tier 4 returns are disposed of at the retailers. We observe that higher tier returns are disposed of because their refurbishing costs are higher. Thus, it is important to consider different categories of returns and customer buying behavior in our model to avoid sub-optimal solutions. The optimal network design for the profit maximization objective is given in the Appendix (available on the CRC Press website: http://www.crcpress.com/product/isbn/9781498708586).

8.5.2 Paired Comparison Method

In this section, we illustrate the interactive solution method using the illustrative example. Let $f_1(x) = Z_1$ and $f_2(x) = Z_2$. We solve the problems (P1) and (P2) as follows:

(P1): Maximize Z_1, subject to constraints (Equations 8.5 through 8.24).

The optimal profit achieved by the model for this example is $12,295,957. The corresponding energy usage for this profit is 1,475,494 kBtu.

By solving the energy objective with the model presented in Section 8.3.4, we get a trivial solution with no shipments and all the returns being disposed of at the retailer. In order to get a realistic value for the energy objective, we incorporate a minimum demand satisfaction constraint in the model (see Equation 8.25).

$$\sum_{w \in W}(QWC_{wc} + RQWC_{wc}) + \sum_{h \in H}(QHC_{hc} + RQHC_{hc}) \ge (0.8 \times d_c) \quad \forall c \in C \quad (8.25)$$

(P2): Minimize Z_2, subject to constraints (Equations 8.5 through 8.25).[*]

The optimal energy consumed by the model for this example is 665,918 kBtu. The corresponding profit obtained for this energy usage is $7,667,994.

---

[*] Constraint (Equation 8.25) is added just to get a realistic value for the energy objective.

We assume a quasiconcave utility function for the DM in order to simulate the interaction process in the algorithm as shown:

$$U[Z_1, Z_2] = \left(\frac{Z_1^{2/3}}{Z_2^{1/2}} \right).$$

Interactive Solution Steps
Step 1:

Solve (P1): Max Z_1, subject to constraints (as defined earlier)

We get v* = 12,295,957.

Solve (P2): Min Z_2, subject to constraints (as defined earlier)

We get w* = w_1 = 665,918.

Step 2:

Solve (P_v): Min Z_2, subject to constraints (as defined for P(2)) & $Z_1 \geq$ v*

We get Min Z_2 = w_u = 1,475,494.

The optimal value of Z_2 lies between 665,918 and 1,475,494.

Calculate $I_0 = w_u - w_1$ = 1,475,494 − 665,918 = 809,576.

Figure 8.6 shows the efficient frontier of the bi-criteria problem. It is used to illustrate the trade-off curve between the profit and the energy objectives in the interactive algorithm. The ideal values for the profit and the energy objectives (v*, w*) are $12,295,957 and 665,918 kBtu, respectively. The corresponding energy usage for v* is 1,475,494 kBtu and the profit obtained for w* is $7,667,994 (see Figure 8.6). Thus, we get the bounds for the profit and the energy objectives as $7,667,994 and $12,295,957 and 665,918 kBtu and 1,475,494 kBtu, respectively. The two extreme solutions, $y^{(p)}$ and $y^{(e)}$, in Figure 8.6 are $12,295,957 and 1,475,494 kBtu and $7,667,994 and 665,918 kBtu, respectively, where $y^{(p)}$ maximizes profit and $y^{(e)}$ minimizes energy. In the interactive algorithm, we are trying to find the best compromise solution between the two extreme solutions using DM's preferences.

Iteration 1 (see Figure 8.6)
Step 3:
Choose w_A and w_B using the golden section search ratios 0.618 and 0.382.

Using the ratios, w_A = 975,176 and w_B = 1,166,236

Solve the problem, P_w: Max Z_1, subject to constraints (as defined for (P2))

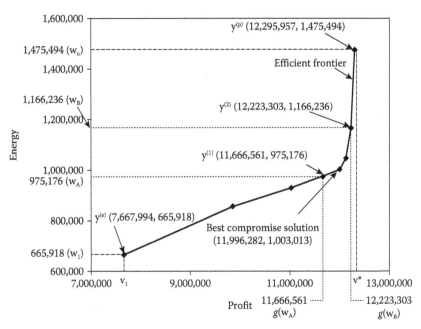

FIGURE 8.6
Illustration of the interactive method.

$$\text{and } Z_2 \leq w \text{ for } w = w_A \text{ and } w = w_B;$$

$$g(w_A) = 11{,}666{,}561 \text{ and } g(w_B) = 12{,}222{,}303$$

Step 4:

$$y^{(1)} = [11666561, 975176] \text{ and } y^{(2)} = [12223303, 1166236].$$

Interact with DM and get his preference between $y^{(1)}$ and $y^{(2)}$.
Assuming the utility function $U[Z_1, Z_2] = \left(Z_1^{2/3} \middle/ Z_2^{1/2} \right)$, $U[y^{(1)}] = 52.09$ and $U[y^{(2)}] = 49.14$. As $U[y^{(1)}] > U[y^{(2)}] \Rightarrow y^{(1)}$ is preferred to $y^{(2)}$.
Eliminate the interval (w_B, w_u). Update $w_u = w_b = 1{,}166{,}236$.

Step 5:
Assuming the interval of uncertainty has to be reduced to 10% we continue the search procedure on the reduced efficient frontier.

Table 8.12 shows the iterations of the algorithm. The best compromise solution obtained by the method is $Z_1 = \$11{,}996{,}282$ and $Z_2 = 1{,}003{,}013$ kBtu in Iteration 5.
In Iteration 1, $U[y^{(1)}] > U[y^{(2)}]$. Thus, the algorithm eliminates the region (w_B, w_u) from the efficient frontier; that is, the best compromise solution does

TABLE 8.12

Interactive Solutions for the Illustrative Example

Iteration #	w_l	w_u	w_A	w_B	$y^{(1)}$	$y^{(2)}$	$U[y^{(1)}]$	$U[y^{(2)}]$	Interval of Uncertainty (%)
0	665,918	1,475,494							
1	665,918	1,166,236	975,176	1,166,236	(11666561, 975176)	(12223303, 1166236)	52.09	49.14	61.80
2	857,039	1,166,236	857,039	975,176	(9852901, 857039)	(11666561, 975176)	49.65	52.09	38.19
3	857,039	1,048,123	975,176	1,048,123	(11666561, 975176)	(12124606, 1048123)	52.09	51.55	23.60
4	930,033	1,048,123	930,033	975,176	(11022459, 930033)	(11666561, 975176)	51.36	52.09	14.59
5	975,176	1,048,123	975,176	1,003,013	(11666561, 975176)	(11996282, 1003013)	52.09	52.33	9.01

not lie in the interval (w_B, w_u). Golden section search rule is used again to generate the next two points between (w_1, w_B) in Iteration 2 (see Table 8.12). We observe that one of the new points is w_A, and $U[y^{(2)}] > U[y^{(1)}]$. Hence, we eliminate the region (w_1, w_A) from the efficient frontier in Iteration 2. The same procedure is continued until the interval of uncertainty is reduced to a specified level. In general, the DM will be able to reduce the interval of uncertainty to less than 10% of the initial interval with just five iterations. The cognitive burden is minimal in each iteration because the DM has to give his preference between two solutions only. For a specified level of uncertainty, this method converges rapidly to the best compromise solution.

The best compromise network design solution by this method is as follows:

- Suppliers 1, 3, 5, 6, 7, 8, 9, and 10 are selected to supply raw materials to the plants for producing new products.
- Plants 1, 2, 3, and 5 are used in new product production, and Plants 1 and 2 are used for refurbishing the return products. Table 8.13 shows the product flows and production of new and refurbished products in the plants.
- Warehouse 12 of size 2 is opened. Warehouse 12 is used to distribute 10,613 units of new products and 4,748 units of refurbished products.
- Recovery centers are not used for distribution in the solution.
- Hybrid facilities 5 and 9, each of size 3, are opened. Hybrid facility 5 is used to distribute 16,381 units of new products and 5,498 units of refurbished products. Hybrid facility 9 is used to distribute 19,542 units of new products and 3,246 units of refurbished products. In the return path, Hybrid facility 5 collects and distributes 7,476 units of return products, and Hybrid facility 9 collects and distributes 6,016 units of return products.
- The retailers' demands are satisfied from Hybrid facility 5, Hybrid facility 9, and Warehouse 12 in the forward channel. The returns at the retailers are shipped to Hybrid facilities 5 and 9 in the return channel.

TABLE 8.13

Product Flows, Production, and Refurbishing in the Plants

	Production and Forward Channel Flow		Return Channel Flow (Units)
	New Products (Units)	Refurbished Products (Units)	
Plant 1	13,030	2,101	2,101
Plant 2	5,359	11,391	11,391
Plant 3	16,381	0	0
Plant 4	0	0	0
Plant 5	11,766	0	0

The percentage deviation of the best compromise solution, obtained in Iteration 5, corresponds to a 2.44% decrease for the profit objective and a 50.62% increase for the energy objective from the ideal values. Energy usage is reduced by 32.02% in the supply chain for a 2.44% decrease in profit when compared to the optimal solution with just profit maximization. These values are based on the best compromise solution obtained for the assumed utility function. The best compromise solution will vary depending on the DM and his relative preference between the profit and energy objectives.

8.6 Conclusions

Integrated operations and management of forward and reverse supply chains is critical to gain economic advantages in a CLSC. In this chapter, we considered an integrated four-stage supply chain network with forward and reverse product flows. The condition of returned products and the cost for refurbishing them varies significantly. Also, the customer behavior toward buying refurbished products is not the same. In this study, we extended our previous work by considering different tiers of return and customer buying behavior in purchasing refurbished products. We also considered two objectives—maximizing profit and minimizing energy usage in warehousing and transportation. We developed a bi-criteria MILP model for the problem. In the model, we considered two customer categories, high-end and low-end customers, and four tiers of returns based on the quality and condition of the products. We considered refurbishing cost based on the tier of return and modeled the acceptance rate of low-end and high-end customers. The model determined optimal locations of facilities and the distribution of new, refurbished, and returned products in the CLSC network.

First, we presented and analyzed the MILP model with the profit maximization objective using an illustrative example. Then, we proposed an interactive optimization algorithm to solve the proposed bi-criteria MILP model. The algorithm was illustrated using an example. The results showed the ability of the method to take the DM's preferences and systematically solve the bi-criteria problem. Also, the method posed less cognitive burden on the DM because the DM only had to compare two solutions and give his preference.

The model can be extended by considering other objectives such as supply chain risk, responsiveness in forward and reverse supply chains, and environmental impact. Interactive optimization methodologies with multiple objectives can be developed. We have not considered any uncertainties in the return parameters. The model can also be extended by considering uncertainties in demand and returned products.

References

Akcalı, E., Cetinkaya, S. and Uster, H. Network design for reverse and closed-loop supply chains: An annotated bibliography of models and solution approaches. *Networks* 53, no. 3 (2009): 231–248.

Amin, S. H., and Zhang, G. An integrated model for closed-loop supply chain configuration and supplier selection: Multi-objective approach. *Expert Systems with Applications* 39, no. 8 (2012): 6782–6791.

Amin, S. H., and Zhang, G. A three-stage model for closed-loop supply chain configuration under uncertainty. *International Journal of Production Research* 51, no. 5 (2013a): 1405–1425.

Amin, S. H., and Zhang, G. A multi-objective facility location model for closed-loop supply chain network under uncertain demand and return. *Applied Mathematical Modelling* 37, no. 6 (2013b): 4165–4176.

Atasu, A., Sarvary, M. and Wassenhove, L.N. Remanufacturing as a marketing strategy. *Management Science* 54, no. 9 (2008): 1731–1746.

De Rosa, V., Gebhard, M., Hartmann, E., and Wollenweber, J. Robust sustainable bi-directional logistics network design under uncertainty. *International Journal of Production Economics* 145, no. 1 (2013): 184–198.

Douthit, D., Flach, M., and Agarwal, V. *A Returning Problem: Reducing the Quantity and Cost of Product Returns in Consumer Electronics*. Accenture Report. 2011. http://www.cas-ag.org/SiteCollectionDocuments/PDF/Accenture-Reducing-the-Quantity-and-Cost-of-CustomerReturns.pdf (accessed on 20 January 2014).

Easwaran, G., and Uster, H. Tabu search and benders decomposition approaches for a capacitated closed-loop supply chain network design problem. *Transportation Science* 43, no. 3 (2009): 301–320.

Easwaran, G., and Uster, H. A closed-loop supply chain network design problem with integrated forward and reverse channel decisions. *IIE Transactions* 42, no. 11 (2010): 779–792.

Ferguson, M. E. Strategic and tactical aspects of closed-loop supply chains. *Foundations and Trends in Technology, Information and Operations Management* 3, no. 2 (2009): 103–200.

Fleischmann, M., Beullens, P., Bloemhof-Ruwaardz, J. M., and Wassenhove, L. V. N. The impact of product recovery on logistics network design. *Production and Operations Management* 10, no. 2 (2001): 156–173.

Geary, S., Disney, S. M., and Towill, D. R. On bullwhip in supply chains—Historical review, present practice and expected future impact. *International Journal of Production Economics* 101, no. 1 (2006): 2–18.

Guide, V. D. R., and Li, J. The potential for cannibalization of new products sales by remanufactured products. *Decision Sciences* 41, no. 3 (2010): 547–572.

Guide, V. D. R., Jr., and Wassenhove, L. V. N. The evolution of closed-loop supply chain research. *Operations Research* 57, no. 1 (2009): 10–18.

Halldórsson, Á., and Kovács, G. The sustainable agenda and energy efficiency: Logistics solutions and supply chains in times of climate change. *International Journal of Physical Distribution and Logistics Management* 40, no. 1/2 (2010): 5–13.

Hasani, A., Zegordi, S. H., and Nikbakhsha, E. Robust closed-loop supply chain network design for perishable goods in agile manufacturing under uncertainty. *International Journal of Production Research* 50, no. 16 (2012): 4649–4669.

Knemeyer, A. M., Ponzurick, G. T., and Logar, M. C. A qualitative examination of factors affecting reverse logistics systems for end-of-life computers. *International Journal of Physical Distribution and Logistics Management* 32, no. 6 (2002): 455–479.

Krikke, H., Bloemhof-Ruwaardz, J., and Wassenhove, L. V. N. Concurrent product and closed-loop supply chain design with an application to refrigerators. *International Journal of Production Research* 41, no. 16 (2003): 3689–3719.

Lee, C. *Analysis of Decision-Making in Closed-Loop Supply Chains.* Doctoral dissertation, Georgia Institute of Technology, 2011.

Masud, A. S. M., and Ravindran, A. Multiple criteria decision making. In *Operations Research and Management Science Handbook,* ed. A. R. Ravindran, Chapter 5. Pages 5–1 to 5–36. Boca Raton, FL: CRC Press, 2008.

Mehrbod, M., Tu, N., Miao, L., and Wenjing, D. Interactive fuzzy goal programming for a multi-objective closed-loop logistics network. *Annals of Operations Research* 201, no. 1 (2012): 367–381.

Mitra, S. Revenue management for remanufactured products. *Omega* 35, no. 5 (2007): 553–562.

Morgan, R. 2006. Tips and Tricks for Recycling Old Computers. SmartBiz. http://www.smartbiz.com/article/articleprint/1525/-1/58 (accessed on 1 December 2013).

Mutha, A., and Pokharel, S. Strategic network design for reverse logistics and remanufacturing using new and old product modules. *Computers and Industrial Engineering* 56, no. 1 (2009): 334–346.

New York Times. Japan recycles minerals from used electronics. 2010. http://www.nytimes.com/2010/10/05/business/global/05recycle.html?pagewanted=all&_r=0 (accessed on 15 November 2013).

Okada, E. M. Uncertainty, risk aversion, and WTA vs. WTP. *Marketing Science* 29, no. 1 (2010): 75–84.

Oscar, F. 2011. *Effect of Weight and Roadway Grade on the Fuel Economy of Class-8 Freight Trucks.* ORNL/TM-2011/471. Oak Ridge National Laboratory, 2011. http://cta.ornl.gov/cta/Publications/Reports/ORNL_TM_2011_471.pdf (accessed on 20 November 2013).

Ovchinnikov, A. Revenue and cost management for remanufactured products. *Production and Operations Management* 20, no. 6 (2011): 824–840.

Palmbeck, E. L. Reducing greenhouse gas emissions through operations and supply chain management. *Energy Economics* 34, no. 1 (2012): S64–S74.

Pishvaee, M. S., Farahani, R. Z., and Dullaert, W. A memetic algorithm for bi-objective integrated forward/reverse logistics network design. *Computers and Operations Research* 37, no. 6 (2010): 1100–1112.

Pishvaee, M. S., Jolai, F., and Razmi, J. A stochastic optimization model for integrated forward/reverse logistics network design. *Journal of Manufacturing Systems* 28, no. 4 (2009): 107–114.

Pishvaee, M. S., Rabbani, M., and Torabi, S. A. A robust optimization approach to closed-loop supply chain network design under uncertainty. *Applied Mathematical Modelling* 35, no. 2 (2011): 637–649.

Pishvaee, M. S., and Razmi, J. Environmental supply chain network design using multi-objective fuzzy mathematical programming. *Applied Mathematical Modelling* 36, no. 8 (2012): 3433–3446.

Pishvaee, M. S., and Torabi, S. A. A possibilistic programming approach for closed-loop supply chain network design under uncertainty. *Fuzzy Sets and Systems* 161, no. 20 (2010): 2668–2683.

Platt, B., and Hyde, J. *Plug into Electronics Reuse*. Washington, DC: Institute of Local elf Reliance, 1997, pp. 13–38.

Pochampally, K. K., Nukala, S., and Gupta, S. M. *Strategic Planning Models for Reverse and Closed-Loop Supply Chains*. Boca Raton, FL: CRC Press, 2009.

Sadagopan, S., and Ravindran, A. Interactive solution of bi-criteria mathematical programs. *Naval Research Logistics Quarterly* 29, no. 3 (1982): 443–459.

Salema, M. I. G., Povoa, A. P. B., and Novais, A. Q. A warehouse-based design model for reverse logistics. *Journal of the Operational Research Society* 57, no. 6 (2006): 615–629.

Salema, M. I. G., Povoa, A. P. B., and Novais, A. Q. An optimization model for the design of a capacitated multi-product reverse logistics network with uncertainty. *European Journal of Operational Research* 179, no. 3 (2007): 1063–1077.

Stock, J. R. *Reverse Logistics*. Oak Brook, IL: Council of Logistics Management, 1992.

Subramanian, P., Ramkumar, N., and Narendran, T. T. Mathematical model for multi-echelon, multi-product, single time-period closed loop supply chain. *International Journal of Business Performance and Supply Chain Modelling* 2, no. 3–4 (2010): 216–236.

Subramanian, P., Ramkumar, N., Narendran, T. T., and Ganesh, K. PRISM: Priority based simulated annealing for a closed loop supply chain network design problem. *Applied Soft Computing* 13, no. 2 (2013a): 1121–1135.

Subramanian, P., Ramkumar, N., Narendran, T. T., and Ganesh, K. A bi-objective network design model for multi-period, multi-product closed-loop supply chain. *Journal of Industrial and Production Engineering* 30, no. 4 (2013b): 264–280.

Subramanian, P., and Ravindran. A. R. Design of closed loop supply chain networks. *International Journal of Business Analytics* 1, no. 1 (2014): 43–66.

Thierry, M., Salomon, M., van Nunen, J. A. E. E., and Van Wassenhove, L. N. Strategic issues in product recovery management. *California Management Review* 37, no. 2 (1995): 114–135.

Torabi, S. A., and Hassini, E. An interactive possibilistic programming approach for multiple objective supply chain master planning. *Fuzzy Sets and Systems* 159, no. 2 (2008): 193–214.

US Energy Information Administration. Documentation for Emissions of Greenhouse Gases in the U.S. 2005, DOE/EIA-0638 (2005), October 2007, Tables 6-1, 6-4, and 6-5.Â [Non-biogenic carbon content and gross heat of combustion for motor gasoline and diesel (distillate fuel)]. 2007. http://www.eia.gov/survey/form/eia1605/coefficients.html (accessed on 20 December 2013).

Uster, H., Easwaran, G., Akçali, E., and Cetinkaya, S. Benders decomposition with alternative multiple cuts for a multi-product closed-loop supply chain network design model. *Naval Research Logistics* 54, no. 8 (2007): 890–907.

Visich, J., Li, S., and Khumawala, B. 2005. A framework for the implementation of radio frequency identification technology in closed-loop supply chains: Impact and challenges. *Innovation Monograph I—Enterprise Resource Planning: Teaching and Research*, SAP University Alliance Program and the Kelley School of Business, Indiana University, Bloomington, IN, November, 7–34.

Vorasayan, J., and Ryan, S. M. Optimal price and quantity of refurbished products. *Production and Operations Management* 15, no. 3 (2009): 369–383.

9

Multi-Objective Multi-Period Supplier Selection Problem with Product Bundling

Vijay Wadhwa

Texas Instruments Inc., Dallas, Texas

CONTENTS

9.1 Introduction

For most manufacturing firms, the purchasing of raw material and component parts constitutes a major expense. A study carried out by the Aberdeen group found that more than 83% of the organizations engaged in outsourcing achieved significant reduction in purchasing cost, more than 73% achieved reduction in transaction cost, and more than 60% were able to shrink sourcing and procurement cycles (Aberdeen Group 2004). Once a decision is made to outsource, the next critical activity is selecting the suppliers. Supplier selection is a key decision in outsourcing, which is prone to errors. The right supplier is one who will meet and complement the organization's needs from its corporate culture to its long-term future needs. The selection of a good supplier is difficult because some suppliers that meet some selection criteria may fail in others. In order to select the right supplier, two basic and interrelated decisions must be made by a firm. The firm must decide which suppliers to do business with and how much to order from each supplier. Weber et al. (1991) refer to this pair of decisions as the supplier selection problem.

Many organizations have found that the only way to align the procurement function with the overall firm's goals is to segregate the purchasing process into different segments based on supply strategies, supply tactics, and supply management approaches. This differentiation process is known as *supply segmentation* (Cavinato and Kauffman 1999).

9.1.1 Supply Segmentation Approach

Supply segmentation provides a mechanism for distinguishing among different items and services that are purchased by a firm with the goal of developing specific strategies to meet the needs of the organization. For constructing a supply segmentation matrix, each firm should carry out a *spend analysis* (Cavinato and Kauffman 1999). In the spend analysis, the total purchasing cost of the products is plotted on the x-axis and market-risk is plotted on the y-axis. The cost represents the importance of the item in terms of annual dollars spent. Each organization also has to define its own risks, which may include technological risks, supply risks, demand risks, environmental risks, and so on. The result of the spend analysis is the supply segment matrix, which is represented in Figure 9.1. Products classified in each of the four quadrants have specific characteristics, as shown in Figure 9.2. In this chapter, we present a supplier selection method for tactical items (Quadrant I).

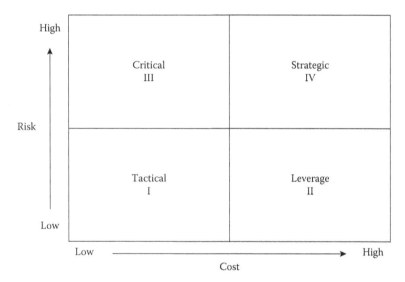

FIGURE 9.1
Supplier selection framework.

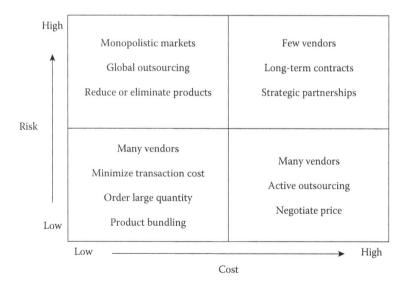

FIGURE 9.2
Purchasing strategy for each quadrant.

9.1.2 Supplier Selection for Tactical Items

Tactical items represented in the first quadrant of the supply matrix are low-risk and low-cost items (i.e., not only the cost of these items to the firm is low but the risk of disruption due to the nonavailability of these items also is low). Maintenance, repair, and operating (MRO) items and office supplies are some examples of products that can be classified as tactical. The largest number of parts and components in any organization will eventually be classified as tactical. There are many suppliers that supply these items; however, due to the low value of these items, it is not beneficial to frequently search and choose suppliers for these products.

9.1.3 Supply Strategy for Tactical Items

In most organizations, the majority of the items are classified as tactical. Although these items are large in number, their overall cost impact is low. The strategy adopted for tactical items includes product standardization, volume ordering, efficient processing, and inventory management. For tactical items, in addition to the selling price of each item, the transaction cost (fixed order cost) is also important because the transaction cost may exceed the quoted price of the supplier. Therefore, tactical items should be consolidated to minimize the transaction cost of procurement.

9.1.4 Problem Definition

In this chapter, we present a multi-period supplier selection problem with product bundling. Due to the advances in information technology (IT), the demand for tactical items is deterministic; therefore, the buyer can forecast demand for various products in each time period with high confidence. These days, most suppliers offer a variable pricing model where the final price may be discounted based on the quantity of product purchased; in this chapter, we model the supplier discount using product bundling. Product bundling is a form of discount where the final price of a product depends on the quantities of different products ordered.

Supplier selection problem is inherently a multi-objective problem, a supplier with the lowest cost may also have very high rejects. In this chapter, we model the supplier selection problem with four objectives. The first objective is to minimize the total cost. The total cost is composed of variable cost, fixed cost, inventory holding cost, and bundling cost. The variable cost is the cost to buy every additional unit. The buyer incurs a fixed cost to order shipments from the suppliers. The fixed cost may include the cost incurred in order requisitions, transportation, and so on. The fixed cost is incurred every time a buyer places an order with the supplier. The buyer also incurs a holding cost to maintain inventory of the procured items. The holding cost is applied to each product in inventory that is carried from one period to another. The last component of the cost is the price reduction due to bundling. If a buyer buys enough quantities of different products from a supplier, then that supplier offers free units of some products that are credited back to the buyer.

The second objective is to minimize rejects over the planning horizon. Every supplier maintains a certain quality standard for each product in each period. The buyer's objective is to decide which products to order from which supplier, in what quantity, and in which period that will minimize the rejects.

The third objective is to minimize the lead time for procurement. Finally, the fourth objective minimizes the value-at-risk (VaR) type risks resulting from transactions with suppliers. VaR type risks are used to model less frequent events that disrupt operations at suppliers that can bring severe impacts to buyers (e.g., a labor strike, terrorist attack, natural disaster, etc.).

In this chapter, we demonstrate the application of a multi-criteria decision-making approach to supplier selection and the use of goal programming (GP) as a solution approach. Supplier selection criteria are conflicting in nature and, because all the criteria/goals cannot be achieved simultaneously by a single supplier, an integer programming solution model might result in an infeasible solution. This problem is overcome by *GP*, which has become a practical method for handling multiple criteria. GP falls under the class of methods that use completely pre-specified preferences of the decision maker in solving the multi-objective optimization problem. The multi-objective problem is solved using four different variants of GP—namely, preemptive GP, non-preemptive GP, fuzzy GP, and Tchebycheff GP. The results of the multi-objective formulations are then compared against each other using the value path approach.

The rest of the chapter is organized as follows: Section 9.2 contains a brief review of supplier selection literature. In Section 9.3, we present the multi-objective supplier selection problem and discuss various GP approaches to solving the problem. Section 9.4 illustrates the application of the solution approach using a numerical example. Section 9.5 contains the conclusion.

9.2 Literature Review

Supplier selection plays a key role in cost reduction and is one of the most important functions of the purchasing department. Several factors affect a supplier's performance. An important review of these criteria has been carried out by Weber et al. (1991) and by Deshmukh and Chaudhari (2011). They assigned rankings based on the proportion of articles that discussed a given criterion. Price, quality, and lead time consistently ranked among the top three over the years. In the 1990s, geographical location was among the top five criteria while, in the first decade of the twenty-first century, it was displaced by technical capability and financial position. Ho et al. (2010) presented a review of multiple criteria approaches mentioned in 78 articles appearing in international journals between 2000 and 2008. Agarwal et al. (2011) offered a different review based on 68 articles published between 2000 and 2011 related to supplier evaluation and selection.

It is necessary to make a trade-off between conflicting qualitative and quantitative factors to find the best supplier(s). Mathematical programming models are the most appropriate methods for multiple sourcing situations (Ravindran and Warsing 2013). They allow the inclusion of constraints related to capacity, delivery time, quality, and others, while suppliers are selected along with their order allocations. Demirtas and Ustun (2008) present a multi-objective model that evaluates total material cost, supplier defect rate, and total purchasing value using the Chebycheff technique to solve the problem. Elahi and Etaati (2011) developed a bi-objective mixed integer non-linear program for allocating orders in a four-echelon supply chain, which maximizes service level and minimizes total costs for multiple periods. Li and Zabinsky (2011) applied two multi-objective models, which included a stochastic programming (SP) model and a chance-constrained programming (CCP) model to determine a minimal set of suppliers and optimal order quantities with consideration of business volume discounts. Sawik (2010) developed a bi-criteria version of an integer programming model that incorporates risk constraints.

Weber et al. (1991), Degraeve (1999), De boer et al. (2001), Wadhwa and Ravindran (2007), Aissaoui et al. (2007), Wadhwa (2008), Ravindran and Wadhwa (2009), and Ravindran and Warsing (2013) provide a comprehensive review of supplier selection methods and solutions.

9.2.1 Supplier Selection with Quantity Discounts

According to Aissaoui et al. (2007), supplier selection problems without discounts are easier to solve compared to the supplier selection problems in the presence of quantity discounts. The most common types of discounts found in literature are all-units and incremental discounts. In this chapter, we model the quantity discount using bundling. Bundling is the practice of marketing two or more products or services (or both) in a single package. Use of bundling is widespread in many products and services. Some common examples of bundling are:

1. Travel websites offer specials price on booking flights and hotels/cars together.
2. Automotive manufacturers offer optional equipment as a package.
3. In the telecommunications industry, the providers offer bundling discounts on cable, internet, and phone.

The two most common bundling practices are *pure bundling* and *mixed bundling* (Rosenthal et al. 1995):

- *Pure bundling:* In pure bundling, the buyer only can buy the entire bundle (i.e., the buyer cannot buy any individual items).
- *Mixed bundling:* Mixed bundling is a more general form of bundling in the sense that the buyer may purchase the entire bundle or individual items. Mixed bundling can be further classified as:
  - *Mixed leader:* In mixed leader, the price of one of the two products is discounted when the other product is purchased at regular price.
  - *Mixed joint:* In mixed joint form of product bundling, the price P_{A+B} is set when two products A and B are purchased jointly (i.e., $P_{A+B} < P_A + P_B$).

Rosenthal et al. (1995) have illustrated three different bundling scenarios.

- In the first scenario, the buyer has the option of buying the entire bundle but not buy any subset of it. This bundling scenario is equivalent to pure bundling.
- In the second scenario, the buyer can get a per unit discount on one product when sufficient quantities of all other items are purchased.
- In the third scenario, the buyer receives free units of some items when sufficient quantities of other items are purchased.

Scenario 3 is the most general form of bundling and can be extended to model the other two bundling scenarios.

9.2.1.1 Illustration of Bundling

Bundling can be illustrated using the following example. Suppose a buyer has a demand of 100 units each of two products A and B. Supplier *s* offers the product A for $1,000 apiece and product B for $100 apiece; the supplier also offers bundling discounts. The bundling scenario states that if the buyer buys 100 units of item A at $1,000 each and 50 units of item B at $100 each, then the supplier will give 50 units of item B free. This concept of bundling can be extended to a case where more than two products are offered on bundle. For example, in the case of four products, a sample bundling case could be as follows: The supplier offers a bundling discount on either all or a subset of all products. For example, if a buyer buys at least 100 units of product 1, 100 of product 2, 100 of product 3, and 100 of product 4, then the supplier provides 0 units of product 1, 5 units of product 2, 10 units of product 3, and 10 units of product 4 free of cost. This means that even though the buyer does not get any free units on product 1, the buyer still has to buy at least 100 units of product 1 to satisfy bundling condition for other products.

9.2.2 Multi-Period Supplier Selection Problem

A vast majority of research in the area of supplier selection considers only a single period problem. According to Aissaoui et al. (2007), although a multi-period supplier selection problem is difficult to solve, the potential benefits of solving such a problem are many. One of the primary advantages of considering a multi-period supplier selection problem is that the buyer can study the trade-off among inventory holding costs, transaction costs, and quantity discounts.

Multi-period problems are usually solved in a rolling format whereby the model is solved at the beginning of each period. For instance, at the end of the first period, the model is moved forward and the second period becomes the first period and so on. Interaction among the periods is obtained by using an inventory decision variable. For example, a buyer buys P_t units in a period t and let I_t and D_t be the inventory left at the end of period t and the demand in period t, respectively, then the material balance constraint for period t is

Beginning Inventory + production − ending inventory = demand

$$I_{t-1} + P_t - I_t = D_t \tag{9.1}$$

Equation 9.1 assumes zero lead time. For the first period I_1 is either equal to 0 or equal to the inventory held in the system at the end of previous cycle. Similarly, at the end of the cycle, the ending inventory could be either equal to 0 or an amount decided by the buyer. In our formulation, the buyer has to trade-off among the fixed order cost (transaction cost), the inventory holding cost, and the benefits of product bundling.

In multi-period inventory selection problem, one or more suppliers can be chosen in each of the periods or the products can be carried forward to a future period incurring holding cost. Inventory lot size and supplier selection are closely related. Supplier selection problem that include multiple time periods can lead to reduction in purchasing price and also can improve inventory management.

9.3 Multi-Objective Multi-Period Supplier Selection Model with Product Bundling

The supplier selection problem involves decisions that need to be made by an organization that would not only minimize total purchasing cost but also minimize rejects, the lead time of the products, and VaR risk. We consider the least restrictive case for modeling as a situation where the buyers can acquire one or more products from any of the suppliers. The mathematical model for the problem is discussed next.

i	Set of products to be purchased $(i = 1... I)$
j	Potential set of suppliers $(j = 1...J)$
t	Set of time periods $(t = 1...T)$, where T is the planning horizon

Data

p_{ij}	Cost of acquiring one unit of demand of product i from supplier j
H_i	Holding cost of product i per time period
F_j	Fixed cost associated with supplier j
D_{it}	Demand of product i in period t
q_{ijt}	Quality that supplier j maintains for product i in period t, which is measured as percent of defects
l_{ijt}	Lead time of supplier j for product i in period t, which is measured in number of days. The lead time of different buyers is not the same because of geographical distance
CAP_{ijt}	Production capacity of supplier j for product i in period t
B_{ij}	Minimum quantity of product i to be purchased from supplier j for satisfying the bundling constraints
VaR_j	Quantified VaR type risk for supplier j
k_{ij}	Free items offered by supplier j for product i when bundling requirements are satisfied

Variables in the Model

x_{ijt}	Number of units of product i supplied by supplier j in period t
I_{it}	Inventory of product i carried from period t to $t+1$
y_{jt}	Binary variable indicating whether or not an order is placed with supplier j in period t
z_j	One binary variable for each supplier, with $z_j = 1$ if $\sum_t x_{ijt} > B_{ij}$ for all products and 0 otherwise

Objective Function

$$\min\left(\sum_i \sum_j \sum_t p_{ij} x_{ijt} + \sum_j \sum_t F_j \cdot y_{jt} + \sum_i \sum_t H_i I_{it} - \sum_i \sum_j p_{ij} k_{ij} z_j\right) \quad (9.2)$$

$$\min \sum_i \sum_j \sum_t q_{ijt} \cdot x_{ijt} \quad (9.3)$$

$$\min \sum_i \sum_j \sum_t l_{ijt} \cdot x_{ijt} \quad (9.4)$$

$$\min \sum_i \sum_j \sum_t VaR_j \cdot x_{ijt} \quad (9.5)$$

The first objective function minimizes the total purchasing cost (Equation 9.2). Purchasing costs have four components: *variable cost, fixed cost, inventory holding cost,* and the *bundling discount*. The first component, the variable cost, is directly proportional to the number of units purchased. The fixed cost, the second component, is incurred if a supplier is chosen irrespective of the number of units purchased. The third component, the inventory holding cost, is incurred for holding inventory from one period to other. The last component is the amount credited to the buyer if the bundling constraints are satisfied.

The second objective is the minimization of the number of rejects (Equation 9.3). Summed over all products and time periods, it minimizes the overall rejects for all supplier-product-time period combinations.

The third objective is the minimization of lead time (Equation 9.4). Summed over all products and time periods, it minimizes the lead time for all supplier-product time periods.

The fourth objective minimizes the VaR type risks resulting from transactions with suppliers (Equation 9.5).

Constraints
Demand/Inventory Constraints

$$\sum_j x_{ijt} + I_{i,t-1} = D_{it} + I_{it} \quad \forall\, i, t \tag{9.6}$$

$$\sum_j x_{ijt} \le \sum_{t=t}^{T} D_{it} \quad \forall\, i, t \tag{9.7}$$

Capacity Constraints

$$x_{ijt} \le CAP_{ijt} \cdot y_{jt} \quad \forall\, i, j, t \tag{9.8}$$

Bundling Constraints

$$B_{ij} \cdot z_j - \sum_t x_{ijt} \le 0 \quad \forall\, i, j \tag{9.9}$$

Nonnegativity and Binary Constraints

$$y_{jt} \in (0, 1) \tag{9.10}$$

$$z_j \in (0, 1) \tag{9.11}$$

$$I_{i,j} \geq 0 \tag{9.12}$$

$$x_{ijt} \geq 0 \tag{9.13}$$

Equation 9.6, the material balancing constraint, states that all the requirements for a period must be satisfied (i.e., shortage and backordering are not allowed). It also specifies that the number of units purchased in any period plus any inventory carried from previous periods must be equal to demand for that period plus the inventory carried forward. Equation 9.7 ensures that the maximum the buyer can buy should not exceed the total remaining demand for that product over the planning horizon. Equation 9.8 models the capacity limit of each supplier and stipulates that a fixed cost is incurred whenever an order is placed with a supplier. The total order placed with a supplier should be less than or equal to the available capacity in that period. Note that the binary variable (y_{jt}) is used to activate the constraint for a supplier j only if supplier j is chosen in that period. Equation 9.9 is used to model the bundling constraint, where z_j is a binary variable, one for each supplier, such that

$$z_j = \begin{cases} 1 & \text{if } \sum_t x_{ijt} \geq B_{ij} \\ 0 & \text{otherwise} \end{cases}$$

The advantage of this model is that z_j could be made a general integer; in that case, the buyer can buy more than one bundle from the same supplier over the planning horizon. Finally, Equations 9.10 through 9.13 force nonnegativity and binary restrictions on the decision variables.

9.3.1 Model Size

For a problem with i products, j suppliers, and t time periods, the size of the problem is as follows:

- Demand/inventory constraints: $i * t + i * t$
- Capacity constraints: $i * j * t$
- Bundling constraints: $i * j$
- Total constraints: $i * (2 * t + j * t + j)$
- Total integer variables: $j * t + j$
- Total continuous variables: $i * t + i * j * t$

This problem size represents the worst case scenario. In most problems, the matrix of variables will be sparse because many variables will be zero; therefore, the computations would be less intensive.

9.3.2 Solution Methodology

One way to treat multiple criteria is to select one criterion as primary and the other criteria as secondary. The primary criterion is then used as the optimization objective function, while the secondary criteria are assigned acceptable minimum and maximum values and are treated as problem constraints. However, if careful considerations were not given while selecting the acceptable levels, a feasible solution that satisfies all the constraints may not exist. This problem is overcome by Goal Programming (GP), which has become a practical method for handling multiple criteria.

In GP, all the objectives are assigned target levels for achievement and relative priority on achieving these levels. GP treats these targets as *goals to aspire to* and not as absolute constraints (Masud and Ravindran 2008). It then attempts to find an optimal solution that comes as "close as possible" to the targets in the order of specified priorities. GP is one of the most commonly used techniques to solve multi-objective optimization problems. We solve the supplier selection problem using four different variants of GP (Ravindran and Wadhwa 2009), namely,

- Preemptive GP
- Non-preemptive GP
- Tchebycheff (min–max) GP
- Fuzzy GP

9.3.2.1 Preemptive Goal Programming

In preemptive GP, priority is assigned for each incommensurable goal and weights are assigned to goals at the same priority. Goals at a higher priority have to be satisfied before lower priority goals are even considered. The preemptive GP formulation for a supplier selection problem is as follows:

$$\min P_1 d_1^+ + P_2 d_2^+ + P_3 d_3^+ + P_4 d_4^+ \tag{9.14}$$

Subject to:

$$\left(\sum_i \sum_j \sum_t p_{ij} x_{ijt} + \sum_j \sum_t F_k \cdot y_{jt} + \sum_i \sum_t H_i I_{it} - \sum_i \sum_j p_{ij} k_{ij} z_j \right) + d_1^- - d_1^+ \tag{9.15}$$

$$= \text{Price goal}$$

$$\sum_i \sum_j \sum_t q_{ijt} x_{ijt} + d_2^- - d_2^+ = \text{quality goal} \tag{9.16}$$

$$\sum_i \sum_j \sum_t l_{ijt} x_{ijt} + d_3^- - d_3^+ = \text{lead time goal} \tag{9.17}$$

$$\sum_i \sum_j \sum_t \text{VaR}_j x_{ijt} + d_4^- - d_4^+ = \text{VaR type risk goal} \tag{9.18}$$

$$d_n^-, d_n^+ \geq 0 \quad \forall n = 1...4 \tag{9.19}$$

All the constraints (Equations 9.6 through 9.13) are also included in the model. The decision maker (DM) provides preference ranking of goals without any weight. In our formulation, price is the more important than quality, followed by lead time and VaR type risk goals. Target values of the goals are to be set by the DM. Variables $d_1^-, d_2^-, d_3^-, d_4^-, d_1^+, d_2^+, d_3^+$, and d_4^+ are the deviation variables representing how far away we are from satisfying each goal. Symbols P_1, P_2, P_3, and P_4 stand for preemptive priorities, determining the hierarchy of goals. Goals of the higher priority levels are satisfied before any of lower priority goals are considered.

9.3.2.2 Non-Preemptive Goal Programming

In the non-preemptive GP model, the buyer sets goals to achieve for each objective, and preference in achieving those goals is expressed as numerical weights, one for each goal as follows:

- Weight w_1 for the price goal
- Weight w_2 for the quality goal
- Weight w_3 for the lead time goal
- Weight w_4 for the VaR type risk goal

Thus, the non-preemptive GP formulation for the supplier selection becomes:

$$\text{Min } Z = w_1 \cdot d_1^+ + w_2 \cdot d_2^+ + w_3 \cdot d_3^+ + w_4 \cdot d_4^+ \tag{9.20}$$

Subject to:

$$\left(\sum_i \sum_j \sum_t p_{ij} x_{ijt} + \sum_j \sum_t F_k \cdot y_{jt} + \sum_i \sum_t H_i I_{it} - \sum_i \sum_j p_{ij} k_{ij} z_j \right) + d_1^- - d_1^+ \tag{9.21}$$

$$= \text{Price goal}$$

$$\sum_i \sum_j \sum_t q_{ijt} x_{ijt} + d_2^- - d_2^+ = \text{quality goal} \tag{9.22}$$

$$\sum_i \sum_j \sum_t l_{ijt} x_{ijt} + d_3^- - d_3^+ = \text{lead time goal} \tag{9.23}$$

$$\sum_i \sum_j \sum_t \text{VaR}_j x_{ijt} + d_4^- - d_4^+ = \text{VaR type risk goal} \tag{9.24}$$

$$d_n^-, d_n^+ \geq 0 \quad \forall n = 1\ldots 4 \tag{9.25}$$

In this model, d_1^+, d_2^+, d_3^+, and d_4^+ represent the overachievement of the stated goals. Due to the use of the weights, goals have to be scaled properly. The weights w_1, w_2, w_3, and w_4 can be varied to obtain different solutions.

9.3.2.3 Tchebycheff (Min–Max) Goal Programming

The Tchebycheff GP model minimizes the maximum weighted deviation from the stated goals. For the supplier selection problem, the Tchebycheff goal program becomes:

$$\text{Min}\left[\text{Max}\left(w_1 \cdot d_1^+, w_2 \cdot d_2^+, w_3 \cdot d_3^+, w_4 \cdot d_4^+\right)\right] \tag{9.26}$$

where w_1, w_2, w_3, and w_4 are the same weights used in non-preemptive GP.
Equation 9.26 can be reformulated as a linear objective by setting

$$\text{Max}\left(w_1 \cdot d_1^+, w_2 \cdot d_2^+, w_3 \cdot d_3^+, w_4 \cdot d_4^+\right) = \text{M}.$$

Thus, Equation 9.26 is equivalent to:

$$\text{Min } Z = M \tag{9.27}$$

Subject to:

$$M \geq \left(w_1 \cdot d_1^+\right) \tag{9.28}$$

$$M \geq \left(w_2 \cdot d_2^+\right) \tag{9.29}$$

$$M \geq \left(w_3 \cdot d_3^+\right) \tag{9.30}$$

$$M \geq \left(w_4 \cdot d_4^+\right) \tag{9.31}$$

$$M \geq 0 \tag{9.32}$$

Constraints (Equations 9.6 through 9.13) and (Equations 9.21 through 9.24) stated earlier will also be included in this model. The disadvantages of this method are (i) the scaling of goals is necessary (as required in non-preemptive GP) and (ii) outliers are given more importance and could lead to poor solutions.

9.3.2.4 Fuzzy Goal Programming

Fuzzy GP uses the ideal values as targets and minimizes the maximum normalized distance from the ideal solution for each objective. An ideal solution is the vector of the best values of each criterion obtained by optimizing each criterion independently, ignoring other criteria. In this example, the ideal solution is obtained by minimizing the price, quality, lead time, and VaR goals independently. In most problem settings, the ideal solution is not achievable because the criteria conflict with one another. Ideal values are also used to scale the different goals.

If M equals the maximum deviation from the ideal solution, then the fuzzy GP model is as follows:

$$\text{Min } Z = M \tag{9.33}$$

Subject to:

$$M \geq \frac{d_1^+}{\text{Ideal value of Price objective}} \tag{9.34}$$

$$M \geq \frac{d_2^+}{\text{Ideal value of Quality objective}} \tag{9.35}$$

$$M \geq \frac{d_3^+}{\text{Ideal value of Lead Time objective}} \tag{9.36}$$

$$M \geq \frac{d_4^+}{\text{Ideal value of VaR Type Risk objective}} \tag{9.37}$$

$$M \geq 0 \tag{9.38}$$

Constraints (Equations 9.6 through 9.13) and (Equations 9.21 through 9.24) stated earlier will also be included in this model.

9.4 Supplier Selection with Bundling and Inventory Management: A Case Study

To illustrate the supplier selection method for tactical items with product bundling and to evaluate the effectiveness of GP as a solution method, we solved several supplier selection models with varying parameters and compared their solutions. This section describes how the problems were generated, computational results, and our recommendation on which GP method works better. In the case study, we assume that every supplier is capable of supplying every product. The scenario where a supplier does not supply a particular product can easily be incorporated into the model. For convenience, we also assume that every supplier offers a similar bundling discount profile. The bundling threshold and quantity of free units is set arbitrarily. The problem formulation in the illustration only considers the price and quality (reject) objective.

9.4.1 Experimental Design

We varied the number of products, number of suppliers, and number of time periods to generate several supplier selection problems. The problems require data on the number of products, number of suppliers, number of time periods, price, capacity, quality, and bundling for various suppliers as well as the holding cost of product and the demand of different products in each time period. The complete data used in the case study are given in Wadhwa (2008). The experimental design is illustrated in Table 9.1.

The number of products is fixed at two different levels—namely, 4 and 8. The number of suppliers and time periods are fixed at 4 and 12, respectively. Data required in the model is generated through a uniform distribution (Jayaraman et al. 1999). We adopt these settings to evaluate a base case of the problem and then parametrically vary them to evaluate the performance of the model. In order to evaluate the effectiveness of the different GP model solutions, we measure their goal achievements. The various parameters used in the model are:

- Demand of each product in each period ~ uniform [100, 200]
- Price that the supplier charges for each product ~ uniform [30, 50]
- Percentage rejections of each product by the supplier in each time period ~ uniform [0.01, 0.09]
- Fixed cost of each supplier ~ uniform [1000, 1200]

TABLE 9.1

Experimental Design by Varying
Product, Supplier, and Time

Set	Products	Suppliers	Time Periods
1	4	4	4
2	4	4	12
3	4	12	4
4	4	12	12
5	8	4	4
6	8	4	12
7	8	12	4
8	8	12	12

- Holding cost of each product ~ uniform [1, 3]
- Capacity of each supplier for each product in each time period ~ uniform [100, 200]

9.4.2 Computational Results

We solve eight different problems using four different variants of GP, as discussed previously. For the purpose of illustration, computational results for the first problem set involving four products, four suppliers, and four time periods are discussed here.

9.4.2.1 Preemptive Goal Programming

In preemptive GP, price is given the highest priority, followed by quality. The target values for each of the objectives are set at 102% of the ideal value. For example, the ideal (minimum) value for price objective is \$86,195; hence, the target value for price is \$87,918.90, and the goal is to minimize the deviation above the target value. Table 9.2 illustrates the solution using the preemptive GP model. Preemptive GP does not require the goals to be scaled. Numbers of units bought from different suppliers in each time period are shown in Table 9.3. Inventory carried on from one period to another is shown in Table 9.4.

Three different suppliers were utilized to supply the different products. Table 9.5 shows the capacity utilization for different suppliers. This is useful in case of a sudden surge in demand or a supply disruption at one or more suppliers.

The bundling conditions for supplier 2 and 3 are satisfied; hence, z_2 and z_3 are 1, and the buyer receives free units from suppliers 2 and 3.

9.4.2.2 Non-Preemptive Goal Programming

In non-preemptive GP, weights w_1 and w_2 are 0.75 and 0.25 for price and quality, respectively. The target values used are the same as in preemptive GP. The solution of the non-preemptive GP model is shown in Table 9.6. Non-preemptive GP requires scaling; the target values are used as scaling constants.

TABLE 9.2

Preemptive Goal Programming Solution

Preemptive GP	Ideal Values	Preemptive Priorities	Scaling Constant	Target for Preemptive Goal (Ideal+2%)	Actual Achieved	Whether Goal Achieved
Price	86195	1	N/A	87918.9	87918.9	Achieved
Quality	80.76	2		82.37	115	Not achieved

TABLE 9.3

Preemptive Goal Programming Solution:
Supplier Allocation

Product	Supplier	Time Period	Quantity
1	1	1	185
1	2	1	60
1	2	3	121
1	3	2	115
1	3	4	163
2	1	1	126
2	2	1	188
2	2	3	135
2	2	4	140
2	3	2	9
2	3	4	49
3	2	1	146
3	2	3	145
3	2	4	102
3	3	1	67
3	3	2	140
3	3	4	89
4	1	1	54
4	2	3	42
4	3	1	196
4	3	2	125
4	3	4	152

TABLE 9.4

Preemptive Goal Programming
Solution: Inventory Decision

Product	Time Period	Inventory
1	1	60
1	2	38
2	1	139
2	2	27
3	1	13
3	2	19
4	1	71
4	2	81

TABLE 9.5

Preemptive Goal Programming
Solution: Supplier Capacity
Allocation

Supplier	Capacity Used (%)
1	15.93
2	44.99
3	48.4
4	0

TABLE 9.6

Non-Preemptive Goal Programming Solution

Non-Preemptive GP	Ideal Values	Weights	Scaling Constant	Target for Non-Preemptive GP	Actual Achieved	Whether Goal Achieved
Price	86195	0.75	87918.9	87918.9	89878	Not achieved
Quality	80.76	0.25	82.37	82.37	91.87	Not achieved

TABLE 9.7

Tchebycheff Goal Programming Solution

Tchebycheff GP	Ideal Values	Weights	Scaling Constant	Target for Tchebycheff GP	Actual Achieved	Whether Goal Achieved
Price	86195	0.75	0.01	87918.9	90782	Not achieved
Quality	80.76	0.25	10	82.37	90.95	Not achieved

9.4.2.3 Tchebycheff Goal Programming

In Tchebycheff GP, the target values used are the same as in preemptive goal programming. Scaling constants are chosen in such a way that both the objectives have a similar magnitude. For example, price target ($87,918.90) when multiplied by 0.01 gives $879.18, and quality (82.37) when multiplied by 10 yields 823.7; this makes price and quality of similar magnitude. Using the Tchebycheff method, the solution obtained is illustrated in Table 9.7.

9.4.2.4 Fuzzy Goal Programming

In fuzzy GP, the ideal values are used as targets for the different goals. The solution obtained using fuzzy GP is shown in Table 9.8.

9.4.3 Value Path Approach for Comparison of Multi-Objective Problems

The presentation of results in a multi-objective problem presents a critical link. Any sophisticated analysis without a good visual can render it useless.

TABLE 9.8

Fuzzy Goal Programming Solution

Fuzzy GP	Ideal Values	Weights	Scaling Constant	Target for Fuzzy GP	Actual Achieved	Whether Goal Achieved
Price	86195	NA	NA	86195	89893	Not achieved
Quality	80.76	NA	NA	80.76	91.85	Not achieved

In the case of multi-objective problems, a lot of information needs to be conveyed that not only includes performance of various alternatives but also trade-offs among different solutions.

The value path approach is one of the most efficient ways to demonstrate the trade-offs among different criteria; this approach was developed by Schilling et al. (1983). The display consists of a set of parallel scales—one for each criterion on which is drawn the value path for each of the alternatives. Value paths have proven to be an effective way to present the trade-offs in problems with multiple objectives.

The value assigned to each solution on a particular axis is that solution's value for the appropriate objective divided by the best solution for that objective. Therefore, the minimum value for each axis is 1. Following are some properties of the value path approach:

- If two value paths representing alternatives A and B intersect between two vertical scales, then the line segment connecting A and B in objective space has a negative slope and neither objective dominates the other.
- If three or more value paths intersect, then their associated points in the objective space are collinear.
- If two paths do not intersect, then one path must lie entirely below the other and is therefore inferior.
- Given any intersecting pair of value paths, a third value path is inferior if it does not lie above the intersecting point.

The four variants of GP models provided different optimal solutions. A summary of the solutions obtained through the four methods is illustrated in Table 9.9.

The following illustrate the value path approach:

1. Find the best solution for each of the criterions. On price criterion, preemptive GP has the best value of $87,918; on quality objective, the best value (90) is obtained through fuzzy GP.
2. For each of the remaining alternatives, divide each solution's value for the appropriate objective by the best solution for that objective.

TABLE 9.9

Goal Programming Solution: Summary

Method	Price	Quality
Preemptive GP	87918	115
Non-Preemptive GP	89878	92
Tchebycheff GP	90782	91
Fuzzy GP	89893	90

TABLE 9.10

Value Path Step 2 Summary

GP Method	Price	Quality
Preemptive GP	1.000	1.278
Non-Preemptive GP	1.022	1.022
Tchebycheff GP	1.033	1.011
Fuzzy GP	1.022	1.000

For example, for the non-preemptive GP alternative, the value of price and quality are $89,878 and 92, respectively. The ideal values for price and quality are $87,918 and 90, respectively. Therefore, the values corresponding to non-preemptive GP are obtained as ($89,878/$87,918) and (92/90), respectively. A similar process is undertaken for the other alternatives.

3. Plot the results, with price and quality on the x-axis and ratios on the y-axis. A summary of the results up to Step 2 is shown in the Table 9.10. The final step is to plot them on a graph for visualization. The graph is shown in Figure 9.3.

From the results, it can be seen that Tchebycheff GP produces an inferior solution compared to fuzzy GP because both the price and quality objectives for fuzzy GP are superior to those of Tchebycheff GP. The solution obtained from preemptive GP, non-preemptive GP, and fuzzy GP form a non-dominated set (i.e., it is impossible to improve on either objective without sacrificing on the other objective).

9.4.4 Discussion of Results

In the problem instance discussed in Section 9.4, preemptive GP was the only method that achieved the price objective; none of the four methods achieved the quality goal. Fuzzy GP achieved the best possible solution for the quality objective. Nonachievement of the quality goal may be due to the target value setting of the quality goal due to inherent trade-off in the supplier's performance. Based upon the preference of the DM, the selection of suppliers and the quantity that is ordered from each supplier can change.

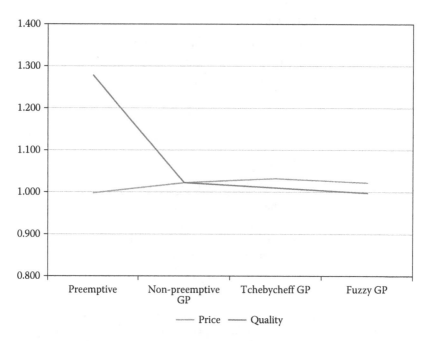

FIGURE 9.3
Price versus quality comparison.

In some cases, the price of the product may dictate the suppliers who are chosen, and in some other cases, quality dictates what suppliers are chosen. By varying the priorities of the goal or by changing the target values, different efficient solutions may be obtained. Another way to compare the trade-off between the price and quality objective is to change the order of the objectives (i.e., solve the problem with price as the highest objective and then solve the problem with quality as the highest objective). These two problem instances will provide lower and upper bounds for the two objectives.

Similar results were obtained for other problem instances as well (Table 9.1). Preemptive GP was able to satisfy the highest goal in all of the instances and hence is the method most suitable to be used in solving the supplier selection problem for tactical items.

9.4.5 Other Results

For tactical items, fixed cost is as important as the variable cost. Table 9.11 shows the fixed cost ratio, which is the ratio of fixed cost to total procurement cost. The result shown is for the preemptive GP method; similar results are obtained using other GP methods also. It can be seen from Table 9.11 that for the four-product case, the fixed cost ratio reduces marginally as the number of suppliers is increased; whereas for the eight-product case, the fixed cost ratio increases as the number of suppliers is increased.

TABLE 9.11

Fixed Cost Ratios for Product, Supplier, and Time Combination

Product	Supplier	Time	Total Procurement Cost ($)	Fixed Cost ($)	Fixed Cost Ratio (%)
4	4	4	87918.9	7500	8.53
4	4	12	265687.6	20552	7.74
4	12	4	85325	6502	7.62
4	12	12	258484	16102	6.23
8	4	4	167551	7450	4.45
8	4	12	506693	25450	5.02
8	12	4	165481	7530	4.55
8	12	12	498219	35640	7.15

TABLE 9.12

Model Scalability and Solution Time

Product	Supplier	Time	Number of Constraints	Number of Variables (Integer Variables)	Solution Time
4	4	4	112	100(20)	1 sec
4	4	12	304	292(52)	17 sec
4	12	4	272	268(60)	10 sec
4	12	12	720	780(156)	37 sec
8	4	4	224	180(20)	24 sec
8	4	12	608	532(52)	3 min
8	12	4	544	476(60)	2.57 min
8	12	12	1440	1404(156)	19.07 min

9.4.6 Model Scalability

As seen from Table 9.12, the model can be solved quickly for moderate-sized problems. The problem was solved using Lingo on a Windows 7 machine with Intel i-5 2.3 GHz processor and 8 GB RAM. The solution times, number of constraints, and variables for the eight problems are shown in Table 9.12.

The model can be solved for reasonable problem sizes without much difficulty. There is a minimal impact on the solution by increasing the number of products or by increasing the number of suppliers. The solution time is most influenced by increasing the number of time periods. As evident from Table 9.12, there is a significant jump in solution time when the number of periods increases from 4 to 12. This is due to the fact that the model needs to evaluate different combinations to assign suppliers to different time periods and to take into account the appropriate bundling criteria. The model also illustrates that there is sufficient spare capacity among the suppliers because some suppliers are not used. Hence, in case of demand fluctuations, back-up suppliers can be used.

9.4.7 Supplier Selection Method for Other Quadrants of the Supply Matrix

In this chapter we presented a supplier selection problem for the tactical quadrant of the supply matrix. The supplier selection methods for other quadrants of the supply matrix are solved differently; the solution method and the criteria chosen to evaluate suppliers depend on the price/risk.

Leverage items in Quadrant 2 are high-priced and low-risk items; supplier selection for leverage items is solved in two phases. In the first phase, called pre-qualification, we reduce the initial set of large number suppliers to a manageable set. Phase one reduces the effort of the buyer and makes the pre-qualification process objective. In the second phase, we analyze the shortlisted suppliers using several known multi-objective problem-solving techniques. We consider three conflicting criteria—namely, price, lead time, and quality.

For the critical items in Quadrant 3, we present a three-step method for global supplier selection. In the first step, we present a GP model for country selection; this step shortlists a country using various qualitative and quantitative criteria. In the second step, we assess the risks of supply using the analytic hierarchy process (AHP). In the final step, we develop a multi-objective model with price and risk as the two conflicting objectives. For every product, we assign three different suppliers—a global supplier, a domestic primary supplier, and a domestic secondary supplier. Order allocation among the suppliers is optimally decided by the model.

Finally, in Quadrant 4, we present a model for strategic supplier selection. In this quadrant, we suggest the buyer establish a strategic partnership with a supplier. For the strategic items, we integrate AHP and total cost of ownership (TCO), using a pairwise comparison method. In most organizations, strategic supplier selection is a group decision-making process; hence, we incorporate multiple decision makers in the supplier selection process.

9.5 Conclusion

In this chapter, we model and solve a multi-period supplier selection problem using a multi-objective optimization technique. We have combined the two most critical aspects of supplier selection activity—namely, inventory management and product bundling. The two aspects, when combined together, can yield more benefits to both the supplier and the buyer than if considered independently. The model assumes that the demand for different products is known in advance. In case of demand fluctuations, the buyer may not be able to buy the required amount to obtain a bundling discount. In that case, the total cost may be higher than the one estimated in the model.

To overcome this problem, demand variability may be implemented in the model. This model also does not take into account the storage space available for the buyer. In the case of limited space, a storage constraint should be added to the model.

Four different GP methods were used to solve the problem. GP methods are flexible in their use and do not present too much of a cognitive burden on the DM. An important characteristic of a multi-objective technique is that it does not provide one solution but a number of solutions—known as efficient solutions. By involving the DM early in the process, the acceptance of the results by management becomes easier. It can be seen from the results that the model can be solved quickly for moderate-sized problems. For very large problems, simple heuristics could be developed to solve problems in a reasonable time.

References

Aberdeen Group. (2004). Outsourcing portions of procurement now a core strategy. *Supplier Selection and Management Report* 4(7): 4.

Agarwal, P., M. Sahai, et al. (2011). A review of multi-criteria decision making techniques for supplier evaluation and selection. *International Journal of Industrial Engineering Computations* 2(4): 801–810.

Aissaoui, N., M. Haouari, et al. (2007). Supplier selection and order lot sizing modeling: A review. *Computers and Operations Research* 34(12): 3516–3540.

Cavinato, J. L. and R. G. Kauffman. (1999). *The Purchasing Handbook: A Guide for the Purchasing and Supply Professional.* New York: McGraw-Hill.

De Boer, L., E. Labro, et al. (2001). A review of methods supporting supplier selection. *European Journal of Purchasing and Supply Management* 7: 75–89.

Degraeve, Z. and F. Roodhooft. (1999). Effectively selecting suppliers using total cost of ownership. *Journal of Supply Chain Management* 35(1): 5–10.

Demirtas, E. A. and Ö. Üstün. (2008). An integrated multiobjective decision making process for supplier selection and order allocation. *Omega* 36(1): 76–90.

Deshmukh, A. J. and A. A. Chaudhari. (2011). A review for supplier selection criteria and methods. *Technology Systems and Management*, Springer, pp. 283–291.

Elahi, B., Etaati, L. and Seyed-Hosseini, S. M. (2011). An integrated modeling for supplier selection and optimal lot sizing: a case study of four-echelon supply chain, *IEEE International Technology Management Conference (ITMC)*, San Jose, CA, June 2011, pp. 877–884.

Ho, W., X. Xu, and P. K. Dey. (2010). Multi-criteria decision-making approaches for supplier evaluation and selection: A literature review. *European Journal of Operational Research* 202(1): 16–24.

Jayaraman, V., R. Srivastava, et al. (1999). Supplier selection and order quantity allocation: A comprehensive model. *Journal of Supply Chain Management* 35(2): 50–58.

Li, L. and Z. B. Zabinsky. (2011). Incorporating uncertainty into a supplier selection problem. *International Journal of Production Economics* 134(2): 344–356.

Masud, A. M. and A. Ravindran. (2008). Multiple criteria decision making. In *Operations Research and Management Science Handbook*, A. Ravindran (Ed.). Chapter 5, 5-1–5-35, Boca Raton, FL: CRC Press.

Ravindran, A. and V. Wadhwa. (2009). Multi criteria optimization models for supplier selection. In *Handbook of Military Industrial Engineering*, A. Badiru and M. U. Thomas (Eds.). Chapter 4, 4-1–4-35, Boca Raton, FL: CRC Press.

Ravindran, A. R. and D. P. Warsing. (2013). *Supply Chain Engineering: Models and Applications*. Boca Raton, FL: CRC Press.

Rosenthal, E. C., J. L. Zydiak, et al. (1995). Vendor selection with bundling. *Decision Science* 26(1): 35–48.

Sawik, T. (2010). Single vs. multiple objective supplier selection in a make to order environment. *Omega* 38(3–4): 203–212.

Schilling, D. A., C. Revelle, et al. (1983). An approach to the display and analysis of multi-objective problems. *Socio-Economic Planning Sciences* 17(2): 57–63.

Wadhwa, V. (2008). *Multi-Objective Decision Support System for Global Supplier Selection*. Doctoral Dissertation, The Pennsylvania State University.

Wadhwa, V. and A. R. Ravindran. (2007). Vendor selection in outsourcing. *Computers and Operations Research* 34: 3725–3737.

Weber, C. A., J. R. Current, et al. (1991). Supplier selection criteria and methods. *European Journal of Operational Research* 50: 2–18.

10

An Analytical Supply Chain Disruption Framework and a Multi-Objective Supplier Selection Model with Risk Mitigation

R. Ufuk Bilsel

The Boston Consulting Group, Istanbul, Turkey

CONTENTS

10.1 Introduction

Globalization of supply chains has brought many benefits, including better growth possibilities for firms and increased access to diverse resources and markets; however, globalization also has resulted in elevated exposure to risks. Many large supply chains have been affected by disruptions in recent years, including the East Japan Earthquake and floods in Thailand, both in 2011. These catastrophic events had massive impacts on global production; it is estimated that up to 10% of total global output was affected by the Japan earthquake alone (Freedman et al. 2011). Repair and preventive measures after Hurricane Sandy in 2012 exceeded $70 billion. Thailand's gross domestic product (GDP) growth declined from 2.6% to 1% after floods that same year (Bhatia et al. 2013).

Suppliers are key elements of supply chains that have been adversely affected by disruptions. Protecting supply chains against supplier disruptions is paramount for the continuation of operations and company profitability. The well-known case of disruption in one Ericsson's chip supplier's plant led to significant sales losses to then-competitor Nokia and to the company's exit from the North American cellular phone market. Building disruption mitigation strategies into supplier selection is one way to reduce the impact of disruptions on the supply chain.

Study of disruptive events is an emerging field of research in supply chain management literature. Current research in disruption management evolved from earlier conceptual frameworks to comprehensive analytical models that assess the possibility and impact of disruptions and suggest managerial countermoves. This chapter presents a review of the recent literature on supply disruption analysis. It builds a statistical framework to model effects of disruption risks and formulates a multi-objective mathematical model to build disruption mitigation strategies into supplier selection decisions.

This chapter is organized as follows. Section 10.2 presents an overview of the recent literature on disruption risk research and multi-objective supply chain management models. An analytic disruption risk quantification framework is presented in Section 10.3. A multi-objective mathematical model for supplier selection under disruption risk is formulated in Section 10.4. Solution methods and a numerical example are discussed in Section 10.5 and Section 10.6, respectively. Concluding comments and future directions are provided in Section 10.7.

10.2 Literature Review

This chapter looks at the past and at current supply chain disruption analysis and supplier selection. Readers interested in more detailed information on those topics can refer to Bilsel (2009), Ravindran and Warsing (2013), and Ivanov et al. (2014) for disruption modeling and to Bilsel (2009), Ravindran and Warsing (2013), and Karsak and Dursun (2016) for supplier selection models.

10.2.1 Disruption Analysis

Earlier research on disruption analysis concentrates on conceptual frameworks, such as in Zsidisin et al. (2004), Hendricks and Singhal (2005), Kleindorfer and Saad (2005), and Ritchie and Brindley (2007). The research is valuable in terms of opening up the supply chain disruption analysis field and providing conceptual basis for future work. The step after conceptual frameworks is analytical models. Tomlin (2006) was among the first to model supply chain disruptions, using stochastic optimization tools. Recently, Bilsel and Ravindran (2012) modeled disruptions as a function of impact, occurrence, detectability, and recovery; they presented analytical methods to quantify each component. Chaudhuri et al. (2013) proposed a group decision-making process to assess supply chain vulnerability during new product development. Hu et al. (2013) discussed incentive mechanisms for suppliers to invest in disruption recovery capabilities. Qi (2013) studied an inventory review problem of a retailer replenishing from two sources—a less costly, but riskier, primary supplier and a more expensive, but reliable, backup source. Ivanov et al. (2014) proposed a framework to analyze ripple effects of disruptive events in supply chains and modeled it as a dynamic optimal control problem. A three-step disruption risk management framework is developed in Kungwalsong and Ravindran (2014), where disruption risk scores for supply chain nodes are calculated based on three factors: hazard, vulnerability, and available risk management practices.

10.2.2 Multi-Objective Supplier Selection Models

The seminal paper in multi-objective supplier selection is Dickinson (1966), who proposed a set of 23 criteria that can be used in supplier selection. Buffa and Jackson (1983) were among the first to model the supplier selection problem using goal programming (GP). They included cost, quality, and delivery as decision criteria. More recent examples include Wadhwa and Ravindran (2007), who formulated a supplier selection problem with quantity discounts and included price, quality, and lead time as objective functions. Then they solved the model using GP. Demirtaş and Üstün (2008) proposed an integrated approach for supplier selection. They first calculated objective weights using the analytical network process and then used those weights in a multi-objective mixed integer program. Yang (2006) included disruption risks into a multi-objective supplier selection model using extreme value theory. He also treated operational risks using Taguchi's loss functions. Ravindran et al. (2010) developed a multi-objective supplier selection model incorporating disruption risk and quantity discounts for the procurement organization of a global information technology (IT) company. They solved their model using different GP techniques. Bilsel and Ravindran (2011) developed a chance constrained multiple objective mathematical programming (MOMP) model to solve supplier selection problems under demand and capacity uncertainty. They also proposed linearization methods for their nonlinear models. Li and Zabinsky (2011) developed two stochastic MOMP models (a two-stage model and a chance constrained model) to optimally select suppliers under demand and capacity uncertainty. Sawik (2013) formulated a MOMP model to optimally select suppliers and to allocate emergency stocks under disruption risks. Conditional value-at-risk is used to model the worst case costs of supply disruptions. Ravindran and Warsing (2013) presented a comprehensive overview of supplier selection and supply chain risks.

10.3 Disruption Risk Modeling

This section introduces an analytical framework for modeling disruption risk as a function of impact and occurrence. Interested readers can refer to Bilsel and Ravindran (2012) and Ravindran and Warsing (2013) for more comprehensive models that include detectability and recovery aspects of disruption risk.

10.3.1 Disruption Impact

Impact from disruptive events is modeled as the economic loss resulting from those events. In civil engineering literature, damages due to cata-strophic events are modeled using heavy tailed statistical distributions, such as Weibull, Gumbel, and Frechet distributions. A more general fam-ily of distributions called generalized extreme value distributions (GEVD) arises as the limit distributions of Weibull, Gumbel, and Frechet distribu-tions (see Castillo et al. [2005] for a comprehensive discussion of those mod-els and applications). There are two GEVDs—one for maximum extremes and another for minimum extremes. Probability density functions (PDF) and cumulative distribution functions (CDF) for the maximum GEVD are given in Equations 10.1 through 10.4. PDF and CDF of the minimum GEVD can be found in Castillo et al. (2005)

$$\text{for } \kappa \neq 0, \quad f_\kappa(x;\lambda,\delta) = \frac{1}{\delta}\exp\left(-\left[1-\kappa\left(\frac{x-\lambda}{\delta}\right)\right]^{\frac{1}{\kappa}}\right)\left[1-\kappa\left(\frac{x-\lambda}{\delta}\right)\right]^{\frac{1}{\kappa}-1} \quad (10.1)$$

$$\text{for } \kappa = 0, \quad f_0(x;\lambda,\delta) = \frac{1}{\delta}\exp\left[-\exp\left(\frac{\lambda-x}{\delta}\right)\right]\exp\left(\frac{\lambda-\exp x}{\delta}\right) \quad (10.2)$$

$$\text{for } \kappa \neq 0, \quad F_\kappa(x;\lambda,\delta) = \exp\left(-\left[1-\kappa\left(\frac{x-\lambda}{\delta}\right)\right]^{\frac{1}{\kappa}}\right) \quad (10.3)$$

$$\text{for } \kappa = 0, \quad F_0(x;\lambda,\delta) = \exp\left[-\exp\left(\frac{\lambda-x}{\delta}\right)\right] \quad (10.4)$$

Table 10.1 provides definitions of the GEVD parameters.

TABLE 10.1

GEVD Parameters

Parameter	Interpretation
κ	*Shape parameter*
	κ > 0, corresponds to a Frechet distribution
	κ = 0, corresponds to a Gumbel distribution
	κ < 0, corresponds to a Weibull distribution
δ	*Scale parameter*
λ	*Location parameter*

The mean of the GEVD can be calculated using Equation 10.5 if the parameter $\kappa \neq 0$,

$$E(X) = \lambda - \frac{\delta}{\kappa} + \frac{\delta}{\kappa} \Gamma(1 - \kappa) \qquad (10.5)$$

where $\Gamma(.)$ is the Gamma function. In the case when $\kappa = 0$, the GEVD boils down to a Gumbel distribution, and the mean can be approximated as $\lambda + \xi\delta$, where $\xi = 0.57721$ is the Euler–Mascheroni constant. The GEVD parameters need to be estimated from disruption impact data. An example using US storm damage data is provided in Bilsel and Ravindran (2012).

10.3.2 Disruption Occurrence

Occurrence is the frequency of a certain disruptive event over a period of time (e.g., a year or several years depending on the event of interest). Tamhane and Dunlop (2000) state that the Poisson distribution is suitable to model the occurrence of rare events, unless they are correlated. The probability mass function of the Poisson distribution is shown in Equation 10.6.

$$P(x) = \frac{e^{-\lambda}\lambda^x}{x!} \qquad (10.6)$$

where λ is the expected number of occurrences over a specific period. An example using real data for λ estimation can be found in Bilsel (2009).

Bogachev et al. (2008) note that the independence assumption required to use the Poisson distribution may not hold for disruptive events that have long-term correlation. Alternative occurrence models need to be developed for cases where disruptive events are correlated. The independence assumption is assumed to hold for the models developed in this paper.

10.3.3 Estimated Disruption Value Function

Estimated values of impact E_i and occurrence E_o should be combined to derive the estimated value of disruptions E_d. It can be easily shown that $E_d = E_i \times E_o$. A formal proof can be found in Bilsel (2009).

10.4 Multi-Objective Sequential Supplier Assignment Model

This section presents a multi-objective mathematical model to optimally assign primary and backup suppliers in a supply chain. The optimal assignment is calculated based on four objectives: minimizing the total cost of operation, maximizing the quality of procured products, minimizing the lead time of procurement, and minimizing the potential losses due to disruption risk. The first three objectives address the most common decisions made in supply chain operations. The disruption risk objective includes the perspective of hedging against rare events that may cause supply chain disarrays. The order in which these objectives would be treated in the multi-objective program solution process depends on the preferences of decision makers (DMs).

Consider a supply chain where a single buyer purchases multiple products from different suppliers. Let $J = 1, ..., m$ represent the set of suppliers, $K = 1, ..., k$ the set of products, and $R = 1, ..., r$ the set of supplier levels. Indices j, k, and r represent suppliers, products, and supplier assignment levels in the sets J, K, and R, respectively. The multi-objective mathematical model assumes that once a supplier is selected to supply a product, it will provide the entire demand for that product. Hence, the model has one set of decision variables, x_{jkr}, defined as follows:

$$x_{jkr} = \begin{cases} 1, & \text{if supplier } j \text{ is assigned as a level } r \text{ supplier for product } k \\ 0, & \text{otherwise} \end{cases}$$

The concept of level r facility is introduced in Snyder and Daskin (2005) to handle sequential allocation of facilities to customers in an incapacitated facility location problem. In the model presented here, a level 1 supplier is responsible of supplying the products as long as there is no disruption and is named as a *primary supplier*. In case of a disruption, a backup supplier replaces the failed primary supplier. A buyer can have only one primary supplier for a given product. Remaining suppliers are then assigned as backups at the m' levels, where $m' \le m$. Other parameters used in the sequential supplier assignment (SSA) model are given in Table 10.2.

It is assumed that suppliers would perform differently depending on their assignment levels; therefore cost, quality, and lead time parameters are indexed over assignment levels r. A supplier, when assigned as a backup, would ask for a higher price, need longer lead times, and would provide lower quality. In other words, a supplier assigned at level r would have higher cost, lower quality, and longer lead times compared to a supplier assigned at level $r - 1$. This is justified because a backup supplier would be used only when a primary supplier fails and would be

TABLE 10.2

SSA Mathematical Model Parameters

Parameter	Description
D_k	Demand for product k
Cap_{jk}	Capacity of product k at supplier j
c_{jrk}	Unit cost of sourcing product k from supplier j when j is a level r supplier
F_{jr}	Fixed cost of working with supplier j at level r
Q_{jkr}	Quality of product k sourced from supplier j
L_{jkr}	Lead time of product k from supplier j when j is a level r supplier
ρ_j	Estimated value of the loss due to disruption at supplier j

on a short notice to satisfy an order. However, the fixed cost of a supplier will increase with the assignment level. Because the buyer will not order from a backup supplier until that supplier is needed, we assume that the fixed costs of backup suppliers would be smaller than those of primary suppliers. The buyer would still need to cover fixed costs for backups because he still may have to sign a contract with the backup suppliers to be able to use them in case of disruptions. Fixed costs of backup suppliers also would include overhead costs. Lastly, the supplier risk value depends on the business environment and is exogenous to the supplier levels. Therefore, independent of its assignment level, a supplier has the same risk value. The multi-objective mathematical formulation of the SSA is given in Equations 10.7 through 10.14:

$$\min z_1 = \sum_{j\in J}\sum_{k\in K}\sum_{r=1}^{m'} c_{jkr}D_k x_{jkr} + \sum_{j\in J}\sum_{k\in K}\sum_{r=1}^{m'} F_{jr}x_{jkr} \tag{10.7}$$

$$\max z_2 = \sum_{j\in J}\sum_{k\in K}\sum_{r=1}^{m'} Q_{jkr}x_{jkr} \tag{10.8}$$

$$\min z_3 = \sum_{j\in J}\sum_{k\in K}\sum_{r=1}^{m'} L_{jkr}x_{jkr} \tag{10.9}$$

$$\min z_4 = \sum_{j\in J}\sum_{k\in K}\sum_{r=1}^{m'} \rho_j x_{jkr} \tag{10.10}$$

Subject to: $\sum_{j\in J} x_{jkr} = 1 \quad \forall k \in K, r = 1,...,m'$ \hfill (10.11)

$$\sum_{r=1}^{m'} x_{jkr} = 1 \quad \forall j \in J, \forall k \in K \tag{10.12}$$

$$x_{jkr}\,(Cap_{jk} - D_k) \geq 0 \ \forall j \in J, \forall k \in K, r = 1, \dots, m' \tag{10.13}$$

$$x_{jkr} \in (0, 1)\ \forall j \in J, \forall k \in K, r = 1, \dots, m' \tag{10.14}$$

The first objective function in Equation 10.7 minimizes total cost. The first summation captures variable cost, and the second summation represents fixed cost. The first summation in Equation 10.7 can be split as $\displaystyle\sum_{j\in J}\sum_{k\in K} c_{jk1}D_k x_{jk1} + \sum_{j\in J}\sum_{k\in K}\sum_{r=2}^{m'} c_{jkr}D_k x_{jkr}$, where the first part represents the variable cost associated with primary suppliers. The second part can be considered as the opportunity cost of assigning a supplier as backup at some level $r > 1$. Hence, the first objective function minimizes the sum of variable cost of primary suppliers, opportunity cost of backup suppliers, and the fixed cost of the overall supplier assignment. The second objective function maximizes the weighted average quality of purchased products and backup supplier assignments; the third objective function minimizes the weighted average lead time, and the last objective function minimizes the risk value associated with supplier selection.

Constraints in Equation 10.11 ensure that the buyer is assigned a level r supplier for each product. These constraints guarantee that there will be one supplier at each level for all products. Constraints in Equation 10.12 prohibit assigning the same supplier to more than one level for the same product. However, the model allows a supplier to be a backup for more than one product. Constraints in Equation 10.13 relate the supplier allocation to capacity restrictions. Given supplier j and product k, if the difference between supply capacity Cap_{jk} and demand D_k is greater than 0 (that is if the supplier has enough capacity to satisfy the demand), the formulation allows the respective assignment variable x_{jkr} to be either 0 or 1. It is important to note that constraints in Equation 10.13 can also be considered as logical relations. If $Cap_{jk} - D_k \geq 0$, then create the relevant x_{jkr} variables; otherwise, do not introduce those x_{jkr} to the model. This logical relation was used when coding and solving the model to eliminate unnecessary x_{jkr} variables and to reduce the size of the model. Lastly, constraints in Equation (14) restrict the decision variables to binary values.

10.5 Solution Techniques

There are many techniques for solving MOMP—compromise programming, the weighted average method, and global criterion and GP methods, to name a few. GP techniques are used in this chapter because they measure objective function performance against the targets set by the DMs; hence, in our opinion, GP methods are more user friendly and implementable than other optimization methods. Readers interested in alternative MOMP solution techniques can refer to Masud and Ravindran (2008).

In GP, each objective is assigned a target value that represents the desired achievement for that objective and deviation variables that model the proximity to each target. The aim of GP is to minimize deviations from the targets. Target values are more natural to managers because they have an aspiration in mind regarding their supply chain's performance. In practice, target values can be provided by DMs, retrieved from business plans, or can be calculated as the ideal solution for an objective with some spread. Ideal solutions in an MOMP are obtained by optimizing each objective individually. There are four GP techniques—preemptive, non-preemptive, min–max, and fuzzy—distinguished by the way the objective functions are prioritized and how deviations from targets are treated. We briefly describe each of the SSA GP models here. Details on the GP formulations and solution techniques can be found in Masud and Ravindran (2008).

Preemptive GP ranks the objective functions with respect to the ordered preferences of the DMs and minimizes the deviations from the target values associated with each objective in the ranked order. Several different techniques can be used to derive preemptive priorities. One convenient way is to use discrete alternative multi-criteria decision-making methods such as rating, Borda count, pairwise comparison, or the analytic hierarchy process (AHP) method (see Ravindran et al. [2010] for an application). These methods also provide a numerical strength-of-preference value that can be used in non-preemptive GP models. The preemptive GP model formulation, assuming that the preference ordering of the objectives is z_1, z_2, z_3, z_4, as follows:

$$\min P_1 d_1^+ + P_2 d_2^- + P_3 d_3^+ + P_4 d_4^+ \tag{10.15}$$

$$\text{Subject to:} \quad z_1 + d_1^- - d_1^+ = T_1$$

$$z_2 + d_2^- - d_2^+ = T_2$$

$$z_3 + d_3^- - d_3^+ = T_3 \tag{10.16}$$

$$z_4 + d_4^- - d_4^+ = T_4$$

$$d_i^+, d_i^- \geq 0 \quad \forall i$$

where P_1, P_2, P_3, P_4 are the respective preemptive priorities. All other SSA constraints in Equations 10.7 through 10.14 are also included. The new T_i parameters for $i = 1, \ldots, 4$ are the assigned target values for the objective functions. Additional variables d_i^- and d_i^+ in Equations 10.15 and 10.16 represent the negative and positive deviations from the target values, respectively. The P_i parameters represent the preemptive priority of each objective function.

For instance, the first objective is to minimize cost; hence, $P_1 d_1^+$ can be interpreted as minimizing the positive deviation from the cost target having the highest priority. Note that the second objective function, quality, is to maximize; hence, the objective function in Equation 10.15 minimizes the negative deviation variable d_2^-.

Non-preemptive GP formulation is very similar to the preemptive GP formulation. The objective function of the non-preemptive GP is given in Equation 10.17, where w_i, $i = 1, \ldots, 4$ are the normalized objective weights. The remainder of the formulation is the same as in Equation 10.16. Note that objective functions need to be scaled for correct implementation of non-preemptive GP because numerical weights are used. Scaling can be achieved by dividing each objective by its ideal solution

$$\min w_1 d_1^+ + w_2 d_2^- + w_3 d_3^+ + w_4 d_4^+ \tag{10.17}$$

The min–max GP minimizes the maximum deviation from the targets. The min–max GP has a nonlinear objective function in Equation 10.18, which can be linearized as in Equation 10.19 with the additional constraints in Equation 10.20 and the original constraints given by Equations 10.7 through 10.14,

$$\min \max \left(d_1^+, d_2^-, d_3^+, d_4^+ \right) \tag{10.18}$$

$$\min M \tag{10.19}$$

$$\text{Subject to:} \quad d_1^+ \le M$$

$$d_2^- \le M$$

$$d_3^+ \le M \tag{10.20}$$

$$d_4^+ \le M$$

Lastly, the fuzzy GP minimizes the maximum deviation from the ideal solution for each objective. In the fuzzy GP objective in Equation 10.21, $I_{z(i)}$ is the ideal solution and $N_{z(i)}$ is the anti-ideal solution for objective i. The anti-ideal solution for objective i is obtained by individually optimizing $-z_i$. The nonlinear objective function in Equation 10.21 can be linearized similar to the min–max objective function. Note that fuzzy GP does not require targets and does not have any deviation variables. Thus, the fuzzy GP formulation requires constraints in Equations 10.7 through 10.14 only,

$$\min \max \left(\frac{z_1 - I_{z(1)}}{N_{z(1)} - I_{z(1)}}, \frac{I_{z(2)} - z_2}{I_{z(2)} - N_{z(2)}}, \frac{z_3 - I_{z(3)}}{N_{z(3)} - I_{z(3)}}, \frac{z_4 - I_{z(4)}}{N_{z(4)} - I_{z(4)}} \right) \tag{10.21}$$

10.6 Numerical Example

Consider a supplier selection problem faced by a buyer with five candidate suppliers and three products to procure. Let the problem data be that from Tables 10.3 through 10.9.

TABLE 10.3

Demand Data Used in SSA (in Units)

Product	1	2	3
Demand	210	250	250

TABLE 10.4

Capacity Data Used in SSA (in Units)

	Product		
Supplier	1	2	3
1	220	250	300
2	250	350	250
3	250	270	260
4	300	400	0
5	200	300	300

TABLE 10.5

Quality Data Used in SSA (in % of Good Items)

Product	Supplier	Level 1
1	1	95
	2	95
	3	90
	4	90
	5	90
2	1	95
	2	97
	3	90
	4	93
	5	92
3	1	93
	2	99
	3	90
	4	90
	5	97

TABLE 10.6

Lead Time Data Used in SSA (in Days)

Supplier	Product	Level 1
1	1	10
	2	9
	3	1
2	1	5
	2	2
	3	8
3	1	8
	2	3
	3	9
4	1	3
	2	4
	3	6
5	1	8
	2	2
	3	4

TABLE 10.7

Variable Cost Data Used in SSA
(in $/Unit)

Supplier	Product	Level 1
1	1	15
	2	10
	3	12
2	1	15
	2	8
	3	9
3	1	10
	2	9
	3	5
4	1	15
	2	16
	3	9
5	1	6
	2	8
	3	18

Quality, lead time, and variable cost data in Tables 10.5 through 10.7 are given for level 1 suppliers only. Quality values for lower level suppliers are modeled by decreasing the level 1 values by 5%. For example, level 2 quality value for supplier 1–product 1 combination is 95% × 0.95 = 90.25%; level 3 quality value is 90.25% × 0.95 = 85.74%. Similarly, lead time and variable cost

TABLE 10.8

Fixed Cost Data Used in SSA (in $)

	Supplier				
Level	1	2	3	4	5
1	100	200	150	150	120
2	75	150	113	113	90
3	56	113	84	84	68
4	42	84	63	63	51

TABLE 10.9

Disruption Risk Loss Values Used in SSA ($)

Supplier	1	2	3	4	5
ρ	400,707	496,028	360,773	937,733	968,962

TABLE 10.10

Non-Preemptive and Preemptive GP Objective Weights and Priorities

Criteria	Weight	Preemptive Priority
Cost	0.343	P_1
Quality	0.338	P_2
Lead time	0.246	P_3
Disruption risk	0.073	P_4

values for the lower level suppliers are modeled by increasing the level 1 values by 5%. Risk values are calculated using the methods presented in Section 10.3. It is assumed that only one disruptive event affects the suppliers each period. Objective weight values and priorities shown in Table 10.10 are taken from Ravindran et al. (2010), were calculated with actual DMs for an IT company and will be used in non-preemptive and preemptive GP models. We set $m' = 4$ to allow only four levels of assignment.

Optimal objective values to all four GP formulations are presented in Tables 10.11 through 10.14. Ideal solutions are calculated by optimizing each objective independently. For an objective function to be maximized, the target is set at 5% less than the ideal values, whereas for the minimization objectives, targets are set at 5% greater than the ideal values.

The status column in Tables 10.11 through 10.13 display the achievement status for each objective function. A target is achieved if the objective value at optimality, reported in the achievement column, is between the ideal value and the target value. The first value in each row of the achievement column is the objective value achieved in the optimal solution. The values in parentheses are the portions of the objective value corresponding to the

TABLE 10.11

Non-Preemptive GP Solution

Objective	Ideal	Target	Status	Achievement
Cost	34,445	36,167	Achieved	36,053; (11,650; 420)
Quality	10.15	9.64	Achieved	10.08; (2.80)
Lead time	58.62	61.55	Achieved	60.26; (11)
Risk	6,616,955	6,947,802	Not achieved	7,185,209; (2,844,427)

TABLE 10.12

Preemptive GP Solution

Objective	Ideal	Target	Status	Achievement
Cost	34,445	36,167	Achieved	36,059; (11,650; 370)
Quality	10.15	9.64	Achieved	10.08; (2.70)
Lead time	58.62	61.55	Achieved	59.56; (18)
Risk	6,616,955	6,947,802	Not achieved	7,185,209; (2,307,402)

TABLE 10.13

Min–Max GP Solution

Objective	Ideal	Target	Status	Achievement
Cost	34,445	36,167	Achieved	34,990; (7,900, 450)
Quality	10.15	9.64	Achieved	10.09; (2.84)
Lead time	58.62	61.55	Not achieved	63.35; (18.99)
Risk	6,616,955	6,947,802	Achieved	6,648,187; (1,834,472)

TABLE 10.14

Fuzzy GP Solution

Objective	Ideal	Anti-Ideal	Achievement	Deviation from Ideal (%)
Cost	34,445	37,093	34,797; (7,900, 450)	1.02
Quality	10.15	10.07	10.11; (2.84)	0.39
Lead time	58.62	71.61	63.85; (19)	8.92
Risk	6,616,955	7,225,144	6,648,183; (1,834,469)	0.47

primary suppliers. Note that the cost objective function has two values within the parentheses: the first value is the variable cost, and the second is the fixed cost for the primary suppliers at optimality.

The most promising results are obtained using non-preemptive, preemptive, and min–max GP solution techniques (see Tables 10.11 through 10.13), where three out of four targets have been achieved. Fuzzy GP, on the other hand, yields cost, quality, and risk results close to the ideal values, but the solution presents significant deviations from ideal values for the lead time objective. For illustration, let us present the preemptive GP optimal solution in Table 10.15.

TABLE 10.15

Preemptive GP Solution

Supplier	Levels				Product
	1	2	3	4	
1	1	0	0	0	1
	0	0	0	0	2
	0	0	1	0	3
2	0	0	1	0	1
	0	0	0	1	2
	0	1	0	0	3
3	0	0	0	1	1
	0	1	0	0	2
	0	0	0	1	3
4	0	1	0	0	1
	1	0	0	0	2
	0	0	0	0	3
5	0	0	0	0	1
	0	0	1	0	2
	1	0	0	0	3

The solution can be interpreted as follows: The first row indicates that supplier 1 is going to be assigned as a level 1 supplier for product 1. The second and third rows further indicate that supplier 1 will not be assigned at any level for product 2 and will be a level 3 supplier of product 3. Analyzing further, we can observe that suppliers 4 and 5 are the other primary suppliers of the buyer and will provide products 2 and 3, respectively. Suppliers 2 and 3 act as backup suppliers. The buyer is assigned a single backup supplier for each product at each level. These backup suppliers will not ship any products unless a primary supplier fails. Finally, note that each product has four suppliers, one primary and three backups, as expected because $m' = 4$.

It is often challenging for managers to interpret the numerical solutions of MOMP. An effective visualization tool is required to compare the optimal solutions obtained using different techniques. The value path approach (VPA) proposed in Schilling et al. (1983) is a simple and effective tool to visualize MOMP optimal solutions. VPA begins by determining the best objective value obtained. Then, other objective values are scaled using the best value. The best objective value is set to one, while all the others have a scaled value greater than one. The larger the scaled objective value, the worse a GP method performs for that objective. Value path calculations for the SSA problem are displayed in Table 10.16, where the first row of each solution technique is the actual objective value, and the second row is the scaled objective value.

TABLE 10.16

SSA Value Path Calculations

	Cost	Quality	Lead Time	Risk
Non-preemptive	36,053	10	60	7,185,209
	1.04	1.01	1	1.08
Preemptive	36,059	10	60	7,185,209
	1.04	1.01	1	1.08
Min–max	34,990	10	63	6,648,187
	1.01	1.01	1.06	1
Fuzzy	34,797	10	64	6,648,183
	1	1	1.07	1

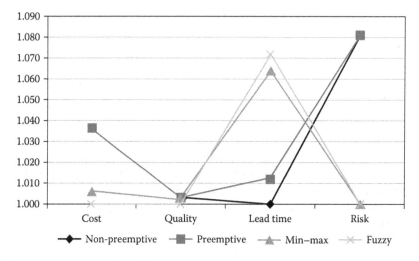

FIGURE 10.1
SSA value path.

Figure 10.1 shows the value path for the SSA solution, and it can be used to determine the dominated and non-dominated solutions. If the value path of one solution is above that of another, then the solution is dominated. If the value paths of two solutions intersect, then these solutions do not dominate each other. None of the GP solutions obtained in the numerical example dominate each other. On the other hand, certain GP methods perform better on a particular objective than the others. For instance, as seen in Figure 10.1, all the methods perform very well for the quality objective. However, min–max and fuzzy GPs yield poor results for the lead time objective, while the best lead time solutions are obtained by preemptive GB and non-preemptive GP. VPA enables managers to easily perform trade-off analyses by visually comparing the different GP solutions and selecting the best compromise solution.

10.7 Conclusions and Future Directions

This chapter presents a disruption risk quantification method and a multi-objective supplier selection model to generate mitigation plans against disruption risks. The proposed risk quantification method considers risk as a function of two components—impact and occurrence. Impact is modeled using GEVD distributions, and occurrence is assumed to be Poisson-distributed. The disruption risk quantification method calculates the estimated value of the loss due to disruptive events at a supplier, which is then used in a multi-objective optimization model. The model minimizes cost, lead time, and risk and then maximizes quality and determines the optimal supplier and order allocation for multiple products. The model is solved using four different GP solution techniques—preemptive, non-preemptive, min–max, and fuzzy GP. Optimal solutions are displayed using the VPA, and the performance of the solution techniques is discussed. We observe that, for the data set we have tested, preemptive GP, non-preemptive GP, and min–max GP achieve three out of four objectives.

Research presented in this paper can be extended in several ways. The assumption that only one disruption event can affect the operations can be relaxed, and more complicated models—as discussed in Bilsel and Ravindran (2012)—can be utilized. Quantity discounts are common in procurement and can be incorporated in the SSA model. Some suppliers may not prefer to be a backup or primary supplier for certain products. Those restrictions can be added to the SSA model to customize it for specific situations.

References

Bhatia, Gurpriya, Charles Lane, and Adrian Wain. *Building Resilience in Supply Chains.* World Economic Forum Reports, 2013. http://www3.weforum.org/docs/WEF_RRN_MO_BuildingResilienceSupplyChains_Report_2013.pdf.

Bilsel, R. Ufuk. *Disruption and Operational Risk Quantification Models for Outsourcing Operations.* PhD dissertation, Pennsylvania State University, 2009.

Bilsel, R. Ufuk, and Ravi Ravindran. A Multi-Objective Chance Constrained Programming Model for Supplier Selection under Uncertainty. *Transportation Research Part B* 45, no. 8 (2011): 1284–1300.

Bilsel, R. Ufuk, and Ravi Ravindran. Modeling Disruption Risk in Supply Chain Risk Management. *International Journal of Operations Research and Information Systems* 3, no. 3 (2012): 15–39.

Bogachev, Mikhail I., Jan F. Eichner, and Armin Bunde. On the Occurrence of Extreme Events in Long-Term Correlated and Multifractal Data Sets. *Pure and Applied Geophysics* 165, no. 6 (2008): 1195–1207.

Buffa, Frank, and Wade M. Jackson. A Goal Programming Model for Purchase Planning. *Journal of Purchasing and Materials Management* 19, no. 3 (1983): 27–34.

Castillo, Enrique, Ali S. Hadi, Narayanaswamy Balakrishnan, et al. *Extreme Value and Related Models with Applications in Engineering and Science.* Hoboken, NJ: Wiley, 2005.

Chaudhuri, Atanu, Bhaba K. Mohanty, and Kashi N. Singh. Supply Chain Risk Assessment During New Product Development: A Group Decision Making Approach Using Numeric and Linguistic Data. *International Journal of Production Research* 51, no. 10 (2013): 2790–2804.

Demirtaş, Ezgi A., and Özden Üstün. An Integrated Multi-Objective Decision Making Process for Supplier Selection and Order Allocation. *Omega* 36, no. 1 (2008): 76–90.

Dickinson, G.W. An Analysis of Vendor Selection Systems and Decisions. *Journal of Purchasing* 2, no. 1 (1966): 5–17.

Freedman, Mark, Satoshi Komiya, Joe Manget, et al. *After Japan's Earthquake: Rethinking the Supply Chain.* BCG Perspectives, 2011. https://www.bcgperspectives.com/Images/BCG_After_Japans_Earthquake_Rethinking_the_Supply_Chain_Jun_11_tcm80-80571.pdf.

Hendricks, Kevin B., and Vinod R. Singhal. Association between Supply Chain Glitches and Operating Performance. *Management Science* 51, no. 5 (2005): 695–711.

Hu, Xinxin, Haresh Gurnani, and Ling Wang. Managing Risk of Supply Disruptions: Incentives for Capacity Restoration. *Production and Operations Management* 22, no. 1 (2013): 137–150.

Ivanov, Dmitry, Boris Sokolov, and Alexandre Dolgui. The Ripple Effect in Supply Chains: Trade-off 'Efficiency-Flexibility-Resilience' in Disruption Management. *International Journal of Production Research* 52, no. 7 (2014): 2154–2172.

Karsak, Ertuğrul E., and Mehtap Dursun. Taxonomy and Review of Non-Deterministic Analytical Methods for Supplier Selection. *International Journal of Computer Integrated Manufacturing* 29, no. 3 (2016): 263–286.

Kleindorfer, Paul R., and Germaine H. Saad. Managing Disruption Risks in Supply Chains. *Production and Operations Management* 14, no. 1 (2005): 53–68.

Kungwalsong, Kanokporn, and Ravi Ravindran. Assessment of Disruption Risks in Supply Chains. In *Encyclopaedia of Business Analytics and Optimization*, Chapter 20, ed. John Wang, (pp. 209–219). Hershey, PA: IGI Global, 2014.

Li, Lei, and Zelda B. Zabinsky. Incorporating Uncertainty into a Supplier Selection Problem. *International Journal of Production Economics* 134, no. 2 (2011): 344–356.

Masud, Abu, and Ravi Ravindran. Multiple Criteria Decision Making. In *Operations Research and Management Science Handbook*, Chapter 5, ed. A. Ravi Ravindran, (pp. 1–35). Boca Raton, FL: CRC Press, 2008.

Qi, Lian. A Continuous-Review Inventory Model with Random Disruptions at the Primary Supplier. *European Journal of Operational Research* 225, no. 1 (2013): 59–74.

Ravindran, Ravi, R. Ufuk Bilsel, Vijay Wadhwa, et al. Risk Adjusted Multicriteria Supplier Selection Models with Applications. *International Journal of Production Research* 48, no. 2 (2010): 405–424.

Ravindran, Ravi, and Donald P. Warsing. *Supply Chain Engineering: Models and Applications.* Boca Raton, FL: CRC Press, 2013.

Ritchie, Bob, and Clare Brindley. An Emergent Framework for Supply Chain Risk Management and Performance Measurement. *Journal of the Operational Research Society* 58, no. 11 (2007): 1398–1411.

Sawik, Tadeusz. Selection of Resilient Supply Portfolio under Disruption Risks. *Omega* 41, no. 2 (2013): 259–269.

Schilling, David A., Charles Revelle, and Jared Cohon. An Approach to Display and Analysis of Multi-Objective Problems. *Socio-Economic Planning Sciences* 17, no. 2 (1983): 57–63.

Snyder, Lawrence V., and Mark S. Daskin. Reliability Models for Facility Location: The Expected Failure Cost Case. *Transportation Science* 39, no. 3 (2005): 400–416.

Tamhane, Ajit C., and Dorothy D. Dunlop. *Statistics and Data Analysis.* Upper Saddle River, NJ: Prentice Hall, 2000.

Tomlin, Brian. On the Value of Mitigation and Contingency Strategies for Managing Supply Chain Disruption Risks. *Management Science* 52, no. 5 (2006): 639–657.

Wadhwa, Vijay., and Ravi Ravindran. Vendor Selection in Outsourcing. *Computers and Operations Research* 34, no. 12 (2007): 3725–3737.

Yang, Tao. *Multi-Objective Optimisation Models for Managing Supply Risks.* PhD dissertation, Pennsylvania State University, 2006.

Zsidisin, George A., Lisa M. Ellram, Joseph L. Carter, et al. An Analysis of Supply Risk Assessment Techniques. *International Journal of Physical Distribution & Logistics Management* 34, no. 5 (2004): 397–413.

11

Multi-Criteria Decision-Making Models in Planning Prevention Services

Yuncheol Kang, Yooneun Lee, Lisa M. Ulan, and Vittaldas V. Prabhu
The Pennsylvania State University, University Park, Pennsylvania

CONTENTS

11.1 Background

Youth prevention services are targeted to prevent youth behavioral and mental problems in advance or to address them in the early stages of development. Specifically, it is known that effective prevention services can reduce delinquency, aggression, violence, bullying, and substance abuse in the youth population (Chilenski et al. 2007). Increased effectiveness of prevention services could potentially lower the risk of substance abuse (tobacco, alcohol, drugs) among youths through better social and emotional health.

Some of the most widely used prevention programs are listed in Table 11.1, and details of the programs can be found on the Blueprints program website (Blueprints for Healthy Youth Development 2015). In Table 11.1, prevention programs are broadly categorized into three different types, *universal, selective*, and *indicated*, according to the target population and intensity/seriousness of the prevention program (Mrazek et al. 1994). A "universal" prevention program is

TABLE 11.1

Examples of Prevention Programs (Blueprints for Healthy Youth Development 2015)

Program Name	Program Type	Program Objectives
Strengthening Families Program 10-14 (SFP)	Universal	Aims to strengthen the relationship between parents and their children by teaching communication techniques, parenting rules, and empathy sharing.
LifeSkills Training (LST)	Universal	Aims to prevent violence and drug abuse, primarily targeted to middle-school-aged students.
Promoting Alternative Thinking Strategies (PATHS)	Universal	Aims to reduce aggressive behaviors in elementary school children through providing a classroom-based social emotional program.
Toward No Drug Abuse (TND)	Universal	Aims to promote drug awareness and prevent drug use through classroom-based high school substance abuse program.
Olweus Bullying Prevention Program (OBPP)	Universal	Aims to create a safe and positive school climate, thereby reducing bullying behaviors among students.
Big Brothers/ Big Sisters (BBBS)	Selective	Aims to prevent youth misbehavior through the support of youth-adult relationships. The term "big" refers to adult volunteers, while "little" refers to youth.
Incredible Years (IY)	Selective	Aims to treat conduct problems through counseling in a small group treatment setting.
Multisystemic Therapy (MST)	Indicated	An intensive intervention aiming to prevent reoccurrences of misbehavior in adolescents who once had contact with juvenile court systems. Participants are treated with cognitive-behavioral therapy, which is provided by trained professionals.
Multidimensional Treatment Foster Care (MTFC)	Indicated	An intensive intervention aiming to prevent misbehaviors such as substance use or violence in a treatment setting. A type of foster care is provided by foster parents through 24-hour on-call assistance, clinical care, mentoring activities, and integrated types of community care.
Functional Family Therapy (FFT)	Indicated	An intensive intervention aiming to prevent any type of misbehavior through engagement and motivational approaches.

the least intensive; it targets a general youth population to provide benefits in a relatively inexpensive way. A "selective" program focuses on a sub-population that is exposed to risks of serious behavioral issues. "Indicated" prevention programs are the most intensive and expensive, dealing with the most serious behavioral issues and targeting early prevention for youth at serious risk of conduct disorder. Prevention services are delivered to youths but may include their families, depending upon the type of prevention program. Delivery can be individualized or in groups, through school or community settings (or both).

Generally, there are three primary roles in the planning and delivery of prevention services, and those include (1) state government policymakers, (2) prevention service providers (i.e., communities), and (3) youth or families needing the services.

Interestingly, the planning and delivery of prevention services can be modeled as a service supply chain involving state government policymakers, service providers, and program participants. The state government as a funding resource supplier, for example, provides financial resources to prevention service providers in response to their requests for funding. In turn, each prevention service provider, as a service supplier, delivers prevention services to its own customers (youths or families) with the budget provided by the state government. After implementing the prevention services, service providers evaluate their program participants' improvements (feedback from customers), estimate annual/biennial demand for the programs, and then request funding from the state government to support the programs in the next delivery period. The planning and delivery of prevention services, however, is expected to face a number of challenges in the near future. As has been pointed out in the literature, policymakers and providers in all areas of health care must consider the most effective planning and delivery, given the limited resources that are available (Brandeau et al. 2004). In other words, planning and delivery on a prevention service supply chain must be organized and implemented in a cost-effective manner in order to face upcoming resource challenges.

From a state government perspective, prevention services—as public services—contribute to the reduction of crime rates, thereby reducing the amount of money that taxpayers have to spend on the justice system, which includes law enforcement salaries, court costs, prisoner care, and prison maintenance (Jones et al. 2008). Several studies have explored the cost-effectiveness and return-on-investment (ROI) of prevention programs in terms of the fiscal benefits derived from successful outcomes (Aos et al. 2004; Miller and Hendrie 2009). In particular, policymakers are interested in evaluating the effectiveness of prevention services given budget constraints, thereby determining the most appropriate prevention services, considering both the needs of the community and the cost-effectiveness of each prevention program (Jones et al. 2008).

In most cases, the planning of statewide prevention services ideally will be based on an accurate estimate of communities' prevention needs, along with optimized allocation of resources for delivering prevention services. As primary input for planning services, prevention needs are estimated by investigating actual beneficiaries, while resource allocation is based on the community's prevention needs. In light of this, the planning problem can be viewed as a hierarchical planning structure, from the youth level to the community level and on to the state level, as shown in Figure 11.1. In Pennsylvania, for example, in order to estimate the demand for prevention programs, communities perform a biennial survey, the PA Youth Survey (PAYS), and examine prevention needs based on the results. The survey results are included in funding requests to the Pennsylvania Commission

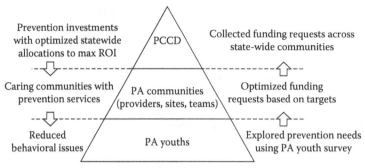

PA = Pennsylvania, PCCD = Pennsylvania Commission on Crime and Delinquency

FIGURE 11.1
Relationships among roles participating in planning and delivery of prevention services in Pennsylvania.

on Crime and Delinquency (PCCD), which collects such requests from 120 statewide communities in Pennsylvania. The collected demand information is then used as primary input for determining long-term plans for supporting prevention programs.

The biggest concern for a state government is to distribute a limited budget over various types of prevention programs, optimizing for effectiveness of overall quality of services. The bottom line is that the assigned budget for each prevention program should be adequate to support the corresponding program, while the total available funds are divided among the desired programs. We may thus consider a "trade-off" in allocating budgets over various prevention programs, considering their relative priorities, economic attributes, and, most importantly, the impact of each prevention program on the public goals set by the state government.

In the planning stages, we must also be aware of the many-to-many relationships among prevention programs and the behavioral patterns addressed. Each prevention program contributes to develop different behavioral aspects of participants. Conversely, each behavioral aspect also can be affected by multiple prevention programs. A behavioral aspect may include either (1) risk factors, which needed to be reduced or prevented, or (2) protective factors, which need to be promoted or enhanced. Those factors will be explained in more detail in the following section. The bottom line is that each prevention service may show different efficacy in reducing some risk factors or in improving some protective factors. Differences in efficacy can result in difficulties in choosing the right set of prevention programs to collectively address multiple behavioral aspects.

We have seen how planning of prevention services may involve complicated structures in terms of (1) varied prevention needs, (2) limited budget, and (3) differing behavioral targets. In this chapter, we show how planning of prevention services can be formulated using multi-criteria optimization approaches considering all aforementioned constraints. For illustrative purposes, we use a real-world example, focusing on Pennsylvania's prevention programs. Thus, we first focus on how to correctly identify prevention needs in communities in Pennsylvania. Then, based on these needs, we suggest how to plan the budgets for supporting prevention services at the program level (state-level planning) and for each prevention community level. In our model, we utilize several methodologies, including the analytic hierarchical process (AHP) and goal programming for solving multi-criteria decision-making problems, in that we consider multiple objectives that need to be met by prioritizing and distributing the limited budget. Although efficient delivery in implementing prevention services is another interesting and important topic, only the planning phase of prevention services will be discussed in this chapter.

11.2 Identifying Needs for Prevention Services

Planning prevention services begins with correctly identifying the needs of communities seeking such services. In this section, we focus on an approach that can quantitatively identify prevention needs arising in communities. Traditionally, the selection of prevention programs has relied heavily on prevention researchers' or decision makers' subjective opinions and knowledge, without a thorough consideration of the actual needs of communities. Such a selection procedure may not capture actual needs, can be biased by researchers' preferences or knowledge (or both), and may in fact result in different subjective recommendations for prevention programs for a given set of risk and protective factors. Furthermore, considering the many types of prevention programs and the many factors involved in program selection, decision makers may be unable to identify appropriate programs among the available options, given the large and complex scale of the selection scheme.

In response to this problem, the AHP, which is an approach for dealing with complex decision making, can be useful. AHP was developed in the 1970s by Thomas Saaty and has been applied in psychological and mathematical problems to determine the best of many options and to rank alternatives. With AHP, instead of striving to reach a correct decision, the decision maker seeks a solution that meets the goals or objectives in solving particular problems. AHP differs from most other decision-making techniques in that it allows diverse, incommensurable elements to be compared in a consistent, rational way based on human judgment.

In this section, we describe an approach for systematically aligning prevention needs with prevention programs using AHP. This approach begins by establishing links among risk and protective factors and candidate prevention services, then prioritizing the potential prevention services by considering the needs of all communities.

11.2.1 The Relevance of Risk and Protective Factors to Prevention Services

PAYS was developed to gather information for assessing the prevalence of risk and protective factors among youth in Pennsylvania. In general, PAYS assesses (1) school climate, (2) alcohol, tobacco, and other drug (ATOD) use, and (3) risk and protective factors (PCCD 2009). PAYS includes more than 100 questions about communities' opinions on numerous topics concerning youth behavioral issues. According to PCCD, protective factors can be considered to be conditions that buffer children and youth from exposure to risk, either by reducing risk impact or by changing how young people respond to risks (PCCD 2009). Protective factors are typically identified as strong bonds with family, school, peers, and community, and encouraging these bonds generally involves teaching skills and the recognition of contributions. At the same time, risk factors can be considered to be conditions that increase the likelihood of a youth's becoming involved in drug use, delinquency, school dropout, or violence (or any combination of these factors) (PCCD 2009). The PAYS 2009 includes 11 protective factors and 23 risk factors, which are listed in Tables 11.2 and 11.3.

TABLE 11.2

List of Protective Factors

Protective Factors	Description
Family Opportunities for Prosocial Involvement	Bonds with family reinforced through children's contribution to their family; children adopt their parents' positive ideas on success and achievement.
Family Rewards for Prosocial Involvement	Bonds with family reinforced through positive participation.
Family Attachment	Bonds with family with reinforced with clear standards, leading children to want to please their parents and engage in fewer activities of which their parents strongly disapprove.
Family Discipline	Growing up with parents who give clear standards.
Family Supervision	Growing up with parents who give clear rules.
Community Opportunities for Prosocial Involvement	Participating in community activities leads to foster relationships with prosocial peers and adult role models.
Community Rewards for Prosocial Involvement	Recognition of children within a community leads to higher self-esteem and less negative behavior.
Belief in Moral Order	Having a strong bond to society leads children to follow society's standards of behavior.
Religiosity	Religious institutions can help instill prosocial beliefs.
School Rewards for Prosocial Involvement	Schools reward students for their involvement, creating a greater bond to the school and reducing incidence of behavioral issues.
School Opportunities for Prosocial Involvement	Opportunities to participate in school activities; helping students bond to their school and adopt the school's standards of behavior.

TABLE 11.3

List of Risk Factors

Risk Factors	Description
Parental Attitudes Favorable toward Antisocial Behavior	Parental attitudes toward violence and law-breaking.
Family History of Antisocial Behavior	Family history of substance abuse and criminal activity, which can lead to exhibiting the same negative behaviors.
Parental Attitudes Favorable toward ATOD Use	Growing up in families where parents are tolerant of substance use and abuse.
Family Conflict	Experiencing high levels of family conflict.
Poor Family Management	Experiencing poor family discipline and supervision.
Transitions and Mobility	Transitions to new environments; becoming less attached to their new environment.
Community Disorganization	Not feeling safe or feeling in disarray in their community, leads to engaging in negative behaviors.
Low Neighborhood Attachment	Low attachment to their community, leads to higher rates of violence, drug use, and delinquency in the communities.
Peer Rewards for Antisocial Behavior	Perception of peers giving positive feedback toward substance use and delinquency.
Early Initiation of Drug Use	Early start with substance use, leads to more consistent use throughout lifetime.
Favorable Attitudes toward ATOD Use	Seeing others who engage in substance use, leads to acceptance of and participation in those behaviors.
Perceived Availability of Drugs	Perceiving drugs to be readily available; can access the drugs easily.
Laws and Norms Favorable to Drug Use	Community standards toward drug use
Low Perceived Risks of Drug Use	Perceiving drug use harm as low, leads youth to easily engage in drug use.
Gang Involvement	Associating with gangs; can increase the chances to engage in negative behaviors.
Friends' Use of Drugs	Associating with peers who use drugs; can increase the chances to engage in the behavior themselves.
Rebelliousness	Not feeling connected to society or bound by rules; can increase risk for delinquency, drug use, and school dropout.
Sensation Seeking	Impulse-driven attitude.
Friends' Delinquent Behavior	Associating with delinquent others increases risk of similar delinquent behavior.
Favorable Attitudes toward Antisocial Behavior	Perceiving others as showing acceptance of negative behaviors.
Low School Commitment	Being less attached to school; can increase risk of developing problem behaviors.
Poor Academic Performance	Poor academic performance can increase developing problems associated with violence, delinquency, and drugs.
Perceived Availability of Firearms	Easy to access to handguns; can increase risk of involving youth with the unauthorized use of them.

TABLE 11.4

AHP Matrix of Family Opportunities for Prosocial Involvement

	MST	SFP	MTFC	FFT	IY	Eigenvector (Priority Vector)
MST	1	1/5	5	5	1/3	0.14
SFP	5	1	9	9	3	0.51
MTFC	1/5	1/9	1	1	1/7	0.04
FFT	1/5	1/9	1	1	1/7	0.04
IY	3	1/3	7	7	1	0.27

As previously mentioned, each protective factor and risk factor can be addressed via prevention services, but little research has been conducted concerning the linkages among these factors and prevention programs. In our previous research, we introduced an approach to examine each protective and risk factor in terms of what it measures, and we compared this with data across the many studies of Blueprints programs (Ulan 2014). First, youth prevention programs shown in the Blueprints programs were investigated thoroughly to determine intensity of involvement with each factor and related outcomes. Based on the findings, prevention programs were then ranked by each factor to determine weight of involvement with different factors. For ranking prevention programs, AHP was used to integrate experts' subjective opinions.

Table 11.4 is an example of AHP analysis on a particular protective factor, family opportunities for prosocial involvement. In this table, the results of pair-wise comparison of each prevention program on the corresponding factor are recorded along with the eigenvector (AHP weight), which can be calculated as the normalized n-th root of the products of each value. In addition, we check consistency of the resulting AHP weights using the threshold (below 0.1) of consistency ratio (CR). In case of family opportunities for prosocial involvement (Table 11.4), CR is measured as 0.06 (random index = 1.12), which shows consistency in terms of evaluating prevention programs.

Table 11.5 summarizes the results for 10 prevention programs (acronyms listed in Table 11.1), along with the weights assigned for each protective and risk factor. For each factor, the sum of weights representing relevance to prevention programs equals 1—the higher the weight of the program, the greater the relevance of the program to the corresponding factor. Such AHP weights can be used as a basis for recommending prevention services for each community, as the following section explains in detail.

11.2.2 The Effectiveness of Prevention Services in the Community

Having obtained the relevance of specific prevention programs to individual protective/risk factors, we now consider how to link the relevance matrix to communities in order to prioritize a set of prevention programs to meet

TABLE 11.5

AHP Weights for Each Individual Protective/Risk Factor by Blueprints Program (Programs Are Listed by Acronym, and a Code Name for Each Risk/Protective Factor Is Displayed in Parentheses. We Use the Code Names to Explain Some Figures Appearing in the Following Section.)

Factor	MST	SFP	LST	MTFC	TND	OBPP	BBBS	FFT	PATHS	IY
Family Opportunities for Prosocial Involvement (xFP2)	0.14	0.51	0.00	0.04	0.00	0.00	0.00	0.04	0.00	0.27
Family Rewards for Prosocial Involvement (xFP3)	0.14	0.25	0.00	0.06	0.00	0.00	0.03	0.06	0.00	0.46
Parental Attitudes Favorable toward Antisocial Behavior (xFR9)	0.26	0.06	0.00	0.00	0.00	0.00	0.00	0.12	0.56	0.00
Family History of Antisocial Behavior (xFR7)	0.02	0.06	0.04	0.00	0.12	0.00	0.12	0.40	0.00	0.24
Parental Attitudes Favorable toward ATOD Use (xFR8)	0.13	0.51	0.26	0.00	0.00	0.00	0.00	0.06	0.00	0.03
Family Attachment (xFP1)	0.22	0.17	0.00	0.03	0.00	0.00	0.40	0.05	0.02	0.10
Family Conflict (xFR6)	0.11	0.31	0.00	0.00	0.00	0.00	0.05	0.05	0.00	0.49
Family Discipline (xFAMDISP)	0.17	0.23	0.00	0.00	0.00	0.06	0.00	0.09	0.02	0.44
Family Supervision (xFAMSUP)	0.08	0.43	0.00	0.00	0.00	0.04	0.00	0.13	0.02	0.29
Poor Family Management (xFR10)	0.07	0.28	0.00	0.04	0.00	0.04	0.00	0.13	0.02	0.41
Transitions and Mobility (xCR5)	0.00	0.00	0.00	0.00	0.00	0.00	0.00	0.00	0.00	0.00
Community Opportunities for Prosocial Involvement (xCP1)	0.33	0.00	0.00	0.33	0.00	0.00	0.33	0.00	0.00	0.00
Community Rewards for Prosocial Involvement (xCP2)	0.33	0.00	0.00	0.33	0.00	0.00	0.33	0.00	0.00	0.00
Community Disorganization (xCR4)	0.50	0.00	0.00	0.00	0.00	0.00	0.50	0.00	0.00	0.00
Low Neighborhood Attachment (xCR3)	1.00	0.00	0.00	0.00	0.00	0.00	0.00	0.00	0.00	0.00
Belief in Moral Order (xIP3)	0.16	0.01	0.09	0.26	0.02	0.09	0.03	0.23	0.07	0.04

(Continued)

TABLE 11.5 (*Continued*)

AHP Weights for Each Individual Protective/Risk Factor by Blueprints Program (Programs Are Listed by Acronym, and a Code Name for Each Risk/Protective Factor Is Displayed in Parentheses. We Use the Code Names to Explain Some Figures Appearing in the Following Section.)

Factor	MST	SFP	LST	MTFC	TND	OBPP	BBBS	FFT	PATHS	IY
Peer Rewards for Antisocial Behavior (xIP7)	0.11	0.08	0.03	0.02	0.01	0.17	0.29	0.05	0.25	0.00
Early Initiation of Drug Use (xIP15)	0.11	0.29	0.25	0.03	0.07	0.02	0.18	0.05	0.00	0.01
Favorable Attitudes toward ATOD Use (xIP9)	0.11	0.22	0.29	0.02	0.18	0.03	0.05	0.08	0.00	0.01
Perceived Availability of Drugs (xCR11)	0.15	0.07	0.32	0.02	0.27	0.03	0.02	0.12	0.00	0.00
Laws and Norms Favorable to Drug Use (xCR9)	0.15	0.07	0.32	0.02	0.27	0.03	0.02	0.12	0.00	0.00
Low Perceived Risks of Drug Use (xIP10)	0.11	0.22	0.29	0.02	0.18	0.03	0.05	0.08	0.00	0.01
Gang Involvement (xIP14)	0.00	0.00	0.00	0.00	0.00	0.00	0.00	0.00	0.00	0.00
Friends' Use of Drugs (xIP6)	0.37	0.02	0.11	0.00	0.11	0.02	0.04	0.11	0.21	0.00
Religiosity (xIP1)	0.00	0.00	0.00	0.00	0.00	0.00	0.00	0.00	0.00	0.00
Rebelliousness (xIP4)	0.28	0.05	0.11	0.21	0.02	0.02	0.02	0.18	0.08	0.04
Sensation Seeking (xIP13)	0.17	0.03	0.31	0.25	0.07	0.00	0.00	0.04	0.02	0.11
Friends' Delinquent Behavior (xIP5)	0.38	0.08	0.00	0.04	0.04	0.21	0.02	0.04	0.17	0.00
Favorable Attitudes toward Antisocial Behavior (xIP8)	0.19	0.02	0.01	0.21	0.04	0.03	0.12	0.06	0.08	0.25
Low School Commitment (xSR4)	0.25	0.00	0.00	0.09	0.00	0.03	0.46	0.05	0.12	0.00
Poor Academic Performance (xSR3)	0.15	0.00	0.00	0.20	0.00	0.48	0.00	0.05	0.03	0.09
School Rewards for Prosocial Involvement (xSP2)	0.11	0.00	0.00	0.11	0.00	0.46	0.03	0.00	0.24	0.05
School Opportunities for Prosocial Involvement (xSP1)	0.13	0.00	0.00	0.00	0.00	0.51	0.03	0.00	0.26	0.06
Perceived Availability of Firearms (xCR12)	0.00	0.00	0.00	0.00	1.00	0.00	0.00	0.00	0.00	0.00

the community's prevention needs. As mentioned earlier, PAYS provides information about the current status of risk and protective factors in a given community. With the PAYS results collected from all communities in Pennsylvania, we compare them with each other to determine relative prevention needs based on specific protective/risk factors. For this, we define need-based factors according to the community's deviation from the Pennsylvania state average for each risk and protective factor. Protective (or risk) factors that deviate negatively (or positively) from the state average are considered. Because protective factors are considered to be positive for a community, higher scores are better. If a community scores lower than the state average (has negative deviation), then it is considered to have a need-based protective factor. By contrast, because risk factors are considered to be negative for a community, lower scores are better in these areas. If a community scores higher on a risk factor than the state average (has positive deviation), then it is considered to have a need-based risk factor. Absolute values of deviations have been used to assess the weight of each factor, and all weights have been normalized based on all need-based factors for the community. As an example, in Table 11.6, we summarize all need-based protective and risk factors for the prevention community of Washington County, Pennsylvania. From the example, we can see Washington County has great needs in "perceived availability of firearms (risk factor)" and in "friends' delinquent behavior (risk factor)" as compared to other factors (both risk factors' weight is greater than 10%). Therefore, the prevention programs chosen for this county should show relatively greater effectiveness for these risk factors.

The effectiveness of prevention programs in a community can be calculated using the AHP weights shown in Table 11.5 and the need-based risk and protective factors of the corresponding community. First, we measure the need-based risk and protective factors for each community. Then, normalized weights for the need-based risk and protective factors are multiplied by AHP weights for how each program addressed the factors, and then they are added together to determine weights for how each program would help the needs of each community. In Table 11.7, we consider Mercer, Washington, Elk, Crawford, and Greene counties as sample communities for this analysis and include a list of prevention programs. In case of Washington County, for example, the relative importance of prevention programs for the community can be calculated by multiplying need-based protective/risk factors for the community (i.e., normalized weight in Table 11.6) and AHP weights of each factor (i.e., Table 11.5).

11.2.3 Cost-Effectiveness Issues in Selecting Prevention Programs

By analyzing PAYS data and Blueprints programs, we have explained how to produce weighted rankings of prevention programs by effectiveness in terms of the needs of five communities in Pennsylvania. In the case of Washington County, for example, "Multisystemic Therapy" (MST) and "Towards No Drug Abuse" (TND) turn out to be the most appropriate prevention programs to

TABLE 11.6

Need-Based Protective/Risk Factor for Washington County

Protective/Risk Factor	P/R	PA Average	Washington Score	Deviation (%)	Normalized Weight
Community Opportunities for Prosocial Involvement	P	1.7819	1.6025	−10.07	0.0611
Perceived Availability of Drugs	R	1.2701	1.3245	4.29	0.0260
Perceived Availability of Firearms	R	0.7086	0.9039	27.55	0.1673
Low Neighborhood Attachment	R	0.9463	1.0133	7.08	0.0430
Community Disorganization	R	0.9267	1.0243	10.53	0.0639
Transitions and Mobility		0.9616	0.9511	−1.09	
Laws and Norms Favorable to Drug Use	R	1.1206	1.2727	13.57	0.0824
Parental Attitudes Favorable toward ATOD Use	R	0.2782	0.2909	4.58	0.0278
Parental Attitudes Favorable toward Antisocial Behavior	R	0.4053	0.4187	3.33	0.0202
Religiosity	P	1.5308	1.3778	−10.00	0.0607
Low Perceived Risks of Drug Use	R	0.9275	0.9984	7.64	0.0464
Sensation Seeking	R	1.2759	1.3247	3.83	0.0232
Gang Involvement	R	0.3577	0.3633	1.57	0.0095
Early Initiation of Drug Use	R	1.2632	1.3487	6.77	0.0411
Belief in the Moral Order	P	2.1277	2.1031	−1.16	0.0070
Rebelliousness	R	0.7516	0.7540	0.32	0.0019
Friends' Delinquent Behavior	R	0.1773	0.2124	19.77	0.1200
Friends' Use of Drugs	R	0.7204	0.7630	5.90	0.0358
Favorable Attitudes toward Antisocial Behavior	R	0.5568	0.5657	1.60	0.0097
Favorable Attitudes toward ATOD Use	R	0.5979	0.5998	0.32	0.0020
School Opportunities for Prosocial Involvement	P	1.9598	1.8284	−6.71	0.0407
School Rewards for Prosocial Involvement	P	1.8065	1.6450	−8.94	0.0543
Poor Academic Performance	R	0.9152	0.9788	6.95	0.0422
Low School Commitment	R	1.3878	1.4187	2.22	0.0135

P, protective factor; R, risk factor.

TABLE 11.7

Relative Importance of Prevention Programs for Each Community

Prevention Program	Community				
	Mercer	Washington	Elk	Crawford	Greene
MST	0.1714	0.2174	0.1549	0.1670	0.2258
SFP	0.1189	0.0569	0.1173	0.1252	0.1144
LST	0.1100	0.0783	0.1216	0.1476	0.1306
MTFC	0.0389	0.0551	0.0322	0.0406	0.0517
TND	0.1792	0.2191	0.2256	0.3642	0.1542
OBPP	0.0415	0.0988	0.0200	0.0187	0.0588
BBBS	0.0717	0.0784	0.0798	0.0799	0.0695
FFT	0.0935	0.0380	0.0698	0.0982	0.0635
PATHS	0.0662	0.0676	0.0614	0.0343	0.0818
IY	0.0615	0.0160	0.0330	0.0483	0.0222

support protective factors and mitigate risk factors in that county. Intuitively, this result makes sense, in that (1) TND is the only prevention program that affects "perceived availability of firearms," which is the highest need-based risk factor for the county, and (2) MST is the most relevant prevention program to reduce "friends' delinquent behavior," which is the second highest risk factor for the county. These two programs are likely to be more effective in addressing the protective and risk factors in the community than others.

This significant effectiveness may not, however, determine the final selection of the prevention programs because it does not consider cost. Because MST is classified as an indicated prevention program (see Table 11.1), the required funding resources are likely to be significant. Thus, allocating prevention funds to MST might not be a cost-effective way to address protective and risk factors in the community. Furthermore, a state budget is limited, and investing in a few expensive prevention programs in a few counties may not be desirable in terms of improving overall public services at the state level. In the next section, we examine these issues further and develop a framework for planning prevention services, including budgeting prevention programs and allocating budgets to each community in a cost-effective manner.

11.3 Multi-Criteria Decision Making for Budget Planning

There exists a serious need to develop a decision-making process for politicians and policymakers in order to generate a quantifiable budget planning process for prevention programs, so that statewide monetary benefits from the prevention programs are maximized. A recent report from PCCD evaluates the cost-effectiveness of the individual evidence-based programs in Pennsylvania, but a collective decision-making procedure for funding allocation needs to be presented. Given limited financial resources, the provincial fund must be efficiently allocated over the prevention programs to satisfy the present needs of local communities. Further, we have seen that a strictly need-based allocation of funds may not be appropriate in terms of implementation cost. Here, we focus on government funding of prevention programs and methods for allocating the state's annual operating budget for prevention programs to communities across the state in such a way as to maximize youth benefits from them.

Economic planning is ever more complex, and a policymaker cannot easily decide how much money should be allocated to each community. Decision making is further complicated by the many-to-many relationships between protective/risk factors and prevention programs mentioned in Section 11.2. Here, we illustrate a two-level goal programming model in which the budget is allocated to prevention programs at the program level and then distributed among sites at the community level. Based on the needs identified by AHP in the previous section, a two-level model can produce cost-effective plans satisfying overall community needs under a limited budget and explain the real-world budgeting process in an intuitive way by providing a quantified analysis of program allocation and benefits.

We explain some assumptions used in the budget planning for prevention services as follows.

- *Assumption 1:* Total budget amount is fixed.
- *Assumption 2:* A prevention service can simultaneously affect the multiple protective and risk factors.
- *Assumption 3:* A prevention program with higher intensity can make a bigger impact in addressing risk and protective factors, but it imposes a larger cost burden.

The state budget is usually fixed and limited, so Assumption 1 is straightforward, and Assumption 2 is described in the AHP result in Table 11.5. Moreover, we introduce the degree of intensity of prevention programs in order to make realistic models in which the impact of each program is different from those of the others, as in Assumption 3. The Institute of Medicine (IOM) categorizes prevention programs into three levels of intensity: universal, selective, and indicated (Mrazek et al. 1994) (see Table 11.1). Universal programs are designed for a general youth population. Because their target populations are broader, the impact of these programs is narrow and limited, while the per capita cost is relatively low. Programs such as the Strengthening Families Program 10–14 (SFP), LifeSkills Training (LST), Promoting Alternative Thinking Strategies (PATHS), Towards No Drug Abuse (TND), and the Olweus Bullying Prevention Program (OBPP) are included in this group. Indicated programs

TABLE 11.8

Intensity of Prevention Programs

Program Type	Intensity	Population Served	Cost	Number of Protective/Risk Factors Impacted	Prevention Programs
Universal	Low	General	Low	Small	SFP, LST, PATHS, TND
Selective	Medium	Sub	Moderate	Medium	BBBS, IY
Indicated	High	Sub	Expensive	Large	MST, FFT, MTFC

are implemented for youths who have exceptionally poor scores in behavior assessments and hence need intense care. These programs are much more expensive, and they make a greater simultaneous impact on a larger number of risk and protective factors, so that the behavior of the youth can be expected to improve. Multisystemic Therapy (MST), Multidimensional Treatment Foster Care (MTFC), and Functional Family Therapy (FFT) are among such programs. Lastly, selective programs, such as Big Brothers/Big Sisters (BBBS) and Incredible Years (IY), are between those two groups in terms of intensity, cost, and the number of risk and protective factors affected by the programs. Table 11.8 summarizes the classification of prevention programs in terms of intensity, cost, and the number of related risk and protective factors.

11.3.1 Program-Level Planning

Based on the assumptions made earlier, we formulate a goal programming model for solving the program-level problem. By deciding the demand for each prevention program, we minimize the weighted sum of overall deviations from the target scores of protective/risk factors. Decision variables and parameters are summarized as follows:

Decision Variables

x_j Demand of the prevention program j
d_i^+ Positive deviations from target score for protective/risk factor i
d_i^- Negative deviations from target score for protective/risk factor i

Parameters

B Total budget
G_i Target score for factor i
R_{ij} Impact matrix of program j on factor i
c_j Cost of prevention program j serving one youth
w_i Weights on positive deviations
v_i Weights on negative deviations

α_j Intensity of prevention program j
γ_i Maximum amount of positive deviation for factor i

The goal program model of program-level planning is given as follows:

$$\min f_i\left(d_i^+, d_i^-\right) = w_i d_i^- - v_i d_i^+, \quad \forall i \tag{11.1}$$

$$\text{Subject to:} \quad \sum_j c_j x_j \le B \tag{11.2}$$

$$\sum_j \alpha_j R_{ij} x_j + d_i^- - d_i^+ = G_i, \quad \forall i \tag{11.3}$$

$$0 \le d_i^- \le G_i, \quad \forall i \tag{11.4}$$

$$0 \le d_i^+ \le \gamma_i, \quad \forall i \tag{11.5}$$

The objective function (Equation 11.1) minimizes the unmet goals of all risk and protective factors, where the goal is set to be the state average score of the factor. The weights w_i and v_i will be adjusted based on the decision maker's judgment as to how much overachievement and underachievement of the factor will be allowed. Constraint (Equation 11.2) ensures that the sum of budget allocation is not allowed to exceed the government's total budget. Constraint (Equation 11.3) describes the amount of money allocated in the specific program to achieve the goal for every factor score based on the program intensity parameters, α_js. Finally, in constraints (Equation 11.4) and (Equation 11.5), the maximum amount of deviations allowed for both negative and positive deviations are defined by a decision maker.

11.3.2 Community-Level Planning

Once the potential demand for each program $\bar{x}_j$ is determined in the program-level planning and budget is allocated accordingly, the next question is how much money has to be distributed throughout the communities for each prevention program. Not every community will necessarily run all programs; selected prevention programs will be implemented utilizing state funds so as to maximize the overall impact of budget allocation. The purpose of community-level planning is to ensure that money is allocated effectively to each site based on the effectiveness of the program.

Decision Variables
y_{jk} Number of participants served by prevention program j on site k

Parameters
A_{jk} Effectiveness of program j at site k identified by AHP
N_{jk} Number of potential participants for prevention program j at site k estimated by PAYS survey

The community-level planning model is as follows:

$$\max \sum_{j} \sum_{k} A_{jk} y_{jk} \tag{11.6}$$

$$\text{s.t.} \quad \sum_{j} \sum_{k} c_{j} y_{jk} \leq B \tag{11.7}$$

$$\sum_{k} y_{jk} \geq \bar{x}_{j}, \quad \forall j \tag{11.8}$$

$$0 \leq y_{jk} \leq N_{jk}, \quad \forall j, k \tag{11.9}$$

The objective function (Equation 11.6) is to maximize the overall impact across the sites based on the needs identified by AHP in the previous section. The total budget constraint (Equation 11.7) remains the same, and constraint (Equation 11.8) enforces the total number of the program participants across all the sites and is at least the number of participants of the program determined in program-level planning. Constraint (Equation 11.9) provides a bound for the number of program participants in the community. The bound, N_{jk} can be estimated by multiplying the number of potential participants of the community k (i.e., N_k) and the relative importance of prevention program j for the community k. For N_k, we refer to the number of PAYS respondents of the community k.

11.3.3 Data Description

In order to illustrate our model, we measure the risk and protective factors in the model using PAYS data collected by the PCCD. From the PAYS data, we calculate state averages of 26 risk and protective factor scores and set decision makers' target score for each factor. Given the current average scores of factors and decision makers' judgment of the situation, we determine a target value for the amount of efforts to be assigned to given factors. Additionally, we assume that a decision maker prefers to focus more on the risk factors whose scores are greater than state average and on the protective factors whose scores are lower than state average. For this illustration, we give such factors twice the weight of other factors that are currently less significant.

Figure 11.2 depicts average scores of protective factors; the decision maker's target score is represented by the straight line. Factors whose scores are below the line are marked in dashed fill. As we can see, average scores for four protective factors, Community Opportunities for Prosocial Involvement (xCP1), Community Rewards for Prosocial Involvement (xCP2), Religiosity (xIP1), and School Rewards for Prosocial Involvement (xSP2), are lower than

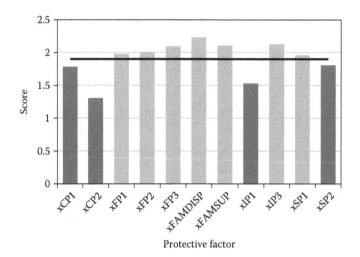

FIGURE 11.2
Average protective factor scores and target score. Dashed fill indicates protective factors that are under the target score, and solid fill indicates those that are over the targeted score.

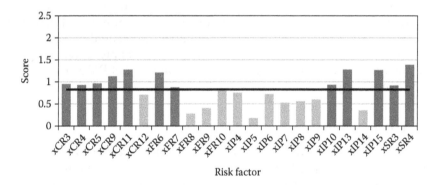

FIGURE 11.3
Average risk factor scores and target score. Dashed fill indicates risk factors that are over the target score. Solid fill indicates risk factors that are under.

the target and hence will benefit from more effort and attention. Similarly, Figure 11.3 depicts average scores and the target score for risk factors; factors whose scores are above the target line are marked in dashed fill. As seen in the figure, 12 risk factors require more effort, while the other 11 factors are within acceptable parameters.

For cost and demand data, we use the cost–benefit assessment performed by the Washington State Institute for Public Policy (WSIPP) (Lee et al. 2012). Using a statistical meta-analysis approach, the report estimates monetary values of benefits and costs of various prevention programs. Moreover, it provides not only measures of juvenile justice but metrics for public policy areas including child welfare and children's mental health, and public health and prevention, in which we are also interested. In order to determine the intensity parameter α_i, we further assume that the program intensity is proportional to the cost of service, based on our earlier Assumption 3. The intensity parameters are log-transformed to adjust scales down to other parameters in the formula. Thus, the intensity parameters are measured by:

$$\alpha_i = \beta \log c_i, \forall i,$$

where β is a scale-adjustment parameter.

Table 11.9 summarizes data for costs per individual and program intensity. The optimal budget allocation of the program-level problem can now be obtained by solving the problem based on the data. Potential demand is calculated by dividing the optimal solution by costs and then is used as a bound parameter in the community-level problem.

11.3.4 Planning Results

Given the data mentioned in Section 11.3.3, a goal programming model is developed at the program level. Because the model includes several parameters subject to administrative decision, the solution can vary depending on the policy of the decision maker. In other words, the solution depends on the total budget, the judgment of policymakers as to the importance of each factor, and the potential demand for prevention services.

For the first program-level problem, we further assume that the administration has a specific preference among the risk and protective factors, and the objective function (Equation 11.1) can be expressed as the following simplest weighted sum (Gass et al. 1955)

$$\min \sum_i \left(w_i d_i^- - v_i d_i^+ \right) \tag{11.10}$$

For the purposes of illustration, we set the weight equal to 1 for underachievement and 0.1 for overachievement, which can be interpreted as the policymaker concerns about underachievement of the goal being 10 times greater than concerns about overachievement.

Changing the total budget allocated to prevention services, we solve the goal programming using IBM® ILog® Cplex® Optimization Studio 12.2. Table 11.10 summarizes the result of the budget allocation among the prevention programs based on the given budget. When the amount of budget is low, the optimization algorithm tends to assign budget to relatively cheaper and less-effective (in terms of the number of factors impacted) prevention programs. This can be interpreted that funding-indicated prevention programs may not be cost-effective when the total budget is low.

TABLE 11.9

Economic Assessment for Prevention Programs and Potential Demand

	SFP	LST	PATHS	TND	OBPP[a]	BBBS	IY	MST	MTFC	FFT
Program Costs (per individual)[b]	$1,077	$34	$115	$14	$32.06	$1,479	$2,074	$7,370	$7,922	$3,262
Program Intensity	6.98	3.53	4.74	2.64	3.47	7.30	7.64	8.91	8.98	8.09
Potential Demand	1,414	2,914	1,774	3,789	3,137	1,431	1,280	1,123	1,105	1,235

[a] Cost information for OBPP is obtained from materials provided by EPISCenter (Evidence Based Prevention Intervention Support Center in Pennsylvania).

[b] The information on program costs (per individual) for all programs except OBPP is obtained from Washington State Institute for Public Policy (WSIPP) (Lee et al. 2012).

TABLE 11.10
Budget Allocation for Prevention Programs

Total Budget ($)	Prevention Programs									
	SFP	LST	PATHS	TND	OBPP	BBBS	IY	MST	MTFC	FFT
10M	1,077	218,858	135,470	53,046	122,886	3,823,215	4,963,082	670,670	7,922	3,262
14M	1,077	203,150	142,830	53,032	110,254	3,406,137	4,676,870	5,394,840	7,922	3,262
18M	1,077	191,522	101,890	53,032	111,376	3,014,202	4,602,206	8,276,510	1,497,258	150,052
22M	17,232	174,828	74,290	53,046	118,398	2,900,319	4,264,144	8,276,510	3,723,340	2,397,570
26M	917,604	128,044	109,020	53,046	116,795	2,441,829	3,287,290	8,276,510	7,280,318	3,389,218
30M	1,522,878	99,076	204,010	53,046	101,726	2,116,449	2,654,720	8,276,510	8,753,810	4,028,570
34M	1,522,878	99,076	204,010	53,046	101,726	2,116,449	2,654,720	8,276,510	8,753,810	4,028,570

In other words, it may be more efficient to assign budgets to universal programs whose targets for covering protective/risk factors are broader with a lower cost burden. As the total budget increases, the algorithm assigns more resources to indicated programs rather than to cheaper and less-effective programs. Figure 11.4 illustrates the budget allocation tendency by changing total budget. Based on our formulation, the total budget to cover the full potential demand of prevention programs is estimated at around $28 million.

Because different decision makers can have different weights on the factors, we now investigate how their judgment makes an impact on the budget allocation. We change the weights of both over- (w_i) and under-achievement (v_i) of the goals and solve the problem to examine the sensitivity of the weights we first set ($w_i = 0.1$, $v_i = 1$). Table 11.11 describes the results of solution when we change the weight vectors w_i and v_i. For this numerical example, we fix the total budget at $28 million, which covers all prevention programs, and change the value of the weight vector. Figure 11.5 depicts that the pattern of assignment remains stable across the region, except for a few programs. As the relative importance of overachievement increases (overachievement is considered as important as underachievement), more of the budget tends to be allocated to MST. Recalling the number of risk and protective factors that are addressed by programs in Table 11.5, we see that MST has a far broader

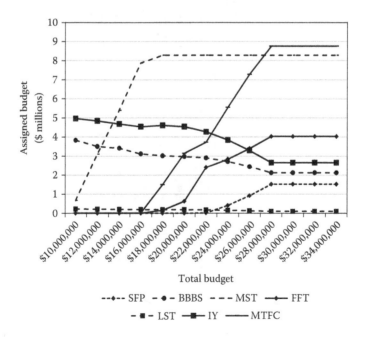

FIGURE 11.4
Budget allocation of various prevention programs given the total budget. (See Table 11.10 for the full list of prevention programs.)

TABLE 11.11

Budget Allocation Based on the Relative Importance of Overachievement (w_i/v_i)

(w_i/v_i)	SFP	LST	PATHS	TND	OBPP	BBBS	IY	MST	MTFC	FFT
0	1,526,109	99,246	207,230	53,018	99,675	2,113,491	2,658,868	8,276,510	8,722,122	4,025,308
0.1	1,522,878	99,076	204,010	53,046	101,726	2,116,449	2,654,720	8,276,510	8,753,810	4,028,570
0.2	1,521,801	99,110	203,895	53,046	101,726	2,116,449	2,654,720	8,283,880	8,745,888	4,028,570
0.3	1,499,184	100,470	216,085	53,046	97,462	2,057,289	2,638,128	9,028,250	8,183,426	3,695,846
0.4	1,523,955	100,504	218,500	53,046	96,982	2,049,894	2,644,350	9,013,510	8,500,306	3,503,388
0.5	1,530,417	100,266	218,500	53,046	97,078	2,048,415	2,640,202	8,998,770	8,531,994	3,500,126
0.6	1,530,417	100,266	218,500	53,046	97,078	2,048,415	2,640,202	8,998,770	8,531,994	3,500,126
0.7	1,535,802	100,028	217,465	53,046	97,270	2,046,936	2,636,054	8,998,770	8,563,682	3,493,602
0.8	1,535,802	100,062	218,270	53,046	97,174	2,046,936	2,636,054	8,991,400	8,563,682	3,493,602
0.9	1,535,802	100,028	217,465	53,046	97,270	2,046,936	2,636,054	8,998,770	8,563,682	3,493,602
1	1,534,725	100,164	218,845	53,032	96,917	2,046,936	2,638,128	8,998,770	8,547,838	3,490,340

Prevention Programs

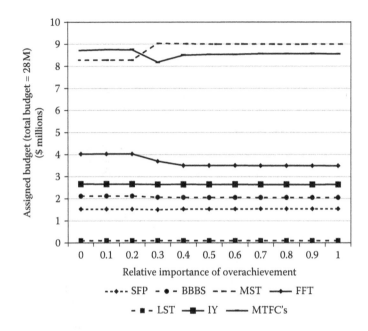

FIGURE 11.5
Budget allocation pattern depending on the relative importance of overachievement compared to underachivement. (See Table 11.11 for the full list of prevention programs.)

impact than MTFC and FFT. Thus, when a decision maker is concerned about overachievement, MST is favored over the other two programs. We can observe that MST receives a higher budget, while a lower budget is allocated to MTFC and FFT.

For the community-level planning problem, an assignment problem is formulated in a linear programming containing 10 dominating prevention programs and 568 communities across Pennsylvania. The optimal solution represents the budget allocation decision that maximizes the overall impact of the prevention programs.

Because the solution obtained is too large to be fully described here, we select one prevention program, SFP, as a representative example of the solution. Based on the optimal solution obtained from the community-level planning, we plot the communities that will support SFP using solid dots on the Pennsylvania map in Figure 11.6. In Chester County, for example, six communities need to operate SFPs to mitigate the risks of the region. Interestingly, but understandably, the trend of the budget allocation from the optimal solution is similar to that of the demographic profile because a much larger number of communities will require prevention services in the more densely populated areas. Figure 11.7 depicts budget for SFP allocated to 14 counties in Pennsylvania (23 local communities in those counties receive budget allocations).

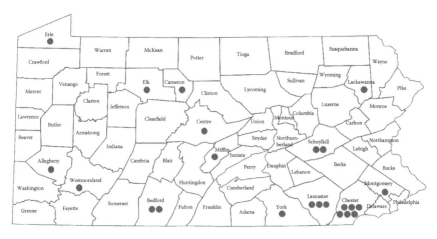

FIGURE 11.6
Budget planning at county level for SFP across Pennsylvania.

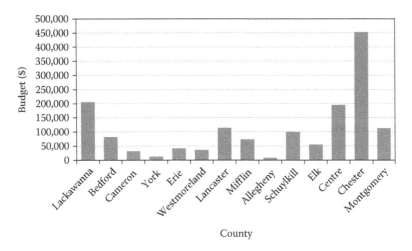

FIGURE 11.7
Budget allocated to counties for SFP.

11.4 Conclusion

In this chapter, we applied multi-criteria optimization techniques, including AHP and goal programming, to solve a state budget planning problem involving prevention services. Using AHP and the goal programming approach, we suggest a decision-making framework that can efficiently allocate the limited state budget to local communities based on their identified needs. Specifically, AHP reveals the relationship among the risk and protective factors to be addressed and each prevention program. With this, we solve a budget allocation problem under the two-level hierarchical structure and examine how the allocated budget for each prevention program would affect the current risk and protective factor scores of each community.

The two-level problem scheme suggested here provides some insights into how to assign a limited budget systematically over a collection of communities whose imminent goals for improving risk/protective factors are different. The numerical result of the program-level problem shows the trend of budget allocation to prevention programs, considering the total budget and the preferences of decision makers. Also, the solution of the community-level problem distributes prevention program funds fairly over the needed communities by considering both regional population and the risk/protective factor scores of the communities.

Although we discuss only the planning phase of prevention programs in this chapter, we also emphasize the importance of efficient delivery in implementing prevention services. Efficient delivery can be achieved by maximizing output performance given the assigned budget and limited resources. Metrics for output performance in prevention services could be defined as, for instance, an increased number of successful completers of the program or a decreased crime rate. We could consider a data envelopment analysis (DEA) approach, which is a well-known multi-criteria decision-making tool, for analyzing the performance of multiple entities (in this example, communities) given multiple inputs and outputs.

The approaches and results presented here are not only for specific problems arising in prevention services. Rather, the proposed model is well-suited to other budget allocation problems in the public service domain, where multiple policies and programs have differing levels of impact on various aspects of a problem and where various multi-criteria decision-making approaches can be useful.

References

Aos, Steven, Roxanne Lieb, Jim Mayfield, Marna Miller, and Annie Pennucci. *Benefits and Costs of Prevention and Early Intervention Programs for Youth*. Olympia, WA: Washington State Institute for Public Policy, 2004.

Blueprints for Healthy Youth Development. Blueprints for Healthy Youth Development Blueprints Programs. http://www.blueprintsprograms.com/ (accessed January 23, 2015).

Brandeau, Margaret L., François Sainfort, and William P. Pierskalla. *Operations Research and Health Care: A Handbook of Methods and Applications*. Vol. 70. New York: Springer Science & Business Media, 2004.

Chilenski, Sarah Meyer, Brian K. Bumbarger, Sandee Kyler, and Mark T. Greenberg. *Reducing Youth Violence and Delinquency in Pennsylvania: PCCDs Research-Based Programs Initiative*. The Pennsylvania State University: Prevention Research Center for the Promotion of Human Development (NJ1), 2007.

Gass, Saul I., and Thomas L. Saaty. Parametric Objective Function (Part 2)-Generalization. *Journal of the Operations Research Society of America* 3, no. 4 (1955): 395–401.

Jones, Damon, Brian K. Bumbarger, Mark T. Greenberg, Peter Greenwood, and Sandee Kyler. *The Economic Return on PCCD's Investment in Research-Based Programs: A Cost-Benefit Assessment of Delinquency Prevention in Pennsylvania*. The Pennsylvania State University: Prevention Research Center for the Promotion of Human Development (NJ1), 2008.

Lee, Stephanie, Steve Aos, Elizabeth Drake, Annie Pennucci, Marna Miller, and Laurie Anderson. *Return on Investment: Evidence-Based Options to Improve Statewide Outcomes*. Olympia: Washington State Institute for Public Policy, 2012.

Miller, Ted R., and Delia Hendrie. *Substance Abuse Prevention Dollars and Cents: A Cost-Benefit Analysis*. DHHS Pub. No. (SMA) 07-4298. Rockville, MD: Center for Substance Abuse Prevention, Substance Abuse and Mental Health Services Administration, 2009.

Mrazek, Patricia J., and Robert J. Haggerty. *Reducing Risks for Mental Disorders: Frontiers for Preventive Intervention Research*. Washington, DC: National Academy Press, 1994.

PCCD. 2009 Pennsylvania Youth Survey. http://www.pccd.pa.gov/Juvenile-Justice/Documents/PAYS/1989-2011%20Reports%20and%20Information/2009%20PAYS%20Report.pdf (accessed January 23, 2015).

Ulan, Lisa. *The Allocation of Blueprints Programs to Pennsylvania Counties Using the Analytical Hierarchy Process*. Master's Thesis, The Pennsylvania State University, 2014.

12

Investigation of Order-Up-To-Policy and Allocation-Rationing Mechanism for Divergent Supply Chains with Multiple Objectives

Kurian John

Indian Institute of Technology Madras, Chennai, India

Chandrasekharan Rajendran

Indian Institute of Technology Madras, Chennai, India

Hans Ziegler

University of Passau, Passau, Germany

CONTENTS

12.1 Introduction

Supply chains exist in almost every industry, and the complexity of the chain may vary from industry to industry and firm to firm. An organization may have many supply chains operational within its various departments or it could itself be part of a larger supply chain (or both). The major drivers of any supply chain's performance are facilities, inventory, transportation, information, sourcing, and pricing (Chopra and Meindl 2007). Inventory exists at every stage of the supply chain as either raw material or semi-finished/finished goods. Inventory stored at different points of the supply chain has a different impact on the supply chain's costs and performance. One of the important issues in supply chain management (SCM) is to decide on the inventory to maintain at different stages in the chain so that the supply chain can achieve the desired levels of responsiveness and efficiency. To achieve this, firms use inventory-control policies or order policies and, for the problem in this work, we assume a periodic review (R), order-up-to (S) policy, that is, a (R, S) policy, at every installation.

If the supply chain is divergent, apart from managing inventory, firms face the additional challenge of rationing resources/products to downstream members. A rationing problem arises when the available resources cannot satisfy all demands, indicating a shortage at the installation, and this is widely observed in industries such as retail, airline, spare parts, and maritime. The product that is rationed varies from firm to firm, but the concept is universal and can be generalized under rationing, and the solutions to rationing are applied with necessary adaptations to suit the respective industry. Allocation is a term often used interchangeably with rationing. However, according to Lagodimos and Koukoumialos (2008), rationing is a special case of an allocation problem and, for multi-period models, allocation decisions for a given day need not involve all available material, whereas rationing allocates all available material to its downstream members, if demanded. Researchers have used these terms interchangeably after stating what they imply by the terminology. In this study, terminology usage is as follows: the quantity used to satisfy the unfulfilled demands of downstream members up to the day of the last review of the upstream member is called *allocated quantity*; and the leftover quantity used to satisfy the demands of downstream members after the day of the last review of the upstream member is called *rationed quantity*. In our model, the quantity allocated by the distributor is calculated in such a manner that the shipment reaches the contemplated retailer for whom the replenishment order has been placed to the manufacturer at the time of the last review of the distributor. Subsequently, the rationed quantity, calculated in case of any shortage in meeting the demand of retailers, necessitates the shipment of the leftover on-hand inventory of the distributor to retailers, and any holding of inventory to satisfy the retailers' demands in future time periods is not allowed. Thus we propose a *two-phase allocation-rationing mechanism* for the distributor. Distinguishing among retailer demands is essential as the distributor places an order to its upstream member contemplating a recipient. If all demands from a retailer are treated alike, then the replenishment may not reach the contemplated recipient (retailer). The proposed two-phase allocation-rationing mechanism ensures that the distributor does not mix-up the demand of one retailer with that of another up to the day of its last review (with the orders received from retailers after the day of the last review of the distributor); hence, the proposed mechanism assures that the shipment corresponds to the contemplated retailer correctly.

The perceived value as well as importance of a product can differ from a customer/retailer to another customer/retailer, and hence the shortage cost (backlog or lost sales cost) that a retailer is set to incur in case of shortage can also vary. Lost sales could mean a loss of profit or a loss of goodwill, and its estimation in monetary terms has practical limitations and difficulties (Nahmias 1989); hence, approximations are widely in use. The costs of holding, handling a product, and ordering can be different for installations based on the location of the installation, machines used by the installation in handling the products, facilities required to store them, and so on. The composition of the total cost, the contribution of each installation to the TSCC, and the conflicting nature of the objectives of the supply chain can have an influence on the central supply chain planner's decisions on acceptable levels with respect to the objectives of the supply chain. According to Stadtler (2005), SCM is the task of integrating organizational units along a supply chain and coordinating material, information, and financial flows in order to fulfill customer demands with the aim of improving the competitiveness of a supply chain as a whole. The aim of maximizing the supply chain profitability can never be achieved by optimizing the operating parameters with any single objective of the supply chain. There always exists a trade-off between the supply chain's responsiveness and its efficiency (Chopra and Meindl 2007). Both responsiveness and efficiency are equally desired by any supply chain, and they hold the key to any supply chain's performance. Along with the supply chain being responsive and efficient, a supply chain planner has to look at the satisfaction of customers because the purpose of any supply chain is to fulfill customer requests. A major task of any supply chain manager is to decide on the level of responsiveness, efficiency, and customer satisfaction that the supply chain should maintain; that is essential for the supply chain, while trying to maximize the chain's profitability. The efficiency of the supply chain is generally measured in terms of costs that the supply chain incurs in the process of fulfilling a customer order. Customer satisfaction levels are very important in some supply chains where an unfulfilled customer request could result in lost sales—and hence loss of good will and also possible loss of future sales. Even though it is extremely difficult to measure penalty costs, they are unavoidable factors while making decisions pertaining to any supply chain. Delivery performance is considered as a measure of customer satisfaction by Sürie and Wagner (2005) and, according to the authors, delivering the right product to the right place at the right time ensures customer satisfaction. According to Klapper et al. (1999), the perfect order fulfillment is one of the measures of customer satisfaction, and the authors break down the metric into orders delivered completely, orders delivered on time, delivery with perfect paper works and procedures completed, and condition of the products in terms of guaranteed features.

The present study addresses the problem of inventory management in a divergent supply chain operating with periodic review (R), order-up-to (S) policy at all the installations, customer sales being lost if unsatisfied, retailer demands rationed in case of shortage at the distributor using the proposed two-phase allocation-rationing mechanism, and the multiple objectives of minimizing the TSCC and maximizing the customer satisfaction, over a finite planning horizon. We formulate the problem as a *mixed integer linear program* (MILP) based mathematical model and also propose a lower bound on the objective function of the problem based on the selective relaxation of some of the assumptions due to the computational complexity experienced while solving the original MILP problem. The MILP-based mathematical model ensures that interchanging or mix-up of retailers' demands does not take place, and the model is solved to obtain installation-specific inventory-control policy parameters (R, S) and allocation-rationing quantities. The organization of the chapter is as follows: There is review of literature in Section 12.2; a discussion on order policy, allocation-rationing mechanism, and problem statement appears in Section 12.3; the model is presented in Section 12.4; the solution methodology is discussed in Section 12.5; Section 12.6 covers the experimental analysis used to test the mathematical model and results of the experiments; and implications and conclusions along with possible future research directions are discussed briefly in Section 12.7.

12.2 Review of Literature

12.2.1 Multi-Objective Models for Inventory Management

Due to the multi-dimensional nature of any supply chain, multiple objectives in supply chains are considered to meet the objective of maximization of supply chain profitability while satisfying customers. Weber and Current (1993) are the authors of one of the earliest papers on the multi-objective approach in supply chains, and they considered three objectives for the vendor selection. Various solution methodologies to the multiple objective problems are explained in detail by Collette and Siarry (2003). According to the authors, the solution methods can be classified as: (1) scalar, (2) interactive, (3) fuzzy, (4) metaheuristic, and (5) decision aided methods. The classical approach and the multi-objective evolutionary algorithm-based approach are explained by Deb (2001). According to the author, the classical approaches to solving multi-objective optimization problems are: (1) weighted sum, (2) ε-constraint, (3) weighted metric, (4) goal programming, (5) Benson's method, (6) value function method, and (7) interactive methods. A review paper on multi-objective optimization for SCM was presented by Aslam and Ng (2010), and Mula et al. (2010) reviewed the mathematical programming models for supply chain production and transport planning. Mansouri et al. (2012) tried to identify the gaps in decision-making support based on multi-objective optimization for build-to-order SCM. Arntzen et al. (1995), Jayaraman and Pirkul (2001), and Amiri (2006) modeled the SCM problem based on the MILP with a single objective. Various studies used genetic algorithms to obtain solutions to multiple objective problems in the SCM; examples are the works of Srinivas and Deb (1995) and Daniel and Rajendran (2006). A detailed survey on multi-objective evolutionary algorithms (MOEA) is presented by Zhou et al. (2011); the authors explain that the algorithm framework is a key issue to the design of any MOEA and the majority of MOEA's share more or less the same framework.

12.2.2 ε-Constraint Method

The ε-constraint method was introduced by Haimes et al. (1971), and Chankong and Haimes (1983) discussed the ε-constraint method in detail. The ε-constraint method optimizes the original problem, after converting all other objectives except one, into constraints within the respective upper/lower bounds. Sabri and Beamon (2000) used the multi-objective approach to undertake strategic and operational planning simultaneously. The authors used the ε-constraint method to solve the problem and considered the multi-objectives of cost, customer service levels (fill rates), and flexibility (volume or delivery). Guillén et al. (2005) used the ε-constraint method for multi-objective supply chain design under uncertainty. The authors considered net present value, demand satisfaction, and financial risk as the various objectives of the supply chain. You and Grossmann (2008) optimized the supply chain design and planning under responsive criterion and economic criterion with uncertain demand. The authors measured the economic criterion in terms of the net present value and responsiveness in terms of transportation times, residence times, and cyclic schedules. They used the mixed integer non linear programming (MINLP) to model the problem and used the ε-constraint method to solve it. Franca et al. (2010) introduced a multi-objective stochastic model that uses six sigma measures to evaluate financial risk. They considered maximization of total profit and increasing quality levels while investigating the effect of uncertainty on the model, and they used the ε-constraint method to solve the model. Liu and Papageorgiou (2013) addressed the problems of production, distribution, and capacity planning of global supply chains and considered costs, responsiveness, and customer service level as objectives. The authors proposed an MILP-based multi-objective approach with total cost, total flow time, and total lost sales as the objectives, and they resorted to the ε-constraint method to solve their model.

12.2.3 Lost Sales Models in Supply Chains

One of the earliest known works that considered lost sales is by Hadley and Whitin (1963), and many researchers over the years have worked on supply chains operating with lost sales. Huh and Janakiraman (2010) and van Donselaar and Broekmeulen (2013) stated that most of the models in inventory-control literature treat unmet demand as backlogged, and the major reason is the knowledge that the analysis of general lost sales systems is difficult and optimal policy for even the single-stage system is complicated. One of the first papers on rationing policies in supply chains operating with lost sales was by Cohen et al. (1988). The authors modeled the problem as a Markov chain and developed a greedy heuristic that minimizes the expected costs subject to fill rate service constraint. Ha (1997) considered the stock rationing problem for a make-to-stock production system with several demand classes, lost sales, and a single product. A critical level-based rationing policy is proposed by the author. Melchiors et al. (2000) and Isotupa (2006) analyzed a lost sales (s, Q) inventory system with two customer classes. Deterministic lead times were considered by Melchiors et al. (2000) and exponentially distributed lead times by Isotupa (2006). Kranenburg and van Houtum (2007) proposed three heuristic algorithms for an $(S-1, S)$ lost sales inventory model with multiple demand classes differentiated by penalty costs for lost sales. The authors considered holding and penalty costs in their study. An ordering policy for a two-echelon inventory system consisting of one warehouse and a number of nonidentical retailers was proposed by Haji et al. (2009). Rationing mechanisms in divergent supply chains, operating over a finite time horizon and with lost sales and costs of review, was studied by Paul and Rajendran (2011). The authors proposed a fractional rationing (FR) policy that makes use of dynamically calculated fractions to arrive at the rationed quantity when a distributor faces a shortage. Cheng et al. (2011) considered a make-to-stock production system with a failure-prone machine and multiple demand classes. The unsatisfied demand was assumed to be lost with a penalty cost associated with lost sales. A dynamic inventory rationing policy was proposed by Wang and Tang (2014) for an inventory system with a mixture of backorder and lost sale demand classes. The authors proposed a heuristic dynamic rationing policy citing the computational complexity of a Markov decision model. A recent work in the area of inventory rationing and lost sales is by Pang et al. (2014). They addressed the problem of inventory rationing in a make-to-stock production system with batch ordering and multiple demand classes. The authors assumed the presence of at least one outstanding order at any point in time and showed that an optimal ordering policy is characterized by a reorder point and time dependent rationing levels.

12.2.4 Rationing Policies

Various rationing policies were proposed by authors in the past for general inventory systems with or without lost sales. The *fair share* (FS) rationing policy was first introduced by Clark and Scarf (1960), and many researchers came up with modifications of the FS policy. The FS policy tries to attain an equal stock-out probability for all the end stock points. Another notable policy is the *consistent appropriate share* (CAS) policy, first introduced by de Kok (1990), who allocated inventory to local stock points based on safety stock ratios. Van der Heijden (1997) proposed the *balanced stock* (BS) policy, which tries to ration the system-wide shortage in a way so that the rationing fractions minimize the average imbalance. *Priority rationing* (PR) policy was proposed by Lagodimos (1992), and *modified echelon stock rationing* (MESR) policy was proposed by Huang and Iravani (2007). Paul and Rajendran (2011) proposed the *fractional rationing* (FR) policy that makes use of dynamically calculated fractions to arrive at the rationed quantity.

_____

12.3 Discussion on Order Policy, Allocation-Rationing Mechanism, and Problem Statement

The present study proposes an MILP-based mathematical model as solution methodology to the problem of inventory optimization in divergent supply chains (over a finite time horizon) with the consideration of minimizing total costs (consisting of order costs, holding costs, and lost sales costs across the supply chain) and maximizing customer satisfaction, and it makes use of the ε-constraint method to solve this problem with multiple objectives. Even though the fill rate has been considered by authors such as Sabri and Beamon (2000) and Guillén et al. (2005), their modeling approach is stochastic and their approach differs from our model's two objectives. In this work, we consider a divergent supply chain operating with lost sales from unsatisfied customer demands and backlogged retailer demands, and we model the problem as an MILP; moreover, the composition of the cost function in our model differs from the earlier works (by addressing all major cost components), and none of them (additionally) addressed the aspect of rationing in a multi-stage divergent supply chain. The earlier work by

Liu and Papageorgiou (2013) proposed an MILP-based solution methodology, but it is different from ours in terms of the cost function and measuring customer satisfaction, and the authors did not address the problem of allocation/rationing that is inevitable in a divergent supply chain. Such earlier authors did not consider the inventory order policy considered in this study. Paul and Rajendran (2011) addressed the problem of inventory rationing with the single objective of minimizing the total supply chain cost (TSCC), and their solution is a lower bound on the objective function (related to the total cost) considered in our model, when solved with this objective as the sole one. Moreover, those authors considered both unsatisfied demands from retailers up to the distributor's day of the last review and demands after the day of the last review equally, and they did not differentiate between these two classes of demands. However, we claim that such an approach could result in a reduced cost with highly unsatisfied retailers; hence, the single-objective approach could affect the performance of the supply chain in the long run due to strained relationships (see our related earlier discussion on the two-phase allocation-rationing mechanism). According to Paul and Rajendran, their rationing approach is superior to the various rationing approaches in literature such as CAS and BS, and it appears similar to FS rule for certain settings. Hence, in this study, we are benchmarking our work with that of Paul and Rajendran (2011), an appropriate representative work related to our chapter. In addition, Paul and Rajendran did not consider multiple objectives in their work, and they solved the supply chain problem with minimizing TSCC as the sole objective. A numerical illustration, comparing the rationing approach of Paul and Rajendran (2011) and the allocation-rationing approach proposed in this study, is provided in the Appendix to aid the reader in understanding the difference between the two approaches.

In this work, we propose a two-phase allocation-rationing mechanism involving allocation (first) and rationing (next), where allocation is inspired by the PR policy and rationing inspired by the FR policy. Lagodimos (1992) discussed the use of a PR rule where a list is used to decide the sequence in which orders are satisfied. The PR rule uses a priority list to satisfy the demands of successor stock points until the stock is exhausted. The first part of our two-phase mechanism is to allocate corresponding to the outstanding orders from the retailers up to the day of the last review of the distributor. The order of distributing unsatisfied demand up to the day of the last review of the upstream member to the downstream members is based on a predetermined priority list. The priority list in this work is developed based on the costs of penalties incurred by retailers in losing a unit of sale. The proposed allocation-rationing mechanism is a step toward reality in the sense that the replenishment received by the distributor is allocated to satisfy the corresponding retailer's unsatisfied demands up to the day of the last review of the distributor, and the leftover quantity is then rationed and used to satisfy the demands from retailers accumulated after the day of the last review of the distributor. The quantity due to downstream members up to the day of the last review of the distributor is completely satisfied in the sequence of decreasing penalty cost rates until the available material is depleted or outstanding orders up to the day of the last review of the distributor are fulfilled. Even though the sequence in which allocation is performed is based on a predetermined priority list, the allocation quantities are dynamic in the sense that they are related to the outstanding shipments to retailers. The PR policy in all the existing works is used for complete rationing, whereas in our study, it is used only to calculate the allocated quantity. To the best of our knowledge, no study published to date has modeled the supply chain along this line (often encountered in real life). We have proposed an exact solution methodology along with a lower bound on the objective function for supply chain operating (R, S) order policy, with multiple objectives of minimizing *total supply chain cost* (TSCC) comprising lost sales (only for retailers), holding and ordering costs, and maximizing the customer satisfaction measured using *product fill rate* (PFR) for a divergent supply chain operating with two-phase allocation-rationing mechanism over a finite time horizon.

12.4 Model

In this work, a periodic review (R), order-up-to (S) policy—that is, (R, S) policy—is assumed to operate at every installation of the supply chain. This policy is assumed owing to its ease in implementation in real life in terms of planning for logistics of inbound and outbound material, and the integrated inventory transportation function can be achieved in a better manner due to a fixed review period leading to fixed shipment/transport frequency (refer to Silver et al. [1998] for a detailed reading on inventory-control policies). The present study considers a divergent supply chain operating with a manufacturer supplying material to a distributor and the distributor serving I retailers; see Figure 12.1.

The unsatisfied demands of retailers are backlogged by the distributor, and the unsatisfied demands of customers are considered as lost sales by the retailer. The distributor uses the two-phase allocation-rationing mechanism proposed in this study to distribute its on-hand inventory to the downstream members. The first phase of the mechanism is used when there are unsatisfied demands of the retailers up to the day of the last review of the distributor. The second phase of the mechanism is used when the leftover inventory available with the distributor (after the allocation) is insufficient to meet the demands from retailers after the day of the last review of the distributor. The main objective of the supply chain is to minimize the TSCC while the maximizing customer satisfaction (measured in terms of the fill rate on a day). The TSCC is comprised of installation-specific holding cost and penalty cost per unit of product sale lost by the retailer and of installation-specific

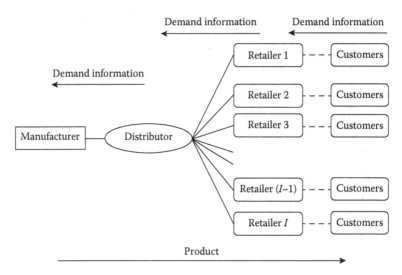

FIGURE 12.1
A schematic representation of the divergent supply chain.

fixed ordering cost. Customer satisfaction is measured in terms of the PFR achieved by the retailer. The PFR is defined by Chopra and Meindl (2007) as the fraction of product demand fulfilled from inventory. The authors explain that it should be measured over specific amounts of demand rather than time. In our work, we measure the PFR achieved by the retailer on a daily basis because the unsatisfied demands of customers are assumed to be lost. The PFR is a measure of a supply chain's β-service level, which is defined as the proportion of incoming order quantities that can be fulfilled from inventory on hand and takes into account the extent to which orders cannot be fulfilled. In this work, we find out the optimum order policy parameters for the periodic review, order-up-to S (R, S) policy at every installation, and the allocated and rationed quantities of the distributor by considering the multiple objectives of minimizing the total supply chain costs and maximizing the PFR over a finite time horizon.

12.4.1 Assumptions

The supply chain model's boundary is specified by a set of assumptions and is explained in this section. The supply chain is assumed to operate with installation-specific ordering policies in the class of periodic review, order-up-to S policy. A single product is assumed to flow in the supply chain from manufacturer to customers. Retailers face deterministic and dynamic customer demand, and the lead time for information processing is assumed to be negligible or zero. The model considers a finite time horizon. Time is assumed to be discrete, and a unit is assumed to be one day. This model does not consider capacity constraints (i.e., installations are faced with no limitations in holding inventory). No discount or lot-sizing is allowed for members. The review period of a retailer is one of $\{1, 2 \ldots Max\_r_i^R\}$, where $Max\_r_i^R$ denotes the maximum possible review period for retailer i, and the review period of the distributor is one of $\{1, 2 \ldots Max\_r^D\}$, where Max_r^D denotes the maximum possible review period for the distributor. For a given installation, the order-up-to S level and the review period take discrete integer values, and they remain constant across the entire finite time horizon, once set by the solver. The product considered in this supply chain neither becomes obsolete nor deteriorates in quality over time periods. Transshipments among installations of the same stage are not permitted. Each installation has its own specific holding cost, shortage (lost sales) cost, and ordering cost (i.e., cost of review). A retailer order is completely or partially satisfied depending on the distributor's available on-hand inventory; if the distributor does not have enough on-hand inventory, then the retailer's order is backlogged. The distributor's order is completely fulfilled after its replenishment lead time because it is assumed to be served by an upstream member (manufacturer) with unlimited capacity.

12.4.2 Mathematical Model

In this section, we present the mathematical formulation of the divergent supply chain model.

12.4.2.1 Terminology

The terminology used in this study is adapted/modified from that used by Zipkin (2000)/Silver et al. (1998).

Indices

t	Current time (unit time period is assumed to be a day).
T	Total number of time periods (planning horizon).
i	Index for retailers, where $i = 1, 2 \ldots I$.
I	Total number of retailers.
R	Retailer.
D	Distributor.
M	Manufacturer.

Parameters

h_i^R	Inventory holding cost-rate of retailer i (in monetary units).
b_i^R	Inventory shortage (lost sales) cost-rate of retailer i (in monetary units).
O_i^R	Ordering cost per order for retailer i (in monetary units).
h^D	Inventory holding cost-rate of the distributor (in monetary units).

O^D	Ordering cost per order for the distributor (in monetary units).
$Max\_r_i^R$	Maximum possible review period for retailer i (in unit of time; day).
Max_r^D	Maximum possible review period for the distributor (in unit of time; day).
LT_i^R	Replenishment lead time of retailer i (in unit of time; day).
LT^D	Replenishment lead time of the distributor (in unit of time; day).
M^R	A large positive value for the retailer.
M^D	A large positive value for the distributor.
$PFR_{i,t}^R$	Product fill rate of retailer i in time period t.
$Dem_{i,t}^R$	Demand from customers to retailer i in time period t (number of units of the product).

Decision Variables

$\Delta_{i,r}^R$	A binary variable that assumes the value of 1 for retailer i when the review period is r; otherwise 0; /*note: r is one of $\{1, 2 \ldots Max\_r_i^R\}$*/.
$\delta_{i,t}^R$	A binary variable that assumes the value of 1 in time period t when an order is placed by retailer i; otherwise 0.
Δ_r^D	A binary variable that assumes the value of 1 for the distributor when the review period is r; otherwise 0; /*note: r is one of $\{1, 2 \ldots Max\_r^D\}$*/.
δ_t^D	A binary variable that assumes the value of 1 in time period t when an order is placed by the distributor; otherwise 0.
$\lambda_{i,t}^D$	A binary variable that assumes the value of 1 when allocated quantity from the distributor to retailer i on day t exists; otherwise 0.
$\gamma_{i,t}^D$	A binary variable that assumes the value of 1 when the intermediate beginning on-hand inventory of the distributor on day t is available to ship the allocated quantity to retailer i; otherwise 0.
α_t^D	A (0, 1) binary variable used to prevent the coexistence of EI_t^D and B_t^D.
$BOI_{i,t}^R$	Beginning on-order inventory of retailer i at the beginning of time period t, after receiving the shipment (if any) from the distributor.
BOI_t^D	Beginning on-order inventory of the distributor at the beginning of time period t, after receiving the shipment (if any) from the manufacturer.
$BI_{i,t}^R$	Beginning on-hand inventory of retailer i at the beginning of time period t, after receiving the shipment (if any) from distributor.
BI_t^D	Beginning on-hand inventory of the distributor at the beginning of time period t, after receiving the shipment (if any) from the manufacturer.
$EI_{i,t}^R$	End on-hand inventory of retailer i at the end of time period t.

EI_t^D	End on-hand inventory of the distributor at the end of time period t.
$EOI_{i,t}^R$	End on-order inventory of retailer i at the end of time period t.
EOI_t^D	End on-order inventory of the distributor at the end of time period t.
$LS_{i,t}^R$	Lost sales of retailer i at the end of time period t.
B_t^D	Backorder of the distributor at the end of time period t.
$QS_{i,t}^R$	Quantity shipped from retailer i to its customers at the end of time period t.
$A\_QS_{i,t}^D$	Allocated quantity that is shipped from the distributor to retailer i at the end of time period t.
$R\_QS_{i,t}^D$	Rationed quantity that is shipped from the distributor to retailer i at the end of time period t.
$QSS_{i,t}^D$	Sum of rationed and allocated quantity (for that time period) shipped from the distributor to retailer i at the end of time period t.
$SQS_{i,t}^D$	Sum of quantity shipped from the distributor to retailer i up to time period t.
$QS_{D,t}^M$	Quantity shipped from the manufacturer to the distributor at the end of time period t.
Dem_t^D	Total demand faced by the distributor from all retailers in time period t.
$OQ_{i,t}^R$	Order quantity of retailer i to the distributor in time period t.
$OQ_{M,t}^D$	Order quantity of the distributor to the manufacturer in time period t.
$NOQ_{i,t}^R$	A dummy variable introduced to maintain feasibility in the mathematical formulation for retailer i in time period t, with respect to the order quantity.
NOQ_t^D	A dummy variable introduced to maintain feasibility in the mathematical formulation for the distributor in time period t, with respect to the order quantity.
$SOQ_{i,t}^R$	Sum of order quantity of retailer i to the distributor up to time period t.
$S\_RP_{i,t}^D$	Sum of order quantity from retailer i to the distributor up to the day of the last review of the distributor, computed with respect to time period t.
$A\_Q_{i,t}^D$	Allocated quantity due from the distributor to retailer i in time period t.
$NA\_Q_{i,t}^D$	A dummy variable introduced to maintain feasibility in the mathematical formulation for the distributor in time period t, with respect to the allocated quantity.
$IBI_{i,t}^D$	Intermediate beginning on-hand inventory of the distributor after allocating the quantity up to retailer i in time period t.

$NIBI_{i,t}^{D}$ A dummy variable introduced to maintain feasibility in the mathematical formulation for the distributor in time period *t* with respect to retailer *i*, with respect to intermediate beginning on-hand inventory.

S_i^R Order-up-to level of retailer *i*.

S^D Order-up-to level of the distributor.

$TPFR^R$ Threshold product fill rate of every retailer for entire time horizon.

$TSCC$ Total supply chain cost over all installations and time periods (in monetary units).

All different forms of inventory and shipment quantity are expressed in terms of number of units of the product.

12.4.2.2 Mathematical Formulation

Objectives:
Minimize *TSCC*

$$TSCC = \sum_{t=1}^{T}\left\{ \left(h^D EI_t^D + O^D \delta_t^D \right) + \sum_{i=1}^{I}\left(h_i^R EI_{i,t}^R + b_i^R LS_{i,t}^R + O_i^R \delta_{i,t}^R \right) \right\} \quad (12.1)$$

TSCC is the sum of holding cost and ordering cost incurred by the distributor and holding, lost sales, and ordering costs encountered by all retailers over the entire planning horizon. The distributor is assumed to backorder the demand quantity from retailers that is not satisfied in a particular time period. The cost associated with backordering by the distributor is assumed to be zero because this study deals with a centralized supply chain and the lost sales/backlog cost is incurred by the retailer that is in contact with its customers.

Maximize *PFR*

$$PFR_{i,t}^R = \frac{QS_{i,t}^R}{Dem_{i,t}^R} \text{ for } i = 1,2...I; \text{ and } t = 1,2...T; \quad (12.2)$$

subject to the following:

{
Constraints with respect to retailer *i*:

[
Constraints to set the review period of retailer *i*: Equation 12.3 ensures that the review period *r* is one of {1, 2 ...$Max\_r_i^R$}, and Equation 12.4 ensures that the binary variable $\delta_{i,t}^R$ is 1 if *t* is the day of review for retailer *i*:

$$\sum_{r=1}^{Max\_r_i^R} \Delta_{i,r}^R = 1 \quad (12.3)$$

$$\delta_{i,t}^{R} - \left(\Delta_{i,1}^{R} + \sum_{\substack{r=2 \\ t \bmod r=0}}^{Max\_r_{i}^{R}} \Delta_{i,r}^{R} \right) = 0 \qquad (12.4)$$

Receipt of material, if any, from the distributor takes place and the installation's information pertaining to: (a) beginning on-order inventory and (b) beginning on-hand inventory are updated:

$$BOI_{i,t}^{R} = EOI_{i,t-1}^{R} - QSS_{i,t-LT_{i}^{R}}^{D} \qquad (12.5)$$

$$BI_{i,t}^{R} = EI_{i,t-1}^{R} + QSS_{i,t-LT_{i}^{R}}^{D} \qquad (12.6)$$

The next step is customer's demand satisfaction by retailer i, and it depends on the retailer's beginning on-hand inventory. If sufficient material is available with the respective retailer, retailer i ships it to the customer instantaneously; otherwise the unsatisfied demand is considered to be lost. The quantity shipped by retailer i does not exceed customer's demand and does not exceed the beginning on-hand inventory of retailer i. We have

$$EI_{i,t}^{R} \geq BI_{i,t}^{R} - Dem_{i,t}^{R} \qquad (12.7)$$

$$QS_{i,t}^{R} = BI_{i,t}^{R} - EI_{i,t}^{R} \qquad (12.8)$$

Constraint to calculate the lost sales:

$$LS_{i,t}^{R} = Dem_{i,t}^{R} - QS_{i,t}^{R} \qquad (12.9)$$

Retailer i makes the decision to place an order based on the following: (a) beginning on-order inventory of the retailer; (b) on-hand inventory of the retailer after satisfying the current day customer demand; (c) order-up-to S level of the retailer; and (d) review period of the retailer. An order is placed by the retailer to the distributor if the current time period is the day of review of the respective retailer and the retailer places the order to raise its inventory position up to S. The order placed is instantaneously communicated to the distributor because the order processing lead time is assumed to be zero. We have

$$NOQ_{i,t}^{R} + OQ_{i,t}^{R} = S_{i}^{R} - EI_{i,t}^{R} - BOI_{i,t}^{R} \qquad (12.10)$$

$$OQ_{i,t}^R \leq M^R \delta_{i,t}^R \tag{12.11}$$

$$NOQ_{i,t}^R \leq M^R \left(1 - \delta_{i,t}^R\right) \tag{12.12}$$

Constraints to update the sum of order quantity and end on-order inventory of respective retailers:

$$SOQ_{i,t}^R = SOQ_{i,t-1}^R + OQ_{i,t}^R \tag{12.13}$$

$$EOI_{i,t}^R = BOI_{i,t}^R + OQ_{i,t}^R \tag{12.14}$$

], $i = 1,2\ldots I$;
Constraints with respect to the distributor:
[

Constraints (Equation 12.15) and (Equation 12.16) set the review period of the distributor. Equation 12.15 ensures that r is one of {1, 2 … Max_r^D} and Equation 12.16 ensures that the binary variable δ_t^D is 1 if t is the day of review of the distributor:

$$\sum_{r=1}^{Max\_r^D} \Delta_r^D = 1 \tag{12.15}$$

$$\delta_t^D - \left(\Delta_1^D + \sum_{\substack{r=2 \\ t \bmod r=0}}^{Max\_r^D} \Delta_r^D \right) = 0 \tag{12.16}$$

Receipt of material, if any, from the manufacturer, takes place and distributor's information pertaining to: (a) beginning on-order inventory and (b) beginning on-hand inventory, and intermediate beginning on-hand inventory is updated:

$$BOI_t^D = EOI_{t-1}^D - QS_{D,t-LT^D}^M \tag{12.17}$$

$$BI_t^D = EI_{t-1}^D + QS_{D,t-LT^D}^M \tag{12.18}$$

$$IBI_{0,t}^D = BI_t^D \tag{12.19}$$

The first phase of the rationing mechanism proposed in this work is realized by constraints (Equations 12.20 through 12.26) and these constraints calculate the quantity to be allocated up to the day of the last review of the distributor. The distributor first satisfies the quantity that is due (if any) to the respective retailer up to the day of its last review:

(

$$A\_Q_{i,t}^D - NA\_Q_{i,t}^D = S\_RP_{i,t-1}^D - SQS_{i,t-1}^D \tag{12.20}$$

$$A\_Q_{i,t}^D \leq M^D \lambda_{i,t}^D \tag{12.21}$$

$$NA\_Q_{i,t}^D \leq M^D \left(1 - \lambda_{i,t}^D\right) \tag{12.22}$$

$$IBI_{i,t}^D - NIBI_{i,t}^D = IBI_{i-1,t}^D - A\_Q_{i,t}^D \tag{12.23}$$

$$A\_QS_{i,t}^D = IBI_{i-1,t}^D - IBI_{i,t}^D \tag{12.24}$$

$$IBI_{i,t}^D \leq M^D \gamma_{i,t}^D \tag{12.25}$$

$$NIBI_{i,t}^D \leq M^D \left(1 - \gamma_{i,t}^D\right) \tag{12.26}$$

) $\forall i \in \Omega^D$ and retailers are considered in the order they appear in Ω^D. Note that Ω^D is an ordered set in which retailers are indexed in a monotone manner such that $b_i^R \geq b_{i+1}^R$.

Demand of the distributor for day t is calculated using Equation 12.27:

$$Dem_t^D = \sum_{i=1}^{I} OQ_{i,t}^R \tag{12.27}$$

Constraints (Equations 12.28 through 12.30) calculate the rationed quantity and the total quantity to be shipped to a retailer, and they update the total quantity shipped to respective retailers, respectively. The distributor satisfies the orders received after the day of the last review, depending on its updated beginning on-hand inventory. If sufficient inventory is available, the order of a retailer is completely satisfied; otherwise, the available on-hand inventory is rationed among the retailers, and the unsatisfied demand is backlogged. The total quantity shipped from the distributor to any retailer reaches it after the elapse of the respective retailer's lead time; that is, LT_i^R. $QSS_{i,t}^D$ is received by retailer i on $\left(t + LT_i^R\right)$, $LT_i^R \geq 1$. We have

(

$$R\_QS_{i,t}^D \leq SOQ_{i,t}^R - \left(SQS_{i,t-1}^D + A\_QS_{i,t}^D\right) \tag{12.28}$$

$$QSS_{i,t}^D = R\_QS_{i,t}^D + A\_QS_{i,t}^D \tag{12.29}$$

$$SQS_{i,t}^D = SQS_{i,t-1}^D + QSS_{i,t}^D \tag{12.30}$$

Constraints to update the sum of order quantity from respective retailers up to the day of the last review of distributor:

$$S\_RP_{i,t}^D \leq S\_RP_{i,t-1}^D + M^D \delta_t^D \tag{12.31}$$

$$S\_RP_{i,t}^D \geq S\_RP_{i,t-1}^D - M^D \delta_t^D \tag{12.32}$$

$$S\_RP_{i,t}^D \leq SOQ_{i,t}^R + M^D \left(1 - \delta_t^D\right) \tag{12.33}$$

$$S\_RP_{i,t}^D \geq SOQ_{i,t}^R - M^D \left(1 - \delta_t^D\right) \tag{12.34}$$

), $i = 1, 2 \ldots I$;

Constraint to ensure that the sum of rationed quantities shipped to all retailers in time period t does not exceed the intermediate beginning on-hand inventory of the distributor (i.e., inventory available with the distributor after allocation to all the retailers in the set Ω^D):

$$\sum_{i=1}^{I} R\_QS_{i,t}^D \leq IBI_{\left|\Omega^D\right|,t}^D \tag{12.35}$$

End on-hand inventory and backlogged demand of the distributor are calculated using constraint (Equation 12.36), and the coexistence of end on-hand inventory and backlogged demand of the distributor is prevented using constraints (Equation 12.37) and (Equation 12.38). This ensures that the supply chain model remains a rationing model and does not transform to an allocation model. The effect of relaxing the binary variable is discussed in the solution methodology. We have

$$EI_t^D - B_t^D = BI_t^D - B_{t-1}^D - Dem_t^D \tag{12.36}$$

$$EI_t^D \le M^D \alpha_t^D \tag{12.37}$$

$$B_t^D \le M^D \left(1 - \alpha_t^D\right) \tag{12.38}$$

The distributor makes the decision to place an order based on the following factors: (a) beginning on-order inventory of the distributor; (b) on-hand inventory of the distributor after satisfying the demand; (c) order-up-to S level of the distributor; (d) total backlogged demands from all retailers; and (e) review period of the distributor. An order is placed by the distributor to the manufacturer if t is day of review of the distributor, and the distributor places the order to raise its inventory position up to S. The order placed is instantaneously communicated to the manufacturer because the order processing lead time is assumed to be zero. We have

$$NOQ_t^D + OQ_{M,t}^D = S^D - \left(EI_t^D + BOI_t^D - B_t^D\right) \tag{12.39}$$

$$OQ_{M,t}^D \le M^D \delta_t^D \tag{12.40}$$

$$NOQ_t^D \le M^D \left(1 - \delta_t^D\right) \tag{12.41}$$

Constraint to update the end on-order inventory of the distributor:

$$EOI_t^D = BOI_t^D + OQ_{M,t}^D \tag{12.42}$$

Constraint to ensure that the total quantity shipped by the distributor to all retailers is the difference between the beginning on-hand inventory and end on-hand inventory of the distributor:

$$BI_t^D - EI_t^D = \sum_{i=1}^{I} QSS_{i,t}^D \tag{12.43}$$

]

Manufacturer's Constraint:
The manufacturer satisfies the distributor's demand completely because it is assumed to have unlimited availability of product. The quantity shipped from the manufacturer reaches the distributor after the lead time with respect to the distributor and the manufacturer, that is, LT^D:

$$QS_{D,t}^M = OQ_{M,t}^D \qquad (12.44)$$

$\}, t = 1, 2 \dots T;$

with the initial conditions:

$$S\_RP_{i,0}^D = 0 \qquad i = 1,2 \dots I; \qquad (12.45)$$

$$EOI_{i,0}^R = B_{i,0}^R = 0 \qquad i = 1,2 \dots I; \qquad (12.46)$$

$$SOQ_{i,0}^R = 0 \qquad i = 1,2 \dots I; \qquad (12.47)$$

$$QSS_{i,t-LT_i^R}^D = 0 \qquad i = 1,2 \dots I; t = 1,2 \dots LT_i^R; \qquad (12.48)$$

$$EI_{i,0}^R = S_i^R \qquad i = 1,2 \dots I; \qquad (12.49)$$

$$SQS_{i,0}^D = 0 \qquad i = 1,2 \dots I; \qquad (12.50)$$

$$EOI_0^D = B_0^D = 0 \qquad (12.51)$$

$$QS_{D,t-LT^D}^M = 0 \qquad t = 1,2 \dots LT^D; \qquad (12.52)$$

$$EI_0^D = S^D \qquad (12.53)$$

$$\delta_{i,t}^R \in \{0,1\} \qquad i = 1,2 \dots I; t = 1,2 \dots T; \qquad (12.54)$$

$$\delta_t^D \in \{0,1\} \qquad t = 1,2 \dots T; \qquad (12.55)$$

$$\alpha_t^D \in \{0,1\} \qquad t = 1,2\ldots T; \tag{12.56}$$

$$\lambda_{i,t}^D \in \{0,1\} \qquad i = 1,2\ldots I; t = 1,2\ldots T; \tag{12.57}$$

$$\gamma_{i,t}^D \in \{0,1\} \qquad i = 1,2\ldots I; t = 1,2\ldots T; \tag{12.58}$$

$$\text{all other variables are} \geq 0. \tag{12.59}$$

The time period t is incremented by a unit of time (i.e., a day), starting from $t = 1$, and the same sequence of events repeats itself for the entire time horizon (until $t = T$).

12.5 Solution Methodology

The ε-constraint method is used to solve the MILP-based multiple objective mathematical programming model. In this study, the objective corresponding to minimizing TSCC is maintained as the sole objective while solving the mathematical programming model, and the other objective is treated as a constraint. The objective of PFR for every retailer is converted to a constraint with a specified lower limit, while solving the mathematical programming model. To develop long-term relationships with customers and to attain a higher level of customer satisfaction, we introduce the PFR as a constraint with a threshold level. The threshold fill rate guaranteed by the supply chain to its customers can be fixed by the supply chain manager, and the solution to our mathematical programming model would aid the decision maker in arriving at the right level of trade-off between cost and customer satisfaction. Because it is difficult to predict the magnitude of the total supply chain cost in terms of monetary units, we refrain from converting the objective, minimizing TSCC as a constraint with bounds. In pilot studies, it is observed that the fill rates achieved by the retailers are as low as zero on certain days, when the model is solved with the sole objective of minimizing the TSCC. It is due to this observation that we consider the fill rate as another objective of the supply chain.

Expression (12.2) calculates the $PFR_{i,t}^R$ for retailer i in time period t. It is reasonable to assume that the PFR is fixed over time (i.e., the same value of PFR is assumed for retailer i for the entire planning horizon because supply chains do not usually offer different fill rates across time periods). In this study, all retailers are assumed to operate with the same threshold

PFR ($TPFR^R$) across time periods, and Expression (12.2) (i.e., objective function) is modified as here and converted to a constraint, while solving the mathematical formulation:

$$\frac{QS_{i,t}^R}{Dem_{i,t}^R} \geq TPFR^R \text{ for } i = 1, 2 \ldots I; t = 1, 2 \ldots T \qquad (12.60)$$

Constraint (Equation 12.60) would ensure that the supply chain model is solved with the objective of minimizing its TSCC, while guaranteeing TPFR for every retailer and for every time period. The major questions for which the inventory-control mechanism in this work provides answers are: How much to order? When to order? How much to allocate and ration? In this study, we present the mathematical programming model (that essentially performs an implicit enumeration) to solve the problem over a fixed time horizon to answer these questions. The number of binary variables increases even with a small increase in the time horizon; hence, limitations and difficulty in executing the mathematical formulation beyond a time horizon are observed. Figure 12.2 is a graphical representation of the relation between the solution time needed to solve the mathematical programming model and its run length.

The time needed to solve the mathematical programming model appears to increase exponentially with an increase in run length. We propose the consideration of a lower bound on the total cost objective, obtained by an LP relaxation technique, when working with heuristics to solve the supply chain problems over a large planning horizon (or for use in a simulation-based heuristic approach). All the solutions, except that for the run length of 110 days, are solved for a maximum solution gap of 0.01% using IBM ILOG CPLEX Optimization Studio solver and a computer with 64 bit, Intel(R) Core(TM) i7-2600 CPU @ 3.40GHz processor and 16GB RAM.

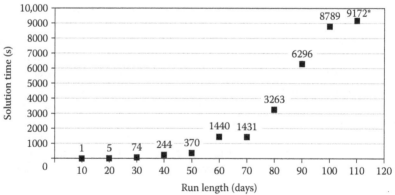

*The solution obtained has a gap of 9.11% from the optimal solution and the solver terminated citing the status as out-of-memory.

FIGURE 12.2
Graphical representation of relation between the run length and the time to solve the mathematical model.

TABLE 12.1

The Time Taken to Solve the Original Problem
and the Lower-Bound Model

Solution Type	TSCC	Time (in Seconds)
Original Problem	181039	8789
LB on TSCC	132018	554

Note: TSCC, total supply chain cost; LB, lower bound.

The lower bound on the objective of the model considered in this study is obtained by the LP-relaxation technique and a selective relaxation of some assumptions/conditions. Even though obtaining lower bounds would mean the relaxation of some of the conditions of the problem defined in this study, such an approach enables the decision maker to execute the model for a larger finite time horizon with considerably reduced computational difficulty. In the mathematical formulation presented in Section 12.3, we relax the binary variable $\left(\alpha_t^D\right)$ that prevents the coexistence of end on-hand inventory and backlog (see Expression 12.37 and 12.38) for the distributor and treat it as a continuous variable in the interval [0, 1] to obtain a *lower bound* (LB) on the objective function (i.e., minimizing TSCC). From Table 12.1, it is clear that the time taken to solve the relaxed problem is considerably lower even for the longest run length for which the original problem has been solved. Therefore, we have not resorted to the relaxation of other binary variables. The time taken to obtain solution to the lower bound on the objective function (i.e., TSCC) and the original problem for a run length of 100 days (pilot study) is reported in Table 12.1.

The relaxation of the binary variable would result in the distributor being able to maintain inventory, and yet incur backlog, in order to minimize the TSCC. Now the original model reduces to an allocation model where it is no longer necessary for the distributor to ship its entire available on-hand inventory in case of shortage, but the distributor reserves the inventory for satisfying high-priority demands in future time periods. The introduction of the binary variable corresponds to a rationing approach, while the relaxation of the binary variable to a [0, 1] continuous variable corresponds to an allocation approach. (See Lagodimos and Koukoumialos [2008] for detailed reading on the difference between allocation and rationing approaches.)

12.6 Experimental Analysis

In order to test the performance of the proposed mathematical model and the solution technology used, we have performed experiments; the next subsection discusses the settings for the experiments. In the subsequent subsection, we present the results and a discussion of the results.

12.6.1 Experimental Settings

The mathematical programming model proposed in this study can handle any number of retailers. However, to evaluate the performance of the solution technique, we have set the number of retailers as four ($I = 4$) for the experiments. The various cost settings used in this study are shown in Table 12.2. The maximum possible value for the review period of any installation in the experiment is set at five; that is, $Max\_r_i^R = 5$ for $i = 1$, 2 … I; and $Max\_r^D = 5$. The shortage cost-rate (lost sales) for any retailer in this study is generalized by $b_i^R = k_i \times h_i^R$ where: $k_i = 20$ for $i = 1, 2, 3$, and 4 in the case of CS1; and $k_i = 20, 18, 16$, and 14 for $i = 1, 2, 3$, and 4, respectively, in the case of CS2. The value of $P = 1.5$ is a parameter and is used to calculate the ordering costs of the installations. $E\left(D_i^R\right)$ is the expectation of customer demand of retailer i and is taken as the mean demand for the particular retailer.

The shortage cost is expressed as a multiple of the holding cost because in a system with very high service level the holding cost is a prominent cost factor, and it can be used to approximate the total installation costs (see Silver et al. 1998). The lead time for all the installations is taken as one in this study because the shipped quantity from an upstream member reaches the downstream member in the beginning of the next period.

The customer demand is sampled from a uniform distribution between the minimum and maximum values and is assumed to be known a priori as the dynamic and deterministic demand over the planning horizon. Hence, the demand stream is given as a deterministic input to the mathematical model. The minimum and maximum values of demand settings used in this study are mentioned in Table 12.3.

Such settings are used with the aim of creating diverse problem instances to test the performance and adaptability of the proposed solution technique. We have set the run length of the study as 40 days. The run length

TABLE 12.2

Cost Settings Used to Perform Computational Experiments

Cost Setting		Distributor	Retailer 1	Retailer 2	Retailer 3	Retailer 4
CS1	HC-R	1	2	2	2	2
	SC-R	0	40	40	40	40
	OC	$\sum_i^I E(D_i^R) \times P$	$\sum_i^I E(D_i^R)$	$\sum_i^I E(D_i^R)$	$\sum_i^I E(D_i^R)$	$\sum_i^I E(D_i^R)$
CS2	HC-R	1	2	2	2	2
	SC-R	0	40	36	32	28
	OC	$\sum_i^I E(D_i^R) \times P$	$\sum_i^I E(D_i^R)$	$\sum_i^I E(D_i^R)$	$\sum_i^I E(D_i^R)$	$\sum_i^I E(D_i^R)$

Note: CS1, Cost Setting 1; CS2, Cost Setting 2; HC-R, holding cost-rate; SC-R, shortage (lost sales) cost-rate; OC, ordering cost.

TABLE 12.3

Demand Setting Across Retailers
for Computational Experiments

	Demand-Setting (DS)		
	A	**B**	**C**
Installation	(Minimum Demand, Maximum Demand)		
Retailer 1	(0, 80)	(0, 80)	(0, 20)
Retailer 2	(0, 80)	(0, 60)	(0, 40)
Retailer 3	(0, 80)	(0, 40)	(0, 60)
Retailer 4	(0, 80)	(0, 20)	(0, 80)

of 40 time units is a reasonably good sample size given the complex nature of the mathematical model. If the model is to be run for very large time horizons, we propose the use of the LP relaxation in evaluating heuristics. M^R and M^D are set as 1000 in this study. We have three demand settings (with the sampled demand stream known a priori and given as an input to the mathematical model when executed) and two cost settings in this study. All the problem instances are solved by using IBM ILOG CPLEX Optimization Studio for a run length of 40 time periods. The $TPFR^R$ is varied from 0.1 to 1, in steps of 0.1. It implies that when $TPFR^R = 0.1$, the solutions to the problem would guarantee a fill rate of minimum 10% for all retailers in every time period; when $TPFR^R = 1$, the solutions from the mathematical programming model would ensure that the supply chain operates with no sales being lost.

12.6.2 Results and Discussions

The results of the problem of inventory optimization and rationing are obtained by solving the mathematical formulation using the solver mentioned in the previous section for a run length of 40 time periods. The correctness, robustness, and adaptability of the mathematical programming model are tested using the various problem instances explained in the experimental settings section. Figures 12.3 and 12.4 are graphs displaying the relationship between the TPFR and TSCC composed of installation-specific holding, lost sales (for retailer), and ordering costs incurred in attaining the TPFR level.

The optimal solutions—in the class of (R, S) policy—for the corresponding demand stream are highlighted in Figures 12.3 and 12.4. The mathematical formulation, when solved, gives the inventory policy parameters of order-up-to levels and review periods for all the installations in the supply chain. In demand-setting-A, all retailers are assumed to operate

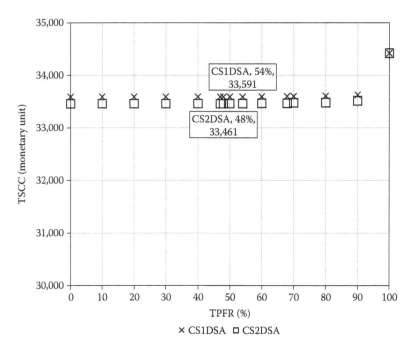

FIGURE 12.3
Relationship between TSCC and threshold PFR for cost-setting-1 and demand-setting-A.

with demands among the same limits across all retailers; demand-setting-B and demand-setting-C represent the case where retailer demands are sampled from a uniform distribution with varying limits across retailers and given as an input to the model while executing it. Cost-setting-1 is the scenario where all retailers have equal cost rates, and cost-setting-2 represents the scenario where one retailer is differentiated from another with respect to profit (i.e., lost sales cost-rate differs from retailer to retailer; refer to Table 12.2).

The results in Figures 12.3 and 12.4 can be interpreted as follows: The markers indicate the TSCC incurred by the supply chain offering the corresponding TPFR level, and the data label is the optimal solution when the supply chain is operating with that particular cost and demand setting for the demand stream. The supply chain operating with a particular cost and demand setting can guarantee a TPFR for the corresponding cost mentioned in the graph; for example, for cost-setting-1 and demand-setting-A (CS1DSA), minimum TSCC equals 33591 (monetary units), and the supply chain can guarantee a TPFR of 54% incurring the minimum TSCC. With the aid of the results in Figures 12.3 and 12.4, supply chain managers can make decisions about the level of customer satisfaction that the supply chain can

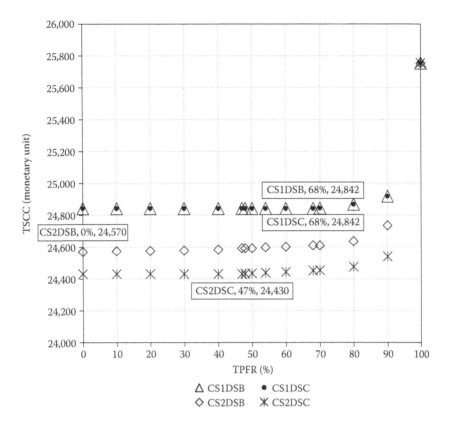

FIGURE 12.4
Relationship between TSCC and TPFR for every set of cost and demand-setting-B and demand-setting-C.

guarantee and the corresponding costs that the supply chain incurs, while attaining the level of customer satisfaction (denoted by the TPFR).

The compositions of TSCC vary with the TPFR levels and are displayed in Figure 12.5 through Figure 12.10 for a given demand stream. Our study helps managers to identify the areas in which to alleviate costs by providing the breakup of the various components of TSCC with respect to every TPFR level. From the bar chart in Figure 12.5, one can observe that the total supply chain shortage cost (TSCSC) component of TSCC is diminishing and is nonexistent when the TPFR of 100% is guaranteed by the supply chain. It should be noted that even though the TSCSC component of TSCC decreases with an increased TPFR, the TSCC is escalating. This is due to the fact that the ordering frequency or ordering quantity (or both) is/are varied to meet the augmented TPFR requirement. The optimal solutions for various supply chain settings are highlighted in

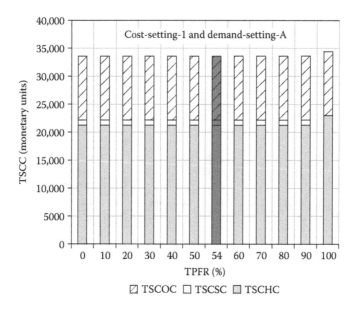

FIGURE 12.5
Bar chart showing breakup of TSCC corresponding to TPFR for cost-setting-1 and demand-setting-A.

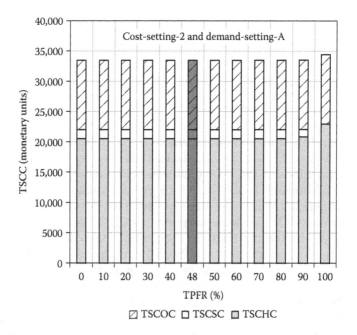

FIGURE 12.6
Bar chart showing breakup of TSCC corresponding to TPFR for cost-setting-2 and demand-setting-A.

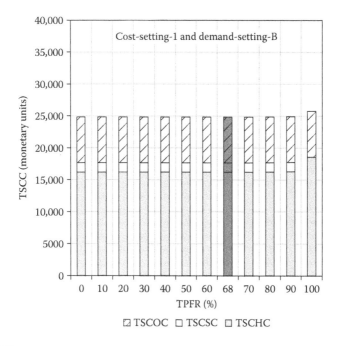

FIGURE 12.7
Bar chart showing breakup of TSCC corresponding to TPFR for cost-setting-1 and demand-setting-B.

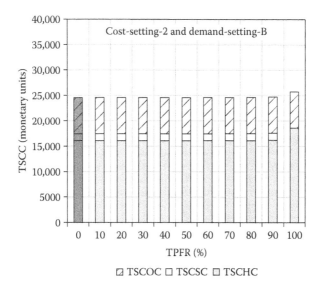

FIGURE 12.8
Bar chart showing breakup of TSCC corresponding to TPFR for cost-setting-2 and demand-setting-B.

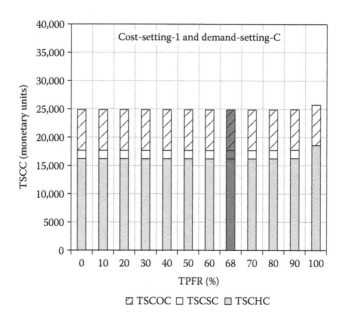

FIGURE 12.9
Bar chart showing breakup of TSCC corresponding to TPFR for cost-setting-1 and demand-setting-C.

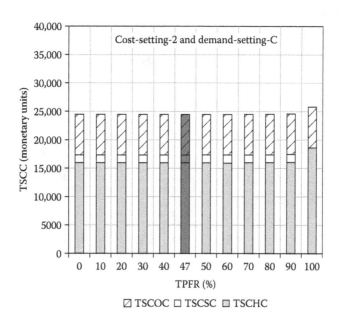

FIGURE 12.10
Bar chart showing breakup of TSCC corresponding to TPFR for cost-setting-2 and demand-setting-C.

TABLE 12.4

Order-Up-To Levels for All the Settings

Setting	Order-Up-To Levels				
	Distributor	Retailer 1	Retailer 2	Retailer 3	Retailer 4
CS1DSA	91	161	154	191	179
CS2DSA	93	159	152	186	177
CS1DSB	166	158	119	79	39
CS2DSB	166	158	119	78	38
CS1DSC	166	39	79	119	158
CS2DSC	166	39	79	117	156

Note: CS1DSA, Cost-Setting-1 and Demand-Setting-A and similarly for all other settings.

Figure 12.5 to Figure 12.10 using a darker shade for the bar corresponding to the minimum TSCC and the TPFR. The breakup of the TSCC and analysis of its various components can bring to the forefront the components of the TSCC that are prominent toward contributing and escalating the total costs; such an analysis can aid decision makers in understanding and resolving the corresponding trade-off issues involving the TSCC and the TPFR.

Table 12.4 displays the order-up-to levels of all the members of the supply chain with respect to all settings. The order-up-to levels and review periods are the decision variables in this study and are set by the solver for respective settings to obtain an optimum solution with the ε-constraint approach.

We present the breakup of the total costs incurred by respective retailers in attaining threshold levels of PFR in Figure 12.11. The breakup of costs pertaining to each retailer for all the problem instances is obtained and is presented for the problem instance with cost-setting-2 and demand-setting-A. An analysis of costs in terms of the various installations' contributions to TSCC will help decision makers in making informed decisions, and it provides them with an enhanced understanding about the functioning of the supply chain.

Figure 12.11 is a collection of bar charts displaying the components of total cost for all retailers, and the optimum for the entire supply chain is depicted using a darker shade for the corresponding bar. The results obtained from cost-setting-2 and demand-setting-A are presented for individual retailers; the minimum TSCC is 33461 (monetary units) and corresponding TPFR is 48% for this setting. In order to develop long-term relationships with its customers and to attain higher level of customer satisfaction, we introduce the PFR as a constraint with a threshold level. The threshold fill rate guaranteed by the supply chain to its customers can be fixed by the supply chain manager, and the solution to our mathematical programming model would aid the decision maker in arriving at the right level of trade-off between the TSCC and customer satisfaction.

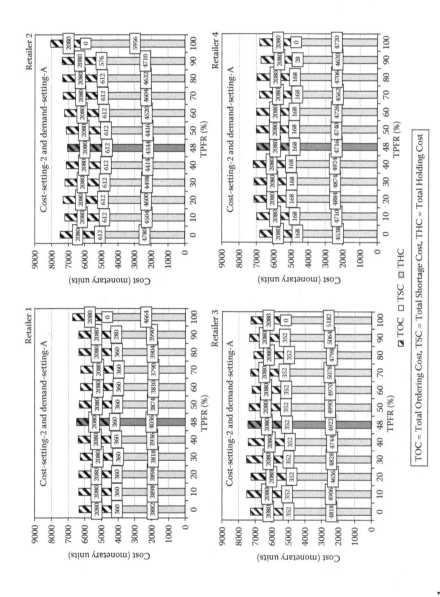

FIGURE 12.11
Bar charts showing breakup of costs incurred by retailers for supply chain operating with cost-setting-2 and demand-setting-A.

12.7 Implications of This Study, Conclusions, and Future Research Directions

It should be noted from the breakup of costs incurred by respective retailers that, given the TPFR, the model does not guarantee minimum costs for each and every retailer but the minimum total cost for the entire supply chain. So the model presented in this study is appropriate for those supply chains where the retailers are owned by the distributor or the manufacturer and for those supply chains where the decision-making power vests with a single supply chain planner such as a dominant manufacturer or distributor capable of dictating terms to retailers. If decision-making power is bestowed on individual retailers, the optimum policy parameters for the entire supply chain and optimum policy parameters for individual retailers could be different, and hence a conflict of interest may arise between the members of the supply chain. If individual retailers are allowed to locally optimize their policy parameters, the entire supply chain will either incur loss in the process or the practice will lead to escalating TSCCs. It can be observed from the bar chart in Figure 12.11 that the optimum point in terms of the TSCC and the TPFR that can be guaranteed by retailer 1 is the TPFR of 70%, incurring a (minimum) total cost of 6230 (monetary units); for retailer 2, it is the TPFR of 48%, incurring a (minimum) total cost of 7036 (monetary units); for retailer 3, it is the TPFR of 20%, incurring a (minimum) total cost of 7068 (monetary units); and for retailer 4, it is the TPFR of 90%, incurring a (minimum) total cost of 6728 (monetary units), compared to the supply chain's optimum of guaranteeing the TPFR of 48% and by incurring a (minimum) TSCC of 33461 (monetary units). The retailers may have a conflict of interest (in terms of the optimum TPFR guaranteed and the total cost incurred in attaining the corresponding TPFR), and hence a revenue sharing mechanism is to be agreed between the members of the supply chain in order to operate within the optimal order policy parameters (in the class of (R, S) policy), if the members of the supply chain are not controlled by a central supply chain planner. The intricacies and specifications of such coordination mechanisms/agreements among the members in the case of the supply chain operating with a separate decision maker for every member of the supply chain can be taken up in future research. However, our study will enable the decision makers to make informed decisions during such agreements or coordination mechanisms because the cost components for respective retailers for various scenarios are presented. Our proposed approach is different from the earlier approaches—such as that by Paul and Rajendran (2011) and, hence, ours is a step toward reality. (See our earlier discussion and the Appendix for a numerical illustration.)

Through the various cost and demand settings, the performance of the mathematical programming model for the supply chain operating with lost sales, review period, rationing, and multiple objectives are analyzed. The model presented in this study is a step closer to reality in the sense that the orders placed by the distributor, corresponding to the contemplated recipient (i.e., retailer), are delivered to the respective retailer. No interchanging (or mix-up) of the replenishment corresponding to the demand from the contemplated retailer is allowed in any time period; in addition, customer satisfaction is considered simultaneously with minimizing TSCC. From a technical point of view, the optimal solution (in the class of assumed inventory policy) obtained from the MILP model can act as a lower bound on the TSCC to evaluate the performance of heuristics, if developed in future. (This is because the MILP model has the complete demand stream as its input and it does the rationing mechanism inherently with multiple objectives, unlike the existing rationing rules.)

This chapter addresses the problem of obtaining the optimal installation-specific inventory-control policy parameters for (R, S) policy in a divergent supply chain operating with multiple retailers, a distributor, a manufacturer, and lost sales of unsatisfied retailer demands, over a finite planning horizon. The model considered in this study does not allow the interchange of orders from/replenishments to retailers, and a two-phase allocation-rationing mechanism is proposed here to ration the inventories to the retailers in case of a shortage. A solution methodology based on the ε-constraint method is used to solve an MILP-based mathematical programming model of the supply chain operating with the conflicting objectives of minimizing TSCC and maximizing customer satisfaction measured using PFR. This study provides an analysis into the costs incurred by the various installations as well as the contribution of the various cost components to total supply chain cost in trying to achieve a threshold level of fill rate. A lower bound on the objective (i.e., TSCC) is proposed by making use of the LP relaxation technique, and this approach can be used in the case of longer run lengths and therefore can be used for future research on heuristics. Multiple products, multiple stages, and multiple distributors can be a possible research extension. Supply chains operating with more than two objectives can be considered in the future. Measuring the performance of the supply chain with other metrics of customer satisfaction also can be research for the future.

Acknowledgments

This research work has been carried out with the financial support from IIT Madras, University of Passau, and DAAD as a part of the joint PhD degree program. The authors are grateful to the two reviewers and the editor for their suggestions and comments to improve the earlier version of this chapter.

Appendix

A hypothetical example to differentiate the model in this study and the model proposed by Paul and Rajendran (2011) is given here, with assumed data and values.

	Distributor	Retailer 1	Retailer 2	Retailer 3
Parameters				
Holding cost rate	1	2	2	2
Shortage cost rate	0	10	100	200
Ordering cost	0	300	300	300
Decision Variables				
Order-up-to level (S)	100	200	250	150
Review period (R)	1	1	1	1
Demand ($t=1$)		150	200	50
Demand ($t=2$)		50	100	150

Approach Used in this Study	Approach Used by Paul and Rajendran (2011)
Day 1:	
$OQ_{1,1}^R = 150$	$OQ_{1,1}^R = 150$
$OQ_{2,1}^R = 200$	$OQ_{2,1}^R = 200$
$OQ_{3,1}^R = 50$	$OQ_{3,1}^R = 50$
$BI_1^D = S^D = 100$	$BI_1^D = S^D = 100$
$A\_Q_{1,1}^D = 0$	—
$A\_Q_{2,1}^D = 0$	—
$A\_Q_{3,1}^D = 0$	—
$R\_QS_{1,1}^D = 0$	$R\_QS_{1,1}^D = 0$
$R\_QS_{2,1}^D = 50\left(\because b_2^R > b_1^R\right)$	$R\_QS_{2,1}^D = 50\left(\because b_2^R > b_1^R\right)$
$R\_QS_{3,1}^D = 50\left(\because b_3^R > b_2^R > b_1^R\right)$	$R\_QS_{3,1}^D = 50\left(\because b_3^R > b_2^R > b_1^R\right)$
$QSS_{1,1}^D = 0$	$QSS_{1,1}^D = 0$
$QSS_{2,1}^D = 50$	$QSS_{2,1}^D = 50$

Continued

Approach Used in this Study	Approach Used by Paul and Rajendran (2011)
$QSS_{3,1}^D = 50$	$QSS_{3,1}^D = 50$
$S\_RP_{1,1}^D = 150$	–
$S\_RP_{2,1}^D = 200$	–
$S\_RP_{3,1}^D = 50$	–
$OQ_{M,1}^D = 400$	$OQ_{M,1}^D = 400$
Day 2:	
$OQ_{1,2}^R = 50$	$OQ_{1,2}^R = 50$
$OQ_{2,2}^R = 100$	$OQ_{2,2}^R = 100$
$OQ_{3,2}^R = 150$	$OQ_{3,2}^R = 150$
$BI_2^D = 400(LT^D = 1)$	$BI_2^D = 400(LT^D = 1)$
$A\_Q_{1,2}^D = 150$	–
$A\_Q_{2,2}^D = 150$	–
$A\_Q_{3,2}^D = 0$	–
$R\_QS_{1,2}^D = 0$	$R\_QS_{1,2}^D = 0$
$R\_QS_{2,2}^D = 0$	$R\_QS_{2,2}^D = 100 + 150\left(\because b_2^R > b_1^R\right)$
$R\_QS_{3,2}^D = 150\left(\because b_3^R > b_2^R > b_1^R\right)$	$R\_QS_{3,2}^D = 150\left(\because b_3^R > b_2^R > b_1^R\right)$
$QSS_{1,2}^D = 150$	$QSS_{1,2}^D = 0$
$QSS_{2,2}^D = 150$	$QSS_{2,2}^D = 250$
$QSS_{3,2}^D = 100$	$QSS_{3,2}^D = 150$

Our approach is different, and this numerical example confirms our claim; $OQ_{M,1}^D(= 400)$ corresponds to $OQ_{1,1}^R$ (i.e., equal to 150 and not satisfied by the distributor), $OQ_{2,1}^R$ (equal to 200 and not satisfied completely by the distributor), $OQ_{3,1}^R$ (equal to 50, and completely satisfied by the distributor), and $S^D(= 100)$. On the second day, out of 400 units of replenishment received from the manufacturer, we first allocate 150 units to retailer 1 (i.e., $A\_Q_{1,2}^D = 150$) and allocate 150 units to retailer 2 (i.e., $A\_Q_{2,2}^{D} = 150$), corresponding to the previous day's retailer order quantities to the distributor. We then ration the leftover inventory of 100 units to retailers. This two-phase mechanism ensures that the replenishment from the manufacturer is shipped by the distributor to the contemplated retailers (orders up to the day of the distributor's last review) with no mix-up or interchange. However, according to earlier attempts such as that by Paul and Rajendran (2011), the quantity received by the distributor from the manufacturer (400 units) is completely rationed between retailer 3 and retailer 2 in order to minimize the TSCC, without considering the unsatisfied order quantities corresponding to retailer 1 and retailer 2 (up to the day of the last review of the distributor) and without considering the due allocation to retailers. Hence, it is evident that our attempt is a step toward real-life situations where the interchange or mix-up of shipments corresponding to retailers' order quantities (up to the day of the last review of the distributor) is not permitted.

References

Amiri, A. 2006. Designing a distribution network in a supply chain system: Formulation and efficient solution procedure. *European Journal of Operational Research* 171: 567–576.

Arntzen, B. C., Brown, G. G., Harrison, T. P., and Trafton, L. L. 1995. Global supply chain management at digital equipment corporation. *Interfaces* 25: 69–93.

Aslam, T., and Ng, A. H. C. 2010. Multi-objective optimization for supply chain management: A literature review and new development. *SCMIS of the Eighth International Conference on Supply Chain Management and Information Systems*, IEEE: Hong Kong. 6–9 October 2010, pp. 1–8.

Chankong, V., and Haimes, Y. Y. 1983. *Multiobjective Decision Making: Theory and Methodology*. New York: Elsevier Science.

Cheng, T. C. E., Gao, C., and Shen, H. 2011. Production and inventory rationing in a make-to-stock system with a failure-prone machine and lost sales. *IEEE Transactions on Automatic Control* 56: 1176–1180.

Chopra, S., and Meindl, P. 2007. *Supply Chain Management: Strategy, Planning, & Operation*. Upper Saddle River, NJ: Pearson Education.

Clark, A. J., and Scarf, H. 1960. Optimal policies for multi-echelon inventory problem. *Management Science* 6: 475–490.

Cohen, M. A., Kleindorfer, P. R., and Lee, H. L. 1988. Service constrained (s, S) inventory systems with priority demand classes and lost sales. *Management Science* 34: 482–499.

Collette, Y., and Siarry, P. 2003. *Multiobjective Optimization: Principles and Case Studies*. Berlin: Springer-Verlag.

Daniel, S. R. J., and Rajendran, C. 2006. Heuristic approaches to determine base-stock levels in a serial supply chain with a single objective and with multiple objectives. *European Journal of Operational Research* 175: 566–592.

Deb, K. 2001. *Multi-Objective Optimization Using Evolutionary Algorithms*. New York: Wiley.

de Kok, A. G. 1990. Hierarchical production planning for consumer goods. *European Journal of Operational Research* 45: 55–69.

Franca, R. B., Jones, E. C., Richards, C. N., and Carlson, J. P. 2010. Multi-objective stochastic supply chain modeling to evaluate tradeoffs between profit and quality. *International Journal of Production Economics* 127: 292–299.

Guillén, G., Mele, F. D., Bagajewicz, M. J., Espuña, A., and Puigjaner, L. 2005. Multiobjective supply chain design under uncertainty. *Chemical Engineering Science* 60: 1535–1553.

Ha, Y. 1997. Inventory rationing in a make-to-stock production system with several demand classes and lost sales. *Management Science* 43: 1093–1103.

Hadley, G., and Whitin, T. M. 1963. *Analysis of Inventory Systems*. Englewood Cliffs, NJ: Prentice Hall.

Haimes, Y. Y., Lasdon, L. S., and Wismer, D. A. 1971. On a bicriterion formulation of the problems of integrated system identification and system optimization. *IEEE Transactions on Systems, Man, and Cybernetics* 1: 296–297.

Haji, R., Neghab, M. P., and Baboli, A. 2009. Introducing a new ordering policy in a two-echelon inventory system with Poisson demand. *International Journal of Production Economics* 117: 212–218.

Huang, B., and Iravani, S. M. R. 2007. Optimal production and rationing decisions in supply chains with information sharing. *Operations Research Letters* 35: 669–676.

Huh, W. T., and Janakiraman, G. 2010. On the optimal policy structure in serial inventory systems with lost sales. *Operations Research* 58: 486–491.

Isotupa, K. P. S. 2006. An (s, Q) Markovian inventory system with lost sales and two demand classes. *Mathematical and Computer Modelling* 43: 687–694.

Jayaraman, V., and Pirkul, H. 2001. Planning and coordination of production and distribution facilities for multiple commodities. *European Journal of Operational Research* 133: 394–408.

Kranenburg, A. A., and van Houtum, G. J. 2007. Cost optimization in the $(S-1, S)$ lost sales inventory model with multiple demand classes. *Operations Research Letters* 35: 493–502.

Klapper, L. S., Hamblin, N., Hutchison, L., Novak, L., and Vivar, J. 1999. *Supply Chain Management: A Recommended Performance Measurement Scorecard*. McLean, VA: Logistics Management Institute.

Lagodimos, A. G. 1992. Multi-echelon service models for inventory systems under different rationing policies. *International Journal of Production Research* 30: 939–958.

Lagodimos, A. G., and Koukoumialos, S. 2008. Service performance of two-echelon supply chains under linear rationing. *International Journal of Production Economics* 112: 869–884.

Liu, S., and Papageorgiou, L. G. 2013. Multiobjective optimisation of production, distribution and capacity planning of global supply chains in the process industry. *Omega* 41: 369–382.

Mansouri, S. A., Gallear, D., and Askariazad, M. H. 2012. Decision support for build-to-order supply chain management through multiobjective optimization. *International Journal of Production Economics* 135: 24–36.

Melchiors, P., Dekker, R., and Kleijn, M. J. 2000. Inventory rationing in an (s, Q) inventory model with two demand classes and lost sales. *Journal of the Operational Research Society* 51: 111–122.

Mula, J., Peidro, D., Díaz-Madroñero, M., and Vicens, E. 2010. Mathematical programming models for supply chain production and transport planning. *European Journal of Operational Research* 204: 377–390.

Nahmias, S. 1989. *Production and Operations Analysis*. Boston: Richard D. Irwin.

Pang, Z., Shen, H., and Cheng, T. C. E. 2014. Inventory rationing in a make-to-stock system with batch production and lost sales. *Production and Operations Management* 23: 1243–1257.

Paul, B., and Rajendran, C. 2011. Rationing mechanisms and inventory control-policy parameters for a divergent supply chain operating with lost sales and costs of review. *Computers and Operations Research* 38: 1117–1130.

Sabri, E. H., and Beamon, B. M. 2000. A multi-objective approach to simultaneous strategic and operational planning in supply chain design. *Omega* 28: 581–598.

Silver, E. A., Pyke, D. F., and Peterson, R. 1998. *Inventory Management and Production Planning and Scheduling*. New York: Wiley.

Srinivas, N., and Deb, K. 1995. Multi-objective function optimization using non-dominated sorting genetic algorithms. *Evolutionary Computation* 2: 221–248.

Stadtler, H. 2005. *Supply Chain Management—An Overview*. Berlin: Springer.

Sürie, C., and Wagner, M. 2005. *Supply Chain Analysis*. Berlin: Springer.

van der Heijden, M. C. 1997. Supply rationing in multi-echelon divergent systems. *European Journal of Operational Research* 101: 532–549.

van Donselaar, K. H., and Broekmeulen, R. A. C. M. 2013. Determination of safety stocks in a lost sales inventory system with periodic review, positive lead-time, lot-sizing and a target fill rate. *International Journal of Production Economics* 143: 440–448.

Wang, D., and Tang, O. 2014. Dynamic inventory rationing with mixed backorders and lost sales. *International Journal of Production Economics* 149: 56–67.

Weber, C. A., and Current, J. R. 1993. Theory and methodology: A multiobjective approach to vendor selection. *European Journal of Operational Research* 68: 173–184.

You, F., and Grossmann, I. E. 2008. Design of responsive supply chains under demand uncertainty. *Computers & Chemical Engineering* 32: 3090–4111.

Zhou, A., Qu, B.-Y., Li, H., Zhao, S.-Z., Suganthan, P. N., and Zhang, Q. 2011. Multiobjective evolutionary algorithms: A survey of the state of the art. *Swarm and Evolutionary Computation* 1: 32–49.

Zipkin, P. H. 2000. *Foundations of Inventory Management*. Boston: McGraw-Hill.

Index

W

Washington State Institute for Public
    Policy (WSIPP), 330
Weighted average cost of capital
    (WACC), 58
Weighted objective problem, 40
Work-in-progress (WIP), 3
World Bank, 193

X

XGS, *see* Exports of goods and services

Z

Zoning, risk of, 58